W9-BYD-568

Designing Professional Development for Teachers of Science and Mathematics

Second Edition

This book is dedicated to our friend and coauthor:

Susan Loucks-Horsley
(1947–2000)

Designing Professional Development for Teachers of Science and Mathematics

Second Edition

Susan Loucks-Horsley
Nancy Love
Katherine E. Stiles
Susan Mundry
Peter W. Hewson

CORWIN PRESS, INC.
A Sage Publications Company
Thousand Oaks, California

Copyright © 2003 by Corwin Press, Inc.

All rights reserved. When forms and sample documents are included, their use is authorized only by educators, local school sites, and/or noncommercial entities who have purchased the book. Except for that usage, no part of this book may be reproduced or utilized in any form or by any means, electronic or mechanical, including photocopying, recording, or by any information storage and retrieval system, without permission in writing from the publisher.

For information:

Corwin Press, Inc.
A Sage Publications Company
2455 Teller Road
Thousand Oaks, California 91320
www.corwinpress.com

Sage Publications Ltd.
6 Bonhill Street
London EC2A 4PU
United Kingdom

Sage Publications India Pvt. Ltd.
B-42 Panchsheel Enclave
Post Box 4109
New Delhi 110017 India

Printed in the United States of America

Library of Congress Cataloging-in-Publication Data

Designing professional development for teachers of science and mathematics / by Susan Loucks-Horsley . . . [et al.] 2nd ed.
    p. cm.
Includes bibliographical references and index.
ISBN 0-7619-4685-3 (cloth: acid free paper)
ISBN 0-7619-4686-1 (paper: acid-free paper)
    1. Science teachers-In-service training-United States.
    2. Mathematics teachers-In-service training-United States.
I. Loucks-Horsley, Susan.
Q183.3.A1 D47 2003
507'.1'55—dc21   2002152752

This book is printed on acid-free paper.

03   04   05   06   07   10   9   8   7   6   5   4   3   2

Acquisitions Editor:	Rachel Livsey
Editorial Assistant:	Phyllis Cappello
Production Editor:	Diana E. Axelsen
Copy Editor:	Kate Peterson
Typesetter/Designer:	Christina M. Hill
Cover Designer:	Michael Dubowe
Production Artist:	Janet Foulger

Contents

Foreword

"Have a simple, clear purpose which gives rise to complex, intelligent behavior, rather than complex rules and regulations that give rise to simplistic thinking and stupid behavior," Visa founder Dee Hock advises organizational leaders. And Hock's advice is nowhere more appropriate than in the planning of powerful professional learning experiences for teachers. Far too often what passes for professional development planning is the identification of a topic for the "inservice" session and the selection of a speaker. The event is judged a success if the presenter has somehow managed to motivate or inspire the audience, with little thought given to its long-term effects on teachers' practice and student learning.

Educators who are no longer content with such slipshod approaches to professional development will find both guidance and inspiration in the second edition of *Designing Professional Development for Teachers of Science and Mathematics* by Susan Loucks-Horsley, Nancy Love, Katherine E. Stiles, Susan Mundry, and Peter W. Hewson. This edition both updates the groundbreaking work presented in the first edition and places the design framework firmly within the context of standards-based reform and a performance-based culture that seeks to continuously improve professional practice and student achievement.

As *Designing Professional Development* points out, there is no formula or single correct way to plan and implement professional development that is intended to improve teaching and student learning. The planning and implementation of successful professional development efforts always occur within a particular setting that presents unique goals, strengths, resources, and barriers. Therefore, as the authors make clear, planning and implementation require the blending of research, "practitioner wisdom," "passionate beliefs," and "a repertoire of strategies from which to choose," with an emphasis always on "a process of thoughtful, conscious decision making."

A particular strength of this edition is the attention it gives to linking professional learning and student achievement. "A major difference those familiar with the original design framework will notice is a tighter link among standards and a vision for student learning, analysis of student learning and other data, and professional development goals and plans," the authors note in Chapter 1. "This change acknowledges the need to clearly connect professional development to student learning and, more particularly, to closing persistent achievement gaps between rich and poor and white and African American and Hispanic students. The change from the word *reflect* to the word *evaluate* was made for similar reasons. It signals the critical importance of rigorous evaluation of professional development." Another strength of this edition is the authors' inclusion of additional strategies such as lesson study, curriculum alignment, and demonstration lessons.

It is noteworthy that Susan Loucks-Horsley, who passed away in 2000, remains the lead author of this book. That fact is a testament to the high regard in which she was held by her coauthors and to the effects she had on their professional lives. It is also a testament to the power of Susan's ideas, which through this book and other venues will continue to affect the field of professional development for many years to come.

—Dennis Sparks
Executive Director
National Staff Development Council

Introduction

Revise—from the root word revidere, which means to "see again."

Revising the first edition of *Designing Professional Development for Teachers of Science and Mathematics* has given us a chance as a team of authors, quite literally, to "see again." We have been able to view the work in a new light and from a number of perspectives. One perspective has been from our own experiences working with professional developers across the country as they made the framework, principles, and strategies in the book come to life in their own programs. Another has been with a wide-angle lens, scanning the field of professional development in mathematics and science over the past five years and noting what has changed and what has not. This revision has also sparked reflection on the deepest personal level, a kind of internal seeing, as we mourned the death of lead author and friend Susan Loucks-Horsley and renewed our commitment to carry forward her work. Finally, much of the revising has been up close, examining the actual words we committed to print, page-by-page, dissecting the original design framework, and updating examples in an attempt to capture what we have learned as well as advances in the field.

The intention of this introduction is to make visible for you, the reader, our own process of revising. If you are familiar with the first edition, you can take this retrospective look with us. If you are new to the book, you will understand its evolution into this revised edition. In either case, you will know why we took on the work of revising *Designing Professional Development for Teachers of Science and Mathematics* and how it has changed.

WHAT HAS HAPPENED
SINCE THE FIRST EDITION

Since 1998, we have been watching with a sense of wonder and delight how *Designing Professional Development for Teachers of Science and Mathematics* has taken on a life of its own. We are professional developers. As such, we knew that writing the book was only the beginning, the easy part, as Susan Loucks-Horsley would say. The hard part, the "real work," was getting it used well. For the past five years, we have been on the ground actively disseminating the ideas in *Designing Professional Development for Teachers of Science and Mathematics* along with many colleagues and collaborators.

Even so, when we first put fingers to keyboards five years ago, we could never have anticipated how well the book would be used. We have seen dog-eared, Post-it-marked copies in the hands of professional developers all over the country, some of whom fondly refer to it as the "yellow book" or the "clouds book" because of its cover design. Equally gratifying, we have worked elbow-to-elbow with professional developers, who have made the principles and processes come to life in the purposeful and imaginative professional development designs they have created, designs that are paying off in powerful learning for teachers and their students.

In the years following the publication of *Designing Professional Development*, the National Institute for Science Education's (NISE) Professional Development Team members, the project that developed the first edition of the book, and its many collaborators, set to work to deepen and spread the knowledge about effective professional development. They investigated three strategies in depth—curriculum implementation, immersion in inquiry and problem solving, and case discussions. They convened another cadre of professional developers who were using the project's research to improve professional development for teachers, and designed more than 40 learning activities to increase professional developers' knowledge of effective professional development.

A long list of products and research that built on and extended the original work resulted from the NISE's work and others' work as well. Two that have been widely disseminated are the Eisenhower National Clearinghouse's (ENC) publications *Ideas That Work: Mathematics Professional Development* (1998) and *Ideas That Work: Science Professional Development* (1999), dubbed the "Professional Development Design Cliff Notes" for their concise synthesis of the book's principles and strategies. In collaboration with the National Staff Development Council (NSDC), ENC has also produced a CD, *By Your Own Design: A Teachers Professional Learning Guide* (2002), which provides a rich array of resources and tools to support the use of the design framework. The newest product to date, *Teachers as Learners: Professional Development in Science and Mathematics, a Video Library* (WestEd, 2003), is a set of videos and learning activities that provide visual examples of powerful professional learning strategies based on those identified in the 1998 edition of this book.

Another important contribution to the professional development field is Horizon Research's creation of the TE-MAT Web site, an online resource that brings together in one place a full array of mathematics and science professional development resources and materials and a conceptual framework to guide purposeful decision making and design (www.TE-MAT.org). In addition, the Eisenhower Mathematics and Science Consortia, under the leadership of the North Central Mathematics and Science Consortium, and the ENC have developed the *Blueprints* CD and Web site, a practical toolkit to help schools, districts, and other providers design and facilitate effective professional development.

One of our reasons for updating the earlier edition of the book was to collect and bring together in one place all that we have learned through many people's efforts to translate the principles, framework, and strategies of the first edition into practice and to deepen our understanding of professional development design through further research and new resources. The original edition evolved by synthesizing and codifying what outstanding and effective professional developers do when they design programs. This edition has the design work of more professional developers from which to draw. It is truly from the field, to the field.

In addition to what we have learned through work that grew directly out of the first edition, the field as a whole is advancing. Capturing these developments is a second reason for this new edition. With a wide-angle lens, we have observed some encouraging changes that have influenced our thinking and informed our revisions.

The knowledge bases about learning, teaching, the nature of science and mathematics, professional development, and change are growing. A veritable explosion of cognitive research has occurred even since the first edition of this book, increasing our understanding about how children construct knowledge in mathematics and science. More also is known about what constitutes and supports transformative learning for teachers. (See, for example, the citations of work from prominent researchers Deborah Ball, David Cohen, Linda Darling-Hammond, Gary Sykes, Charles Thompson, and John Zeuli in this volume.) We now better understand when and how professional development improves practice and student learning and the nature of systems and cultures that makes that outcome possible. Our vision for professional development has been strengthened by the revised NSDC's *Standards for Staff Development* (NSDC, 2001b) along with the council's executive director Dennis Sparks's (2002a) eloquent synthesis of the best thinking in the field—*Designing Powerful Professional Development for Teachers and Principals*.

Many other researchers and practitioners, among them Carne Clark, Kathy DiRanna, Catherine Lewis, Judy Mumme, and Margaret Smith, have provided us with new, rich examples of practice that bring to life our vision of job-embedded and practice-based professional learning. Through the work of Horizon Research, Inc., Inverness Associates, Thomas Guskey, and others, the field has also made strides in evaluating professional development. These developments are reflected in our substantial revision of Chapter 2, "Knowledge and Beliefs Supporting Effective Professional Development," and in chapters throughout the book.

National, state, and local standards are more widely known and consulted as school districts shape their vision of teaching and learning. Since we first convened as a team of authors and collaborators in 1996, the National Council of Teachers of Mathematics (NCTM) standards were only three years old, and the National Research Council's (NRC) *National Science Education Standards* had just been published. "The 1990s," we wrote, "are certain to be known as the decade in which standards became commonplace among educators and policymakers in the United States" (Loucks-Horsley, Hewson, Love, & Stiles, 1998, p. 215). We were right; standards are now commonplace. Most states and many school districts have adopted standards, some more closely aligned with national standards than others. For the most part, today the debate has shifted from whether or not standards should guide mathematics and science education to which particular standards to embrace, how to implement them, and how to ensure that they are met. Many more resources, including the NCTM's revised *Principles and Standards for School Mathematics* (2000), new tools from the American Association for the Advancement of Science (AAAS) such as the *Atlas of Science Literacy* (2000), the NRC's *Inquiry and the National Science Education Standards: A Guide for Teaching and Learning* (2000) and other publications supporting standards implementation, are now available. The consensus that has been reached around standards sets the context for the other advances in the field we discuss below.

Professional development has become more purposeful and is being designed more often with the clear intention of improving student learning. While "hodge-podge" and "hit-and-run style" professional development are far from a thing of the past, we find more examples than we did five years ago of professional development that is being designed and implemented for the purpose of helping students to achieve standards. In these programs, goals for student learning are determined by studying standards and analyzing student learning data; student goals influence the purpose and content of professional development, which is tied to improving practice. It has been especially gratifying for us to witness the design framework described in the first edition of this book being widely used to stimulate dialogue about important inputs into the design process and to produce more thoughtful and powerful professional development programs. In writing this edition, we had the benefit of many examples of the design process in action from which to choose. We have seen the design framework used to guide the development of programs in many grain sizes, from single institutes to complex multiyear programs.

Science and mathematics content and pedagogical content knowledge are playing a greater role in professional development programs. Another positive development has been a shift from providing teachers with opportunities to learn generic instructional strategies such as cooperative learning to designing professional development around the essential knowledge teachers need to teach the mathematics and science embodied in the standards. We see more examples of professional development that engages teachers in understanding the content they teach, deepening their knowledge about how to teach this content in particular, and learning about ways that students think about and learn this content.

"Job-embedded," "practice-based," and "collegial" forms of professional development are more widely accepted, researched, and practiced. One of the original purposes of our work was to create "thick and rich descriptions of practice" so that when professional developers envisioned professional development, they could imagine many alternatives to short-term workshops. We described 15 powerful development strategies, including strategies that draw on artifacts of practice such as student work, instructional materials, lessons, and cases and strategies that rely on learning from collegial reflection and dialogue as much as from outside expertise. Today, it was easier to find examples of these strategies. New strategies that embed professional learning into the daily work of teachers and enable teachers to learn "in and around their practice" (Ball & Cohen, 1999, p. 4) are emerging, such as lesson study.

THE ENDURING CHALLENGES OF PROFESSIONAL DEVELOPMENT

Despite these positive developments, the challenges of professional development for mathematics and science education are greater than ever. The first challenge is *raising the performance of all students in mathematics and science and closing achievement gaps between rich and poor, white and minority students.* Given that future innovation, global finance, and our very standard of living depend on mathematics and science knowledge, our students' unacceptable performance in these subjects constitutes nothing short of a national crisis. The report from the National Commission on Mathematics and Science Teaching for the 21st Century (2000; also known as the Glenn Commission), aptly named *Before It's Too Late*, states:

> Our children are not just losing the ability to respond to the challenges already presented by the 21st century but to its potential as well. We are failing to capture the interest of our youth for scientific and mathematical ideas. We are not instructing them to the level of competence they will need to live their lives and work at their jobs productively. Perhaps worst of all, we are not challenging their imaginations deeply enough. (pp. 4-5)

Most alarming are gaps in performance between rich and poor, white and minority, which, after a decade of investment in systemic reform, are maddeningly persistent. The challenge we face is to make breakthroughs in educating an increasingly diverse student population with different histories and cultural perspectives, experiences and expectations, and styles and approaches to learning and organizing information—"before it's too late."

The second challenge is *enhanced goals for student learning*. According to the Glenn Commission, "Students' grasp of science as a process of discovery, of mathematics as the language of scientific reasoning is often formulaic, fragile, or absent altogether" (National Commission on Mathematics and Science Teaching for the 21st Century, 2000, p. 10). Moving students beyond superficial understandings requires a fundamental shift in the goals that school communities embrace for their diverse students: goals proposed in national standards that focus on deep understanding, inquiry, and problem solving rather than on acquisition of facts; application of knowledge across subject areas; collaboration among learners; and alternatives to traditional assessment that measure progress of individuals in relation to new learning goals while providing accountability for the effectiveness of teaching and schools.

The most direct route to achieving these enhanced goals for students is *better teaching* (National Commission on Mathematics and Science Teaching for the 21st Century, 2000), the third enduring challenge. Standards and assessments are not enough, say Stigler and Hiebert (1999), who call teaching "the new frontier in the struggle to improve schools" (p. 2). Teaching in ways that will realize enhanced goals for diverse students requires a great deal of teachers. They must know their subjects more deeply. They must become students of their students' thinking and learn how to connect new learning to the knowledge their students bring. They also are students of their students' cultural backgrounds, examining their own biases, recognizing students' strengths, and reaching diverse learners with a relevant and rigorous curriculum. Teachers need to become designers of learning environments that are sufficiently flexible to accommodate varying needs of learners, with the full array of tools currently available and access to others as new tools emerge. Furthermore, teachers need to view themselves and behave as members of a community working intensely together for the benefit of its youth. The knowledge, skills, abilities, and attitudes required by this new vision of education and roles of educators are simultaneously broad and deep. Like their students, educators must become lifelong learners, with the understanding that there will always be important things to learn.

A fourth challenge involves *new organizations*: the necessity for teachers and other educators to not only function well in but to actually help to create new organizations—organizations that are flexible, organized for improvement, and riveted on producing results for students. In such settings, collaboration is critical; teachers become colearners and cocreators of learning communities both in their classrooms and with their colleagues. If teaching is the "new frontier," as Stigler and Hiebert said, then the pioneers are not just individual, competent teachers but skilled collaborators who function as part of a learning community, taking collective responsibility for every student's learning.

These challenges underscore the urgency of transforming the nature of professional development. There is little dispute in the research community that improving teaching and learning depends on sustained, high-quality professional development (Darling-Hammond, 1997; U.S. Department of Education, 2000, 2002). Moreover, there is a great deal of consensus about what constitutes effective professional development (Loucks-Horsley, Stiles, & Hewson, 1996; NSDC, 2001b). Still, the gap between common knowledge and common practice is wide. It was our sense of urgency about closing that gap that led us to write the first edition. We wrote then, "The purpose of this book is to engage individuals involved in professional development in careful examination of how professional development needs to change to meet the challenges ahead and how to make it an indispensable fixture in our educational systems of the future" (Loucks-Horsley et al., 1998, p. x). Today, the need for more extensive and effective approaches to professional development is greater than ever. Far from being an "indispensable fixture," professional development is still marginalized and mired in outmoded practices that serve neither teachers nor their students. While the changes in professional development we noted above are encouraging, they in no way amount to the sea change in behavior or results we hoped for five years ago.

Then, we characterized the current state of professional development in these ways: "(a) significant numbers of teachers who have few or no professional development opportunities; (b) a large percentage of the opportunities in the form of workshops, courses, and institutes that may not be appropriate to the learning goals nor provide sufficient support over time for teachers to apply what is learned in classrooms; (c) a focus on individual development, one teacher at a time, without attention to organization (e.g., department, school, district) development; and (d) some pockets of innovation, but with minimal means for greater impact, both within their own system or beyond. Students will fall far short of the national standards in science and mathematics if their teachers' learning opportunities are so restricted" (p. xi).

The fact that these conditions persist and in fact still dominate practice is not just cause for concern. It is cause for alarm. Our third reason for revising *Designing Professional Development* is that the original purpose and intent of the book has yet to be fulfilled and is, in fact, more urgent than ever. Since the writing of the first edition, we have been in classrooms that are alive with inquiry and learning. We have seen transformative professional learning, where teachers shed deeply held beliefs and assumptions and embrace new understandings of the nature of mathematics and science and how students learn. We have been in schools where teachers' learning is as much a part of their daily life in schools as school buses and books. We have, in fact, lived some of the images that you will find in Resource A at the end of this book. We know from these experiences that it is within our reach to achieve the "stretch goals" of a competent and caring teacher in every classroom, producing powerful learning for every student (Sparks, 2002a). Every day that this goal eludes us, students, especially from poor and minority backgrounds, and their teachers pay a huge price.

CARRYING ON THE WORK OF SUSAN LOUCKS-HORSLEY

Our commitment to these stretch goals relates to our fourth reason for undertaking the revision: to carry forward the work of our close friend, mentor, and coauthor, Susan Loucks-Horsley, who died in a tragic accident in 2000. *Designing Professional Development for Teachers of Science and Mathematics* was Susan's vision. In her usual generous way, she brought collaborators into the process so that we could learn with her. Learning was Susan's passion—students' learning, teachers' learning, her colleagues' learning, and her own continuous growth. The project grew out of her commitment to create "thick and rich descriptions of robust professional development" that could transform old notions of what she called "cafeteria style" or "hit and run" professional development. She led the project with extraordinary clarity of thinking and purpose, yet surprised us with her eagerness to listen and learn from us. Susan did more than write about collegial learning; she created it wherever she went. When anyone would call *Designing Professional Development* Susan Loucks-Horsley's book, she was quick to correct them, saying, "It is *our* book." Benjamin Disraeli said that the mark of a truly great person was not just someone who gave her gifts, but someone who brought out the gifts in others. Because Susan brought out our gifts, we produced this new edition—"*our* book"—as our gift to her.

In describing the central idea for *Designing Professional Development for Teachers of Science and Mathematics,* Susan Loucks-Horsley used the simile of a bridge. She wrote, "A bridge, like professional development, is a critical link between where one is and where one wants to be" (1999, p. 2). We find her simile apt in several ways. Susan was herself a bridge builder—building bridges between the research and practitioners, between the professional development and the science and mathematics education communities, and between educators and scientists and mathematics. She intended for *Designing Professional Development for Teachers of Science and Mathematics* to build strong bridges as well.

The book's organizing principle is that professional development is a complex design undertaking. Susan wrote: "Each bridge requires careful design that considers its purpose, who will use it, the conditions that exist at its anchor points (beginning, midway, and end), and the resources required to construct it" (p. 2). In part, *Designing Professional Development* is a practical manual for bridge building. While there is consensus about the general characteristics of effective professional development, there is much less known about how to put those principles into practice. *Designing Professional Development* bridges research and practice by providing rich descriptions of effective programs constructed in various contexts addressing common challenges in unique ways.

The book, like Susan's life, also bridges the professional development and science and mathematics education communities. Until recently, research and theory building in professional development have not been driven by subject matter concerns, but rather by those concerns generally regarding adult growth and development. The book connects the literature on adult learning and staff development to the disciplines of mathematics and science and has as its linchpin designs that enhance teachers' knowledge of these subjects and their ability to teach them well, as the dynamic, evolving subjects they are. Finally, by carrying on her work, we as Susan's coauthors and friends serve as a bridge, connecting our readers to her prodigious legacy and profound vision.

PURPOSE AND EVOLUTION OF THE BOOK

The book is intended to help professional developers construct strong bridges—between theory and practice, professional development and mathematics and science education, and the current and desired state of teaching and learning these subjects. It brings together in one place a rich discussion of the practices and issues of professional development for mathematics and science education. It is at once a "primer" on principles of effective professional development and a conversation among experienced professional developers about ways they address the many barriers to creating programs that emulate those principles. The book gets inside the thinking of designers, illuminating their purposes, strategies, triumphs, and failures.

The idea behind this book—and the professional development project at the National Institute for Science Education that produced it—evolved as experienced professional developers examined their practice. The purpose of the book as originally conceived was to offer a few distinct and robust models of professional development, ones that provided alternatives to traditional formats such as inservice workshops. As we examined the "models" in use by each of the project's collaborators, we realized that, rather than offering distinctly different approaches, each program or initiative was a unique combination of professional development strategies whose choice was influenced by the professional learning goals and the particular context—and those strategies changed over time as learning occurred, goals and context changed, and various issues developed. We determined that professional development, like teaching, is about decision making—designing optimal learning opportunities tailored to the unique situation. Rather than offering a few models for professional developers to adopt or adapt, we could instead provide guidance about professional development design. Drawing on research, the literature, and the wisdom of experienced professional developers, we could offer multiple "best practices" to assist professional developers in designing and strengthening their programs. More specifically, this book is designed to

- Offer a framework to assist professional developers in considering key inputs and combining strategies uniquely tailored for their contexts and their particular goals in improving science and mathematics teaching and learning

- Summarize key knowledge that informs professional development design such as the characteristics of effective professional development for teachers of science and mathematics

- Provide guidance on how to assess one's context to prepare to design professional development

- Discuss critical issues that cut across professional development programs and initiatives and ways these issues can be addressed

- Describe different strategies for professional learning that go beyond the most common workshops and institutes

- Provide examples of how elements of the design framework were used to create real-life professional development initiatives for teachers of mathematics and science

- Offer references and resources for further exploration and inquiry

CHANGES IN THE SECOND EDITION

While the fundamental purpose of the book remains the same, you will find significant changes in the book's content and organization. Most important, we have reconceptualized the design framework, which was and still is the core organizing concept of the book. The design framework is an attempt to describe the professional development design process: that is, what professional developers think about as they design, and what helps them to make good decisions about goals and strategies for their programs. The new design framework more closely connects standards and a vision of student learning to professional development goals and plans. Also, the use of student learning and other data figure more prominently in the new model, as does evaluation of professional development's impact on teachers, students, and schools.

We have also provided more guidance to professional developers in both Chapters 1 and 3 about what kinds of questions they need to ask about their context as they design and what data sources and resources might help them answer those questions, drawing especially on the guidebook *Using Data/Getting Results: A Practical Guide for School Improvement in Mathematics and Science* (Love, 2002). Reflecting advances in professional development practices, this edition describes three more strategies for professional learning: lesson study, aligning and selecting curriculum, and demonstration lessons. The book is now peppered with up-to-date examples of powerful professional learning, including new uses of technology for professional learning and data-driven designs. A completely new chapter, Chapter 7, "Putting the Professional Development Design Framework to Work," synthesizes our current thinking about how the design framework can and has been used to design a wide range of programs and highlights myths for professional developers to dispel. In addition, the structure and organization of the book have changed. The strategies chapter, for example, comes after all of the other inputs, knowledge and beliefs, context, and critical issues, to reinforce the message that professional development design is not about grabbing at strategies (as exciting as they are!), but about carefully considering a number of inputs to inform decision making. Finally, formatting and graphic enhancements make this edition more user-friendly.

THE UNIQUENESS OF THIS BOOK

The book has maintained its many unique features. The information in it was gleaned from a wide variety of sources, including the general professional development literature and information in science and mathematics education, as well as general education journals, Web sites, and unpublished "fugitive" documents that few beyond the authors knew existed including program evaluations and project descriptions and stories by dozens of professional developers, most of which were not written. Accumulating and making sense of this material has been a challenge, and it is also a unique contribution of this book: it offers "one-stop shopping" for busy practitioners who have limited time themselves to search in this wide variety of places.

A second feature of this book is its intent to go beyond descriptions of characteristics of professional development programs and offer rich images of what is possible. These images are presented in two ways: in the form of vignettes, which are not always real situations but a composite of what the authors have learned or a vision for what could be. The images are also in the form of cases or case illustrations: descriptions of real programs or program features that illustrate ideas as they play out in the world. We in no way pretend that this book is a "how to" guide, but it does bridge between theory and such a step-by-step manual. It also suggests where to go for specific guidance.

Finally, the focus on mathematics and science makes this book unique in a different way. Characteristics of these two disciplines directly correspond to the new directions professional development is taking. The paradigm shift in professional development (Hawley & Valli, 1999; Loucks-Horsley, 1995; Sparks, 1994) suggests a change in emphasis from transmission of knowledge to experiential learning, from reliance on existing research findings to examining one's own teaching practice, from individual-focused to collaborative, and from mimicking best practices to problem-focused learning. These shifts are the very backbone of the reforms in science and mathematics education because they mirror the practice of these disciplines. Furthermore, the important connections between professional learning and student learning are clear: We are not only talking about the *process* of professional learning but also the way that learning mirrors and extends to deep and new understanding on the part of students. Looking at best practices in mathematics and science professional development reminds us and reinforces for us the most important ideas in the reforms.

THE AUDIENCE FOR THIS BOOK

The primary audience for this book is professional developers: those who design, conduct, and support professional development for practicing teachers of mathematics and science and those learning to do so through coursework, mentoring, and collegial support groups. Our focus is at the *inservice* level, although many of the ideas presented in the book can be used to redesign preservice teacher education programs. These professional developers are found in schools (as teacher leaders, advisers, mentors, administrators, members of leadership teams); school district offices (as curriculum supervisors, coordinators, staff developers); intermediate and state agencies; colleges and universities in faculties of education, science, and mathematics; professional associations such as the National Science Teachers Association (NSTA) and the National Council of Teachers of Mathematics (NCTM), and their affiliated leadership organizations; state and federally funded projects and initiatives, such as those focused on teacher enhancement, systemic reform, and materials development, funded by the National Science Foundation, the U.S. Department of Education, and individual states; independent training and development firms; museums and other informal education organizations; and research labs and other organizations. There are several secondary audiences for the book: funders, sponsors, evaluators, policymakers, and mathematics and science teachers in their roles as consumers of professional development. All should find this book useful as it depicts best practices and how critical issues can be dealt with within different contexts.

ORGANIZATION OF THE BOOK

Chapter 1, "A Framework for Designing Professional Development," introduces the design orientation of this book. This chapter discusses why, with the wide variety of professional development goals and contexts in which they are pursued, it is most fruitful to think of professional development as a dynamic decision-making process rather than as a static set of models. The design framework, which can be used to design new programs or analyze and improve existing programs, is described. Driving the process is a commitment to a vision for students and their learning and analysis of student learning and other data to set specific goals for professional development. These goals will serve as the basis for evaluating the program. Inputs of knowledge about effective teaching, learning, and professional development; alternative strategies for professional development; and the nature of the disciplines of mathematics and science are combined in unique ways, given the goals, audience, and context of a particular professional development initiative. A case of professional development is used to illustrate the design process.

Chapter 2, "Knowledge and Beliefs Supporting Effective Professional Development," describes what is currently known about learning, teaching, professional development, the change process, and the disciplines of mathematics and science—knowledge that can form the foundation for a professional development initiative.

Chapter 3, "Context Factors Influencing Professional Development," discusses several dimensions of a context that influence the design and nature of professional development, including the nature of the students and teachers (their needs, backgrounds, abilities, motivations, etc.), current practices in teaching and professional development, the nature of the culture of the school and district, the organizational structures and quality of leadership, policies that constrain or support professional learning, and available resources. How differences in these dimensions influence design and implementation of professional development is illustrated by a variety of examples from different contexts.

Chapter 4, "Critical Issues to Consider in Designing Professional Development," discusses issues that need to be addressed in professional development initiatives if they are to be effective and successful over time. Seven issues are defined and illustrated (what it is and why it is an issue), the existing literature is cited, and questions and actions are suggested for professional developers to consider as they grapple with these issues.

Chapter 5, "Strategies for Professional Learning," describes 18 strategies that are widely used for professional development of mathematics and science educators. They are grouped into six clusters: aligning and implementing curriculum, collaborative structures, examining teaching and learning, immersion experiences, practicing teaching, and vehicles and mechanisms. Each strategy is described by its key elements and implementation requirements. Specific examples are given throughout.

Chapter 6, "The Design Framework in Action," illustrates how the different parts of the design framework influenced the decisions and professional development designs in five settings. The five settings are summarized as cases of professional development, written by the book's collaborators: Hubert Dyasi and Rebecca Dyasi of City College of New York; Susan Friel of the University of North Carolina/Chapel Hill; Judy Mumme of the Mathematics Renaissance at WestEd; Cary Sneider of the Museum of Science, Boston; and Karen Worth of the Educational Development Center (EDC) and Melanie Barron of the Cambridge (Massachusetts) public schools. These cases are referred to throughout the book.

Chapter 7, "Putting the Professional Development Design Framework to Work," uses the initiatives of experienced professional developers to illustrate the process of design: who is involved, and how a plan including the unique combination of strategies is developed, implemented, monitored, and adjusted. It also provides guidance on the use of the design framework for developing goals and plans for different types of programs. More examples illustrate a variety of design configurations from a single-strategy effort for one department within a school to a large-scale, districtwide mathematics and science initiative combining multiple strategies over several years.

"Resource A: Images of Learning and Professional Development" uses vignettes of classrooms and professional development experiences to illustrate the vision of teaching and learning on which the book is based. These images are not strategies to replicate, but a way to communicate a sense of where we need to be and to demonstrate our commitment to a new paradigm for student and teacher learning.

HOW TO USE THIS BOOK

There are a variety of ways this book can be used. The design framework itself, introduced in Chapter 1 and discussed with illustrations in Chapter 6, can be used by professional developers to design new programs or improve current programs. Beginning with these chapters will immerse the reader immediately into the dynamic world of decision making about professional development. An alternative is reading the chapters sequentially, in which case different inputs into professional development programs are introduced one by one—the knowledge base, context, critical issues, and strategies—combining increasingly more considerations about professional development design by the time the actual planning and implementation process is described in Chapter 6. Another alternative, one that may be more immediately helpful to professional development planners, is to review the section in Chapter 2 on the knowledge base in professional development and then to turn to Chapter 5, which describes each of the 18 strategies and suggests under what circumstances they might be best used. A final path is to "begin with the end in mind" (Covey, 1989, p. 95) by going to Resource A before turning to Chapter 1. Because professional development is a complex and dynamic process, we believe that each chapter has something new to offer the reader, but the order in which chapters are read is not critical.

VALUES SHARED BY THE AUTHORS

Early in framing this book, we realized that what we were creating was based very much on our shared beliefs and that a book by another set of authors might read quite differently. Therefore, we decided it was important to be explicit about our beliefs, as a form of "truth in packaging." Readers who share these beliefs should find the contents quite compatible; we hope that those who do not will be challenged to consider an alternative perspective and direction, and its value in their work. The values that underlie this book include the following:

1. *Professional development experiences need to have students and their learning at their core. And by that we mean all students.* Science and mathematics education reforms and the national standards on which they are based share a common commitment to learning for all, not the privileged or talented few. This not only implies a whole new perspective on the content that students should learn but also the teaching and learning strategies that need to be employed by their teachers (especially ways of knowing what students know). We believe that, given the scarcity of resources, including time, for teacher learning,

all those resources must be focused on learning and developing the best means for reaching all students.

2. *Excellent science and mathematics teachers have a very special and unique kind of knowledge that needs to be developed through their professional learning experiences.* Pedagogical content knowledge, that is, knowing how to teach specific scientific and mathematical concepts and principles to children at different developmental levels, is the unique province of teachers and must be the focus of professional development. Knowledge of content, although critical, is not enough, nor is knowledge of general pedagogy. There is something more to professional development for science and mathematics teachers than generic professional development opportunities are able to offer.

3. *Principles that guide the reform of student learning should also guide professional learning for educators.* Professional development opportunities need to "walk their talk." People teach as they are taught, so engaging in active learning, focusing on fewer ideas more deeply, learning collaboratively—all of these principles must characterize learning opportunities for adults.

4. *The content of professional learning must come from both inside and outside the learner, and from both research and practice.* Traditionally, knowledge that is officially due respect has come from external sources such as research or the consultant from at least 50 miles away. More recently, the wisdom that teachers themselves have gained over time has received more attention, often to the neglect of external knowledge. We believe that internal and external knowledge and knowledge from practice as well as from research are all valid and important. It is the artful professional development design that combines these most effectively.

5. *Professional development must both align with and support system-based changes that promote student learning.* Professional development has long suffered from separation from other critical components of education, with the common result that new strategies and ideas are not implemented. While professional development cannot be expected to cure all the ills of the system, it can support changes in such areas as standards, assessment, and curriculum, creating a culture and capacity for continuous improvement so critical to facing current and future challenges.

With these values explicit, the reader is now invited to explore a new direction for professional development for mathematics and science. We hope that you will, as we have in revising this edition, see with fresh eyes the possibilities for powerful professional learning.

Acknowledgments

From its conception, this book has been a complex undertaking. It originally represented a year of collaboration among people from vastly different "communities": practitioners and researchers; scientists, mathematicians, and educators; people working in elementary, middle, and high schools and higher education settings; and those with school, district, state, and national perspectives. Our challenge has been to avoid simply gathering and describing efforts to support professional learning, but to examine and understand those efforts, search for common themes and struggles, and write a book that represents the collective wisdom of the field. Our success in this undertaking rests in large part on the contributions of hundreds of voices.

Hearing these voices was made possible by a five-year grant from the National Science Foundation for the creation and funding of the National Institute for Science Education (NISE). The NISE was a partnership between the Wisconsin Center for Education Research at the University of Wisconsin–Madison and the National Center for Improving Science Education, now at WestEd. It was headquartered in Madison, Wisconsin, from 1996 to 2001. The work of the NISE was carried out by several different teams, one of which was the Professional Development team, whose members authored the first edition of this book.

First and foremost, we are grateful to our original collaborators: Hubert Dyasi, who, along with Rebecca Dyasi, contributed the case on the Workshop Center at City College, New York; Susan Friel, who contributed the case on Teach-Stat; Judy Mumme, who contributed the case on the

Mathematics Renaissance; Cary Sneider, who contributed the Global Systems Science case; and Karen Worth along with Melanie Barron, who contributed the case on the Cambridge public schools. These exceptional professional developers shared their learning, their struggles, and their enthusiasm for their work. Their stories weave through this book and illustrate the main ideas we formulated together.

For their careful reviews and substantive contributions to the first edition, we thank Joan Ferrini-Mundy, Iris Weiss, Deborah Schifter, Josefina Arce, Ed Silver, Ned Levine, Mark St. John, and Vernon Sells. We are grateful for the vision and guidance of the leadership of the NISE—Andy Porter, Terry Millar, and Denice Denton—and the National Center for Improving Science Education—Senta Raizen and Ted Britton. We appreciate the support from the National Science Foundation, especially that of Susan Snyder, Margaret Cozzins, Larry Suter, and Daryl Chubin.

In the years following the publication of the first edition, four projects and many individuals were instrumental in extending the work of *Designing Professional Development for Teachers of Science and Mathematics*. The NISE Cases Group—Ned Levine, Ed Silver, Margaret Smith, and Mary Kay Stein—worked with NISE Professional Development project staff to develop four cases of professional development practice that elucidated the ways in which the design framework is implemented in different contexts. Through their participation on the NISE Strategies Working Group, Carne Barnett-Clarke, Virginia Bastable, Mark Driscoll, David Hartney, Barbara Miller, Judy Mumme, Lynn Rankin, Ann Rosebery, Susan Jo Russell, Mary Kay Stein, and Jo Topps enriched our understanding of three professional development strategies—curriculum implementation, immersion in inquiry and problem solving, and case discussions. The NISE professional development cadre disseminated the first book to thousands of educators and provided new insights from the field that are reflected in this book. We thank them for their commitment to getting the ideas in the book into the hands of so many practitioners; thanks especially go to the regional directors of the K–12 Alliance in California and staff at Learning Innovations/ WestEd in Massachusetts. In addition, we are grateful to the many professional developers who opened their doors to video cameras so that WestEd and WGBH's Teachers as Learners project could capture images of effective professional development in action and teach us all more about teachers as learners.

Many people enthusiastically contributed descriptions and analyses of their programs and initiatives, many of which we have used as examples and cited as resources. Special thanks go to Kirsten Daehler, Perry Davis, the Dover-Sherborn (Massachusetts) School District, Mark Driscoll, Kathy Dunne, Linda Gregg, Page Keeley, Grace Kelemanik, Mayumi Shinohara, Jim Short, Joyce Tugel, Liz Van Cleef, and the MSAD 52 (Greene, Leeds, and Turner, Maine). For their patience and encouragement as our editors, we thank Rachel Livsey and Diana Axelsen at Corwin Press. We are especially grateful to Deanna Maier, who worked her magic once again, formatting the manuscript in record time and maintaining good spirits and high standards throughout the process. Thanks also to Mark Kaufman, director of the Regional Alliance at TERC, for his kindness and understanding.

Finally, for their unflagging support through the difficult period of juggling writing this second edition with the usual demands of our work and personal lives, we thank our families.

The contributions of the following reviewers are gratefully acknowledged:

Harold Pratt
President
Educational Consultants, Inc.
Littleton, Colorado

Susan Koba, Ph.D.
Professional Development Coordinator
Banneker 2000: CEMS, Omaha Public
    Schools
Omaha, Nebraska

Gay Gordon
Associate Director, Publishing
Eisenhower National Clearinghouse
Columbus, Ohio

Page Keeley
Science and Technology Specialist
Maine Mathematics and Science
    Alliance
Augusta, Maine

Kathy DiRanna
Statewide Director
K–12 Alliance/WestEd
Santa Ana, California

About the Authors

Susan Loucks-Horsley was the lead author of the first edition of *Designing Professional Development for Teachers of Science and Mathematics* and she directed the Professional Development research for the National Institute for Science Education on which the book is based. At the time of her death in 2000, Susan was Associate Executive Director of Biological Sciences and Curriculum Study (BSCS) and Senior Research Associate for Science and Mathematics at WestEd. She had previously served as Director of Professional Development and Outreach at the National Research Council's Center for Science, Mathematics, and Engineering Education, where she promoted and monitored standards-based education, especially the *National Science Education Standards*. Susan was a leading researcher, writer, and professional developer who enjoyed collaborating with others to address education's toughest problems. She was the senior author of several books, including *Continuing to Learn: A Guidebook for Teacher Development; An Action Guide for School Improvement;* and *Elementary School Science for the 90s.* In addition, she wrote numerous reports on teacher development for the National Center for Improving Science Education, as well as chapters and articles on related topics. While at the University of Texas/Austin Research and Development Center for Teacher Education, she worked on the development team of the Concerns-Based Adoption Model (CBAM), a classic framework for understanding and leading change efforts.

Nancy Love is Principal Investigator and Director of the Using Data Project at TERC, in Cambridge, Massachusetts, where she works with schools and mathematics and science education projects nationally to improve mathematics and science teaching and learning through effective and collaborative use of school data. Before coming to TERC in 1996, Nancy worked at The NETWORK, Inc, in Andover, Massachusetts, where as staff of the National Institute for Science Education Professional Development Project, she coauthored the first edition of *Designing Professional Development for Teachers of Science and Mathematics* (1998). She has been very active since then in working with professional developers and school leaders nationally to design professional development that is based on research, draws on a repertoire of robust strategies, and is tailored to local needs and goals for student learning. Nancy is also the author of *Using Data/Getting Results: A Practical Guide to School Improvement in Mathematics and Science* (2002) and *Global Perspectives for Local Action: Using TIMSS to Improve U.S. Mathematics and Science Education Professional Development Guide* with Susan Mundry (2001).

Katherine E. Stiles is a Senior Research Associate and Project Director at WestEd, where she leads projects focused on professional development, leadership development, and evaluation in science education. She is Principal Investigator of the Academy for Professional Development in Science and Mathematics, a project to design an academy to support the NSF-funded Mathematics/Science Partnerships. She is Codirector of WestEd's National Academy for Science and Mathematics Education Leadership, designed to enhance the knowledge, skills, and strategies of leaders of science and mathematics education reform. As staff on the National Institute for Science Education Professional Development Project, she coauthored the first edition of *Designing Professional Development for Teachers of Science and Mathematics* (1998). She has coauthored several articles and publications, including *Leading Every Day: 124 Actions for Effective Leadership* (2002). Prior to her work at WestEd, Katherine was a Curriculum Development Specialist at the National Science Resources Center in Washington, D.C., where she developed and wrote elementary science curriculum for the Science and Technology for Children project. She also worked as the K–12 Professional Development Specialist at the National Research Council's Center for Science, Mathematics, and Engineering Education, where she designed and implemented State Leadership Institutes for state science and mathematics supervisors.

Susan Mundry is a Project Director at WestEd, where she directs several leadership development programs and develops products to improve the quality of adult learning. She consults with many educational and nonprofit organizations around the United States to enhance their performance and effectiveness. She also conducts coaching, facilitates strategic planning, and leads workshops on systems thinking, organizational development and change, professional development, and leadership. Prior to her work at WestEd, she was Associate Director of The NETWORK, Inc., where she managed many large-scale research and development projects focused on improving organizational effectiveness and innovation. Susan is codeveloper of the *Teachers as Learners* videotape series and of two widely used simulation games that help people learn the processes and pitfalls of change management, *Making Change* and *Systems Thinking/Systems Changing.* She is the coauthor of several books, including *Leading Every Day: 124 Actions for Effective Leadership* (2002), and *Designing Successful Professional Meetings and Conferences in Education* (2002), as well as many articles and book chapters.

Peter W. Hewson is Professor of Science Education at the University of Wisconsin–Madison. He is also the director of a project to develop collaborative research in science and mathematics education between South Africa and the United States. He has been a principal investigator on several other federally funded multiyear projects in science education. As Codirector of the Professional Development Project of the National Institute for Science Education, he coauthored the first edition of *Designing Professional Development for Teachers of Science and Mathematics* (1998). He teaches in the undergraduate teacher education and graduate science education programs and coordinates a professional development school in Madison. He has been deeply involved in the development of a conceptual change framework and its application to the learning and teaching of science. He has also studied initial teacher education and the continuing professional development of practicing teachers. He has published numerous articles on these and related topics. He received his D.Phil. in theoretical nuclear physics from Oxford University, and he taught physics and science education in South Africa before moving to the United States.

1

A Framework for Designing Professional Development

I n the years that followed the development of the original design
framework, in the 1998 edition (see Figure 1.1), it has been heartening to
see how extensively the framework has been used by professional developers to design programs and by researchers to analyze and describe professional development. Through these experiences, as well as developments in
the field of professional development design and evaluation, we have arrived at some new thinking about professional development design that is
reflected in a modified design framework. A major difference those familiar
with the original design framework will notice is a tighter link among standards and a vision for student learning, analysis of student learning and
other data, and professional development goals and plans. This change acknowledges the need to clearly connect professional development to student learning and, more particularly, to closing persistent achievement
gaps between rich and poor and white and African American and Hispanic
students. The change from the word *reflect* to the word *evaluate* was made
for similar reasons. It signals the critical importance of rigorous evaluation
of professional development both to inform redesign and to document the
impact of professional development on student learning, teacher learning,
teaching practice, and organizations. Reflection, we believe, is still a vital
part of professional development design, informing the work not only after
implementation but also during and before. Another change in the professional development landscape since the first edition of this book is that new
and promising strategies for professional development have emerged and

Figure 1.1.   Original Professional Development Design Framework

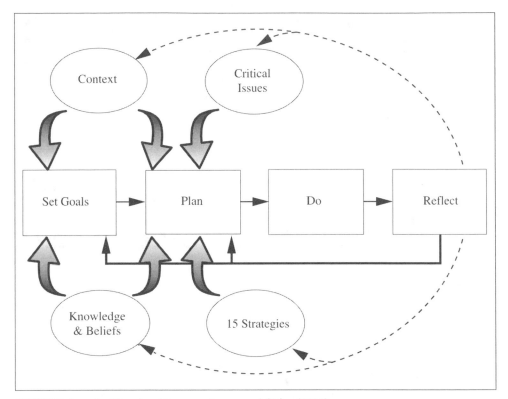

SOURCE: Loucks-Horsley, Hewson, Love, and Stiles (1998).

caught our attention, including lesson study, curriculum alignment and instructional materials selection, and demonstration lessons, and are now included in an expanded description of professional learning strategies. Coaching and mentoring, identified as one strategy in the 1998 edition, are now treated as two different strategies.

These changes strengthen the framework for use as a guide to the process of designing and providing quality professional development. The framework emerged originally from collaborative reflection with outstanding professional developers about their programs for both mathematics and science teachers. These professional developers felt very strongly that what they had to offer were not "models" that others could admire and adopt. Their programs were more complex than that, combining elements of different models, evolving and changing over time. They emerged out of and were uniquely suited to their own particular goals and context.

Equally complex was the process they used to develop their programs. As professional development "designers," they consciously drew on research and "practitioner wisdom" and were guided by their own passionate beliefs about the nature of mathematics and science and student and adult learning. They had a repertoire of strategies from which to choose. They grappled with challenging, critical issues related to the "big picture" of mathematics and science education reform. They analyzed student learning data and student work and studied their own unique contexts to deliberately set goals to improve student and teacher learning and classroom practice. They thought carefully about what approach would be best in a particular time and place to advance their goals. Drawing on all of these elements, they carefully crafted their goals and plans. Once implemented, their designs never stopped evolving. As they learned from their mistakes, as teachers developed, and as their contexts shifted, their programs changed as well. Finally, they evaluated their programs not just in terms of teacher satisfaction but also on the basis of whether teacher and student learning goals were met. For these "designers," professional development was not about importing models or following formulas. It was a process of thoughtful, conscious decision making.

It is this process of decision making that we have attempted to capture, albeit greatly simplified, in Figure 1.2. At the center of the framework, illustrated in the rectangles connected with horizontal arrows, is a generic planning sequence, incorporating the following actions: committing to a vision and a set of standards, analyzing student learning data, goal setting, planning, doing, and evaluating. The circles above and below the planning sequence represent important inputs into the design process that can help professional developers make informed decisions. They cue designers to consider the extensive knowledge bases that can inform their work (knowledge and beliefs), to understand the unique features of their own context, to draw on a wide repertoire of professional development strategies, and to wrestle with critical issues that mathematics and science education reformers will encounter, regardless of their contexts.

The arrows from the input "bubbles" into the boxes in the center of the graphic indicate when in the planning sequence these inputs are most important to start to consider. For example, note that strategies are most important to consider after goals are clearly established. Otherwise, there is the danger of grabbing at strategies that may not align with your goals, meet student learning needs, or fit your context. Once an input feeds into the system, it is assumed that it will continue to inform all subsequent stages in the process. For example, knowledge and beliefs informs "commit to vision" and every subsequent step, including how the plan is designed, implemented, and evaluated. Context determines what kind of data you consider in the data analysis phase and what student, teacher, and organizational learning needs the goals should address. Plans are made and implemented based on a solid understanding of contextual factors such as available time, resources, leadership, and school culture and are evaluated, in part, by the

Figure 1.2. Design Framework for Professional Development in Science and Mathematics

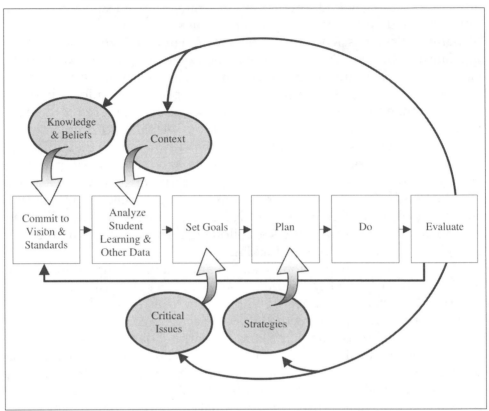

extent to which these and other context factors are positively impacted. Planners consider critical issues like equity, scaling up, and building capacity early on as they set goals and develop plans, and they continue to attend to them later as they are implementing and evaluating the program. Finally, in the design framework graphic, an arrow connects evaluation back to vision to illustrate how evaluating leads to rethinking the vision, plans, goals, and actions. The feedback loop also connects back to the inputs of context, critical issues, and strategies to reflect how inputs may change. For example, professional developers may unearth new critical issues, develop new knowledge as a result of their experience, identify the need for a different strategy, or document changes in context. Designs continue to evolve as professional developers learn from both their experiences and evaluation results.

The process mapped out in the design framework can be used to design both small- and large-scale professional development, from an individual school's program to a statewide or national initiative. It can guide designs that involve a single strategy such as a workshop or study group or a complex program, combining several strategies either simultaneously or over time. Whatever the grain size, the design framework provides a map for crafting professional development to achieve the desired goals for students and teachers. (See Chapter 7 for further discussion.)

The framework describes professional development design at its very best—an ideal to strive toward, rather than an accurate depiction of how it always happens or a lockstep prescription for how it should. Given limited resources, especially time, professional developers may not always have the luxury of giving their full attention to every input in the model. The professional developers who helped to develop the framework extracted its components from what they actually did and what they wished they had done better. With the benefit of hindsight, they helped to construct a tool that alerts planners to important bases to cover and pitfalls to avoid. For programs just being designed, planners can take advantage of the knowledge and experience of others who have preceded them down the path. If programs are already under way, the framework can stimulate reflection and refinement. Wherever planners are in their process, they can hone in on the parts of the framework that best serve their purposes, knowing that no planning process is perfect, and that even the "best laid plans" are subject to the whims and serendipity of change.

This chapter briefly describes each element of the design framework, using examples primarily from the Cambridge (Massachusetts) public school curriculum implementation initiative, to make the process come alive. Chapters 2, 3, 4, and 5 provide more detail on each of the major inputs into the design process. While the design framework looks rational and analytical, professional development design is more art than science. It is fueled by vision and passion; requires great skill, knowledge, and creativity; and continues to evolve as the designer strives for greater mastery—better results for students, teachers, and schools.

KNOWLEDGE AND BELIEFS

"How long did it take you to make that pot?"
someone asked the potter. "A lifetime," the potter
replied.
                                        —Source unknown

Skilled professional developers, like skilled artists, come to the task of designing professional development with knowledge that has evolved over many years of research and practice. Much is known about effective professional development for mathematics and science education, and more is being learned every day. Taking advantage of this knowledge can help

Figure 1.3.   Knowledge and Beliefs Supporting Effective Professional
Development

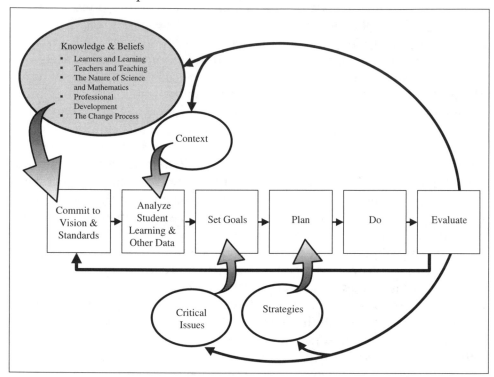

planners jump-start their efforts, put them on solid footing, and avoid unnecessary and costly mistakes.

Five distinct, but related knowledge bases inform the work of professional developers. (See Figure 1.3.) First is what we know about learners and learning. An explosion of cognitive research in the past 20 years has resulted in a rich body of knowledge about learners and learning in general and in mathematics and science in particular (Bransford, Brown, & Cocking, 1999). A second knowledge base is what is known about teachers and teaching. Third is the nature of the disciplines of mathematics and science. Fourth are the principles of effective professional development. Last is the knowledge base about change and the change process. In Chapter 2, we argue that there is a growing consensus about what is known in each of these domains and summarize key principles. That is not to say that these principles constitute the final word but that there is a substantial body of evidence to support them. Professional development designers tap this reservoir of knowledge to inform the initial planning and whenever they face dilemmas that research has addressed. In the design framework (see Figure 1.2), knowledge and beliefs are delineated as an important input into every phase of design, from the initial vision to the evaluation.

For example, the Cambridge team planning its curriculum implementation program brought a wealth of knowledge and experience to the table. The science staff development teachers on the team had been practicing inquiry-based science in the classroom for years. Some members had been involved in urban school change and science education reform since the 1960s. They knew the research on effective professional development and change and have been living it for 30 years. Everyone was steeped in standards work, from their science education consultant, Karen Worth, who was involved in developing national science education standards, to the staff themselves, who had drawn heavily on national and state standards to develop their own curriculum frameworks. Even so, one of the first decisions the team made was to find out more about successful science systemic change efforts. Team members wanted to know who was doing what, where, and what was working. They were determined not to reinvent the wheel or go down the wrong path.

Guiding beliefs about each of the five knowledge bases are important inputs into the vision and goals that drive professional development planning. Beliefs are the ideas people are committed to. Sometimes called core values, fundamental choices, or mental models, beliefs shape one's ways of perceiving and acting. Many researchers have found that organizations that are deeply committed to a clear set of beliefs and that act consistently with them experience the greatest success (Deal & Kennedy, 1982; Fritz, 1996; Peters & Waterman, 1982; Schwahn & Spady, 1998). As designers clarify and articulate their beliefs, these beliefs become the "conscience" of the program. They shape goals, drive decisions, create discomfort when violated, and stimulate ongoing critique.

This was certainly true for the Cambridge team members, who shared a strong belief in inquiry science for all students and a common image of what that meant. They knew why they were there—to see their vision of science learning enacted in their schools. These beliefs were reflected in the vision and goals for the program and helped to sustain leaders through the difficulties of implementation.

CONTEXT

There is no prescription for which designs are right for which situations—no "paint by numbers kit" for professional development. Skillful planners have one foot planted firmly in theory (knowledge and beliefs and vision) and the other in reality. As professional developers design their program, they are influenced by their vision of what science and mathematics teaching, learning, and professional development should look like, but they also carefully analyze and study their own context. (See Figure 1.4.)

They must know who the students are and what standards are in place for them. They need data about student performance, about performance

Figure 1.4.   Context Factors Influencing Professional Development

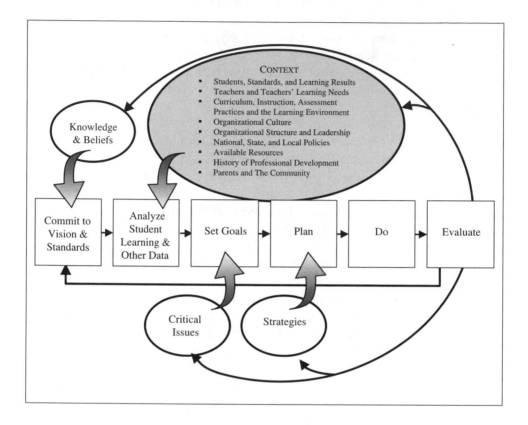

gaps between rich and poor, white and minority, boys and girls, and about practices that are contributing to these gaps. They also need to know about teachers and their knowledge and beliefs about teaching and learning as well as their learning needs as they relate to students' learning needs. They rely on information about current curriculum, instruction, and assessment practices and about the culture of the organization. This information serves as the basis for professional development goals for students, teachers, teaching, and the organization and helps to ensure that professional development is linked with learning results. It is so crucial to the design process that the revised design framework (Figure 1.2) includes "analyze student learning and other data" as an essential step before arriving at goals for professional development. (See the section Analyze Student Learning and Other Data below.)

Other features of the context that are important to consider are organizational structures and leadership; national, state, and local policies; available resources such as time, money, and available expertise; the history of professional development; and parents and community. (See Chapter 3 for a fuller discussion of each of these.) Considering these factors helps designers make better decisions as they plan, implement, and evaluate programs. Each of the cases discussed in this book (see Chapter 6), from Cambridge, Massachusetts, to the state of California, illustrates how different contexts influence the creation of very different programs. The design process entails filtering all of the other inputs—knowledge and beliefs, strategies, and critical issues—through one's own context to arrive at the most appropriate approach for a given setting.

Context is complex, comprising many interconnected and dynamic influences. Some contextual factors were readily apparent to the professional developers and drove their designs from the outset. For example, in Cambridge, the design team knew that the schools had a history of autonomy, and, therefore, opted for a school-based strategy with liaisons from each school. Other context factors required more study and analysis. When the Cambridge team members surveyed curriculum practices, they learned that there was little continuity from grade to grade and that the quantity and quality of science being taught was uneven. Some teachers in kindergarten through sixth grade were not teaching science at all. This led them to a decision to start slowly, phasing in a few units of the new curriculum at a time. Still other context factors were overlooked entirely, in some cases, to the program's peril, such as public perception of mathematics reform in the Mathematics Renaissance program in California. (See Chapter 6.)

CRITICAL ISSUES

As we looked at professional development programs throughout the country, we discovered some common issues that designers were facing. These issues seemed to be critical to the success of programs everywhere, regardless of the context (although context will heavily influence how they take shape): time for professional development, equity and diversity, professional culture, leadership, capacity building for sustainability, scaling up, and garnering public support. (See Figure 1.5.) Proactive planners anticipate these issues and begin grappling with them in the initial design phase. As the program is implemented, they keep these issues in the forefront, confronting obstacles and creating opportunities to better respond to these challenges. For example, during several years of implementing the new science curriculum in Cambridge, professional developers kept their focus on developing capacity by supporting building liaisons and district staff developers in moving along the continuum from novice to expert science educators and taking greater responsibility for leading the effort.

The critical issues defy easy solutions. They are the "tough nuts" that professional developers work to crack as they design and provide learning experiences for teachers. Chapter 4 examines these issues in all of their

Figure 1.5. Critical Issues

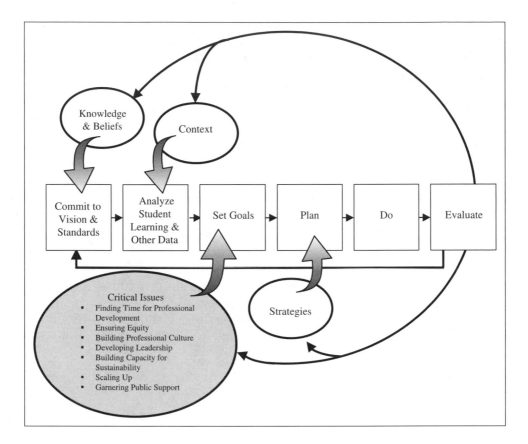

complexity, summarizing research, offering examples of best practice, and posing enduring, unresolved questions.

STRATEGIES FOR PROFESSIONAL LEARNING

After developing goals for the program, professional developers consider another important input, proven strategies for professional learning. Like classroom teachers, effective professional developers have a variety of strategies to draw on and skillfully select and combine to achieve their goals and to support change over time. Professional developers with such a repertoire to select from are in a much better position to come up with a strategy or combination of strategies to suit their purposes than designers who have only one move—the workshop. That is not to say that workshops cannot be effective. They can, if implemented well and linked to other strategies that sustain learning. The problem comes about when doing a workshop

Figure 1.6. Strategies for Professional Learning

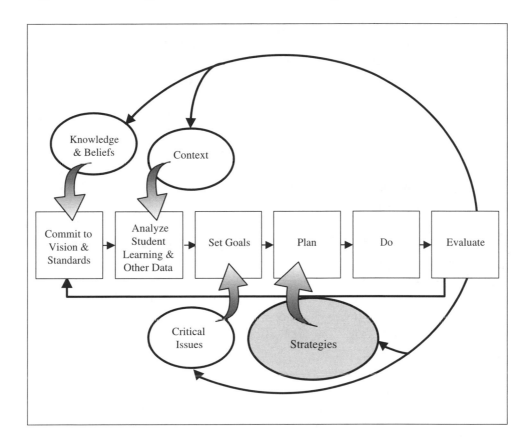

becomes a knee-jerk reaction, not a conscious choice from among alternatives. With a repertoire of strategies, professional developers can design programs that embed professional learning into the daily lives of teachers. (See Figure 1.6.)

Chapter 5 describes 18 different teacher learning strategies clustered around six categories: aligning and implementing curriculum, collaborative structures, examining teaching and learning, immersion experiences, practicing teaching, and vehicles and mechanisms. (See Table 1.1.) These strategies are included in this book because they are robust examples of professional development in mathematics and science and are consistent with the principles of effective professional development discussed in Chapter 2. With each strategy, a set of key elements and implementation requirements is provided to assist planners in matching strategies to their own contexts and purposes. A professional development program can be made up of multiple strategies offered simultaneously to different groups of teachers to meet their different needs or accommodate varied learning styles. For example, novice teachers might benefit from an inquiry immersion

TABLE 1.1   Eighteen Strategies for Professional Learning

Aligning and implementing curriculum
- Curriculum alignment and instructional materials selection
- Curriculum implementation
- Curriculum replacement units

Collaborative structures
- Partnerships with scientists and mathematicians in business, industry, and universities
- Professional networks
- Study groups

Examining teaching and learning
- Action research
- Case discussions
- Examining student work and thinking, and scoring assessments
- Lesson study

Immersion experiences
- Immersion in inquiry in science and problem solving in mathematics
- Immersion into the world of scientists and mathematicians

Practicing teaching
- Coaching
- Demonstration lessons
- Mentoring

Vehicles and mechanisms
- Developing professional developers
- Technology for professional development
- Workshops, institutes, courses, and seminars

experience followed by mentoring. More expert teachers might follow up on the immersion experience with an action research project to study how students learn through inquiry. Different strategies can also be phased in over time, such as in Cambridge, where professional development evolved from workshops led by external experts to more teacher-directed study groups as teachers' confidence and skill increased. Or strategies can be bundled together for the same group of teachers, like when a study group is facilitated by a university partner who also coaches study group members in the classroom. Rather than models, these 18 strategies are the palette from which professional developers can select and blend individual colors to give life and form to their professional development programs.

Figure 1.7. The Implementation Process: Commit to Vision and Standards→Analyze Student Learning and Other Data→Set Goals→Plan→Do→Evaluate

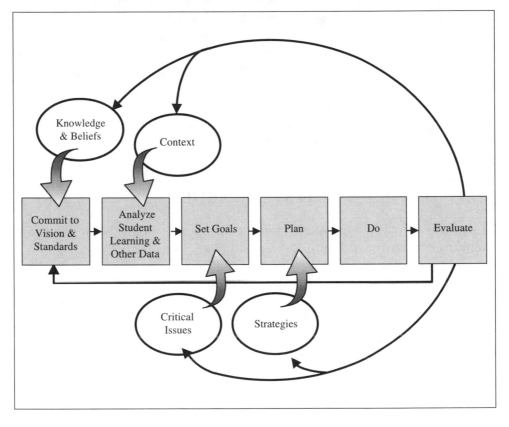

THE IMPLEMENTATION PROCESS

The components of the framework described above—knowledge and beliefs, strategies, context, and critical issues—are important influences on the professional development design process. While taking these into account, the design process has a life of its own. It sometimes follows a logical sequence from committing to a vision, to analyzing student learning data, to goal setting, planning, doing, and evaluating. It often does not. Action can often help to clarify the vision or the goals, for example. But, eventually, in some fashion, the implementation of a professional development program, from its initial conception to its postmortem, unfolds over time. A brief look at each of the phases of the implementation (commit to vision and standards→analyze student learning and other data→set goals→plan→ do→evaluate) follows (see Figure 1.7).

Create a Structure

Before beginning, designers need a structure for ongoing professional development planning and decision making. Creating that structure involves asking the following questions: Who sits at the table? Who makes the decisions? Who has input into the decisions? What do decision makers need to know and be able to do to effectively carry out their roles? How do decisions get made? How will designers communicate with stakeholders and build support for the plan? In Cambridge, for example, it was very important to the design process that teachers were brought in from the very beginning. The Cambridge team also employed an outside expert and established a collaborative decision-making process.

COMMIT TO VISION AND STANDARDS

The reform of mathematics and science education rests firmly on a commitment to enhance the teaching and learning that is currently the norm in our nation's classrooms. The new vision of mathematics and science teaching and learning, based on the standards developed by the National Council of Teachers of Mathematics (NCTM, 1989, 1991, 1995, 2000), the National Academy of Science's National Research Council (NRC, 1996a), and the American Association for the Advancement of Science (AAAS, 1993), is one in which all students engage in inquiry into significant questions in science and investigate complex problems in mathematics in supportive, collegial communities. Students come to deeply understand important science and mathematics ideas and master complex skills and reasoning processes that are essential to scientific and mathematical literacy. To achieve this vision teachers also need new knowledge, skills, behaviors, and dispositions. Teachers need to have ownership in the new vision and feel competent to create appropriate learning environments for their students. This includes feeling secure in their knowledge of the content they will help their students learn.

For this to happen, teachers need opportunities for professional growth—ones in which they learn what they need to know to achieve this new vision, in ways that model how they can work with their students. The National Staff Development Council's (2001b) professional development standards and the teaching standards and professional development standards in the NCTM and NRC documents clearly articulate a vision for science and mathematics teaching and professional development. Because it is difficult if not impossible to teach in ways that one has not learned, teachers also need opportunities to inquire into significant questions in science and to learn challenging mathematics and reflect on their own learning and teaching in supportive, collegial communities. What do classrooms look like in which the new vision of science and mathematics teaching and learning, based on local, state, and national standards, is playing out? And, following from that question, what do professional development opportunities look like in which teachers learn in that way, and learn to teach in that way? In Resource A, we include vignettes that create images of alternatives to the dominant practices in both teaching and professional development.

The original design framework included "Supporting Standards and Frameworks Through Professional Development" as a critical issue, which was discussed in Chapter 6 of the first edition of this book. Our decision to incorporate commitment to vision and standards as the first essential step in the design framework reflects our new understanding that supporting standards is more than a critical issue to be considered; standards set the course for professional development. (See Figure 1.7.) Providing teachers with the knowledge and skills they need to help every student achieve high standards is the central purpose of professional development. Standards guide the selection of content for professional development, which helps teachers explore the "big ideas" of the disciplines and deepen their content knowledge. Standards themselves are often the subject of professional development, as teachers immerse themselves in studying what the standards mean and what their implications are for learning, teaching, schooling, and professional development. And standards serve as the foundation of the vision that inspires the professional development design process from beginning to end.

Dennis Sparks (1997) wrote, "It's been said that someone who has a 'why' can endure any 'how'; few things are more important to motivation than purpose that is regarded as profoundly and morally compelling" (pp. 24-25). The vision of learning, teaching, and professional development based on standards is the "why" of professional development design. It is the desire to reach the vision that motivates professional developers to create powerful learning opportunities for teachers. It is the tension between the vision and the current reality that fuels goal setting and planning, drives the desire to change, and gives meaning to the daily tasks of implementing professional development programs. And, as professional developers reflect on and evaluate their programs, they gauge how well the school community is moving closer to its vision and recommit to the future they want for students, teachers, and schools.

What actually happens in the phase "commit to vision and standards" of the design process? How does a school community solidify its commitment to a vision and a set of standards for science and mathematics reform? Many educators have experienced the process of developing a vision as a meaningless exercise of putting words on paper that are either promptly ignored, written and embraced by only a few, or so general as to inspire no one. Because the vision for science and mathematics reform is rooted in deeply held beliefs and assumptions, developing a truly shared and compelling vision is a complex and long-term process. Notice in the design framework that an important input to the vision is knowledge and beliefs—

TABLE 1.2   Questions to Consider in Committing to a Vision and Standards

1. What is our vision for science and mathematics teaching and learning?
2. What do students need to know and be able to do in mathematics and science?
3. How will we know they have gained this knowledge?
4. What will we do if they do not gain this knowledge?
5. What do classrooms in which this new vision is playing out look like?
6. What do teachers need to know and be able to do if students are to achieve these standards?
7. What is our vision for teachers' learning?
8. What does professional development in which this new vision is playing out look like?
9. What kind of organization do we need to be to support this vision of science and mathematics teaching, learning, and professional development?

the knowledge bases about teaching, learning, the nature of science and mathematics, professional development, and change. It is important that the vision statements are written based on shared knowledge, not shared ignorance, and that school staff take the time to study relevant research and national standards and supporting documents. Without exception, the professional developers who worked on this book reported drawing on these knowledge bases to formulate the purpose, guiding principles, and core outcomes for their work.

A recent example in one author's experience is a kindergarten through Grade 12 mathematics committee in Turner, Maine, that began its curriculum development project with a yearlong study of *Principles and Standards for School Mathematics* (NCTM, 2000). Committee members read and discussed each content strand, solved mathematics problems together related to that strand, provided similar problems to their students, and studied the student work together. In this case, the professional development design had as its goal building teachers' knowledge of national standards and strengthening their commitment to a different kind of classroom.

Richard DuFour and Robert Eaker (1998) offer another strategy for building collective ownership of a vision and set of commitments based on using data. First, staff paint a picture of the current conditions of the school using a variety of data, including student achievement, behavior, participation data, satisfaction surveys, and staff activities. Then they answer the question, "If, within the next five years, you achieve everything you describe in your vision, what changes would you expect to see in the data?" (DuFour, 2000, p. 72). "When a faculty begins to struggle with that question," says DuFour, "they begin to develop the results orientation of a learning community."

Creating opportunities for constructive dialogue around the questions in Table 1.2 can also contribute to developing a shared vision for science and mathematics reform. The vignettes with reflective questions in Resource A may act as a catalyst to this dialogue.

Although a shared vision is essential for a productive learning community, this does not mean that professional development cannot proceed until the entire school community is united around a common vision. Michael Fullan (1993) reminds us that "vision emerges from, more than it precedes, action" (p. 28) and that "ready, fire, aim" may be a more productive sequence (p. 31). *Ready* implies that professional development design starts with some notion of purpose, especially for those designing the effort, but does not bog down in perfecting the shared vision. *Fire* is implementing the professional development program. It is through doing, learning, reflecting, and applying new knowledge and skills that the vision is clarified. *Aim*, according to Fullan, is crystallizing new beliefs and clarifying and strengthening the sense of shared purpose. While commitment to vision and high standards for all students come first in the sequence of the design framework, this phase is in fact iterative and interactive with all other phases of the process.

ANALYZE STUDENT LEARNING AND OTHER DATA

In this phase of the professional development design process, analyze student learning and other data, professional developers take stock of their reality as they explore the gap between the current and the desired state and set targets for improvement. (See Figure 1.7.) When a school community has a shared commitment to high standards for all students, it is better prepared to take an honest look at student learning data and is more likely to experience dissatisfaction with results that fall short of its commitments, rather than complacency, resignation, or defensiveness. The purpose of analyzing student learning and other data is to identify specific targets for improving student learning that will determine the goals for teacher learning and form the basis for a professional development program clearly focused on results for students. When designing professional development for a local school or district, it is crucial that the professional development plan is linked with school or district goals for improving mathematics and science learning.

Most important in this phase, professional developers examine multiple sources of student learning data to determine what essential knowledge and skills students are and are not learning and what performance gaps exist between rich and poor, white and minority, and boys and girls. Data

RELEVANT DATA

- **Demographic data about students and teachers**
- **Multiple measure of students' achievement of standards**
- **Student learning data disaggregated by racial, economic, language, and gender groups**
- **Data about classroom practice and students' opportunity to learn**
- **Data about professional development, the school culture, and leadership**

analysis can begin with readily available data such as state and district assessments, including both standards-based and norm-referenced test results. These assessments, however, do not provide adequate evidence of achievement of all the knowledge, skills, and dispositions that local communities may value and that national standards and many state and local standards call for, such as mathematical reasoning, problem solving, and communication, inquiry skills, or in-depth understanding of important mathematical and scientific concepts.

An important part of enacting a vision based on standards is putting into place a comprehensive local assessment system that complements high-stakes tests with assessments tied to local standards and curriculum and includes performance tasks, portfolios, and scoring and examination of student work as well as short-answer and multiple-choice tests. For example, schools or districts implementing standards-based curriculum can use assessments that are part of the program, such as in the Fresno (California) Unified School District, where teachers administer assessments from their FOSS units, which are collected and analyzed by the district (Love, 2002). In addition to classroom and school or district local assessments, common assessments administered periodically by teachers who teach the same grade level or course can provide teachers with timely and relevant feedback on the extent to which students are mastering agreed on standards (DuFour & Eaker, 1998; Love, 2002; Schmoker, 2002). Figure 1.8 illustrates the dynamic interplay among different parts of a comprehensive assessment system.

By using multiple measures, professional developers verify their hunches about student learning needs with more than one data source. Goals for professional development are not arbitrary or based on individuals' pet issues but instead are grounded in the needs that are showing up consistently in the data. Another advantage of using both classroom and common-grade-level assessments along with state and district assessments to target needs is that teachers become actively involved themselves in data analysis and data-driven dialogue. A professional learning experience in itself, the process of collecting and analyzing student learning data, using assessments that are aligned with their curriculum, increases teachers' ownership of student learning problems. When teachers embrace the problems, they are more willing participants in the professional development programs designed to solve them. They also become active agents in testing

Figure 1.8. A Dynamic, Local Assessment System Informing
Professional Development Design

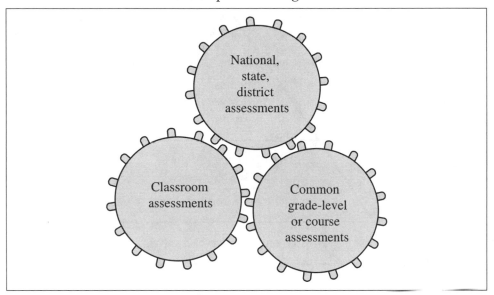

SOURCE. Love, N. (2002). © TERC, Cambridge, MA.

out new instructional strategies and monitoring progress toward improvement (DuFour & Eaker, 1998; Love, 2002).

Digging Deeper Into Student Learning Data

It is important not only to use multiple assessments of student learning
but also to go beyond superficial analyses of summary or aggregate reports
to derive the maximum value for goal setting. Figure 1.9 illustrates a process
for digging deeply into state and local assessment results to gain a fuller
picture of how students are performing in relation to the standards set by
the school community. The process begins with examining aggregate or
summary reports. These reports provide the headlines such as, overall,
what percentage of students met standards in mathematics or science (on
standards-based assessments) or what percentage of students are at or
above the 50th percentile (on norm-referenced assessments).

They also reveal trends over time, such as progress in increasing the percentage of students who meet standards. To explore performance gaps, professional developers need to go beyond the aggregate or summary reports
to examine disaggregated results, results separated out by subgroups such
as students receiving lunch assistance and those not, racial groups, language groups, and boys and girls.

Figure 1.9. Digging Into Student Learning Results

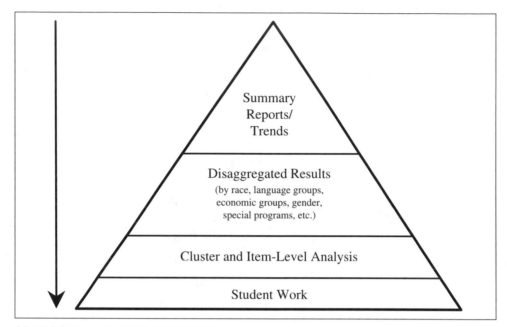

SOURCE: Love, N. (2002). © TERC, Cambridge, MA.

Digging deeper into the data in this way enables professional developers to uncover achievement gaps so that equity issues take center stage in the professional development plan. Often schools do not even recognize that they have race, economic, or cultural performance gaps until they examine disaggregated data. By uncovering these gaps, professional developers can direct attention to improving the achievement of specific groups of students who are not learning well. Their designs may include opportunities for teachers to better understand the racial and cultural backgrounds of their students and challenge educators' beliefs, practices, and policies that act as obstacles to poor and minority students achieving standards.

The next level of analysis is examining cluster or strand and item-level data. This kind of analysis requires looking at how students performed on content clusters or strands such as number sense or geometry and on particular test items. By getting inside the actual items, analyzing what knowledge and skills the assessment items were actually measuring and looking for patterns in correct and incorrect answers, planners gain a much better sense of what mathematics and science knowledge and skills students are struggling with as well as what vocabulary and test-taking skills they may be lacking. This enables professional developers to pinpoint needs more precisely, not just, for example, at mathematics problem solving in general, but at specific aspects of problem solving that are most challenging for students. Finally, examining student work often proves to be the most fruitful data source, providing rich insights into students' thinking, as the following example illustrates.

"Our mathematics department meets weekly," explained a teacher at City On A Hill. "There are two meetings a year where we *don't* look at student work." The team uses a process for examining work that begins with defining a clear purpose for looking at the work. They always do the mathematics task themselves and share their strategies before digging into the student work. Then they closely examine pieces of work the teachers bring, first making observations, then drawing inferences and identifying questions for further investigation.

For the past two years, they focused on this question: Why are our students doing so poorly on the open-response problems on the state mathematics assessment when we do these kinds of problems regularly as part of our Interactive Mathematics Program? As they studied student work and thinking over time, they identified some key reasons. First, there was some basic mathematics vocabulary the students did not have. Second, teachers were hovering too much over the students in the classroom, explaining the problem to them, breaking it down, coaching them step-by-step. So even though the students were familiar with mathematics problem solving, they did not have enough independent practice. Teachers worked on these areas and over a two-year period quadrupled students' average score on open-ended questions. This example illustrates how careful analysis of student work led to a clear focus for improvement and how examining student work is in itself a powerful professional learning strategy. (See Chapter 7 for more on City On A Hill and see Chapter 3, Table 3.1, for questions to consider, data sources, and resources for investigating students and student learning.)

Opportunities-to-Learn Data/Data About Practice

Underlying performance gaps are often inadequate opportunities for particular student groups, particularly racial and language minorities and poor students, to learn a rigorous mathematics and science curriculum. A study by Weiss, Banilower, McMahon, and Smith (2001) found that ability grouping was still widely practiced in mathematics and science and that classes labeled low ability are more likely to contain a high proportion of minority students. Another study by Weiss, Matti, and Smith (1994, as cited in Weiss, 1997) found that students in low-ability classes had fewer opportunities to do inquiry-based science or write about reasoning when solving mathematical problems. Professional development programs should be geared not just to closing achievement gaps but also to closing opportunities-to-learn gaps. In this phase of the design process, professional developers can also use data about course enrollment, special program placement, teachers' qualifications, and curriculum, instruction, and assessment practices to uncover what practices may be preventing some students from achieving standards (Love, 2002). (See also Table 3.3 in Chapter 3.)

Complementing data about student achievement and opportunities to learn are data about teachers' needs. What knowledge and skills do teachers need if students are going to reach specific standards? These can be assessed through surveys, classroom observations, interviews, and content assessments. (See Table 3.2 in Chapter 3.) Finally, professional developers will want to consider data about the school, district, or organization that helps them assess the quality of leadership, the strength of the professional learning community, and the capacity of the organization to implement and sustain mathematics and science reform. (See Tables 3.4 and 3.5 in Chapter 3.)

When designing professional development programs not for individual schools or districts but for teachers from many different schools and districts or for large-scale state or national programs, professional developers can draw on state-level data and national data from sources such as the National Assessment of Educational Progress (NAEP) and from the Third International Mathematics and Science Study (TIMSS) to identify trends in student learning, achievement gaps, and classroom practice. Whether using local, state, national, or international data, professional developers ground their design in data about student learning, opportunities to learn, and classroom practice to ensure that their programs focus on critical areas of need for student and teacher learning.

SET GOALS

Rigorous analysis of student learning and other data sets the stage for setting goals for the professional development program. (See Figure 1.7.) If the vision describes the desired future and the data analysis describes the current reality, goals are the benchmarks or milestones to assess progress toward the vision. "Vision may inspire, but goals foster immediate accountability," says Richard DuFour and Robert Eaker(1998), who liken goals to the "ports of call on the journey toward improvement" (p. 203). A few clear, concrete, and attainable goals motivate, energize, and focus professional development and school improvement. On the other hand, according to Michael Schmoker (1999), the absence of explicit learning goals is "the most striking, self-defeating, contradictory characteristic of schools and our efforts to improve them" (p. 23). If professional development is to be linked to gains in student achievement, four kinds of goals are relevant: goals for student learning; goals for teacher learning; goals for teaching practice; and goals for the organization. The following were the broad goals for the curriculum implementation program in Cambridge:

- To improve science learning for all kindergarten through Grade 9 students in the Cambridge public schools (student learning)

- To implement an inquiry-based, modular science curriculum throughout the district (teaching practice)
- To build teacher leadership and expertise within the system (teacher learning)
- To develop a structure that would permanently sustain the science program (organization)

The driving force behind a professional development program is a small number of specific, attainable, and measurable student learning goals. Learning goals, according to Schmoker (2002), should target the lowest-scoring subjects or courses and target specific standards where achievement is low. For example, a professional development program might target students' understanding of fractions, decimals, and percentages or problem solving in mathematics, as in the example from City On A Hill above. Improvement efforts

> **FOUR KINDS OF GOALS FOR PROFESSIONAL DEVELOPMENT**
> - **Goals for student learning**
> - **Goals for teacher learning**
> - **Goals for teaching practice**
> - **Goals for the organization**

can bog down with long laundry lists of goals or vague or overly ambitious goals. As designers set goals for student learning, they tap into knowledge about teaching and learning and the nature of mathematics and science treated explicitly in the national and some state standards. In Cambridge, planners developed a conceptual framework for science in the elementary years, based on state and national standards, which eventually led to the selection of the curriculum they implemented. In addition, setting goals for students involves analyzing students' needs and confronting disparities in achievement between boys and girls or among racial or cultural groups. It is essential that goals for student learning specifically address closing achievement gaps and expanding learning opportunities to all students.

Goals for teachers flow directly out of goals for students. If students are going to develop a set of understandings, skills, and predispositions, then what do teachers need to know and be able to do to realize those outcomes for students? Learning goals for teachers are also informed by referring to the standards, as well as data about teacher performance, knowledge and skills, needs, and supports available. Planners in Cambridge considered what knowledge and skills, professional development, and structural support teachers needed to successfully implement the new science curriculum.

Professional development that is linked to improving student learning should also set goals for teacher practice. How will teachers translate the new knowledge and skills they are gaining into classroom practice? In the

Cambridge example, the goal was for teachers to implement the new science curriculum as intended by the curriculum developers.

Professional development goals can also encompass goals for the organization, such as the development of leadership or the strengthening of the learning community. In Cambridge, for example, a goal was to put in place a structure that would sustain the implementation of the science program. This goal reflected the designers' attention to the critical issues of sustainability and professional culture as well as their knowledge and beliefs about effective professional development and change. These are important inputs into goal setting as are contextual factors such as the history of professional development, the resources available, and local, state, and national policies. In Cambridge, the decision to focus on leadership development early on in the program arose in part because resources limited reaching every teacher. Knowledge of context helps designers formulate goals that are realistic, attainable, and forward moving. "You want to both be realistic and push the system at the same time," explained Karen Worth.

Clarifying clear and worthwhile outcomes for student learning, teacher learning, teaching, and the organization not only brings focus and coherence to the professional development program but also lays the groundwork for future program evaluation. An important part of the goal-setting process, according to Thomas Guskey (2000), is to consider how goals will be assessed and what evidence will be used to determine if goals are met.

PLAN

Once goals are set, planners begin to sketch out their design. All of the other inputs described above—critical issues, context, knowledge and beliefs, and strategies—are strong influences in the planning phase. (See Figure 1.7.) Planners scan their context, unearthing important factors to consider as they tailor their program to their own circumstances and review the student learning and other data they have collected to connect plans to goals. This is when they may decide they need more information about learning, teaching, mathematics or science, professional development, and change. Having a research-based vision of what effective programs can look like can also generate some ideas for their plans. (See the profiles in *Enhancing Program Quality in Mathematics and Science* by Kaser and Bourexis, 1999, for one source.) Learning about other similar districts' plans can also be helpful.

Planning is also the time to revisit and clarify the beliefs that underlie the program. Critical issues enter in, as planners consider how to confront challenges like scaling up or building leadership. And, finally, during planning, professional developers think strategically about which strategy or combination of strategies to employ, much like a skillful teacher selects from a repertoire of instructional strategies.

The design framework has been used to plan short-term and long-term and small- and large-scale programs. Planners for small-scale and short-term efforts pick and choose among the contextual factors, critical issues, and knowledge and beliefs that are most relevant for their initiative but can still use the design framework to be more thoughtful and deliberate about their planning. For example, staff members at Biological Sciences Curriculum Study (BSCS) use the design framework to plan institutes, which are part of their National Academy for Curriculum Leadership. For a small-scale, shorter-term effort such as one institute, they do not consider every context factor but think carefully about the most relevant ones, especially about the participants' backgrounds and their learning needs. Since they are working with high school teachers in district teams who are implementing standards-based high school curriculum, they consider participants' need to plan during the institute; planning time is hard to come by once the teams return to their districts. To make the planning time as productive as possible, they have participants bring their own student achievement data to the institute, which they analyze and use to guide the goals for the curriculum selection process and subsequent professional development. Based on selective inputs and their goals for a particular institute session, they plan to use a mix of strategies. For example, participants are engaged in an immersion in inquiry experience both to increase the participants' science content knowledge and for staff to model a professional development strategy to be implemented in the teams' districts. Participants also engage in examining student work during the institutes to enable them to effectively select instructional materials. Whether large scale or small scale, short term or long term, professional developers draw on the most relevant inputs into the design process to craft a plan that will soon be put to the test of implementation—the "do" phase of the design process.

DO

Having made the best decisions they can, designers move from "sketching" to "painting"—the actual implementation of their plan. (See Figure 1.7.) In this phase, they draw on their skills as change facilitators and knowledge about implementation and the change process (e.g., Fullan, 1991, 2001; Hall & Hord, 2001; Loucks-Horsley et al., 1990). For fundamental change to happen, teachers need to experiment with new behavior and gain new understandings, and that takes time. They will move through predictable developmental stages in how they feel and how they are using new approaches. Frequently, things get worse before they get better, as teachers experience what Fullan (1991) calls the "implementation dip." And, despite professional developers' best efforts to "manage" change, it is, by nature, unpredictable. Often the best that can be done is to expect the unexpected and problem solve along the way. Taking these and other important principles of change into consideration can help prevent the all too common failure of professional development programs at this stage in the process.

Despite the "best laid plans," it is impossible to predict how the initial design will work. As the action unfolds, designers discover what works and what doesn't. Like artists stepping back from the canvas and examining their work from different perspectives, professional developers continuously monitor their plan, using a variety of data sources. They ask questions such as: Is this working? Are we moving toward our goals of improved student learning in mathematics and science? Are we meeting participants' needs? Is our program, in fact, a good match with our context? What conditions, if any, have changed, and how should we respond? What critical issues do we need to address now? Sometimes their reflection is enhanced by interested "visitors" (sometimes called "critical friends") who sensitize professional developers to important aspects of their programs seen from different perspectives.

Based on this feedback, planners often go back to the drawing board. It is rare that an entire program is carried out exactly as planned. As the examples in this book will illustrate, the most successful programs do not start out with flawless designs. They begin with a sound idea that then goes through many revisions and continues to evolve. Programs change over time both because planners figure out a better way and because conditions change, sometimes as a direct result of the professional development program. For example, as teacher leaders in Cambridge became more self-assured and experienced, they wanted fewer workshops and more self-directed study groups. Professional development changed the culture, which in turn created the conditions for a different strategy. There is a live interplay between context and implementation.

None of the inputs, in fact, remains static over time. The knowledge base about learning, teaching, the nature of mathematics and science, professional development, and the change process is constantly growing. As professional developers learn from their experiences, they become active contributors to the knowledge base, as the professional developers featured in this book have. And, as their needs and interests change, they look to research for new ideas. Beliefs change, too. Seeing the impact of their work, professional developers begin to think differently about students, teachers, their disciplines, professional development, and change. Critical issues are just as dynamic. Experience may lead designers to consider new issues or gain deeper understandings of the ones they have grappled with. Far from linear or lockstep, implementing professional development is recursive and usually messy, demanding flexibility and continuous learning throughout the process.

EVALUATE

An essential but often overlooked or underutilized part of the professional development design process is evaluation. (See Figure 1.7.) Professional development opportunities are designed for a wide variety of purposes. It is the role of evaluation to determine whether and in what ways they are successful.

Fulfilling that role, however, is rarely easy for several reasons. First, regardless of the purpose of a given program, people typically jump to measure what is easiest: satisfaction of participants. Because of this norm it is difficult to get people to think more broadly about outcomes and measures. Second, there is increasing demand to assess the value of professional development based on the achievement of the students of those teachers who participate. This demand is well founded, given the large investment of resources that has been made in professional development and the critical need to improve student learning and close achievement gaps. The challenge here is not to expect student learning outcomes prematurely, before the professional development program has been fully implemented and teacher learning and change in practice have been well supported over time. Nonetheless, it is important that professional developers broaden the valued outcomes for in-depth, long-term professional development to include change in classroom practice and in student learning results. Finally, evaluation needs attention because it is underutilized as a valuable learning experience for professional developers, participants, and others. Reflection on evaluation results, as they are being gathered as well as when synthesized, is an important contributor to continuous improvement. There are several questions that professional developers can ask themselves that may help them address the challenges of evaluation of their programs and initiatives.

- What are the goals or desired outcomes?
- How do you assess the accomplishment of the outcomes?
- How do you acknowledge and evaluate how a professional development initiative and its participants change over time?
- How do you take advantage of evaluation as a learning experience in itself?

What are the goals or desired outcomes of the program or initiative?

Professional developers typically have a wide range of goals, but they are often not skilled at articulating them as outcomes. What would you see if you were successful? What would have changed for whom? It is easier to think of activities than accomplishments, for example, conducting a summer institute and a series of follow-up problem-solving sessions is often cited as a goal, rather than teachers using inquiry-based strategies in their classrooms. The range of possible outcomes is quite large: development of new abilities (knowledge, skills, strategies, dispositions) by a variety of people (teachers, students, administrators) and organizations (departments, teams, schools, districts) in a variety of areas (teaching, leadership, change management). Being clear about desired outcomes, articulating what they would look like if they were present, not only lays important groundwork for evaluation but also results in a more focused and purposeful program.

How do you assess the accomplishment of the program's outcomes?

Evaluation helps collect evidence of the extent to which a program's aims have been met. Although paper and pencil in the hands of the participants in professional development have traditionally been the tool of choice in evaluation, a wide range of instruments and sources of information are preferable. Evidence from interviews, observations, product (e.g., lesson plan) analysis, performance tasks, focus groups—all can contribute evidence. Teachers, students, colleagues, administrators, scientists and mathematicians—all can be sources of information about the outcomes of a professional learning experience. Obviously there are trade-offs for every instrument and source of information, for example, in cost, time, degree of self-report, or amount of inference required (Guskey, 2000). These are all considered in designing an evaluation keyed to a particular purpose, audience, and budget.

The National Science Foundation has funded many local school districts to reform the teaching of mathematics and science throughout their systems. Horizon Research, Inc. developed and is supporting the use of evaluation instruments so that each of these projects does not have to create its own, and so data can be aggregated across projects. The framework for data collection includes such outcomes as the quality of the professional development activities; extent of teacher involvement in the activities; changes in teacher attitudes and beliefs; changes in science and mathematics curriculum, instruction, and assessment; nature of the culture or context for teaching; and the sustainability of the professional development system (Horizon Research, 2001).

How do you acknowledge and then evaluate how a professional development initiative and its participants change over time?

The impact of professional learning activities looks different at different times. This is why it is foolhardy to either expect or focus on measuring student learning when teachers have just begun to learn and experiment with new ideas and strategies. Well-designed evaluations unfold with expectations for change. For example, one might focus on measuring participants' satisfaction and whether they are developing basic understanding early in a program; change in classroom behavior and in the professional culture midway; and then on various kinds of student change, beginning with attitudes and evolving to demonstrating new, deeper understandings of concepts.

To address this issue, evaluators have used concepts and tools of the Concerns-Based Adoption Model (Hall & Hord, 2001) to answer questions about the implementation of changes in mathematics and science education (Loucks-Horsley et al., 1990; Pratt & Loucks-Horsley, 1993). Three kinds of questions can be asked: How do teachers' concerns about the new program or teaching strategy change over time? How does their use of the new program or teaching strategy change over time? To what extent do teachers implement the critical components of the new program or teaching strategy over time? Two developmental scales—Stages of Concern (assessed using paper-and-pencil instruments) and Levels of Use (assessed through a focused interview procedure)—provide criteria for assessing progress along the change continuum. Components of the program or strategy can also be defined and assessed using a combination of interview and observation; the different "configurations" that the program components take on in different classrooms can then be represented and monitored over time.

After sufficient time has elapsed for teacher change to result in improvement in student learning, students are an appropriate focus for professional development evaluation. A unique evaluation scheme was used by the Mathematics Renaissance (see Chapter 6) in its final and fifth year to evaluate the impact on students of the professional development it provided to middle school teachers throughout the state of California. As part of TIMSS, hundreds of hours of classroom instruction have been videotaped in mathematics classrooms throughout the United States (U.S. Department of Education, 1996), which have been compared to those of classrooms in Japan and Germany using a very sophisticated coding and analysis procedure. Videotapes of classrooms of teachers participating in Mathematics Renaissance professional development were made, and similarly coded and analyzed. They were compared with a sample of the TIMSS tapes of U.S. classrooms to address the question, "Do students of Mathematics Renaissance teachers have a greater opportunity to develop the kinds of mathematical understandings, skills, and attitudes called for in the NCTM Standards and the California Mathematics Framework, than do students of teachers not involved in Mathematics Renaissance?"

Another resource for evaluating professional development comes from Thomas Guskey's (2000) book *Evaluating Professional Development*. Guskey identifies five critical levels of professional development evaluation ranging from simple to more complex. Each level builds on the one before it.

- Level 1: Participants' reaction

- Level 2: Participants' learning

- Level 3: Organizational support and change

- Level 4: Participants' use of new knowledge and skills

- Level 5: Student learning outcomes

For each level, Guskey lays out what questions are addressed, what information will be gathered through which evaluation methods, what is measured or assessed, and how the information will be used.

How do you take advantage of evaluation as a learning experience in *and of itself?*

Increasingly, evaluators are becoming partners with professional developers in a commitment to continuous improvement of programs and their results. Involvement is the key word here, through such activities as

- Engaging program staff as well as participants in specifying and discussing desired outcomes and identifying and prioritizing evaluation questions
- Involving staff and participants in the design or review of instruments or procedures for assessing outcomes
- Sharing responsibility with staff and participants for collecting data
- Engaging staff in analyzing and interpreting data
- Sharing responsibility for reporting learning from evaluation with a variety of audiences using a variety of formats

Each of these activities can contribute to staff and participant understanding of their own learning and that of others; of a variety of methods to assess important learning outcomes as well as interpret information gathered; of ways to specify and then to investigate the answers to important questions; and of how to communicate to a variety of audiences and develop arguments for new ways of acting.

A DISCLAIMER AND A PITCH

The design framework presented above is not perfect. It creates artificial distinctions among components like critical issues and context, which are far more interconnected than separate circles depict. It simplifies an enormously complex process. And it may miss important feedback loops and connections. With that disclaimer, allow us to advocate strongly for the use of a design framework such as this to guide professional development. Since the publication of the first edition of this book in 1998, we have seen the design framework lead to more purposeful and reflective professional development designs. Its use helps professional developers make conscious choices and resist the quick-fix approach. We are more convinced than ever that only through thoughtful and careful design, based on sound principles and strategies, can professional development be elevated from its current state.

2

Knowledge and Beliefs Supporting Effective Professional Development

Chapter 1 introduces and describes a comprehensive framework for designing professional development. One of the first and very important inputs to the design process is the knowledge base related to professional development. The *knowledge base* refers to two different kinds of information—*knowledge* and *beliefs*. Knowledge refers to information that is sure, solid, dependable, and supported by research. It is distinct from opinions that are points of view that may not be supported by evidence. Beliefs are what we think we know (Ball, 1996) or may be coming to know based on new information. They are supported by experience, and people are strongly committed to them. What people know and believe informs the choices they make about professional development.

New knowledge and beliefs based on research and practice are transforming the way educators think about teaching and learning and teacher professional development. Knowledge in the areas of learning, teaching, the nature of science and mathematics, professional development, and how change occurs provides a valuable framework for shaping decisions about the design and provision of professional development. (See Figure 2.1.)

Since the publication of the first edition of this book, we have worked with hundreds of educators to promote the idea that effective professional development is designed based on research and on the particular needs,

Figure 2.1. Knowledge and Beliefs Supporting Effective Professional
Development

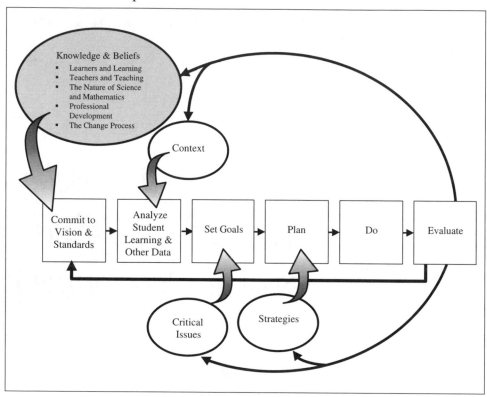

contexts, and circumstances of the participants. As part of this work, we
have asked scores of people what makes learning powerful in mathematics
and science. Time after time their responses are right on target with the research. They say: "Learning has to be active," or "You need to connect what
you are learning to what you already think and know," or "Learners have to
want to learn—it has to be meaningful and relevant to them." Then we ask
how many of them have professional development opportunities with
these same features. The inevitable response is "none" or "a few."

The fact remains that the field of education is living in a paradox of
knowing one thing and doing another. For example, we say we know that
learning experiences should be active, coherent, and relevant; yet too much
of student learning and teacher professional development is still not interactive or reflective and remains disconnected from practice and what the
learners know and need. We need to make common knowledge our common practice, starting with professional development that reflects the
knowledge base. At every juncture designers should ask themselves, "What

does the research say?" and "How well does our design reflect the knowledge from research?" In this chapter, we outline key knowledge and beliefs related to professional development to encourage all to make common knowledge a key input into the vision setting, planning, and provision of professional development for teachers of science and mathematics.

LEARNERS AND LEARNING

All professional development programs need to consider the knowledge base on learners and learning as a major input to their designs. This is critical on at least two levels. First, when teachers have learning experiences that help them understand how children best learn mathematics and science, they are better able to provide such experiences to their students. On another level, we need professional development designs that reflect how people learn so that the adult learners are supported to learn in a sustained and in-depth way. Too often the cognitive research on learning is forgotten when it comes to teachers' learning. (See Figure 2.1.)

Developing proficiency in mathematics and science requires learners to develop conceptual understanding as well as procedural information in the subject and be able to apply and transfer knowledge of the content flexibly (Bransford, Brown, & Cocking, 1999). Such learning is complex and involves developing and revising ideas over time. Five general concepts summarize the knowledge base about learners and learning that should inform the design of professional development:

> **LEARNERS AND LEARNING**
>
> - **New knowledge is built on the learner's prior knowledge.**
> - **Learning is an active process.**
> - **Knowledge is constructed through a process of change.**
> - **New knowledge comes from experiences and interaction with ideas and phenomena.**
> - **Learning needs to be situated in meaningful and relevant contexts.**
> - **Learning is supported through interaction among students about the ideas of science and mathematics.**
>
> **SOURCE: Bransford, Brown, and Cocking (1999).**

- What learners already know influences their learning.

- Learners acquire new knowledge by constructing it for themselves.

- The construction of knowledge is a process of change that includes addition, creation, modification, refinement, restructuring, and rejection.

- Learning happens through diverse experiences.

- All students regardless of race, culture, and gender are capable of understanding and doing science and mathematics.

What Learners Already Know Influences Their Learning

Research into student thinking and understanding in science and mathematics has documented ideas that students hold about concepts and how concepts build on each other (American Association for the Advancement of Science [AAAS], 2000; Pfundt & Duit, 1994). This research demonstrates that what learners know is an important foundation for their future learning. When consistent with conceptions that are currently accepted by mathematics and science communities, this prior or informal knowledge is a strong base on which to build new understandings. Sometimes, however, learners' conceptions are inconsistent with accepted knowledge—they are misconceptions.

Misconceptions are tenacious and resistant to change using conventional teaching strategies. The existing ideas interact with and even filter new knowledge, resulting in a variety of learning outcomes—some desired by the teacher and others, unintended. What learners already know or think they know plays a much more important role in teaching and learning than previously recognized. We know through cognitive research that learning involves building on or modifying existing ideas, rather than just adding new disconnected information (Wandersee, Mintzes, & Novak, 1994). This understanding of how prior knowledge influences how learners interpret and interact with new information has had a profound influence on the design of learning experiences.

Learning is also influenced by the learners' expectations, attitudes, and beliefs about themselves and about learning, schooling, and the community in which they live. When individuals are learning effectively, they are engaged in what they are doing and expect that it will make sense to them. They do not expect learning to be easy and instantaneous, but have confidence that understanding will come from persistence, interaction with ideas and natural phenomena, dialogue with peers and teachers, attention to other possible ideas, and a willingness to change their view on the basis of compelling new evidence.

Since learning is influenced by what learners already know and think they know, and by their view of themselves as learners, it is essential that learning experiences be designed to connect with or challenge prior knowledge and provide opportunity for interaction with people and ideas.

Learners Construct New Knowledge

Contructivist theory has changed how educators think about teaching in fundamental ways. The theory sees learning as a process through which learners construct their knowledge by modifying or rejecting existing ideas (Bransford et al., 1999; Cobb, 1994; Driver, Asoko, Leach, Mortimer, & Scott, 1994). This idea is based on the knowledge that learning is a very personal and active process through which the learner interacts with information and experiences and filters them through what they already know (Bruner, 1966). Learning comes from thinking through and often struggling with problems and situations to arrive at new understandings, which are built on learners' current ideas. The learner interacts in a very active sense with ideas and experiences, rather than just passively taking in facts or memorizing data (Bransford et al., 1999).

Viewed through constructivism, learners are not empty vessels to be filled by knowledge imparted by others. Rather, they hold their own ideas that help them make sense of their world, and these ideas are the link to new learning. Teaching involves drawing out the ideas learners hold and making useful connections between new ideas and existing ones. Learning environments that reflect how people learn help learners make these connections and provide collaborative forms of learning so people can interact with one another and make sense of new concepts and ideas (Jonassen, 1994).

> **FEATURES OF PROFESSIONAL DEVELOPMENT BASED ON THE KNOWLEDGE OF LEARNING**
>
> - **Make useful connections between teachers' existing ideas and new ones.**
> - **Provide opportunity for active engagement, discussion, and reflection to challenge existing ideas and construct new ones.**
> - **Situate the learning in contexts teachers find familiar.**
> - **Challenge current thinking by producing and helping to resolve dissonance between new ideas and existing ones.**
> - **Support teachers to develop a range of strategies that address learning for all students.**

Another important aspect of learning is the process of personal reflection. Effective learners are able to monitor their own ideas and thought processes, compare and contrast them with those of others, and provide reasons why they accept one point of view over another. The research literature also supports the idea that learning is mediated by the culture and the social environments in which learners interact with their peers, teachers, parents, and others. It is from this interaction that learners acquire (very often implicitly) the norms, expectations, and values that influence whether, how, and what they learn (Silver, Kilpatrick, & Schlesinger, 1990).

Learning in this way is very person specific and supported through interaction with other learners. These two concepts have greatly challenged the perspective that people acquire concepts by receiving and memorizing information from other people who know more than they do or that students will learn what their teachers know by listening to what they say and that the presence of other students is incidental to learning (Schifter, 1996a).

Knowledge Is Constructed
Through a Process of Change

Learners evolve from their current state of knowledge in four different ways: (1) when new ideas fit naturally with existing ideas and are added to them; (2) when learners create a new idea out of existing knowledge; (3) when new ideas extend and challenge existing knowledge, leading to its minor modification or wholesale restructuring; and (4) when learners see that new ideas are powerful but irreconcilable with existing knowledge, leading to the rejection of their existing knowledge.

As learners confront new information their initial questions relate to defining it. They ask: "What is it? Do I know what it means? Can I represent it?" Once a new perspective becomes clear to learners, they can consider if it is plausible and useful. They ask: "Do I believe it? Does it fit with other things I believe to be true? Does it achieve anything for me? Does it solve problems I have been grappling with? Does it suggest approaches I hadn't thought of?" (Posner, Strike, Hewson, & Gertzog, 1982). If all these conditions are met, the new idea will gain higher status for the learner. This entire process happens as learners assess, adopt, or reject new ideas, often unconsciously.

Even if learners find that a proposed change has a high status for them, they may still not consider it worth the trouble and effort to adopt it. Individuals are more likely to change, rejecting their existing ideas and adopt new ones—that is, transforming their thinking—when the new idea has high status *and* they have reason to be dissatisfied with their existing ideas (Hewson & Thorley, 1989).

> **LEARNING IS A
> PROCESS OF CHANGE**
>
> - **Add new knowledge that fits easily with their existing ideas.**
> - **Create new ideas out of their existing knowledge.**
> - **Modify existing ideas based on new information.**
> - **Reject existing knowledge in the face of powerful new ideas.**

Learners may become dissatisfied with their current knowledge when they confront new ideas that do not support their current thinking, also referred to as experiencing *cognitive dissonance*. For example, a teacher may examine student work and assessments and see that the students did not learn the concepts the teacher thought she taught. The teacher may ask herself if the methods she is using can really be effective when so many students failed to learn. She may then begin to question her practice or become dissatisfied with her current ideas about how to teach.

When such dissatisfaction emerges, the learner works hard to resolve it by either rejecting the new information (this is often the case) or by beginning a process of reorganizing their prior knowledge (Bransford et al., 1999;

Thompson & Zeuli, 1999). Transformational learning occurs when learners reject deeply held ideas, reorganize what they know, and restructure their basic assumptions and frameworks for learning (Mezirow, 1991, 1997).

New Knowledge Comes From Experiences

Learning arises in different ways as learners inquire into natural phenomena, grapple with challenging problems, raise and address questions, interact with other people directly in conversation or indirectly through resources (e.g., books or videotapes), and reflect on their own thoughts and ideas. These diverse experiences include direct observation of and experience with phenomena and ideas and input from experts, such as through teachers' explanations, instructional materials, and mathematicians and scientists.

All Students Can Learn Science and Mathematics in the Ways Described Above

National standards for mathematics and science education reflect a vision in which all students are provided with opportunities and support to learn challenging content. The rich knowledge base on learners and learning shows that all learners from very young ages come to school with conceptions about the world, are curious about phenomena, and can inquire into them and make meaning of them. When all children have access to quality teaching and high expectations, they are able to meet standards for content learning (Campbell, 1995). Schools keep the flame of learning alive by challenging all students to learn these subjects that are most critical for the future.

Educational equity and opportunity for learning are enhanced when teachers, students, and parents hold high expectations for student learning. High expectations, however, are not enough (National Council of Teachers of Mathematics [NCTM], 2000). To support all learners means creating access to courses and effective teaching and support structures for non-English speakers and students with disabilities. It means having diversity among faculty and adults to act as role models, and it means ensuring that children in high-poverty districts have access to the curriculum and instructional and laboratory materials needed for them to succeed in science and mathematics (Britton, Raizen, Kaser, & Porter, 2000).

TEACHERS AND TEACHING

Teaching is the act of organizing and shaping learning experiences for students. In recent years, higher standards for student learning have caused educators to reexamine the teaching routines common in our schools. Many

TEACHERS AND TEACHING

- The purpose of teaching is to facilitate learning.
- Teaching is a profession requiring specialized knowledge.
- The practice of teaching is complex and demanding.

do not support students to reach the high standards we now hold for learning. For example, from an in-depth look at the teaching of mathematics in eighth-grade classrooms in the United States, Japan, and Germany, researchers found American mathematics teaching to be focused narrowly on having students develop isolated skills through repeated practice (Stigler & Hiebert, 1999). This has prompted a rethinking of what it looks like to teach concepts in depth and to all students. To do so, teachers must be proficient in their content areas, understand how students learn, and have a wide range of instructional strategies to facilitate learning (NCTM, 2000; National Research Council [NRC], 2001). Furthermore, they must be skilled at assessing student learning and using assessment information to make hundreds of instructional decisions every day. Quality professional development focuses on supporting the improvement of teaching by enhancing knowledge and skills in these critical areas. (See Figure 2.1.)

Three general concepts frame what we currently know about teachers and teaching (see the box titled "Teachers and Teaching"). Together, these concepts support a view of teaching that is reflected in national standards and that many schools are working hard to bring about. It is a view of teaching that coherently builds on the concepts of learners and learning previously outlined. In particular, this view contrasts sharply with teaching approaches used in the past in which teachers outlined procedures they expected students to follow, provided authoritative explanations they expected students to memorize, and evaluated students' work only to see if information had been reproduced correctly (Schifter, 1996a). It also underscores the requirement that teachers be highly skilled and knowledgeable in their subject matter so they can create coherence and connections across the content, know the next best questions to ask, and facilitate learning with understanding (Schifter, 1999).

The Purpose of Teaching Is to Facilitate Learning

This may seem so obvious that there is no need to state it. Yet there are still many examples of teacher learning that focus on preparing teachers to deliver content without attention to whether their students have learned this content (Sparks, 2002a). Increasingly, educators are interested in linking teaching to learning and using ongoing assessment to adjust and enhance teaching and increase student learning (Black & William, 1998).

Learning lies at the heart of any conception of teaching. Teachers need to match learners and what they know with the intended curriculum in ways that make learning achievable. A teacher cannot assume it is solely the learners' responsibility to make the necessary connections between where they are and where the teacher intends them to go. Rather, effective teaching involves continually assessing where the learners are, choosing appropriate learning activities based on the assessment, and assessing again to inform the next instructional decisions (Black & William, 1998). This includes engaging the students in self-assessment and monitoring of their own learning (Carlson, Humphrey, & Reinhart, 2003).

> ## EXPERT TEACHERS
>
> - **Know the structure of the knowledge in their disciplines.**
> - **Know the conceptual barriers that are likely to hinder learning.**
> - **Have a well-organized knowledge of concepts (content knowledge) and inquiry procedures and problem-solving strategies (based on pedagogical content knowledge).**
> - **Continuously assess their own learning, knowledge, and practices.**
>
> **SOURCE: Bransford, Brown, and Cocking (1999, p. 230).**

This view of teaching has obvious implications for professional development. Teachers committed to ensuring learning need advanced knowledge in their content, an understanding of what they can learn by examining student work and thinking, a diverse array of assessment strategies, and a range of instructional strategies.

Teaching Is a Profession Requiring Specialized Knowledge

Practice of any profession is complex and uncertain and draws upon expert knowledge bases particular to the profession (Schön, 1983, 1988). The complexity and uncertainty stem from the fact that professionals are constantly being called on to make decisions in unique circumstances without "absolute" knowledge. Past experience and a base of expert knowledge do not provide a set of fixed rules to follow but only heuristics that can guide professional judgment and decision making. To make decisions that are informed rather than reactive, a key characteristic of professional practice is reflection on past and current actions to inform future decisions.

The current view of teaching as a profession requiring specialized knowledge is in sharp contrast with the outmoded perspective of teachers as skilled technicians who, rather than have their own body of knowledge, simply apply bodies of disciplinary knowledge produced by others. It is now recognized that the teaching profession constitutes its own large body of knowledge. This includes knowledge of the content of the disciplines, of students, and of a variety of instruction and assessment strategies (Coble &

Koballa, 1996; National Commission on Mathematics and Science Teaching for the 21st Century, 2000; NCTM, 2000; NRC, 1996a).

These three key areas of teacher knowledge are continually consulted and integrated by teachers as they make hundreds of professional decisions every day (Ball & Cohen, 2000). Shulman's (1986) and others' research on teacher knowledge (Cochran, De Ruiter, & King, 1993; Fernández-Balboa & Stiehl, 1995; van Driel, Verloop, & De Vos, 1998) refer to teachers' specialized knowledge as *pedagogical content knowledge*. It is an understanding of what makes the learning of specific concepts easy or difficult for learners, awareness of what concepts are more fundamental than others, and knowledge of ways of representing and formulating subject matter to make it accessible to learners. Developing pedagogical content knowledge requires subject matter knowledge (Smith & Neale, 1989). For example, in mathematics, in order for teachers to demonstrate the highest levels of pedagogical content knowledge, they must have sufficient subject matter knowledge. With limited mathematical understanding, teachers' pedagogical content knowledge is restricted.

Like other professionals, teachers expect to continue learning throughout their careers to deepen their expertise and enhance their practice. They recognize that they practice in uncertain circumstances, that much of their knowledge is embedded in their practice rather than in codified bodies of knowledge, and that their extensive, complex knowledge, particularly with respect to their understanding of how learners learn, profoundly influences how they teach. Based on this, teachers need learning opportunities that focus on their practice. They need to engage with other teachers to learn what works under what circumstances to develop as "connoisseurs" of effective practice. As Ball and Cohen (1999) write:

> The opportunity to engage in such conversation can provide a means for teachers to represent and clarify their understandings, using their own and others' experiences to develop ideas, learn about practices, and gain a more solid sense of themselves as contributing members of a profession, as participants in the improvement of teaching and learning and their profession, and as intellectuals. (p. 17; see also Pfeiffer, 1998; Stein, Silver, & Smith, 1994)

The Practice of Teaching Is Complex

Teaching involves a complex cycle of planning, acting, observing, and reflecting. It occurs in a highly dynamic atmosphere characterized by interactions happening second to second. It requires teachers to process information on multiple levels simultaneously and to make meaning and decisions constantly. To do so, they must draw on their ability to apply knowledge about students, content, the curriculum, instruction, assessment, and their schools and communities.

To succeed in such a complex environment, teachers need opportunities to develop their pedagogical content knowledge through critical reflection on their own and others' classroom practice and to develop rich repertoires of practice that support them through the complexity of teaching and learning. Currently, there is a growing emphasis on professional development that engages teachers in examining practice with experts and colleagues to develop the specialized knowledge of the profession (Smith, 2001; Stigler & Hiebert, 1999). Specifically, professional development strategies such as case discussions and examination of student work (see Chapter 5) are contributing to the development of a rich appreciation for the complexity of teaching and have been shown to develop teachers' content knowledge and sophisticated pedagogical reasoning skills and to increase student achievement (Barnett & Tyson, 1993; Heller, Kaskowitz, Daehler, & Shinohara, 2001).

Teaching is complex because learning is complex. Developing rote and factual knowledge is simpler than developing in-depth understanding of science and mathematics concepts. The latter requires teaching characterized by posing challenging tasks more often than providing succinct explanations. Teachers encourage their students to articulate their ideas and question each other about their reasons for holding them, rather than only correct their mistakes. Teachers and students set goals for instruction and create appropriate contexts for classroom activities. Students engage in meaningful projects, problems, and inquiries.

Teachers who embrace the complexity of teaching organize activities in which students do much of the talking and doing, often in small groups without the teacher. They watch students' actions and listen carefully to students' arguments and explanations in order to understand what sense the students are making. They monitor classroom activities and decide if, when, and how to intervene. When they intervene, they frequently do so by opening the topic up in ways that elicit more questions rather than prompting premature closure. Their knowledge of the subject matter and the students' developmental level helps them ask the next best question. They facilitate different levels of discourse needed in the classroom, being concerned not only with what students say about the topic but also why they say it. They establish and maintain a classroom environment that provides opportunities for students to explore their own and others' ideas individually and collectively without fear of ridicule or sanction. Teachers build on and guide students to new understanding by challenging their thinking and recognizing and addressing their confusion (NCTM, 2000; NRC, 1996a).

These teachers create opportunities for all students to learn. They know learning is not simple and that students all learn differently. They establish the learning environment as a place where students are respected and engaged, where students' questions and ideas are valued and respectfully challenged, and where students have the time, resources, and space necessary to explore and learn. They have a repertoire of strategies for responding appropriately to the variety of knowledge and experience brought by their students, and they work to ensure equal access to equitable teaching for all students.

THE NATURE OF SCIENCE AND MATHEMATICS

As professional developers plan activities to increase teachers' abilities to teach science and mathematics in ways consistent with national standards and state frameworks, it is important for them to keep the nature of the disciplines in mind. Just as professional development programs should reflect what is known about learning and teaching, so, too, should they reflect the nature of the disciplines. For example, national standards documents call for these subjects to be experienced and learned in ways that reflect how they are practiced in the real world (NCTM, 2000; NRC, 1996a). (See Figure 2.1.)

> **THE NATURE OF SCIENCE AND MATHEMATICS**
>
> - **Mathematics and science are dynamic disciplines that continue to produce new knowledge.**
> - **Science is practiced through active engagement and inquiry into phenomena in the world.**
> - **Mathematics involves complex reasoning, problem solving, and communication.**

Mathematics and science were long viewed as bodies of established knowledge, comprising true facts known for a long time. Science of this kind has been called a rhetoric of conclusions and final-form science (Duschl, 1990). It represented a static conception of the discipline. People expressed similar conceptions of mathematics in the past when they said, "All the mathematics there is, is already out there" (Schifter & Fosnot, 1993, p. 12).

In the past few decades, there has been explosive development in technology leading to new understanding and applications of science and mathematics that have challenged and changed the view of these disciplines as static bodies of knowledge. They have come to be seen as dynamic disciplines that are a necessity for all to learn.

With regard to mathematics, the need to be able to think and reason mathematically has become essential for everyday life (NCTM, 2000). Mathematics develops the ability to reason, to solve complex problems— often from different perspectives—and to analyze and communicate about patterns and relationships. It is used to answer fundamental questions and find solutions to practical problems (AAAS, 1993). The ability to understand and manipulate quantitative information is a basic skill for all.

With regard to science, scientists use processes to produce knowledge and make judgments of whether it is valid knowledge. This involves careful use of the processes of observing, describing, conjecturing, testing, explaining, revising hypotheses, and explaining, applied repeatedly to investigations. These processes are critical for scientifically literate individuals to make informed decisions and understand the complex advances in science that impact their lives on a daily basis.

The characteristics of the work of scientists and mathematicians are finding their way into classrooms in which students solve challenging mathematical problems and engage in scientific inquiry (NCTM, 2000; NRC, 1996a). Educators have come to appreciate that the learning of mathematics and science should reflect what it means to "do" mathematics and science and an understanding of where knowledge comes from. This is a dynamic conception of these disciplines, recognizing science and mathematics as human pursuits—as much invention as discovery—with a long history in which schools of thought compete, fashions change, and some questions may never be settled (Schifter & Fosnot, 1993).

Effective professional development in science and mathematics reflects the nature of the disciplines. For example, the teachers are engaged in doing challenging science and mathematics. They dialogue with each other and with their facilitators about what they are observing and learning. They speak, listen, and respond as they construct new meanings and formulate arguments. Through this process, they grapple with fundamental concepts in the discipline, not only learning what they are, but also why they take the form that they do. In the process of developing these higher-order ideas and capabilities, teachers are also learning important information such as facts and formulas and doing exercises and procedures. These facts and procedures are not, however, ends in themselves but serve as integral parts of a broader context that gives these pieces of information their meaning. Teachers in turn can create experiences with their students in the classroom that reflect the nature of doing and learning science and mathematics.

PROFESSIONAL DEVELOPMENT

The knowledge base on professional development has grown considerably since the first edition of this book. We now have more evidence linking quality professional development and teacher expertise with students' opportunity to learn challenging mathematics and science (Cohen & Hill, 1998; Darling-Hammond, 1997; Garet et al., 1999; Weiss, Banilower, McMahon, & Smith 2001). Contextual factors such as professional culture, leadership, systemic support, and time for teacher learning influence the type and quality of professional development (Darling-Hammond, 1997; Sparks, 2001).

EFFECTIVE PROFESSIONAL DEVELOPMENT

- Is driven by a well-defined image of effective classroom learning and teaching.
- Provides opportunities for teachers to build their content and pedagogical content knowledge and examine practice.
- Is research based and engages teachers as adult learners in the learning approaches they will use with their students.
- Provides opportunities for teachers to collaborate with colleagues and other experts to improve their practice.
- Supports teachers to serve in leadership roles.
- Links with other parts of the education system.
- Has a design based on student learning data and is continuously evaluated and improved.

Professional development has remained a key strategy in the educational reform movement, yet its focus and means of delivery have shifted and continue to shift in some fundamental ways. For example, science and mathematics reform initiatives have been challenged to increase the content and pedagogical content understanding of teachers. They have reached out to highly competent mathematics and science specialists to build this understanding, often immersing teachers in mathematical problem solving and scientific inquiry and sustained programs that increase teachers' understanding of their curriculum. They are realizing that simply providing different and more collegial forms of professional development is not the answer. Rather, the professional development must address substantive content and pedagogy within the teacher learning program (Ball, 1996; Garet et al., 1999). (See Figure 2.1.)

Educators now see the value of placing learning and student thinking at the center of professional development and, as a result, have adopted many practice-based strategies such as examining student work and using cases of student learning to deepen understanding of content and how children learn it (Ball & Cohen, 1999; Smith, 2001). These practices flow from a new appreciation of what it takes to develop what was described previously as teachers' specialized pedagogical content knowledge.

Professional development programs, such as the curriculum support initiatives at organizations like the Education Development Center, TERC, and Biological Sciences and Curriculum Study (BSCS), use knowledge from how people learn not only to help teachers add new skills but also to transform their thinking and deeply held beliefs about teaching and learning. From the hallmark study of mathematics reform in California, educators learned that reform focused only on adding new materials and changing some practice can result in a patchwork quilt of reform where some reform practices—often the ones that fit with a teacher's prior ideas—are adopted and others ignored (Cohen & Hill, 1998). What is needed is for teacher learning programs to engage teachers in strategies that produce "transformative" learning, that is, "changes in deeply held beliefs, knowledge, and habits of practice" (Thompson & Zeuli, 1999, p. 342). According to Thompson and Zeuli, transformative learning experiences for teachers have five requirements:

Requirement 1: Create a high level of cognitive dissonance to upset the balance between teachers' beliefs and practices and new information or experiences about students, the content, or learning. For example, a teacher might engage in a scientific inquiry that disrupts what she thought she knew about a scientific concept, such as how electric current moves through a circuit.

> ## REQUIREMENTS FOR TRANSFORMATIVE LEARNING EXPERIENCES
>
> - **Create a high level of cognitive dissonance.**
> - **Provide sufficient time, structure, and support for teachers to think through the dissonance experienced.**
> - **Embed the dissonance creating and resolving activities in teachers' situations and practices.**
> - **Enable teachers to develop a new repertoire of practice that fits with their new understanding.**
> - **Engage teachers in a continuous process of improvement.**
>
> SOURCE: Thompson and Zeuli (1999, pp. 355-357).

Requirement 2: Provide sufficient time, structure, and support for teachers to think through the dissonance they experience. They need opportunities to discuss, challenge, read about, and make sense of what they experienced.

Requirement 3: Embed the dissonance creating and resolving activities in teachers' own situations and the practices of teaching and learning by using student work, videotaping, or engaging in student investigations as a learner.

Requirement 4: Enable teachers to develop a new repertoire of practice that fits with their new understanding. This moves teachers from new understanding to change in practice. Teachers need to answer the questions: "Now that you have new understanding, what will you do differently in the classroom?" and "What could you do to help students come to new understanding?"

Requirement 5: Engage teachers in a continuous process of improvement, including (a) identifying new issues and problems with teaching and learning, (b) engaging with these to come to new understanding, (c) making changes in their practice, and (d) recycling through this process (Thompson & Zeuli, 1999, pp. 355-357, citing Huberman, 1995).

Transformative learning is different from "additive" learning through which teachers develop new skills or learn new things to integrate with what they currently know (Thompson & Zeuli, 1999). Historically, professional development has focused on only adding new skills and knowledge without helping teachers to rethink and discard or transform thinking and beliefs. Many teachers have reported that this practice leaves them overwhelmed with an increasingly overflowing plate of new things to know and do. There is a place for both additive and transformative learning in teacher professional development, but there needs to be conscious choices of what is being added and what is being discarded, and why. Unless teachers have learning opportunities that help them see the basic intentions of reform and of their curriculum and how both fit with knowledge of how people learn, they run a high risk of inadvertently making choices that detract from student learning. For example, teachers may grab at the hands-on activities in a kit-based science program without using these activities to build students' conceptual understandings.

These new developments in the knowledge base on effective professional development are quite significant. They enrich the basic principles of effective professional development that are reflected in earlier works (Loucks-Horsley, Hewson, Love, & Stiles, 1998) and support the common vision of effective science and mathematics education (NCTM, 1989, 2000; NRC, 1996a) and standards for teacher professional development (National Staff Development Council [NSDC], 2001b). The common vision is of several principles that are present in quality professional development experiences:

- Effective professional development experiences are driven by a well-defined image of effective classroom learning and teaching, for example, commitment to all children learning mathematics and science, an emphasis on inquiry-based learning, investigations, problem solving and applications of knowledge, an approach that emphasizes in-depth understanding of core concepts and challenges students to construct new understandings, and clear means to measure meaningful achievement.

- Effective professional development experiences provide opportunities for teachers to build their content and pedagogical content knowledge and skills and examine practice critically. They help teachers develop in-depth knowledge of their science or mathematics as well as pedagogical content knowledge (understanding how children learn the content, listening to students' ideas, posing questions, recognizing misconceptions), and help in choosing and integrating curriculum and learning experiences.

- Effective professional development experiences are research based and engage teachers as adult learners in the learning approaches they will use with their students, for example, start where teachers are and build from there; provide ample time for in-depth investigations, collaborative work, and reflection; and connect explicitly with teachers' other professional development experiences and activities.

- Effective professional development provides opportunities for teachers to work with colleagues and other experts in learning communities to improve their practice, for example, continuous learning is a part of the school norms and culture, teachers are rewarded and encouraged to take risks and learn, teachers learn and share together.

- Effective professional development experiences support teachers to serve in leadership roles, for example, as supporters of other teachers, as agents of change, as promoters of reform.

- Effective professional development experiences provide links to other parts of the education system, for example, professional development is integrated with other district or school initiatives, district or state curriculum frameworks, and assessments and have active supports within the community.

- Effective professional development experiences are designed based on data that determine their focus and priority as they relate to student learning, and they are are continuously evaluated to ensure a positive impact on teacher effectiveness, student learning, leadership, and the school community.

These principles demonstrate how beliefs about professional development have changed during the past 30 years. In the early 1970s, professional development was called inservice training; its goal was to bring outside expertise to teachers to increase their knowledge, often about a discrete new program or approach. This was strictly additive learning with little attention to changing underlying assumptions or building professional culture. The contemporary focus of professional development has widened to embrace not only the teacher but also the organization to which the teacher belongs (Loucks-Horsley, 1995). Many schools now see that ongoing teacher learning must become a permanent part of a school's systems and structures to support continuous learning (Sparks, 2002a). Designing professional development so that it promotes continuous teacher and organizational learning requires ensuring its fit with a school's vision and goals, that it is equitable for teachers and students, builds the leadership and infrastructure needed, fits with the school context, and gives teachers the range of experiences they need to learn. The design framework presented in this book is aimed at guiding schools to create such effective systems and structures for professional development.

THE CHANGE PROCESS

Professional developers can be guided by the extensive body of knowledge about how effective change happens in education settings (Evans, 1996; Fullan 1991, 1993, 2001; Hall & Hord, 2001). (See Figure 2.1.) Change is both an individual and an organizational phenomenon, affecting each and every educator, as well as the schools, districts, universities, and other organizations to which they belong. Principles that derive from the knowledge base on change include those shown in the box titled "The Change Process."

> ### THE CHANGE PROCESS
>
> - Change is a process that takes time and persistence.
> - At different stages in the change process, individuals need different kinds of support and assistance.
> - Change efforts are effective when the change to be made is clearly defined and communicated, support and assistance are available, and leaders and policies support the change.
> - Most systems resist change.
> - Organizations that are continuously improving analyze data, set goals, take actions, assess their results, and make adjustments.
> - Change requires communication about complex topics in organizations that are, for the most part, large and structured.

All educational changes of value require individuals to act in new ways (demonstrated by new skills, behaviors, or activities) and to think in new ways (beliefs, understandings, or ideas). The question of the relationships between thoughts and actions is therefore important for professional development. The conventional wisdom has been that changing teacher beliefs should be the primary work of professional development, for when one believes differently new behaviors will follow. Research on teacher change, however, indicates that changes in beliefs often come later when teachers use a new practice and see the benefits to their students (Ball & Cohen, 1999). Instead of being linear, changes in ideas and attitudes, and actions and behaviors, occur in a mutually interactive process. On the one hand, people's current thoughts influence what choices they make and what they attend to as they plan and carry out educational activities. On the other hand, people's reflections on these activities and their outcomes influence their thoughts about educational matters. Change in attitudes and behaviors is iterative; well-conceived professional learning experiences address both, knowing that change in one brings about and then reinforces change in the other.

A study of sites engaged in mathematics or science reform found that when the intervention was focused primarily on changing teachers' philosophy and beliefs, changes in actual practice and use of new curriculum were disappointing. Likewise, in sites where the intervention focused on practice to the exclusion of developing new philosophy and beliefs needed to embrace new curriculum, the desired changes were not achieved. Only in sites where the professional development provided a balance between pragmatic application and development of new philosophy did the use of the new curriculum take root (Mundry & Loucks-Horsley, 1999).

Fundamental beliefs are formed over time, through active engagement with ideas, understandings, and real-life experiences. This explains why many teachers find it difficult to change how they teach: because they learned mathematics or science in ways that are very different from those reflected in the national science and mathematics standards. They learned by memorizing information and others' explanations through a transmission model. These experiences served as powerful models for their own teaching and created a script that they followed in their own teaching (Stigler & Hiebert, 1999). Deep change occurs only when beliefs are restructured through new understandings and experimentation with new behaviors.

Effective professional development experiences are designed to help teachers build new understandings of teaching and learning, and try the teaching strategies that help students learn in new ways. They guide teachers to construct knowledge in the same ways as do effective learning experiences for students. Yet it is surprising to note how often the principle of constructivism is conveyed to teachers in the context of how they should help their students learn, without its being the basis for how they learn themselves (e.g., there are still too many lectures on constructivism). Experiencing learning in ways that hold to constructivist principles is the only way for teachers to understand deeply why it is important for their students to learn in this way and for them to break their old models of teaching (Little, 1993; Loucks-Horsley et al., 1990).

It should come as no surprise, then, that when change occurs, it does not happen in one step, but is progressive. Studies of individuals who change their practice over time report that individuals go through stages in how they feel about the change and how knowledgeable and sophisticated they are in using it. The questions that people ask evolve from early questions that are more self-oriented (What is it? How will it affect me?) to questions that are more task-oriented (How do I do it? How can I use these materials effectively? How can I organize myself? Why is it taking so much time?) to questions focused on impact (Is this change working for my students? Is there something that will work even better?) (Hall & Hord, 2001; Hord, Rutherford, Huling-Austin, & Hall, 1987).

Professional development initiatives that are designed with the change process in mind have distinct characteristics (Fullan, 1991; Loucks-Horsley & Stiegelbauer, 1991; Sparks, 2002a). First, they are informed by the ongoing monitoring of the concerns, questions, and needs of teachers and focus interventions and support on what is learned. Second, they pay attention to implementation for several years in order for teachers to progress from an early focus on management to a later focus on measuring student learning. Tied to this is the way they create realistic expectations in the system. It can take several years (most research indicates three to five) for teachers to fully implement a new practice or program, and, therefore, expecting student achievement to change in a short period of time is unrealistic. Yet clear expectations for student learning should be established from the beginning and data collected to assess student growth over this time. Third, once changes in teachers' practice become routine, other demands on their time may distract them from focusing on student learning. Effective professional development designs anticipate this and build in opportunities for organizational priority setting and ongoing monitoring of student learning (Loucks-Horsley, 1995; Sparks, 2002a).

Although a major focus of change efforts is on the individuals changing, professional development can succeed only with simultaneous attention to changing the system within which teachers and other educators work. In the earlier wave of mathematics and science reform, impact studies reported the disturbing finding that many teachers who had experienced exemplary professional development returned to their schools to find no support for the kinds of changes they wanted to make and, therefore, no change ultimately occurred. Education and businesses alike have learned a great deal from similar experiences over the past two decades, and what has emerged is new attention to the structures in the system that support or block innovation and change. In organizations, five factors contribute to successful change efforts: leadership, effective communication, a tight alignment of people and organizational goals, adequate training and funding, and a clear definition of the compelling reasons for change (Kotter, 1996).

Change cannot happen in isolation—it must be part of the strategic direction of the organization that is planned and managed (Sparks, 2002a). With organizational change the unit of change is the system and not the individual. A major premise of systems thinking is that the behavior of individuals in systems is dictated by underlying structures in organizations such as incentive systems, culture, and rules. Individuals are not to blame for breakdowns in the system that are caused by the system itself (Patterson, 1993; Senge, 1990). Effective change thus requires the organization to strive for continuous learning, to adopt new approaches and strategies quickly in response to new needs in the system. Educators at all levels are seeing the need to pay attention to "systemic change" by aligning components of the system, strengthening the relationship of the components to one another, and focusing their efforts on high standards for student learning (Smith & O'Day, 1991). Professional development is viewed as a critical component of reform, one that must be linked to those same clear goals for students, as well as assessment, preservice teacher education, school leadership, and resources and staffing (National Commission on Teaching and America's Future, 1996).

SUMMARY

The knowledge base discussed in this chapter provides important guidance to the design of professional development experiences. It encourages professional developers to know the knowledge base on the relevant areas affecting professional development and to embed this knowledge into the visions and designs for teacher learning in science and mathematics.

3

Context Factors Influencing Professional Development

A group of teachers from a large urban center's archdiocese schools attended a two-day professional development session on peer coaching. They were excited about the peer coaching session, but when it came time to attend a follow-up meeting, most admitted they had not tried peer coaching at all. In talking with the teachers, the staff development coordinator discovered that several factors were at play. School schedules made it extremely difficult for teachers to be released from their classrooms for observations and pre- and postconferences. Teachers had high anxiety about being observed by other teachers. Norms of risk taking and collegiality simply were not strong enough for teachers to overcome the obstacles to implementing peer coaching.

Professional development does not come in one-size-fits-all. It needs to be tailored to fit the context in which teachers teach and their students learn. In the example above, the strategy and the context were a mismatch, and the program failed. A program that is a great success in one place may fail in another. What makes the difference is the context in which the program operates. Richard DuFour (2001) writes, "In the right school context, even flawed professional development activities (such as the much maligned single-session workshop) can serve as a catalyst for professional growth. Conversely, in the wrong school context, even programs with solid content and training strategies are unlikely to be effective" (p. 14). What is the context for professional development? How can professional developers

Figure 3.1. Context Factors Influencing Professional Development

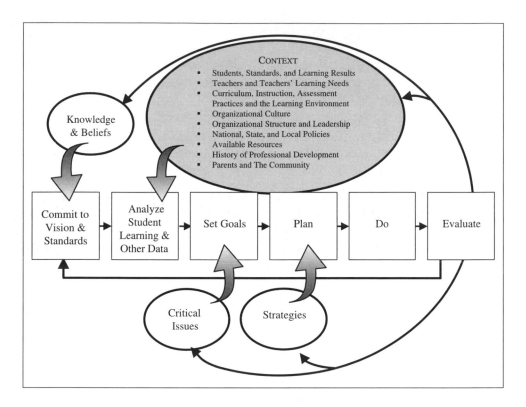

design programs that both suit and positively impact their local context? What contextual factors do they consider?

Professional developers rely on knowledge about many dimensions of their context to guide them in designing professional development that is appropriate and realistic while advancing the organization's vision and goals. They do what business leader Max DePree (1989) calls the "first responsibility of leaders"—to define and assess their current reality (p. 11). This chapter discusses nine context factors that influence professional development design: (1) students, standards, and student learning needs; (2) teachers and teacher learning needs; (3) practices, that is, curriculum, instruction, assessment, and the learning environment; (4) organizational culture; (5) organizational structures and leadership; (6) national, state, and local policies; (7) resources; (8) history of professional development; and (9) parents and the community. (See Figure 3.1.) For each of these factors, we identify key questions to consider and data sources and resources to guide professional developers' assessment of their context. Given the complex and variable nature of contexts, no single list will adequately capture every situation. Readers are encouraged to generate their own list of contextual factors that will help them ground professional development designs in their own reality.

Professional developers use information about their context throughout the design process. At the outset, they use data about student and teacher learning as the basis for program goals. For example, in one school district, students performed poorly in statistics and probability on their state and local assessments and teachers reported feeling unprepared to teach this content. This led the district to adopt new instructional materials that engaged students with statistics and probability concepts in the elementary years and to focus professional development on helping teachers, as adult learners, to increase their own understanding of statistics and probability and use the new materials effectively. The history of professional development will also come into play in the goal-setting phase so that teachers' prior knowledge and experience as well as their experiences with prior professional development are considered from the beginning.

In the planning phase, professional developers consider what factors might support or constrain their program, such as structures for collaborative work, leadership, the history of professional development, or local, state, or national policies. They may discover that some aspect of their context will so impede effective professional development that it must be changed before planning can move forward. For instance, if the only time currently available for professional development is three districtwide inservice days, solving the time problem will need to happen before designers can implement a quality program. The implementation phase is a time to be acutely aware of all contextual factors and notice what factors are shifting in part as a result of the professional development and what critical issues may be emerging. (See Chapter 4.) Finally, evaluation of professional development will show what changes have occurred in the context, such as any impact on the professional culture or the quality of leadership as well as teacher and student learning.

It is difficult to draw sharp lines between context factors, critical issues, and principles of effective professional development. Some context factors overlap with these other inputs into the design framework, and they are also treated in other chapters of this book. For example, the knowledge base on professional development (Chapter 2) reinforces how important contextual factors such as professional culture, leadership, system support, and time are to powerful teacher learning. Contextual factors of time, professional culture, and public support also crop up in Chapter 4 as critical issues, which regardless of the particularities of local context will need to be addressed successfully.

Chapter 1 describes the process of collecting and analyzing disaggregated student learning and other data as the basis for setting program goals. This chapter on context reiterates the importance of using student learning and other data to understand students and student learning, teachers and teacher learning, and other dimensions of context. What matters is not which context factors fall into which abstract categories in the design framework, but that professional developers design with the best possible understanding of the multiple dimensions of their local context, beginning with the students themselves.

STUDENTS, STANDARDS, AND LEARNING RESULTS

The most direct route to improving mathematics and science achievement for all students is better mathematics and science teaching.
—National Commission on
Mathematics and Science Teaching
for the 21st Century (2000, p. 7)

Although students are not the clients of professional development, they are its ultimate beneficiaries. The goal of professional development is improved student learning. At the same time, student performance will not improve unless staff and organizational performance improves. It follows that a logical starting point for planners is to gain a clear picture of who the students in the system are, what standards are in place for them, and how they are performing in relation to those standards. (See Figure 3.1.) Rigorous analysis of student learning data is a prerequisite for planning any professional development program. (See Chapter 1 for a fuller discussion of using student learning data.) For example, a large urban district in California identified that well over 60% of its students lacked an understanding of physical science concepts. In examining enrollment data, they identified that fewer and fewer students were taking the physics courses offered in Grades 11 and 12. They established as a goal to introduce physics for all students in Grade 9. This required professional development for the many more teachers who were now needed to teach physics if every ninth-grade student was to have access to the course. The district designed a professional development program that combined learning to use new curriculum through workshops and demonstration lessons with mentoring by members of a leadership team comprised of veteran physics teachers.

Table 3.1 summarizes questions, data sources, and resources to use to investigate students' needs and to inform professional development design.

TEACHERS AND TEACHERS' LEARNING NEEDS

Clearly, teachers have the most direct impact on student learning. Student learning depends on teacher knowledge. Research studies confirm a close link between teacher content knowledge in mathematics and science and student performance in these disciplines (Darling-Hammond, 2000;

TABLE 3.1 Students, Standards, and Learning Results

Questions to Consider	Data Sources	Resources
1. Who are our students? What are their cultural backgrounds? Learning styles?	Student demographic data, student and parent interviews and surveys, learning styles inventories	*A Framework for Understanding Poverty* by Ruby K. Payne, Aha Process, 2001 *Other People's Children* by Lisa Delpit, New Press, 1995
2. What standards are in place for student learning?	Local, state, and national standards	*Global Perspectives for Local Action: Using TIMSS to Improve U.S. Mathematics and Science Professional Development Guide,* National Research Council, 1999
3. How are students performing in relation to standards? What particular concepts, skills, dispositions are students not learning well?	Norm-referenced, standards-based, performance-based assessments, student work; national, district, school, and classroom data	State and national assessments, e.g., National Assessment of Educational Progress (NAEP) Third International Mathematics and Science Study (TIMSS) (Web site: nces/ed.gov/timss) *Using Data/Getting Results* by Nancy Love, Christopher-Gordon Publishers, 2002
4. What gaps in achievement exist among racial, socioeconomic, language, or gender groups?	All of the above sources disaggregated by race, socioeconomic status, language groups, and gender	*Using Data to Close Achievement Gaps: How to Measure Equity in Our Schools* by Ruth Johnson, Corwin Press, 2002
5. What specific goals for improving student learning and closing achievement gaps in mathematics and science does the school, district, or program have?	District and school improvement and professional development plans	

Goldhaber & Brewer, 2000). If student learning is going to improve, what do teachers need to know and be able to do and what kind of support do they need to be successful? As planners consider tailoring professional development to their context, no factor is more important to consider than teachers themselves. (See Figure 3.1.) How many professional development efforts have fallen flat, insulting and alienating teachers because they failed to honor their knowledge, skill, cultural background, or experience? How many others have missed the mark by attempting to impose new ideas about mathematics or science education on teachers without considering their own beliefs about teaching and learning these disciplines? How many programs have failed to target the specific knowledge that teachers need to improve their students' learning?

To avoid these pitfalls, professional developers take time, as they plan, to find out about the teachers' background and experience, knowledge and beliefs, and goals and needs. They are especially focused on assessing teacher needs as they relate to student learning needs. For example, if students are struggling with mathematics problem solving, staff developers investigate what content, pedagogical content knowledge, and instructional materials teachers need so that their students can become better problem solvers. Frequently, teachers have learned to teach mathematics as a set of procedures. They often need to experience learning mathematics through problem solving themselves as they expand their understanding of mathematics teaching and learning. They need to deeply understand mathematics concepts so they can help students explore them. They need to know how to help students make their thinking visible; how to orchestrate discourse in the classroom; when to clarify, model, and lead; and when to let students struggle with difficulties (Killion, 1998; National Council of Teachers of Mathematics [NCTM], 2000).

Similarly, in science, professional developers consider what teachers need to help students learn challenging concepts and processes. For example, when Kirsten Daehler and Mayumi Shinohara from WestEd were developing science case discussions, they decided to focus on physical science concepts that students often had difficulty understanding (e.g., directional flow of electricity and strength of flow in parallel and series circuits). Evaluations of the science case discussions showed that teachers improved their content knowledge and deepened their pedagogical reasoning and that their students' achievement improved (Heller, Kaskowitz, Daehler, & Shinohara, 2001).

Taking stock of the teachers' learning needs, particularly as they relate to students' learning needs, lays the groundwork for setting realistic and meaningful goals, gathering baseline data to assess progress, and helping to ensure that the program will in fact meet students' and teachers' needs. Table 3.2 summarizes guiding questions, data sources, and resources for investigating teachers and their learning needs.

TABLE 3.2   Teachers and Teachers' Learning Needs

Questions to Consider	Data Sources	Resources
1. Who are the teachers (demographics, years of experience, cultural background)?	Teacher demographic data	Report of the 2000 National Survey of Science and Mathematics Education by Horizon Research by Iris Weiss et al. (Web site: 2000survey. horizon-research. com/reports/status.php)
2. How well prepared are teachers to teach challenging science and mathematics content (course work, credentials, professional development experiences, perceptions)? What percentage are teaching subjects for which they are not certified?	Teacher credential, course work, and professional development records, interviews, surveys, observations, content assessments, lesson plans	Surveys of the Enacted Curriculum from Council of Chief State School Officers (Web site: www.ccsso.org) *By Your Own Design: A Teacher's Professional Learning Guide,* a CD-ROM (Eisenhower National Clearinghouse and National Staff Development Council, 2002) *Concerns-Based Adoption Model (CBAM).* See *Implementing Change: Patterns, Principles, and Potholes* by Shirley Hord and Gene Hall, Allyn & Bacon, 2001
3. How are new teachers inducted and supported?	Teacher interviews, surveys, focus groups, state and local policies, and programs for new teachers	Local Systemic Change Through Teacher Enhancement: 2001 Teacher Questionnaires from Horizon Research (Web site: www.horizon-research.com) 2000-2001 Local Systemic Change Classroom Observation Protocol from Horizon Research (Web site: www. horizon-research.com) TIMSS Teacher Survey on Pedagogy (Web site: www.steep.bc. edu/timss)

(Continued)

TABLE 3.2 (Continued)

Questions to Consider	Data Sources	Resources
4. What goals do teachers have for their learning?	Teacher interviews, surveys, individual professional development plans	*Global Perspectives for Local Action: Using TIMSS to Improve U.S. Mathematics and Science Professional Development Guide,* National Research Council, 1999
5. What are their beliefs, perceptions, concerns related to the professional development program? To mathematics and science improvement based on national standards?	Teacher interviews, surveys, classroom observations, lesson plans, student learning data, student work	*Using Data/Getting Results: A Practical Guide for School Improvement in Mathematics and Science* by Nancy Love, Christopher-Gordon Publishers, 2002
6. What are their strengths in mathematics and science content and pedagogy? What specific content knowledge and pedagogical skills do teachers need if students are to achieve the learning goals for the program?	Teacher interviews, surveys, classroom observations, lesson plans, content assessments, student learning data, student work	
7. What specific goals is the professional development program targeting for students? For teachers?	Professional development plans	
8. What have been their experiences implementing new programs?	Teacher interviews, focus groups, surveys	

CURRICULUM, INSTRUCTION, ASSESSMENT PRACTICES, AND THE LEARNING ENVIRONMENT

For a campus or school district to make changes in any program, it must first examine the current state of the program to determine the type of change that is needed. Only then can the campus or district make appropriate plans to implement the change.
—Charles A. Dana Center's AP Equity Initiative Web site
(www.utdanacenter.org/ap/math/APCAT.html)

If professional development is going to improve mathematics and science learning, then it must improve classroom practice. (See Figure 3.1.) But what is the state of practice, and where are the improvements needed? When designing programs to improve classroom practice, professional developers seek to understand four dimensions of classroom practice: curriculum (what is being taught), instruction (how it is taught), assessment (how learning is measured), and the learning environment (the physical facilities and arrangements as well as the culture within the classroom). A learning environment that supports students in learning a rigorous mathematics and science curriculum encourages appreciation of students' diversity, active participation, respect for students' ideas and contributions, collaborative working relationships among students and between students and the teacher, and intellectual rigor (Horizon Research, 2000).

Equally important, professional development designers probe what inequities may persist in students' opportunity to learn. For example, is tracking practiced? Are poor and minority students overrepresented in low-track mathematics and science classrooms or underrepresented in advanced mathematics and science courses? Do English-language learners have access to a rigorous science and mathematics curriculum? Data about practice can be as important in shaping a professional development program as student learning data.

The Charles A. Dana Center's Advanced Placement (AP) Equity Initiative is a good example of a professional development program that uses data about practice to customize the design of the initiative for participating schools and to monitor program results. The overall goal of the program is "to increase students' access to AP courses and actively recruit and support students who have historically been underrepresented in these courses" (Dana Center Web site). The Advanced Placement® Capacity Assessment Tool (APCAT) for Schools with AP is an instrument for collecting and analyzing data on several dimensions of the current AP program, including staffing and professional development, curriculum and instruction, resources, exam participation, and support for teachers, students, and the school. Based on responses, an APCAT team, made up of high school AP teachers, regular teachers, counselors, campus administrators, district office staff, and middle school teachers and counselors, identifies priorities and strategies for expanding student access to AP courses.

Over the past several years, a variety of tools have been developed to help mathematics and science reformers assess classroom practice, monitor changes, and evaluate the impact of reform on curriculum, instruction, assessment, and learning environments and opportunities. Examples of tools and the questions they can help answer are outlined in Table 3.3. The results of investigating practice in these ways have important implications for both the design and evaluation of the professional development program.

ORGANIZATIONAL CULTURE

> *Culture and professional development enjoy a symbiotic relationship. Professional development activities contribute to a culture of collegiality, critical inquiry, and continuous improvement; the school culture, in turn, stimulates ongoing professional development—a mutually reinforcing relationship. Attending to this aspect of context, assessing its strengths and weaknesses and planning accordingly, can yield a rich harvest both for professional and organization development.*
>
> —Hord and Boyd (1995, p. 10)

School culture is the norms, values, beliefs, rituals, ceremonies, symbols, and stories that make up the "persona of the school" (Peterson, 2002, p. 10). A growing body of research is converging on this finding: Schools that improve and where professional development "takes" have strong collaborative cultures and professional learning communities. Characteristics of a professional learning community include (1) a shared mission, vision, and values; (2) norms of continuous learning and improvement; (3) collective responsibility for and a relentless focus on learning for all students; (4) collaborative and collegial relations and the deprivatization of teaching, that is, moving teaching out from behind closed doors so teachers share ideas and practice with one another; (5) regular opportunities for collective inquiry, and reflective dialogue (DuFour & Eaker, 1998; Fullan, 2001; Hord, 1998; Lambert, 1998; Louis, Kruse, & Marks, 1996; Stein, 1998).

It is impossible to overestimate the impact of school culture on professional development design and implementation. Because the culture can make or break a professional development program, strengthening the learning community must be a central and consistent goal of all professional development. The organizational culture also figures heavily in the selection of professional learning strategies. Strategies that presume a high level of collaboration and shared norms and values (e.g., study groups and lesson study) will likely fail if the culture cannot support them. On the other

TABLE 3.3 Curriculum, Instruction, Assessment Practices, and the Learning Environment

Questions to Consider	Data Sources	Resources
1. To what extent is the written and taught curriculum aligned with standards? How are the specific content standards targeted for improvement treated in the written and taught curriculum? To what extent is the curriculum focused, rigorous, and coherent?	Local curriculum documents, curriculum maps, teacher and student interviews, teacher and student surveys, classroom observations, instructional materials, student work	NCREL curriculum mapping Web site (Web site: currmap. ncrel.org) Advanced Placement Capacity Assessment Tools (APCAT) from the Dana Center (Web site: www. utdanacenter.org/ ap/math/apcatprod.html) Surveys of the Enacted Curriculum from Council of Chief State School Officers (Web site: www. ccsso.org)
2. To what extent do some students (poor, minority, second-language learners, special needs students, girls) have less opportunity to learn a rigorous curriculum than others? Is tracking practiced? Who is taking AP courses?	Disaggregated data from teacher and student interviews, surveys, classroom observation, instructional materials; disaggregated course-enrollment data, special program placement, teacher qualifications by course or program; master schedules (Love, 2002)	Concerns-Based Adoption Model (CBAM). See *Implementing Change: Patterns Principles, and Potholes* by Shirley Hord and Gene Hall, Allyn & Bacon, 2001 Local Systemic Change Through Teacher Enhancement: 2001 Teacher Questionnaires from Horizon Research (Web site: www.horizon-research.com) 2000-2001 Local Systemic Change Classroom Observation Protocol (Web site: www. horizon-research. com) TIMSS Teacher Survey on Pedagogy (Web site: www. steep.bc.edu/timss) *Global Perspectives for Local Action: Using TIMSS to Improve U.S. Mathematics and Science Professional Development Guide,* National Research Council, 1999

(Continued)

TABLE 3.3   (Continued)

Questions to Consider	Data Sources	Resources
3. To what extent are students in science classes involved in active, hands-on learning approaches? Are some groups of students receiving more of this type of instruction than others?	Same as 1 and 2	*Using Data/Getting Results: A Practical Guide for School Improvement in Mathematics and Science* by Nancy Love, Christopher-Gordon Publishers, 2002 *Using Data to Close Achievement Gaps: How to Measure Equity in Our Schools* by Ruth Johnson, Corwin Press, 2002
4. To what extent are students in mathematics classes learning problem solving and reasoning skills and learning how to apply knowledge to novel problems (Council of Chief State School Officers [CCSSO], 2001)? Are some groups of students receiving more of this kind of in-instruction than others?	Same as 1 and 2	
5. What methods of student assessment are used in class, and are the strategies consistent with goals of learning in content standards (CCSSO, 2001)? Are varied assessment strategies being used more with some student groups than others?	Same as 1 and 2, sample assessments	
6. Is the learning environment respectful of students and their diversity and conducive to all students' active participation and collaboration?	Same as 1 and 2	

hand, professional development programs can be carefully designed to strengthen the culture by creating positive, collaborative learning experiences for teachers that are linked to results for students. Finally, collaborative cultures are the soil in which teacher leadership emerges and changes in teaching and learning can take hold and thus are key to the sustainability of professional learning. For all of these reasons, it is essential that professional developers "test the soil" and understand the culture of the organizations with which they work. (See Figure 3.1.)

One of the best examples of diagnosing and then transforming an organization's culture is the story of Community District 2 in New York City. In 1987, District 2 ranked tenth in the city in reading and fourth in mathematics out of 32 districts. Eight years later, it ranked second in both reading and mathematics at the same time the student population grew more linguistically diverse and economically disadvantaged. During those eight years, under the leadership of former superintendent Anthony Alvarado, the district mounted a coherent and sustained effort to improve instruction in first reading and then mathematics through professional development. "Central to Alvarado's strategy in District 2 is the creation of a strong belief system, or a culture, of shared values around instructional improvement that binds the work of teachers and administrators into a coherent set of actions and programs" (Elmore & Burney, 1999, p. 266). Alvarado underscores the importance of professional culture in this way:

> Our vision of instructional improvement depends heavily on people being willing to take the initiative, to take risks, and to take responsibility for themselves, for students, and for each other. You get this kind of result only when people cultivate a deep personal and professional respect and caring for each other. We have set about finding and hiring like-minded people who are interested in making education work for kids. We care about and value each other, even when we disagree. Without collegiality on this level you can't generate the level of enthusiasm, energy, and commitment we have. (Quoted in Elmore & Burney, 1999, p. 270)

There are many ways of assessing an organization's culture that range from listening to the stories teachers and administrators tell about the school to observing how new teachers are treated. Table 3.4 suggests some questions to ask and tools to use to investigate organizational culture.

ORGANIZATIONAL STRUCTURES AND LEADERSHIP

If you want to change an organization, change
the people who come to meetings.
                                                    —Bailey (1995)

TABLE 3.4   Organizational Culture

Questions to Consider	Data Sources	Resources
1. Do teachers and staff meet and work together to solve instructional, organizational, and curricular issues? (Phillips, 1993)	Interviews, observations, surveys	Self-Assessment of Implementation of NSDC Standards of Staff Development (Web site: www.nsdc.org) *Practice-Based Professional Development for Teachers of Mathematics* by Margaret Smith, National Council of Teachers of Mathematics, 2001
2. Are school staff members focused on student learning goals?	Improvement plans, interviews, observations, surveys	Self-Assessment: School Culture Triage from Penelope Masden-Copas, *Journal of Staff Development*, Summer 2002
3. Do people enjoy working together, support one another, and feel value and included? (Phillips, 1993)	Same as 1	School Culture Audit from Christopher Wagner, *Journal of Staff Development*, Summer 2002
4. Are people in this school because they want to be? Do they work to improve their skills as professionals, or do they see themselves as victims of a large and uncaring bureaucracy? (Phillips, 1993)	Same as 1	School Culture Survey by Joan Richardson, *Tools for Schools, 3*, National Staff Development Council, April/May 2001 *The School-Culture Audit* by G. Phillips, Eduserve, British Columbia School Trustees Publishing, 1993 *The School Portfolio: A Comprehensive Framework for School Improvement, 2nd edition* by Victoria Bernhardt, Eye on Education, 1999 *Using Data to Close Achievement Gaps: How to Measure Equity in Our Schools* by Ruth Johnson, Corwin Press, 2002

Closely related to culture is the structure of the organization—procedures for decision making, rules and regulations, resource allocation, incentive and accountability systems, collective bargaining agreements, assignment of people, and scheduling of time. Just as organizational culture asserts a powerful and pervasive influence on individual behavior and professional learning, so do the organizational structure and the quality of leadership. (See Figure 3.1.) Robert Fritz describes how organizational structures can be oscillating or advancing. "Oscillating behavior is that which moves from one place to another but then moves back toward its original position," writes Fritz (1999, p. 6, as cited in Sparks, 2002a). An example of oscillating behavior is when, after a three-year funded initiative to reform mathematics education ends, the support structures fade away, the champions of the program move on, and the new mathematics curriculum is abandoned. When the system is working against high performance for students and teachers, the school snaps back to its original state, "almost as if it were pulled back by a strong rubber band" (Sparks, 2002a, ch. 4, p. 4).

An "advancing structure" is characterized by a compelling vision, a thorough assessment of current reality, and powerful strategies to lead the organization to achieve its vision (Fritz, 1996). The organizational structures are aligned with high-quality professional development and continuous improvement. For example, new teachers are supported through a mentoring program and given assignments that are realistic and based on their experience. Student groups that are not achieving at high levels have access to the most capable teachers and best practice. Time is set aside regularly during the school day for teachers to collaborate on instructional improvement. Adequate resources are allocated for materials, modeling, coaching, and professional development. The district has an improvement infrastructure, including permanent positions for professional developers, coaches, and curriculum specialists, in much the same way that businesses have permanent research and human resource development departments (St. John, 2002).

While schools and districts are complex systems with interconnected parts that should be working together, they often do not function in this way. In school staff members' efforts to respond to myriad grants and mandates, they may have literally dozens of professional development plans and initiatives managed by different people. Coordination across these initiatives is rare, resulting in duplicated efforts, mixed messages, and wasted resources. Some parts of the system may be moving toward change while others are working against it. For example, a district makes a decision to implement a kit-based science program, but fails to set up a system and allocate resources for refurbishing kits. Soon using the kits becomes too much of a classroom management chore, and use of them is abandoned.

How decisions are made is another important aspect of the organizational structure. Loucks-Horsley and her associates (1987) emphasize the importance of having the "right people" at the table making professional development decisions, those that meet the criteria of relevance (most affected by professional development decisions), expertise, and jurisdiction (authority to carry out decisions). Decision makers can be formal or informal leaders such as curriculum supervisors, principals, teacher leaders, or university personnel involved in grant-supported programs "The roles of instructional leadership are not exclusive, and the more people in the education community who can take on leadership roles, the more likely their sense of commitment and responsibility will lead to real school improvement" (Loucks-Horsley et al., 1987, p. 13).

Equally important is the quality of the leadership. Effective leadership of professional development combines clear direction with ample support. Leaders champion professional development by setting the context. They articulate clear expectations, outcomes, and purposes for the program; link development to other important goals and initiatives; model continuous learning themselves; delegate development responsibilities; and focus the effort. Supports include rallying the resources, freeing up time, actively participating in professional development programs, and encouraging risk taking in the classroom (Loucks-Horsley et al., 1990). Leaders help to build a community of learners who share a vision of where they are going and why. They actively filter everything through the vision to create coherence and connections (Kaser, Mundry, Stiles, & Loucks-Horsley, 2002). In addition, Fullan (2002) identifies five characteristics of effective leadership: moral purpose, understanding change, relationship building, knowledge creation and sharing, and coherence making.

The role of the principal is key. Carol Schweitzer (2000) describes the school leader as the "primary culture carrier for the organization" and concludes that "the leader and the culture must be in synch" (p. 35). In addition to helping others acquire new values and skills, effective principals have an inclusive and facilitative leadership style, focus on student learning, and provide efficient management. They have the ability to attack incoherence and innovation overload by focusing and prioritizing (Fullan, 2002; Sebring & Bryk, 2000). If principals are to succeed in these new and challenges roles, then the organizational structures, such as the duties principals are assigned and opportunities provided for their own professional learning, need to change to support them (Cross & Rice, 2000; Sparks, 2002a).

Aligning the system in support of instructional improvement and strengthening leadership at every level, especially among principals, are two hallmarks of the success of professional development in District 2 in New York City. "We expected principals to have a clear vision of what they wanted to have happen in teaching and learning in their schools and to be willing to question themselves and their capacity to deliver," Alvarado said (quoted in Elmore & Burney, 1999, p. 265). To support principals in enacting this vision, the district provides principal support groups, monthly principals' conferences organized around instructional issues, and active district oversight and site visits to schools.

Having a clear picture of the organizational structure will help professional developers initially to navigate the system and determine the leverage points. Inevitably, structural changes will be necessary to support a professional development system that is aligned with district mission and goals, designed for results, and systemic. Table 3.5 lists questions to consider, data sources, and resources for examining organizational structures and leadership.

NATIONAL, STATE, AND LOCAL POLICIES

Most plans for systemic reform or restructuring underestimate the sustained impact of long-standing policy and practice.
—Little (1993, p. 140)

The system that influences professional development extends beyond the school or district to the state and national contexts. Professional development programs swim in a stream of state and national policies as well as local mandates. No school is unaffected by federal policies such as the No Child Left Behind Act of 2002, which calls for sweeping changes in state and national accountability systems, new certification requirements and procedures, and incentive systems for mathematics and science teachers. Policies at all levels exert a strong, if not readily apparent, influence on professional development design. (See Figure 3.1.)

In the best of circumstances, policies are in synch with improving student and teacher learning. In their study of ten years of mathematics reform in California, researchers David Cohen and Heather Hill (2001) found that the state standards and accountability system positively impacted student learning when teachers had new curriculum, new assessments, and good professional development in how to use them. Linda Darling-Hammond (2000), in her research, has found that states experiencing progress in increasing student learning are taking two clear policy steps: (1) They are identifying teaching standards that identify what teachers should know and be able to do at different points in their career, and (2) they use these standards to develop more thoughtful certification and licensing systems, more productive teacher education and induction programs, and more effective professional development.

Unfortunately, prevailing state and national policies often are inconsistent with powerful and effective professional development. In many places, professional development is not even acknowledged as a legitimate activity for teachers; policies reflect the attitude that teachers are doing their jobs only when they are in the classroom teaching. Where professional development is legitimized, it is often viewed as a way of helping teachers acquire knowledge and skills they are lacking by participating in training provided by external experts. Rarely are teachers given the opportunity to learn as a part of their daily experience, engage in inquiry with their colleagues, or

TABLE 3.5 Organizational Structures and Leadership

Questions to Consider	Data Sources	Resources
1. What are the organization's decision-making structures, schedules, calendars, incentive systems, accountability systems, policies, and teacher contracts?	Contracts, organizational charts, calendars, schedules, policy statements, budgets, interviews, observations, surveys	Leadership Audit Tool: A Participatory Management Checklist (NCREL) (Web site: www.ncrel.org) ASCD Survey (Web site: www.ascd.org: 8108/ trainingopportunities/ossa/ survey-questions.cf.org)
2. To what extent do these structures support professional development? Constrain it?	Same as 1	Self-Assessment of Implementation of NSDC Standards of Staff Development (Web site: www.nsdc.org)
3. Who in the organization makes decisions about professional development? How?	Same as 1	See the profiles in *Enhancing Program Quality in Science and Mathematics* by J. S. Kaser and P. S. Bourexis with S. Loucks-Horsley and S. A. Raizen, Corwin Press, 1999
4. What improvement infrastructure is in place (time for collegial learning, professional developers on staff, mentoring and coaching programs)?	Same as 1	*How to Help Teaching Succeed* by Carl D. Glickman, ASCD, 2002 *Leadership Practices Inventory* by J. M. Kouzes and B. Z. Posner, Jossey-Bass/Pfeiffer, 2001
5. To what extent do leaders at the district and building levels provide clear direction and support for professional development? How committed are they to mathematics and science improvement?	Interviews, focus groups, observations, surveys	See surveys in *Building Leadership Capacity in Schools* by Linda Lampert, ASCD, 1998
6. To what extent are teachers developing as leaders?	Interviews, focus groups, observations, surveys	

(Continued)

TABLE 3.5   (Continued)

Questions to Consider	Data Sources	Resources
7. What professional development efforts are currently under way? How are multiple efforts coordinated? How are teachers and others being helped to address multiple and conflicting priorities?	Interviews, focus groups, school improvement and professional development plans, schedules, budgets, consultant contracts, a timeline and map of past efforts	

actively shape the content and context of their own learning experiences (Little, 1993; McDiarmid, 1995).

In many cases, policies need to be revamped to support high levels of student and teacher learning. Obviously, changes at the district level are easier to bring about than at the state and national levels. For example, districts participating in the Equity 2000 program, a College Board initiative to provide all students with access to a rigorous mathematics program, issued district policy statements eliminating tracking and requiring that all students enroll in algebra. This mandate gave teeth to professional development that prepared teachers and guidance counselors to implement the program.

Policies can limit or broaden options, impede or support progress. In any case, professional developers need to carefully examine the local, state, and national policies that will affect the success of their professional development program. Table 3.6 provides questions to consider, data sources, and resources to guide exploration of national, state, and local policies.

AVAILABLE RESOURCES

*We want to revamp our science curriculum,
but we can't afford to purchase the hands-on
materials required.*

No one who plans professional development needs to be reminded about the need for adequate resources, especially time, money, and materials. (See Figure 3.1.) More often than not, these resources are scarce and stand as a

TABLE 3.6   National, State, and Local Policies

Questions to Consider	Data Sources	Resources
1. What policies impact professional development at the local, state, and national levels?	National, state, and local policies; interviews; surveys; research studies	*Learning Policy: When State Education Reform Works* by David K. Cohen and Heather C. Hill, Yale University Press, 2001
2. What accountability systems are in place at the state and national levels? How do they support or impede on teacher learning?	Same as 1	National Staff Development Council Web Site on Policy (Web site: www. nsdc.org/ educatorindex.htm)
3. What are state and local policies for recertification? For support of beginning teachers? For attracting and retaining qualified mathematics and science teachers?	Same as 1	*Teacher Quality and Student Achievement: A Review of State Policy Evidence* by Linda Darling-Hammond (Web site: epaa.asu. edu)
4. How do policies impede or support collegial learning? A focus on core problems of teaching and learning? Equity? Teacher leadership?	Same as 1	*Teaching for High Standards: What Policymakers Need to Know and Be Able to Do* by Linda Darling-Hammond and Deborah Ball, National Commission of Teaching & America's Future and the Consortium for Policy Research in Education, 1998 (Web site: www.cpre.org)
5. How is professional development defined by local, state, and national policies? Does the definition focus on workshop hours? Designate who will "deliver" professional development? Allocate or restrict time for professional development?	Same as 1	
6. What incentives are provided for professional development, both extrinsic and intrinsic?	Same as 1, incentive systems	

barrier to results-driven and job-embedded professional development. As demands for school accountability increase, so too must the resources allocated to professional development. The National Staff Development Council (NSDC) recommends that at least 10% of a school district's budget be devoted to professional development and that 25% of an educator's work day be used for staff development (NSDC, 2001b). If professional learning is to become embedded in the fabric of the school day, schools need to rethink the "three annual release days" approach. Teachers need significant chunks of pupil-free time. An important insight from the Third International Mathematics and Science Study (U.S. Department of Education, 1996) is the substantial amount of time spent on professional development by teachers in countries such as Japan, whose students demonstrate high levels of science and mathematics learning. Japanese educators have up to 40% of their day when they are not with pupils and can work with other teachers to improve instructional practice. (See Chapter 4 for a discussion of finding time as a critical issue.)

Professional developers themselves need time to design professional development in the thoughtful way this book advocates. They cannot be burdened with so many responsibilities that they are unable to give professional development the attention it requires. They need time and other resources to plan, implement, monitor, and evaluate professional development as well as time for their own professional growth.

Time is not the only resource that is necessary for professional development. Teachers need professional materials, teaching materials, computers for themselves and their students, and laboratory facilities. Expertise is another valuable resource that can be found in many places. University and community college faculty, scientists and mathematicians from industry, government agencies (e.g., geological surveys, agricultural extension offices), and environmental organizations can provide valuable content expertise. Experienced teachers are a resource for helping other teachers develop pedagogical content knowledge.

Professional developers are, simultaneously, visionaries and realists. They work toward a vision of professional development that is adequately supported. In the short run, they scan their environment for available resources, make efficient use of what they have, and aggressively seek out more. They consider what resources they need and what resources they have available as input into the design of their program. Table 3.7 offers questions, data sources, and resources to use for identifying and locating available resources.

HISTORY OF PROFESSIONAL DEVELOPMENT

Another contextual factor that professional developers consider is the history of professional development in the school or district. (See Figure 3.1.) Teachers' past experiences with professional development will influence

TABLE 3.7 Available Resources

Questions to Consider	Data Sources	Resources
1. What time do teachers have available for professional development and collegial work?	Schedule, contract, district policies, interviews, surveys	Self-Assessment of Implementation of NSDC Standards of Staff Development (Web site: www.nsdc.org)
2. Does professional development happen mostly during the school day? What percentage of the school day is devoted to professional development?	Schedule, contract, district policies, interviews, surveys	
3. What resources are allocated in the budget for professional development? What additional resources, including those currently designated for courses, credit reimbursements, or teacher evaluation, could be rechanneled for professional development?	Budgets, interviews	
4. What grant funds are available?	Budgets, national and state programs and mandates, foundations	
5. What community support, partnerships (such as universities or businesses), collaboratives, and other sources of external expertise are available?	Guides to local communities, local speaker bureaus, regional service providers, state departments of education	
6. What local expertise can be tapped?	Teacher surveys and interviews	
7. What instructional and professional development materials, equipment, supplies, and technology do teachers have?	Materials audits, surveys, observations, interviews	

how they view new initiatives. If past efforts were a "waste of time," resulted in few or no changes, or failed to support teachers after initial training, professional development planners need to help teachers see how new efforts will be more effective. If teachers have been "inserviced to death," they may need to experience very different professional development strategies. On the other hand, designers will want to know what professional development initiatives have been successful and how they can be built upon. Knowing where expertise from universities and other organizations outside of the school have contributed to teacher learning can also be helpful.

Planners can also take a close look at the current state of professional development, mapping out the range of current activities and their histories. It may be useful to identify at what stage of development each activity is— from a brand-new initiative, to one just taking hold, to an old friend. It is often surprising to planners to realize how many initiatives are under way and how few have really taken hold over the long term. In mathematics and science reform, it is important to understand what priority these content areas have in the larger picture of school and district improvement. Is the organization overloaded with competing initiatives? The goal of investigating professional development history is to build on past successes and avoid past mistakes. Table 3.8 suggests some questions to consider as professional developers reflect on past practice and the impact it will have on current designs.

PARENTS AND THE COMMUNITY

One final contextual factor should be considered when planning professional development activities: parents and the community. (See Figure 3.1.) Mathematics and science reform calls for major changes in what and how students learn. As reformers make these changes, they must be careful to consider the views of parents and community members and gain public support for reform. One of the most important lessons learned about systemic reform is that it is "at least as much a political challenge as it is a technical challenge" (Heck, Weiss, Boyd, & Howard, 2002, p. 3). Political strategies include involving key players and addressing their interests, communicating with stakeholders, and positioning the initiative in the initial planning. During implementation, political strategies are used to gain broad support and establish credibility. Sound political strategy requires keeping closely attuned to the "ebbs and flows of shifting opinions and interests and responding to major changes in the political landscape" (p. 4).

Parents have many questions about new approaches to science and mathematics education. They worry that their children will not develop basic skills. They are concerned that the school may be changing for change's sake or that innovations such as inquiry-based science education are just "fun and games." They want to know if new approaches will hurt their children when they take a college entrance exam or state assessment. In

TABLE 3.8 History of Professional Development

Questions to Consider	Data Sources	Resources
1. What have teachers' experiences been with professional development? How have their experiences shaped their views of professional development?	Interviews, focus groups, surveys, evaluation reports	Self-Assessment of Implementation of NSDC Standards of Staff Development (Web site: www.nsdc.org) Local Systemic Change Through Teacher Enhancement: 2001 Teacher Questionnaires from Horizon Research and other resources at Horizon Research (Web site: www.horizon-research.com) SRI International Online Evaluation Resource Library (Web site: www.oerl.sri. com) Staff Development Program Review in *What Works in the Middle: Results-Based Staff Development* by Joellen Killion, National Staff Development Council, 1999 Surveys in Designing Effective Professional Development: Lessons From the Eisenhower Program, U.S. Department of Education, 1999 (Web site: www.ed.gov/teacherquality/eisenhower/title.html) *Using Data to Close Achievement Gaps: How to Measure Equity in Our Schools* by Ruth Johnson, Corwin Press, 2002
2. What is the range of initiatives currently under way? What is the relative priority of mathematics and/or science initiatives?	Interviews with district leadership, school improvement and professional development plans, schedules, budget	
3. What has been tried and abandoned and why?	Interviews, focus groups, surveys, evaluation reports	
4. What was the nature and scope (who and how many involved) of past efforts, both successful and unsuccessful? Who initiated them? What consultants or partners were involved?	Interviews, focus groups, school improvement and professional development plans, schedules, budgets, consultant contracts Construct a timeline and map of past efforts	
5. To what extent have the professional development activities in the school or district reflected the attributes of effectiveness discussed in Chapter 2? Addressed equity issues?	Interviews, surveys, observations, evaluation reports, self-assessments	

Harlem, Hubert Dyasi reported, parents were concerned that "experimenting" on their children with inquiry-based science was discriminatory. (See Chapter 6.) Dyasi's experience points to the critical need for professional developers to bridge the gap that separates schools from culturally diverse families.

Community members other than parents have concerns as well. They want their tax dollars to be spent wisely (or less of them to be spent). They may be confused about conflicting reports that teachers need to spend more time with students as well as needing more time for their own learning. Some may worry that the reforms in science and mathematics will not provide students with the rigorous skills they need to be productive citizens. Others wonder why schools have not embraced new programs that will provide students with the problem-solving, teamwork, and decision-making skills they will need for future employment. Many mathematics and science educators know too well how fear and mistrust on the part of the public can thwart a program. Effective public engagement can invigorate and help sustain it.

As they design, professional developers take public perception into consideration in several ways. Striving for two-way communication—listening and talking—they bring parents and community members into the dialogue as they plan. If parents or community members have resisted a mathematics or science initiative before, they investigate why and how to avoid the same reaction again. Throughout implementation, professional developers monitor public perceptions informally and formally through surveys, interviews, or focus groups. They include in their designs strategies for proactively engaging the public rather than just responding to criticism and attacks. The program may also include professional development for teachers and administrators in how to more effectively engage the public. See Table 3.9, page 78, for suggestions on how to investigate the contextual factor of parents and community.

SUMMARY

Having scanned these nine contextual factors, planners now have a better sense of what they need to consider in their own settings as they plan for professional development. In answering the many questions posed, professional developers have become aware of the constraints and the supports operating within their systems. They know which aspects of their context are givens—the mountains that cannot be moved (at least for now)—and what "landscaping" needs to happen as they develop their professional development programs. They are ready to design professional development that fits their context.

TABLE 3.9 Parents and Community

Questions to Consider	Data Sources	Resources
1. What are parents' and the community's interests and concerns about the science and mathematics education program?	Parent and community surveys, interviews, focus groups	*Effective Public Engagement* by the Public Agenda Foundation for the New Standards Project (phone: 1-888-361-6233) *Supporting Reform in Mathematics: A Public Relations Sourcebook,* National Council of Supervisors of Mathematics, 1997 (Web site: www. ncsm.org)
2. To what extent do parents, school board, and community members understand/support the national standards' vision of science and mathematics teaching, learning, and professional development?	Same as 1	
3. How effective is the organization's approach to public engagement? To what extent have they reached out to diverse cultural groups?	Same as 1	
4. How well prepared are teachers and administrators to communicate and work effectively with diverse parents and community members?	Teacher, administrator, and parent surveys; interviews; focus groups	
5. Where in the community can you find support for your mathematics and science education program and use this as a resource for professional development?	Contact and interview education and business alliances, community foundations, and university partners and faculty	

4

Critical Issues to Consider in Designing Professional Development

Seven critical issues need to be considered as one designs and provides professional development for teachers: finding time for professional development, ensuring equity, building a professional culture, developing leadership, building capacity for sustainability, scaling up, and garnering public support. (See Figure 4.1.) Readers who are familiar with the first edition of this book will notice the absence of two critical issues—evaluating professional development and supporting standards and frameworks. To emphasize the critical role of ongoing evaluation of professional development, we incorporated evaluation as one of the major steps in the design framework. Similarly, supporting standards and frameworks was incorporated into the design framework to show how important it is for professional development design to be driven by a vision of standards-based teaching and learning. (See Chapter 1 for a discussion of the stages of committing to a vision and standards and evaluation in the design framework.)

Each of the seven issues discussed in this chapter is important, and lack of attention to any one of them can ultimately doom a professional development initiative. As Susan Loucks-Horsley repeatedly warned when sharing the design framework with professional developers, "Ignore these at your own peril." The seven critical issues play an important role at different

Figure 4.1. Critical Issues Influencing Professional Development

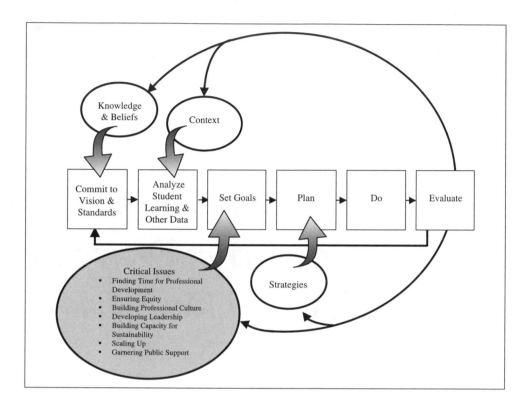

stages in the life of a professional development program or initiative, but designers can be assured that each will influence the effectiveness of the program at some point. For this reason, it is important to consider each of them during the "set goals" stage in the design process and not only when the program or initiative is well under way. Anticipating that each issue will have an impact on the way in which the professional development program is implemented and sustained can enable designers to plan for ways to address each of them. For example, when setting goals and identifying specific learning outcomes to be achieved, it is imperative to consider the issue of finding time for professional learning. If designers intend to conduct collaborative study groups with grade-alike teachers during the school day, such a strategy will fail if policies and structures are not adjusted beforehand that provide the necessary time. In another example, inviting teachers to examine student work or engage in lesson study in a school in which isolation is the prevalent norm will meet with defeat if designers do not plan early to address ways to enhance the professional learning culture in the school.

This chapter discusses each of the seven critical issues and recognizes that entire books have been written on each. The intent of this chapter is to raise the awareness level of professional development designers to ensure that the issues are not ignored and to suggest questions for professional developers to ask themselves as they design or reflect on their programs.

FINDING TIME FOR PROFESSIONAL DEVELOPMENT

It is clear that, for science and mathematics professional development to be effective, experiences for teachers must occur over time, provide ample time for in-depth investigations and reflection, and incorporate opportunities for continuous learning. (See Figure 4.1.) Finding adequate quality time to effectively carry out professional development programs or initiatives is a challenge faced by every professional developer. In fact, time has emerged as one of the key issues in virtually every analysis of school change appearing in the past decade (Fullan & Miles; 1992; Garet et al., 1999; Little, 1993; Loucks-Horsley et al., 1987;

> **FINDING TIME FOR PROFESSIONAL DEVELOPMENT**
>
> • How do you find ways to make more effective use of the time currently available within the school calendar for ongoing teacher learning?
>
> • How can you work toward influencing state policies and public perceptions that support professional development?

Loucks-Horsley, Stiles, & Hewson, 1996; National Council of Teachers of Mathematics [NCTM], 2000; National Research Council [NRC], 1996a; Sparks, 1994). The issue, however, is not just *finding* time but assessing how time is used, allocated, and distributed throughout the school day and throughout the academic year. Simply finding more time does not ensure more effective professional development opportunities for teachers. It is critical to use the time that is available in creative and unique ways to provide diverse learning opportunities for teachers. As the National Partnership for Excellence and Accountability in Teaching (2000) notes, "The one major reason for failure of schoolwide change models is the lack of teacher time focused on the right things. Districts actually may be providing sufficient support and time for professional development, but the results are less than desired because the time is not used well" (p. 11).

One challenge educators face is overcoming the traditional ways in which teachers, administrators, and the public view how time is spent in schools. Most schools are organized around the value—whether explicitly or implicitly acknowledged—that the most worthwhile use of time in schools is spent in direct contact with students. Although student learning *is* the most valuable outcome of schools, teachers' professional development greatly contributes to that learning. Until the view of learning for all, including teachers and students, changes, educators will continue to bemoan the fact that "there isn't enough time!" As Tom Guskey (1999) notes, "If the additional time for professional development is to yield truly meaningful improvements, we must ensure that time is used wisely, efficiently, and effectively. This will require deep and profound changes in the organizational culture of most schools and in the perspectives of educators who work within them" (p. 11).

Advocating for quality time for teacher learning in schools is the responsibility of all educators. Fortunately, there is mounting evidence and research to support educators in their efforts to promote professional development embedded within the school day and the life of teachers. It will take devoted time to address the reforms in science and mathematics professional development and student learning being heralded by national standards. It cannot happen in one-shot workshops, during three professional development inservice days a year, or by attending several seminars that are disconnected from each other in their content and focus. As discussed in Chapter 2, the idea of building new understandings through active engagement in a variety of experiences over time, and doing so with others in supportive learning environments, is critical for effective professional development.

National standards are not the only impetus for moving the reform of professional development forward; the relationship between time and learning, for both teachers and students, was reviewed in depth by a nine-member commission of the National Education Commission on Time and Learning. The resulting report, *Prisoners of Time*, clearly stated that time for professional development is

> urgently needed—not as a frill or an add-on, but as a major aspect of the agreement between teachers and districts. They [teachers] need time to read professional journals, interact with their colleagues, and watch outstanding teachers demonstrate new strategies. (National Education Commission on Time and Learning, 1994, p. 36)

Almost ten years later, time for high-quality professional development continues to be a barrier. For example, the recent report from the National Commission on Mathematics and Science Teaching for the 21st Century (2000) supports and reconfirms the essential need for schools and districts to allocate time and institutionalize structures that support teacher learning. The report noted:

> Many people erroneously believe that teachers are not working unless they are standing in front of a classroom. In fact, preparation time, individual study time, as well as time for peer contact and joint lesson planning, are vital sources of both competence and enrichment for all teachers. But teachers are granted precious little time for

any of these activities. Equally rare are extended periods of time set aside for teachers to have challenging educational experiences of their own. Everyone connected with and touched by the U.S. education system is responsible for changing the character of professional development and its impact. The place to begin improving mathematics and science teaching is with a *system* that promotes high-quality professional development opportunities for all teachers. (pp. 24-25)

Both reports reflect the continued emphasis throughout the country on the value and need for professional development for teachers.

Although changes have been made in numerous schools and districts throughout the country, professional developers still face challenges in reallocating time for professional development. One barrier is the current structure of schools. Teachers typically have only their lunch or planning period designated as time away from their students. Rarely are teachers able to use this time to collaborate or consult with their peers, reflect on either their teaching or their students' learning, or connect with others outside of the school environment. Implied in this statement is that teachers' own time is "designated" for them; rarely, however, are teachers empowered, or trusted, to "use their noninstructional time wisely and [historically they] have had virtually no control over the structure or use of their time" (Castle & Watts, 1992, p. 2).

Given the organizational structure of schools and the perception of how teachers should spend their working hours, what can professional developers do? How do professional developers design programs and initiatives that overcome the obstacles and allocate the necessary time needed to create continuous learning opportunities for teachers of science and mathematics? The following section suggests questions for professional developers to ask themselves as they tackle the issues surrounding time for professional development.

How do you find ways to make more effective use of time currently available within the school calendar? Even with the current structure and organization of schools, professional developers have been able to find ways to "creatively restructure" the time that is already available to teachers within the school day and the calendar year. A review of the literature finds that the solutions being implemented fall into several categories: released time, restructured or rescheduled time, common time, better-used time, and purchased time (Castle & Watts, 1992; Darling-Hammond, 1999; Guskey, 1999; Murphy & Lick, 2001; WestEd, 2000).

• *Released time.* This strategy entails freeing teachers from their regular instructional time with students. The most obvious approach is to provide substitute teachers so that teachers can participate in professional development. Some schools have recruited principals and other administrators, parents, and volunteers to serve as substitute teachers; other schools use specialist teachers, such as art, music, or part-time teachers. Other options include team teaching and instituting community-based learning experiences or library research for students that free individual teachers from instructional responsibilities.

• *Restructured or rescheduled time.* This solution requires formally altering overall instructional time—the school day, the school calendar year, or teaching schedules. For example, some schools are implementing schedules in which students attend school one hour longer on four days and are released early on the fifth day or in which students arrive one hour later in the morning and stay one hour longer at the end of day, providing time in the morning for teachers to meet with one another. Some schools combine this approach with teachers arriving 30 minutes early, creating additional nonteaching time. Others have combined and reallocated the small amount of time that teachers are required by contract to stay after school each day to "buy" one or two 45-minute periods for collegial work before school each week. Others group students and teachers, using a team teaching approach, so that groups of teachers have scheduled time outside of the classroom. Year-round scheduling is increasingly being used by many districts, which creates larger blocks of time during semester breaks (e.g., three or four weeks) for professional development.

• *Common time.* To move teachers out of individual preparation time, schools are reorganizing time so that teachers have "common" times together. Common planning or preparation times can enable teachers to meet by grade level or by discipline or subject areas or as interdisciplinary teams. This arrangement is used for mentor and mentee teachers, creating a regular time for them to conference. Many schools are organizing planning time to follow or precede lunch time, giving teachers as much as 90 minutes of nonteaching time when they can interact with colleagues informally and/or in learning activities such as study groups, case discussions, and examining student work.

• *Better-used time.* Often, teachers' time outside of the classroom during the school day is consumed by faculty meetings and administrative tasks that limit their opportunities for collaborating with peers. Schools are finding ways to reduce the administrative nature of this time, allowing teachers to focus on their own professional development. For example, using e-mail for routine communication between teachers and administrators can save time typically spent in faculty or management council meetings discussing administrative issues. Other schools designate one staff meeting each month for professional development. A unique solution has been to move "nonessential" student-oriented activities, such as assemblies and club meetings, to after-school time or to recruit staff other than teachers to participate in activities, thus providing more time for teachers to meet. Also, professional developers can closely examine the days that are formally scheduled for professional development (often only three or four days a year) and reassess whether they are being used to best meet the teachers' needs and are designed around a comprehensive plan. In addition to examining existing professional learning time, professional developers are turning to technology for teachers' professional development. This avenue for learning allows teachers to engage in reflective, in-depth, and collegial learning via online courses, online study groups, or online book study.

• *Purchased time.* Even in the face of limited funds, professional developers have found ways to reallocate existing funds to provide time for professional development. Many schools and districts have taken advantage of the funding opportunities for professional development by obtaining grants from agencies, such as the National Science Foundation, or private foundations. Some schools and districts have established a "pool" of permanent substitutes or provide stipends for teachers to attend professional development activities outside of the school day, usually in the evenings and on weekends.

How can you work toward influencing state policies and public perceptions that support professional development? The suggestions described previously primarily focus on implementing solutions at the school or district level. Inherent in those solutions is the assumption that schools and districts do in fact have control over their own programs, have budgets for professional development, and can institute the kinds of restructuring identified—reorganizing school days and calendar years. Many professional developers, however, are faced with policies and perceptions that further impede their efforts to create meaningful learning opportunities for teachers, such as limited numbers of days allocated by state boards of education for professional development or public concern about teachers' time out of classrooms.

Professional developers can do much toward moving the reform of professional development forward. One step is convincing key stakeholders and policymakers that new forms of professional development are essential to support improved student learning and that providing time for professional development is critical. To accomplish this, professional developers must identify and define what is considered professional development at their local sites. Schools and districts that investigate their current professional development practices (inservice days, Saturday workshops, and after-school presentations) often find that they do not meet the teachers' needs for growth and learning. By redefining professional development to include teacher learning experiences such as case discussions, summer months spent in a scientific research lab, or action research conducted in the classroom, schools have reallocated funds budgeted for the annual inservice days to support these alternative forms of teacher learning.

Increasing public awareness of and support for teachers' professional development includes conveying the importance of teachers' ongoing learning outside of the classroom and emphasizing how this enhances student learning. The literature abounds with studies and reports that reflect the benefits of teacher professional development on student learning (Cohen & Hill, 1998; Klentschy, Garrison, & Amaral, n.d.; National Education Goals Panel, 2000; Sparks, 2002a; U.S. Department of Education, 2000; Wenglinsky, 2000; WestEd, 2000). Changing perceptions about what professional development "looks like" and how it benefits student learning can increase parents' and communities' understanding of its importance.

For time for professional development to be valued, all involved—including teachers, administrators, policymakers, and the public—must begin to reconceptualize school time. As Margaret Wheatley (2002) states,

> Schools that are truly learning communities for students and teachers alike require time for teachers to study and collaborate during the school day. If we want our world to be different, our first act needs to be reclaiming time to think. (p. 99)

ENSURING EQUITY

Ensuring equity in a diverse society has become extremely important as science and mathematics reform has shifted from producing a relatively few highly skilled scientists and mathematicians to promoting literacy in these disciplines for all citizens. Numerous reports document the underrepresentation of women, persons of color, individuals from low socioeconomic groups, and persons with disabilities in various aspects of science and mathematics, including careers, higher-level coursework, and opportunities to learn from adequately prepared teachers. The inadequacies of curriculum materials and instructional approaches for such a diverse population are often cited as a problem, particularly with the movement to build new learning on the learner's experiences and context. Widespread strategies such as tracking have come under attack as obstructing access to mathemat-

ENSURING EQUITY

- Is access to the professional development experience equitable? Is this opportunity available to all or does it favor people in certain locations, with certain lifestyles, and from certain cultural, gender, or racial groups?
- Does the design of the professional development invite full engagement and learning by participants?
- Does the content of the professional development experience include the issues of equitable opportunity for all students to learn science and mathematics and participate in careers in science and mathematics?

ics and science learning for a large portion of the student population.

How does equity relate to a discussion of effective professional development? A major issue involves equity for the participants in professional development: equal access for all teachers to quality professional development. (See Figure 4.1.) Access is only the beginning, however. Another issue is whether the programs are designed to support educators to examine and challenge their beliefs about who can learn and how diverse groups of students best learn. Programs must accommodate the diverse characteristics of educators, who have a wide variety of needs, learning styles, cultural backgrounds, and experiences. A final issue relates directly to the students: ensuring that what teachers learn in professional development provides them with the skills, resources, and sensitivities necessary to help a diverse student body gain literacy in science and mathematics. Thus, the issues relate to both the design and the content of professional development. The discussion here is organized around these three areas and proposes questions that professional developers can ask about their programs.

Is access to the professional development experience equitable? Is this opportunity available to all or does it favor people in certain locations, with certain lifestyles, and from certain cultural, gender, or racial groups? Access is a simple concept, but it is often ignored by professional development designers, who are not aware of the inequities that can be created when opportunities are offered to teachers. They may think they offer the same chance to everyone to participate in professional development, but many factors, some of which are in their control, inhibit participation. Some of these factors include scheduling, distance, and resources required to use what is learned. For example, there are many opportunities for teachers to participate in research during the summer and work side by side with scientists and mathematicians. Unfortunately, these opportunities are not always accessible to all teachers. Many teachers have summer jobs, and others have family obligations that prohibit them from enrolling in an intensive professional development program that will keep them away from home for multiple days or weeks.

States with a large number of rural schools struggle with the challenge of providing quality professional development for all teachers in all schools. Many districts, regions, and states have addressed this issue by instituting online professional learning and networking opportunities for teachers. For example, the Maine Governor's Academy for Science Education Leadership addresses the need to reach science teachers throughout the state. The program provides in-person learning sessions complemented by online study group and book study discussions and electronic networking, ensuring that teachers in the most remote regions, serving the poorest of students, have access to quality professional development. In other instances, videoconferencing allows isolated teachers to participate in common learning experiences even when they are dispersed throughout a region.

Inequitable policies and practices in school funding can create unequal opportunities for professional development. Just examining the variation in how professional development funds are distributed and then used in different schools, districts, and states is enlightening. Resource-rich schools, which are unlikely to be those serving underrepresented groups, can better support the learning of their staff, considered by some to be a luxury or frill when lab equipment and books are in short supply. Access to professional development is restricted when teachers do not have the resources to buy the new materials the professional development program requires or recommends.

Does the design of the professional development invite full engagement and learning by participants? Making professional development accessible is a necessary first step, but the adequacy of its design will determine if it is truly equitable. Professional development strategies should be chosen to meet the diverse needs and learning styles of participating teachers. Unfortunately, professional development planners are not always aware of the characteristics of programs that could be problematic. Cultural norms may create barriers to some professional development activities, such as modeling and giving critical feedback. Programs that require consumption of large volumes of reading materials do not serve auditory and kinesthetic learners well.

Demonstrating equity in the design of professional development programs also involves who is chosen to play leadership roles. The designation of leaders sends a strong message about the priority of equity and its role in what and how educators learn. Schools need to select professional development leaders who represent the diversity in both the teacher and student population, understand and value equity and diversity, and proactively involve teachers in professional development efforts who are from underrepresented groups and/or teach underrepresented students.

In California, Carne Barnett Clarke and Alma Ramirez have actively recruited and supported teacher leadership development among African American, Latino, Native American, and other underrepresented groups through WestEd's Mathematics Case Methods Project. In the initial stages of the project, Clarke found relatively few minority teachers volunteering to participate in the professional development sessions that use mathematics case discussions to enhance teachers' pedagogical content knowledge. Since one of the explicit goals of the project is to reach a diverse audience of teachers and to develop a diverse group of teacher leaders as case facilitators, Clarke examined the ways in which teachers were recruited and invited to participate. She found that the practice of contacting schools and sending out fliers resulted in recruitment of the "usual suspects"—the most active, frequently engaged teachers were the ones who attended or were nominated by their principals and were most often not representative of a diverse group of teachers. For example, Clarke found that in the initial case discussions most teachers were white, shared a common pedagogy and philosophy of teaching and learning, and were more experienced teachers. There were few teachers of color and no new and inexperienced teachers, and there was a lack of diverse perspectives about teaching.

To address the lack of diversity among participating teachers and the resulting pool of people to develop into case facilitators, Clarke and her staff began to personally invite teachers from more diverse backgrounds, contact previous case discussants asking them to nominate teachers, and encourage and support leadership among diverse participants. Case discussions were also designed to help teachers move from low-risk engagement to higher-risk participation, such as sharing the facts and details of the case before critically examining the teaching beliefs or behaviors of the case teacher. These strategies resulted in case discussions characterized by diverse perspectives, confident case discussants, and case facilitators who represent varied cultural backgrounds and experiences (Ramirez & Barnett Clarke, 2000).

Does the content of the professional development experience include the issues of equitable opportunity for all students to learn science and mathematics and participate in careers in science and mathematics? The goal of equitable science and mathematics education is to equalize outcomes for all students regardless of their race, ethnic heritage, gender, disability, class, or learning style. How can professional development help teachers improve their strategies for reaching all students with effective science and mathematics education? One way is to introduce tools that assess student progress and allow teachers to identify differential impact on groups of students; areas of identified weakness can be the focus of professional development. Research-based programs that show results for increasing motivation and achievement among minority children and females can be included in professional development. Support groups can explore the problem of equity through reading and discussing research and evaluation reports. Schools can carefully examine their student learning data and data on structures, such as tracking, to identify imbalances in equitable opportunities for student learning.

In addition, research increasingly shows that "the professional development that makes a difference for students of color is professional development that deepens teachers' knowledge of the curriculum they are teaching, helps them find or create effective lessons, and enables them to assess and respond to student performance" (Haycock & Robinson, 2001, p. 18). In other words, *effective* professional development—professional learning opportunities that embody the characteristics of practice-based learning for teachers—leads to enhanced learning of *all* students. The content of professional development should focus squarely on the practice of teaching and learning; that focus in and of itself can enhance equitable learning for students. In fact, in Pittsburgh, Briars and Resnick (2001) found that African American students in schools whose teachers were involved in ongoing curriculum-based, mathematics professional development performed better on standardized tests than did Anglo students in schools that were not considered "high-implementation" schools.

Issues of equity in mathematics and science education reveal themselves in many elements of education; opportunities for educators to become aware of the current situation and ways to think about change are very appropriate as content for professional development. Exploration of how students best learn challenging content in a second language, the impact of tracking on opportunities to learn, cooperative learning as an alternative pedagogical approach, testing, and parent and community collaboration can all be important issues for professional development for mathematics and science teachers, administrators, and other educators.

Numerous programs have been developed in recent years to specifically address equity in teaching, learning, and schools, including the work of the Education Trust (www.edtrust.org), the Dana Center's Advanced Placement Equity Initiative (www.utdanacenter.org, and TERC's Weaving Gender Equity Into Math Reform. Many Web sites, books, and journals, including publications by the NCTM and the National Staff Development Council (NSDC), are now devoted to the topics of equity and diversity. In addition, Weissglass's (1996) early work in mathematics education remains a good example of addressing the issues of equity for both education in general and professional development. His work suggests the need to make equity the central focus of the reform effort. His professional development goal is to help educators understand the relationship of mathematics and culture and to increase their capacity to provide mathematical experiences that meet both the needs of a diverse student population and the NCTM standards. Through reading, discussion, and observation, educators in Weissglass's programs explore how cultural values and ways of understanding can affect mathematics learning and teaching; understand the culture of mathematics and the value of building classroom mathematics on children's own experiences; examine instructional materials though an "equity filter"; and experience the application of mathematics to understanding important social issues, such as hunger, poverty, and teen pregnancy. These kinds of experiences help educators to better understand the issues of equity as part of their own professional development.

BUILDING PROFESSIONAL CULTURE

The culture of a school contributes to the learning of all within its walls. As described in Chapter 3, a school that embodies a collaborative culture and professional learning community is characterized by a strong vision of learning, is focused on continuous learning, promotes a community of learners who all take responsibility for learning, "deprivatizes" teaching through collaborative and collegial interactions, and routinely supports and engages in collaborative inquiry and dialogue (DuFour & Eaker, 1998; Fullan, 2001; Love, 2002). Without a supportive culture, professional learning of teachers has little chance of survival

> **BUILDING PROFESSIONAL CULTURE**
>
> - **What is a good starting place for building a professional learning culture?**
> - **What can professional developers specifically do to build professional communities among teachers?**

vival —teachers' newly gained knowledge and skills have little chance of having a lasting impact on their practice. What can professional developers who aim to help teachers foster improved learning of science and mathematics do? Especially in instances in which the professional development opportunity is neither inside the school nor connected with the school or district in any way, professional developers have special challenges for nourishing professional cultures. The first step in that direction, however, is to understand what is known about professional culture and why it is important. (See Figure 4.1.)

Rosenholtz (1991) aptly coined the terms *learning enriched* and *learning impoverished* to describe elementary schools in which students, teachers, and other members of the school community either learned and grew in an exciting, supportive environment or languished with none of the expectations, norms, and rich learning experiences to help them grow. Little's (1982) early work on professional development pointed out differences between schools in which teachers talked continuously about their teaching and their students, experimenting with new strategies and sharing successes and failures, and those in which teachers were isolated, private, and not prone to innovation. Both researchers found student learning differences that favored schools in which teachers also learned. More recently, researchers (Bransford, Brown, & Cocking, 1999) have identified four characteristics of effective learning environments:

- Learner-centered environments that focus on the knowledge and experiences learners bring to the situation

- Knowledge-centered environments that emphasize teaching new content and concepts in ways that align with how people learn the discipline

- Assessment-centered environments that provide learners with ongoing feedback on their learning and promote self-reflection on learning

- Community-centered environments that nurture learning communities characterized by collaboration, collegial interaction, and reflection

Schools that develop learning environments that incorporate all four aspects of professional communities provide a *learning enriched* environment for both students and teachers.

In their studies of high school departments, McLaughlin and Talbert (2001) determined that strong professional cultures are "essential" to changing norms of practice and pedagogy. This happens when teachers examine assumptions, focus their collective experience on solutions, and support efforts on the part of everyone to grow professionally. Professional communities with norms of privacy and unchallenged sacred principles or personal beliefs breed embittered, frustrated teachers. Interestingly, departments within a single high school can have such different professional cultures that the influence of school leadership seems much less important.

Researchers with the Qualitative Understanding: Amplifying Student Achievement and Reasoning (QUASAR) project have examined teacher development and change in middle schools through a "community of practice" framework (Stein, Smith, Henningsen, & Silver, 2000), which was originally developed by Lave and Wenger (1991). The notion of a "community of practice" helps describe how teacher learning occurs in collaborative, school-based communities. For example, in looking at ways in which "newcomers" to a school were participating in the community, QUASAR found that simply being a "member of a community of practitioners provides meaning and context to newcomers' learning experiences" (Stein et al., 2000). The community provided opportunities to observe teaching strategies in action, to hear stories about the process of changing, and to become immersed in the "language" of reform. Rather than teacher collaboration being simply a contextual variable that enhances individual change and growth, it also nurtures and supports learning and change in the community. It is the culture of the community itself that contributes to both individual and group changes and learning.

These findings about the power of professional community cut across levels of schooling. They provide clues to what professional developers working with teachers of science and mathematics can do to foster deeper learning and development. The following paragraphs provide questions that professional developers can ask themselves to improve the impact of their programs by building professional culture.

What is a good starting place? Professional developers have used three strategies to build professional communities. First, they have increasingly required teacher participants to bring colleagues and principals with them to share in learning. For example, teachers are asked to participate in pairs or teams with an administrator. Having an administrator present can be important in creating both the culture and the structures to support professional community back at the school. In other cases, the professional development is for the whole department (as in high schools and some middle schools), whole school, or even whole district so that an entire staff learns together. Community District 2 in New York City (see Chapter 3) is an example of an entire district transforming the culture of both individual schools and the way in which teaching and learning are perceived throughout the district.

A second strategy is for professional developers to build their own professional communities outside the boundaries of departments, schools, or districts. The professional networks described in Chapter 5 provide examples. The professional developers supporting these networks take pains to build relationships among their members that lack only the physical proximity of an intact teaching staff. A critical ingredient of what some call "temporary systems" is that they continue overtime, purposely nurturing the relationships between their members in an ongoing way rather than severing them after a "main event," such as an institute or workshop experience.

A third strategy that professional developers have used to nurture professional community is to work with individual participants to equip them with ways to build their own professional communities "back home." This is not the "each one, teach one" strategy that some use, largely unsuccessfully, in which teachers learn new skills and strategies and are expected to return to their schools and teach others the same skills and strategies. In the case of developing a professional community, professional developers suggest and encourage sharing of strategies for teachers to use in their schools to (a) initiate and sustain dialogues about what they have learned, (b) work with their administrators to build realistic expectations and garner support, and (c) encourage others to participate in similar, complementary learning experiences. For example, teachers may return home with study guides for examining articles or videos that engage others in what they are learning. They practice "reentry" behaviors that keep them from becoming isolated by virtue of their changing beliefs and values and enthusiasm for new ideas and approaches and that allow them to respond constructively to questions and issues raised by others. They may also learn how to work collegially with peer teachers and how to coach prospective teachers who are placed with them for practice teaching. These kinds of strategies help teachers make inroads in building or strengthening their own professional communities.

What can professional developers specifically do to build professional communities among teachers? Research indicates that professional communities thrive where collaboration, experimentation, and challenging discourse are possible and welcome (Elmore & Burney, 1999; Fullan, 2001; Hord & Boyd, 1995; Little, 1993; Norris, 1994; Sparks, 2002a; St. John & Pratt, 1997). Collaboration is fostered through finding time for professional learning (see the section Finding Time for Professional Development above). Also, collaboration must meet the needs of participants; there must be something in it for each of them, and it must have a purpose that is better served by collective rather than individual work or expertise. The purpose of collaboration must be improving student learning; clear goals for students coupled with use of student learning data, including student work, help teachers to maintain that focus. Effective collaboration requires special skills—in communication, "data-driven dialogue," decision making, problem solving, and managing meetings. Finally, collaboration requires a genuine caring about others that can be strengthened through opportunities to do constructive work together and to share interesting and stimulating experiences. Professional developers can foster collaboration through structuring experiences of shared learning and special skill development.

It is important to note that collaboration as a vehicle for learning and community building can be a negative as well as a positive force. Fullan and Hargreaves (1991) point out that "contrived collaboration" can take teachers away from valuable time with students, and "groupthink" can stifle rather than stimulate innovation and imaginative solutions. McLaughlin's (1993) research has found collegiality can focus on being critical of students and reinforcing norms of mediocrity. The chances of collaboration taking a more "learning-enriched" path are increased when it is accompanied by experimentation and challenging discourse.

Experimentation requires skills and dispositions toward inquiry, norms that recognize and support failure, and ideas with which to experiment. Although this does not refer specifically to formal action research, insights into fostering inquiry are provided in the discussion of action research as a professional development strategy in Chapter 5. Professional development programs can be sources of new ideas and practices with which to experiment and can assist teachers to do so in ways that increase their potential for learning. More difficult is the issue of making it okay to fail. Teachers, who are often perfectionists, have traditionally been expected to be the source of knowledge and thus must always have the right answers. Learning to accept and learn from failure is harder for some than others. It can be enhanced by having a critical mass of people who value it, a structured way to reflect on both successes and failures, and a clear picture of which situations are low stakes and which are high—that is, the ability to analyze the consequences of failure for different situations.

Finally, challenging discussions are not very common among teachers, who often equate criticism with personal inadequacies. Building professional cultures, however, by the very definition of *professional*, carries with it a commitment to effective practice in oneself and in others who share the profession. Desiring high-quality teaching for all students requires teachers to challenge their own practices and the practices of others to improve the learning opportunities for all. Teachers need skills and practice in applying standards of effectiveness to their and others' practice; in gathering, analyzing, and explaining the evidence for their convictions; and in communicating criticisms to each other, both positive and negative. It cannot be otherwise because the science and mathematics teaching promoted by the standards requires challenging what the learner thinks he or she knows to reorganize or deepen understanding. What we want for students, we should want for ourselves as learners. Often, difficult discussions are the ones we learn from most.

Professional developers can purposely build structures that promote a positive professional culture by breaking down isolation through strategies such as study groups, coaching, mentoring, lesson study, examining student work, networks, and case discussions (see Chapter 5). They can teach teachers skills of collaboration, problem solving, and inquiry. Also, they can equip teachers with tools and techniques to build and maintain supportive, professional communities in their schools.

DEVELOPING LEADERSHIP

Leadership is a critical issue in professional development for two reasons. First, leadership development is an explicit goal of a large majority of professional development initiatives in science and mathematics. Numerous science and mathematics projects design professional development experiences for principals and administrators, teachers, and other educators involved in the improvement of science and mathematics education. The extent to which the goal of developing leaders is achieved, however, varies greatly. Second, from research on professional development and change in schools it is clear that leadership and support are required for professional development experiences to be turned into changes in teaching and learning (Bybee, 1993; Fullan, 1991; St. John & Pratt, 1997). The support and advocacy of leaders for the professional learning of teachers legitimize changes, provide resources, and create expectations that changes will occur. (See Figure 4.1.)

> ### DEVELOPING LEADERSHIP
>
> - **Is leadership development a goal of the professional development program or initiative?**
> - **If developing leaders is important, what is meant by a leader and what roles do leaders play?**
> - **What specific roles of teacher leaders are we interested in developing?**
> - **How can these and other roles be developed?**
> - **Are there roles other leaders must play for professional development to be successful? If so, how can they be developed?**

In this section, leadership is addressed from these two perspectives, and questions to attend to in designing professional development are suggested.

Is leadership development a goal of the professional development program or initiative? The answer to this question should be "yes." In Chapter 5, developing leadership is identified as one of the major purposes of professional development programs; it should influence the selection and combination of strategies. Currently, most professional development programs or initiatives identify developing leaders as a goal of their work in education based on the overwhelming literature that emphasizes the critical role that leaders play in reforming science and mathematics education. For example, in an examination of national standards focused on professional development for science and mathematics teachers, professional development in general for teachers and principals, and professional development for technology for teachers and administrators, leadership development is a component of effective professional development mentioned in all of the documents. Studies also indicate that leadership is an essential element of educational change. St. John and Pratt (1997) found that in sites in which science and mathematics reforms were successful, there was one or more long-term, highly skilled leader involved. There are hundreds of institutes and academies that have been initiated in recent years to focus on the professional learning of leaders, from classroom teachers to principals and other administrators. The key issue for professional developers designing programs is to ensure that individual leadership efforts align with and complement the entire design of the program.

If developing leaders is important, what is meant by a leader and what roles do leaders play? Effective leaders are connected to networks through which they gain access to resources and support for continuing the work of reform. They primarily focus on issues of educational substance such as supporting new curriculum and instructional and assessment practices, while remaining smart about the politics and organizational and cultural issues that may thwart them (Kaser, Mundry, Stiles, & Loucks-Horsley, 2002). They see standards not as a lockstep formula to be followed but rather as guideposts to lead and direct efforts. They anchor change efforts in a vision of effective learning and build support for the vision and the practices needed to support it. They continuously reflect on and inquire into teaching and learning and engage in professional discourse. They use research-based models as a way of understanding and leading change (Anderson & Pratt, 1995). They have moral purpose, actively build relationships, create coherence, and encourage the creation and sharing of knowledge (Fullan, 2001).

Kouzes and Posner (2001) identify five practices exemplary leaders use:

- Challenging the process: Searching for opportunities to change the status quo and innovative ways to improve.

- Inspiring a shared vision: Seeing the future and helping others create an ideal image of what the organization can become.

- Enabling others to act: Fostering collaboration and actively involving others.

- Modeling the way: Creating standards of excellence and leading by example.

- Encouraging the heart: Recognizing the many contributions that individuals make, sharing in the rewards of their efforts, and celebrating accomplishments.

All leaders need to develop the knowledge, skills, and abilities previously identified—teachers, principals, district administrators, policymakers, and other educators involved in science and mathematics education. Leaders play different roles at different times. Leadership implies that there are others to lead and, thus, a leader must have authority whether it be vested in the position itself; in the personality, character, or expertise of the person; or in the vision that is espoused. They recognize and accept the responsibilities of leadership. Teacher leaders and administrators alike share leadership roles of advocating for science and mathematics education with parents and the community. Although the specific roles that leaders play varies, as Michael Fullan (1993) notes, for change to be successful, everyone must be a leader.

What specific roles of teacher leaders are we interested in developing in science and mathematics education? Increasingly, teachers are taking on formal and informal roles as educational leaders. Through the National Academy for Science and Mathematics Education Leadership at WestEd, we have seen firsthand the passion and power that are unleashed when talented teachers take responsibility for changing the quality of teaching and learning in their schools. Using data to guide them, they become superb diagnosticians focusing in on what needs to be done, who needs to be involved, and where to start the "treatment." New forms of teacher leadership are resulting in teachers who believe they can do something about the crisis in education. As Crowther, Kaagan, Ferguson, and Hann (2002) write: "Ultimately, teacher leadership as we intend it, is about action that transforms teaching and learning in a school, that ties school and community together on behalf of learning, and that advances social sustainability and quality of life for a community" (p. xvii). Teachers are playing key leadership roles in supporting the learning of their colleagues, including the following:

- *Teacher development.* Many professional development programs support teachers to conduct presentations or workshops for other teachers in the new practices they themselves are learning. In addition to the role of presenter, teachers can act as coaches and facilitators of various kinds of professional learning experiences, such as study groups, case discussions, or demonstration lessons. As professional development opportunities shift from workshops offered by external experts to job-embedded forms rooted in teaching practice, teachers' ability to guide these efforts is increasingly important. They can also plan and initiate professional development for others, even if they do not conduct it themselves.

• *Curriculum, instruction, and assessment.* As an extension of their involvement in professional development, teachers can play leadership roles in curriculum, instruction, and assessment. Teachers play key roles as members of school and district committees that plan curriculum, adopt textbooks and other instructional materials, select or develop assessments, and respond to new initiatives—for example, a call to implement national and state standards for the teaching of science and mathematics. Finally, teachers can use their mathematics or science expertise by being a resource teacher for their peers.

• *School improvement.* Teachers can play additional leadership roles beyond their classrooms by facilitating communication among teachers, serving on school leadership or management councils, and addressing political problems with administrators and community members that relate to new ways of teaching and learning science and mathematics (Ferrini-Mundy, 1997). They can participate in or facilitate networks within or across schools, both in person and through electronic means.

Leadership roles provide teachers with numerous benefits, both personally and professionally. As Roland Barth (2001) states,

> Teachers win something important. They experience a reduction in isolation; the personal and professional satisfaction that comes from improving their schools; a sense of instrumentality, investment, and membership in the school community; and new learning about schools, about the process of change, and about themselves. All of these positive experiences spill over into their classroom teaching. These teachers become owners and investors in the school, rather than mere tenants. They become professionals. (p. 449)

How can these and other roles be developed? Professional developers in mathematics and science have made it increasingly clear that good teachers of students do not necessarily make good leaders of adults. Although even the business literature increasingly views effective leaders as those who can teach and coach (Senge, 1990), experienced teachers require special development opportunities to effectively take on roles of leadership (Ball & Cohen, 1999; Darling-Hammond & McLaughlin, 1999; Friel & Danielson, 1997; Grady, 1997; Katzenmeyer & Moller, 1996). Furthermore, professional developers must be clear about their expectations of the roles participating teachers are to play during or after their professional development experiences (Joyner, 1997). Often, teachers are surprised by the expectation that they are responsible for leading others in the new practices they are learning. In Chapter 5, the strategy in the section Developing Professional Developers describes the skills that teachers find useful as they take responsibility for the professional development of others. As they take on additional leadership roles, however, teachers need more. They need an understanding of leadership, including the bases of power and different leadership styles. They also need skills in decision making, building and managing teams, conflict resolution, using data as a guide to instructional improvement, problem solving, vision building, communicating, and managing diversity. They need to be astute about how to operate as leaders among their peers. Especially in the absence of a professional culture, teacher leaders can become targets and find that their colleagues are reluctant to accept them in their new roles.

Developing leadership does not stop with learning new knowledge and skills. As in any other professional development, teachers learning to be leaders require ongoing support and opportunities to learn over time and to experiment with some of their new skills and strategies, receive feedback, discuss problems that arise, and make appropriate changes. Professional development designers have found it useful to structure regular meetings of teacher leaders for these and other purposes (see especially the Cambridge school district and Mathematics Renaissance cases in Chapter 6).

Are there roles other leaders must play for professional development to be successful? If so, how can they be developed? Administrator leadership is required for professional development to promote learning and changes in classroom practices. Principals, for example, support changes in school mathematics and science through such roles as advocate, facilitator of curriculum selection or development, provider of funds and other resources, broker of professional development and other support, monitor of progress, and troubleshooter (Mechling & Oliver, 1983). They also must understand their role in supporting teachers by learning to anticipate how teachers will feel and behave as they change their practices; what help teachers are apt to need and when; what materials, other supplies, and support staff are required; and what outcomes they can expect from the changes teachers are implementing. In addition, principals must become instructional leaders and therefore must develop their own in-depth understanding of science and mathematics standards, instructional strategies, professional development, the change process, assessment, and curriculum (Fullan, 2000, 2002; Institute for Educational Leadership, 2000). Their own professional development, in fact, mirrors effective professional development for teachers: It should be long term and planned, focus on student achievement, job-embedded, supportive of reflective practice, and provide opportunities to work, discuss, and problem solve with peers (Educational Research Service,

1999). All these leadership activities and experiences reinforce the importance of building a learning community around new ways of learning and teaching and of working together to change perspectives and expectations. Learning together, when it is done in an open and trusting environment, can build respect for different roles and relationships that help school staffs with the difficulties of significant change.

Leadership is required for professional development to make its impact felt in schools and classrooms. Professional development programs can address this by building the leadership knowledge, skills, and dispositions of participating mathematics and science teachers, as well as in administrators, at all levels of schooling.

BUILDING CAPACITY FOR SUSTAINABILITY

Often, professional developers view their role as more than providing opportunities for individual teachers, or even all teachers within a school or a district, to learn and grow. Indeed, they see an important role in building the capacity of the system—whether of a school or a district or some combination of those and universities, and other members of the community— to support teacher learning and development in an ongoing way. What would it mean to build capacity? What would it look like if there were capacity to sustain ongoing professional learning? This section suggests some questions that professional developers can use to determine how they do or could contribute to the capacity of their systems to sustain ongoing professional growth. (See Figure 4.1.)

Would you know capacity if you saw it? A conference of mathematics and science educators pondered this question (and others) in the fall of 1994 (for the full report, see Friel & Bright, 1997). The conference proceedings concluded that components of capacity, which can be present at any system level from local to national, are the following:

- People who can work with teachers in supporting their learning and teaching

BUILDING CAPACITY FOR SUSTAINABILITY

- Would you know capacity if you saw it?
- Do you employ and develop people who can work with teachers to support their learning and teaching?
- Do you build support systems for professional development providers?
- Do you recognize, study, and apply the knowledge base of professional development theory and practice and help others do so?
- Does your professional development program support "subcultures" in which professional development can flourish?
- Do you work to create and influence policies, resources, and structures that make professional development a central rather than a marginal activity?

- Support systems for professional development providers
- A knowledge base of professional development theory and practice
- Supported subcultures in which professional development flourishes
- Policies, resources, and structures that make professional development a central rather than a marginal activity

These elements constitute an "infrastructure" for professional development. Without a strong infrastructure, professional development can be of uneven quality and insufficient quantity, is not cost-effective, and comes in the form of projects that are not sustainable, accessible, or inclusive.

The Consortium for Policy Research in Education (CPRE) conducted a study of 22 schools districts to examine the ways in which school districts effectively support sustained capacity for student and teacher learning. The report (Massell, 2000) notes four strategies common to all of the districts: (1) interpreting and using data to drive decisions about teaching and learning, (2) building teacher knowledge and skills through professional development, (3) aligning curriculum and instruction with both state policies and other reform efforts in the schools and districts, and (4) targeting additional interventions on low-performing students or schools.

Do you employ and develop people who can work with teachers to support their learning and teaching? In the previous section, leadership for professional development was discussed. Here, the importance of leadership is underscored. Traditionally, most of the individuals responsible for staff development were located in higher education and midlevel school district administration. The current view of professional development calls for a much broader range of individuals who can facilitate and lead professional development experiences for and with teachers. These include teachers who are in leadership positions, science and mathematics resource teachers, staff developers within school systems, and principals. Building capacity for mathematics and science reform means developing a wide range of opportunities for individuals in all these roles to expand their existing professional knowledge to work with teachers in facilitating learning.

Professional development initiatives that are invested in building the capacity of the system to sustain the gains they help teachers make must identify individuals who are willing and able to provide leadership and must provide professional development that assists them in understanding and taking on expanded leadership roles. The previous section on leadership and the Developing Professional Developers section in Chapter 5 discuss how this might be done.

Do you build support systems for professional development providers? In addition to teachers, professional developers also need support and opportunities for ongoing learning and development. The development of a larger and more cohesive cadre of professional development providers is of critical importance to sustaining effective professional development. They need opportunities to learn, network with others in similar roles, and confront challenges and solve problems together that are too large for them as individuals. Building capacity and sustainability for mathematics and science education thus means developing and maintaining a diverse array of structures to provide this ongoing support.

Do you recognize, study, and apply the knowledge base of professional development theory and practice and help others do so? As described in Chapter 2, there is a substantial knowledge base for professional development theory and practice that covers a wide range of both the contexts for professional development and the kinds of professional development experiences that can occur. This knowledge base includes psychological studies of teachers in the process of changing their beliefs, mathematics and scientific knowledge, and classroom practice; research on the process of staff development itself; studies of teachers in subject matter collaboratives and networks; studies of a variety of strategies of professional development; and teachers' own writing about their practice and about changed classrooms.

Professions are defined, in part, by shared knowledge, both practical and theoretical, that becomes a common language with which to communicate and improve. In fact, creating and sharing knowledge is one of the key roles of leaders (Fullan, 2000). Building the profession of professional development, and thus building capacity in the system to initiate and sustain ongoing learning, requires that the knowledge base be recognized, built on, shared, and implemented.

Does your professional development program support "subcultures" in which professional development can flourish? Increasing systems' capacities to sustain the continuous learning and growth of teachers is not limited to increasing the number of programs in which teachers can participate for specific lengths of time. It also includes making opportunities available to teachers on an ongoing basis in which they can "join" a subculture that embodies the values of high-quality teaching and inquiry about teaching. Such subcultures provide ongoing support for teachers who have participated in a particular program and those who might join one again but currently choose a different form of learning. They also provide "rampways" for teachers who have not previously been engaged in intensive professional development but would like to try it on a limited basis. Finally, they provide contexts that can sustain teachers over the long term and in which continuous questioning and learning about teaching are encouraged.

The nature of the reform movement that is embodied in the mathematics and science standards not only requires change and learning on the part of a large number of teachers but also implies a different intellectual culture for schools than is typical. Therefore, capacity must be built not only for each teacher to reflect on and examine his or her own teaching but also for the culture of teaching and schooling itself to change. Viewing reform as a cultural matter, as well as an individual psychological one, opens new avenues. The deliberate creation of supportive subcultures in different parts of the system would begin the process of cultural change.

Thus, building capacity for sustainability means initiating, developing, and supporting teacher subcultures at social and organizational levels that will complement efforts designed to build capacity at individual levels.

Do you work to create and influence policies, resources, and structures that make professional development a central rather than a marginal activity? In addition to adding a variety of structures and activities to what is currently available for teachers' learning, it is clear that certain current state and local policies and financial arrangements constrain the degree to which teachers can participate thoughtfully in the professional development opportunities available. This means that to increase what is available to teachers, it is necessary to identify and institute policies that increase the capacity of teachers and schools to take advantage of what is available. As long as structures and financial policies marginalize professional development, whatever capacity can be built will be underutilized.

For example, educational systems are plagued by schedules that impede professional development during the school day, a major obstacle to promoting job-embedded learning. Schedules also challenge teachers' ability to work in teams, often a condition that supports job-embedded learning. Schools and districts often lack a commitment to long-term and consistent priorities for teacher learning that would support teachers to develop in any one content area over time.

Professional developers must work with policymakers at all levels to develop and institute policies that recognize that professional development for all educational personnel is an essential component of an effective school system rather than an add-on activity that can be eliminated in difficult times. Strategies for developing supportive policies are also addressed in Chapter 3 and in this chapter in the sections Garnering Public Support and Finding Time for Professional Development.

SCALING UP

Scaling up becomes an area of great concern as school districts implement new teaching and learning strategies. At the school level, programs are often initiated with vol-

SCALING UP

- Is the innovation clearly defined and based on a sound foundation?
- How do you provide professional development opportunities to large numbers of people?
- Does each teacher have sufficient support to change his or her practice?
- What mechanisms are in place for quality control of the professional development for all?
- Is there a plan at each unit of implementation (department, school, district, state, etc.) for ongoing use, support, and institutionalization?

unteer teachers or the "early adopters." Many resources are invested in this first wave of users, often without a plan for bringing the rest of the faculty on board—which can be a bigger challenge. There is a need to scale up the use of effective practice throughout the school district. (See Figure 4.1.)

At state and regional levels, there are some districts or schools that have benefited from educational changes while others have been untouched. There is a need to scale up to reach those that have not been served. Since there are about 100,000 schools and more than 3 million educators in this country, the challenge of reaching these large numbers is daunting.

The particular challenge for many professional developers is how to design programs and initiatives so that they are able to reach a significant number of teachers. In the past, many have been able to work with the volunteer teachers in summer institutes, help a school select and get training in a new curriculum or instructional practice, or work with one or two teachers from each of several schools who then return and help their schools implement changes. None of these strategies have worked particularly well for reaching large numbers of teachers however, except in the most superficial ways. Furthermore, funding agencies are less interested in creating "pockets of innovation" and are impatient to spread reform more broadly. Witness the large percentage of resources from the National Science Foundation that are currently supporting systemwide initiatives, such as the Mathematics and Science Partnerships, designed to provide in-depth professional development to all teachers in a school district or region.

How can professional developers address this need to reach large numbers—that is, to scale up from a few to many? Although there is no single answer to this question, several factors, discussed in this section, can contribute to success.

Is the innovation clearly defined and based on a sound foundation? The literature reflects different ways of thinking about what is being scaled up. In the implementation literature, the "innovation" is a program or practice new to the setting (Fullan, 1991; Wilson & Davis, 1994). School improvement and reform efforts refer to a vision or purpose (Olson, 1994). Others refer to standards or "normative practice" (Elmore, 1996). The common theme is that it is important to articulate what the change is supposed to look like when it is being practiced: what teachers and students are doing (and not doing) and what one would see in classrooms and schools if the program was working well (Hall & Hord, 1987, 2001). This does not necessarily imply a highly prescriptive set of teaching behaviors and materials, although it could; even the national standards for science and mathematics are specific enough to reveal themselves in teachers' practices and students' responses. One knows them when one sees them.

Therefore, clarity is important but so are utility and practicality because unless a change seems possible, it will not be attempted. There must be evidence that it does not require superhuman efforts, skills that few have or can develop, exotic equipment, or special classroom or school situations (e.g., extra staff), or that it does not rely on a specific teacher or a unique situation. Finally, the change must be credible and backed by evidence that if this change were to occur, clear benefits would ensue for teachers, students, and schools. These attributes of a change make it better able to be shared from one place to another, to be picked up by larger numbers of people, and to be communicated to those whose support is needed for it to become common practice (Fullan, 1991).

How do you provide professional development opportunities to large numbers of people? This is a particularly difficult question to address. Rarely does professional development succeed when it is "delivered en masse" because it usually lacks attention to individual needs, person-to-person interaction, and opportunity for in-depth study and experimentation. Several strategies, however, are being used to reach large numbers. One is technology for professional development (as discussed in Chapter 5). Technology enables teachers from throughout the country to engage in ongoing professional learning with other teachers, facilitators, scientists and mathematicians, and course instructors. In some instances, such as a videoconference course, there is no limit to how many people can participate, especially when combined with smaller group learning strategies, such as online book study or online study groups. Other means of providing professional development through technology, as noted in Chapter 5, have limitations similar to other in-person professional learning strategies: They are limited by how many participants a single moderator or instructor can respond to and engage in learning.

Another strategy is to use a *multiplier*, which is referred to by many names, including *certified trainers, teacher leadership cadres,* or *teachers on special assignment*. This strategy is discussed in Chapter 5 in the Developing Professional Developers section, in the cases in Chapters 6 and examples in Chapter 7, and in this chapter in the Developing Leadership section. Here, a cadre of teachers or other educators learn science or mathematics content and pedagogy, master the new practice(s) in their own classrooms, and are prepared to work with adult learners and are given time to do so. This can have a *multiplier* effect, enabling larger numbers of teachers to be reached.

Professional development does not have to be "one size fits all" but rather should be a combination of strategies. For example, teachers can learn new teaching practices through workshops, institutes, coaching, study groups, case discussions, and immersion experiences. Reaching large numbers is not about everyone having the same experience and having that experience in a constrained period of time. When teachers are offered a variety of strategies from which to learn, and these are offered over an extended period of time, many people can be reached. Here, the issue may be one of focus. When schools or districts decide to focus their professional development resources on one particular change or area of change, teachers have the opportunity to learn fewer new practices more in depth (Bennett & Green, 1995; Elmore, 1996). They can be engaged intellectually, rather than superficially, in the change (Klein, McArthur, & Stecher, 1995).

Does each teacher have sufficient support to change his or her practice? Klein and associates (1995) note that "economies of scale operate only weakly in educational reform" (p. 145). Although it may be economical to supply teachers with materials in large numbers, such as in the use of science kits in elementary schools, it is still the case that each teacher needs professional development, follow-up support, time to learn and experiment, and ways to assess results with students. Scale-up cannot occur if teachers lack what they need to change. Furthermore, it may take increasingly more resources, largely in the form of time and energy on the part of "change agents," to reach those who come to a change at the end of the line—that is, the "late adopters." These schools or individuals may require more evidence to be motivated, assistance to develop new knowledge and skills, and lower assister-to-teacher ratios to troubleshoot during implementation (Klein et al., 1995). These are all issues that need to be anticipated in a support plan for all those who will ultimately be involved. The support plan must accurately estimate and ensure provision of the resources that are necessary to reach everyone.

This points out the importance of coordinating different components of the system and multiple actors in ways that will focus support on the change that is to become widespread. Curriculum and assessment practices, school administration and policies, school structures (including time, materials support, and teaching assignments), and other change initiatives must be coordinated and focused for scale-up to succeed.

What mechanisms are in place for quality control of the professional development for all? This is a particularly important issue, especially where a multiplier strategy is being used. When a particular change has been chosen that promises certain outcomes if all of its critical elements, however generally defined, are in use, it is important that all who are involved in the change learn those elements well. This requires professional developers who have mastered the required knowledge, practiced the strategies, and demonstrated their abilities to work with adults. They are both competent and conscious of their competence; therefore, they are not on "automatic pilot" with no ability to communicate to others and help them change.

Previously noted was the preparation professional developers require to be effective. Some programs fail because they expect teachers with limited professional development to return to their schools and share what they have learned with other teachers. Since the teachers have not had the opportunity to practice and reflect on what they have learned, they are ill prepared to help other teachers. This results in the use of the practice becoming watered-down or distorted. Quality control requires intense attention to developing professional developers, coaching them to develop their content and professional development skills, and supporting them over time as they work with increasing numbers of teachers and encounter different kinds of challenges and problems.

Other quality control mechanisms include clear expectations for the roles of professional developers, written guidelines for professional development activities (e.g., workshop plans and materials, cases and facilitator notes, coaching guides, and immersion activities), and tools for monitoring and evaluating the work of professional developers.

Is there a plan at each unit of implementation (department, school, district, state, etc.) for ongoing use, support, and institutionalization? Plans at each level acknowledge that successful change is simultaneously top down and bottom up (Fullan, 1991). Individual progress in learning and changing can be anticipated (Loucks-Horsley & Stiegelbauer, 1991), as can the management and policy moves that each unit of organization will need to make to support increasing numbers of people involved in the change. Institutionalization, the stage at which a change becomes "how we do things around here," requires attention to such issues as routine professional development for new teachers or those who change grade levels; support networks; routine ordering of required materials and equipment; continuous reflection, monitoring, evaluation, and commitment to changes based on what is learned; and ensuring a line item in the budget for support of the change (Miles, 1983).

Scaling up is a challenge that many are currently taking on in an effort to provide all students with challenging science and mathematics programs. This challenge has inspired innovative, creative, and entrepreneurial approaches by many professional development initiatives (Education Commission of the States, 1995).

GARNERING PUBLIC SUPPORT

Constantly shrinking resources are a sign of the times and nowhere is it felt more keenly than when the public (often through the eyes of school board members) scrutinizes an education budget. What stays and what goes is based on what is valued. Keeping time and funding for professional development in the budget requires public support. (See Figure 4.1.)

GARNERING PUBLIC SUPPORT

- How can professional developers build awareness of the importance of mathematics and science education reform and of effective professional development?
- How can professional developers engage the public in improving mathematics and science teaching and learning?

Public support for professional development is needed at times other than when budgets are being determined. When substitute teachers are in classrooms, school is out because of professional days, or teachers are attending a conference far from home, the public needs to voice its support for ongoing teacher learning and know the benefit it has on student achievement.

Public support for professional development is intimately related to public support for science and mathematics education. A public that values quality science and mathematics learning for all children knows that teachers need opportunities to continually update their knowledge and skills to support students. Such supporters acknowledge and commit to playing an ongoing role of advocacy and support for the science and mathematics education over time.

Professional developers can address the dual purpose of garnering public support for science and mathematics education reform and for teacher professional development. They can do so by paying attention to three areas: (a) increasing awareness of the importance of effective teaching and learning of science and mathematics as well as effective professional development and what they entail, (b) involving the public in learning situations (of both students and teachers) and in various roles, and (c) gathering and publicizing the results of teaching and professional development.

How can professional developers build awareness of the importance of mathematics and science education reform and of effective professional development? The first step is to clarify why reform and the public's support for it are essential. There are several reasons; many relate directly to parents, who are an important segment of "the public." The reasons include the following:

- Parents and the general public can benefit from a better understanding of science and mathematics—for example, they can see how it is used to understand and propose solutions to everyday problems and to better understand technological developments happening all around us.

- Parents can help by supporting their children to learn in new ways—for example, parents can help their children use inquiry and problem solving by asking and investigating questions that arise in everyday life.

- Schools can benefit from the contributions of committed parents and community members, such as scientists and mathematicians, who have expertise to contribute. In addition, generating their interest could increase the resources available to the school.

- An informed public will be more skeptical about and able to address misinformation about science and mathematics education—for example, be able to address issues that arise regarding the teaching of evolution in science or problem solving and computation skills in mathematics.

- Authentic partnerships between schools and parents and the community benefit students' learning.

Mathematics and science educators are clear about the need for public engagement around the future of science and mathematics education. For example, in its charge to groups writing the *National Science Education Standards*, the NRC (1996a) stated the following:

> The traditions and values of science and the history of science curriculum reforms . . . argue for a large critique and consensus effort. Science is tested knowledge; therefore, no matter how broadly based the perspective of the developers, their judgment must be informed by others' responses . . . particularly teachers, policymakers, and the customers of education systems—students, parents, business, employers, taxpayers. One of several reasons for the limited impact of past reform efforts was the weakness of their consensus building activities. (p. 2)

Professional developers can help teachers and other educators understand the importance of improved mathematics and science teaching and learning and, more important, become articulate about it. They can help educators communicate with parents and the public about the benefits of a mathematically and scientifically informed populace.

Mathematics and science educators have found that parent involvement is essential in their reform initiatives. As Parker (1997) notes, "Parents become strong advocates for change if they are kept informed of the need to change and the nature of the change needed in mathematics education" (p. 240). Staying informed, however, is only one step in the process toward developing authentic relationships and partnerships with parents who can be strong advocates for science and mathematics education. Schools must develop a broader conception of what "parent involvement" means and expand the roles of parents beyond volunteering for field trips or helping out in classrooms. As Mike Murphy (2001) notes, too often "parent involvement can merely be empty rhetoric or window dressing" (p. 3). If parents and families are viewed as true partners in children's education, their involvement includes activities such as participating in school planning and governance, engaging in decision-making processes regarding the ways structures and policies influence students' learning, examining their child's work with the teacher to better understand what the child is learning, and participating in science or mathematics "curriculum and concept awareness" activities to enhance their understanding of the instruction their students receive. Numerous schools and districts have found that when parents and families are truly engaged as partners in children's learning, they are advocates for the school and the ways in which their students learn.

The University of Washington's professional development project for elementary school teachers directly addressed the issue of garnering public support for science education through a three-day mini-institute for teachers. During that time, teachers learned how to craft messages to address the questions and concerns of various audiences, including parents, principals, business executives, and city council members. They interacted with a panel representing these groups regarding the question, "What would motivate you to support science education?" They identified the common threads and the unique needs of the various groups (C. Kubota, personal communication, July 1996).

In addition to awareness of effective mathematics and science education, the public must have awareness of the importance and nature of effective professional development. It helps to state how little education systems invest in their employees compared with corporations. Again, clear articulation of what professional development is for, what it entails, and what its benefits are can help to increase the public's support. Linking professional development to student learning—as in the statement, "the more teachers know and are able to do, the more students can learn"—is an effective motivator for parent and community support. Sharing recent research and literature on the relationship between teacher professional learning and student learning can also increase the community's understanding of and support for teachers' learning. More important, local school or district data on the ways in which students' learning is increasing in science or mathematics and the relationships to their teachers' professional learning can "convince" and motivate the community to support time and resources for teacher professional development.

How can professional developers engage the public in improving mathematics and science teaching and learning? Another strategy for garnering public support is by actually engaging people from the community in mathematics and science education. This can be done in several ways. First, parents and community members can be invited into the professional development experiences as learners; for example, they may join teams from schools or districts for professional development during summer institutes. In other cases, parents and community members can collaborate together in learning experiences, such as study groups to examine and understand national or state standards. Second, they can be invited in as "teachers," working with students in classrooms and teachers in professional development settings. This is of particular benefit when they have science or mathematics expertise and experiences to share. Examples of how this can happen were discussed in the section on Finding Time for Professional Development.

5

Strategies for Professional Learning

The decision about which strategies for professional learning to include in your design is informed by all other inputs into the process of designing. (See Figure 5.1.) The goals of the professional development program—which are grounded in the vision and in data analysis—drive the selection of specific strategies. Strategy choices are also informed by the knowledge and beliefs the designers hold about the change process, teaching, learning, professional development, and the nature of science and mathematics. The context within which the strategies will be implemented shapes the selection, combination, and sequence of the learning opportunities provided. The critical issues that influence the successful implementation and outcomes of any professional development program play a role in determining the selection of strategies. For example, building capacity for sustainability may lead to a decision to combine strategies such as immersion, curriculum implementation, and technology for professional learning to meet different teachers' needs at different times. Finally, professional learning opportunities are often the specific components of the design that are evaluated and assessed.

A word of caution—strategies in isolation do not constitute effective professional development. Strategies are frequently what professional developers "grab at"; this book emphasizes why different strategies are better choices within different contexts, for different goals and purposes, and for different circumstances. As noted above, it is the intricate interplay of all

Figure 5.1. Strategies for Professional Learning

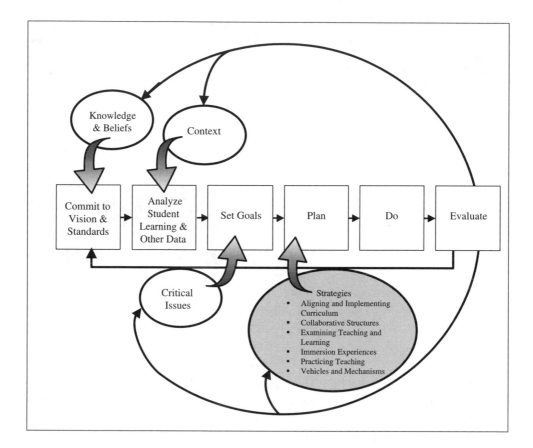

components of the design framework that informs the selection of strategies for professional learning.

This chapter describes 18 specific professional development strategies. The chapter describes each strategy according to its (a) key elements, the components of the strategy that help answer the question: How will I know it when I see it? and (b) implementation requirements, the resources and support needed to use the strategy, such as time, facilities, materials, and additional staff. Following this are various examples of ways in which the strategy has been implemented and a discussion of some of the issues and challenges faced when selecting and using the strategy. In addition, for each strategy, there are several resources noted—articles, books, and Web sites—for obtaining further information and learning about specific programs or initiatives that use the strategy.

The 18 strategies are grouped into six clusters: (1) aligning and implementing curriculum, (2) collaborative structures, (3) examining teaching and learning, (4) immersion experiences, (5) practicing teaching, and (6) vehicles

TABLE 5.1   Eighteen Strategies for Professional Learning

Aligning and implementing curriculum
    Curriculum alignment and instructional materials selection
    Curriculum implementation
    Curriculum replacement units

Collaborative structures
    Partnerships with scientists and mathematicians in business, industry,
        and universities
    Professional networks
    Study groups

Examining teaching and learning
    Action research
    Case discussions
    Examining student work and thinking and scoring assessments
    Lesson study

Immersion experiences
    Immersion in inquiry in science and problem solving in mathematics
    Immersion into the world of scientists and mathematicians

Practicing teaching
    Coaching
    Demonstration lessons
    Mentoring

Vehicles and mechanisms
    Developing professional developers
    Technology for professional development
    Workshops, institutes, courses, and seminars

and mechanisms. (See Table 5.1.) The strategies within a cluster share common underlying assumptions about teaching, learning, and professional development. Therefore, the clusters provide a framework for organizing the strategies and considering their selection and use.

As noted in previous chapters, professional development is more than offering isolated strategies. Every program, initiative, and professional development plan uses a variety of strategies in combination with one another to form a unique design. Each strategy is one piece of the puzzle, and how a designer fits strategies together depends on his or her particular circumstances. The professional development designer's challenge is to assemble a combination of learning activities that best meets the designer's specific goals and context.

From work with professional developers in science and mathematics, we identified four interconnected outcomes that often drive professional development designs in science and mathematics education:

- Increasing science and/or mathematics content knowledge
- Increasing pedagogical content knowledge
- Building a professional learning community
- Developing leadership (NISE Professional Development Strategies Working Group, 1999)

If districts are working to promote these four outcomes, as many are, it is easy to see that one strategy will not be sufficient. Instead, the designer combines different strategies to address the different outcomes, with some strategies addressing more than one outcome. Increasing teachers' content knowledge is often best accomplished by immersing teachers in content as learners themselves. This can be accomplished through the immersion strategies, through partnerships, and in workshops/institutes. But learning content alone will not lead to changes in teaching, so designers must build in opportunities for teachers to put the content they learn into the context of teaching and provide opportunities to develop pedagogical content knowledge. This is accomplished through different strategies, such as examining student work, case discussions, curriculum work, and lesson study. Engaging in such collegial arrangements helps to address the third outcome—building a professional learning community, which can also be developed through teachers' participation in lesson study, demonstration lessons, and study groups. The final outcome is often addressed through the use of the developing professional developers strategy.

In addition to using the intended outcomes of a professional development program to guide the selection of strategies, another guide is knowing the purpose each strategy best addresses and matching it to the needs of participating teachers. Different strategies can be more appropriate for people depending on where they are in the change process. At the beginning of the process, teachers need concrete information and "how to" advice. Later they want ways to collaborate with others and assess impact.

For example, some strategies are more appropriate for building knowledge (e.g., workshops/institutes and partnerships), whereas others help teachers reflect on learning and teaching (e.g., action research, examining student work, and lesson study). The following are some different purposes for strategies:

- Strategies that focus on *developing awareness* are usually used during the beginning phases of a change, which call for introducing teachers to new approaches or content. The strategies are designed to raise awareness through the introduction of new information and to elicit thoughtful questioning on the part of the teachers concerning the new information. Examples of strategies that help to raise awareness include professional networks, demonstration lessons, and study groups.

- Strategies that focus on *building knowledge* provide opportunities for teachers to develop science and mathematics content knowledge and pedagogical content knowledge. Examples of strategies often used to build knowledge include case discussions, immersion experiences, workshops, technology for professional development, and partnerships with scientists or mathematicians.

- Strategies that help teachers *translate new knowledge into practice* engage teachers in drawing on their knowledge base to plan instruction and improve their teaching. Examples of strategies often used to help teachers translate knowledge into practice include coaching, mentoring, curriculum implementation, and demonstration lessons.

- Strategies that focus on *practicing teaching* help teachers learn through the process of using a new approach, practice, or process with their students. As they practice new moves in their classrooms, they increase their understanding and their skills. Examples of strategies often used to practice teaching are examining student work, lesson study, coaching, mentoring, and demonstration lessons.

- Strategies that provide opportunities to *reflect deeply on teaching and learning* engage teachers in examining their experiences in the classroom, assessing the impact of the changes they have made on their students, and thinking about ways to improve. These strategies also encourage teachers to reflect on others' practice, relating it to their own and generating ideas for improvement. Examples of strategies often used to help teachers reflect on their practice include action research, study groups, lesson study, case discussions, and examining student work.

The above schema is adapted from a framework devised by researchers in the Qualitative Understanding: Amplifying Student Achievement and Reasoning (QUASAR) project (Brown & Smith, 1997) to describe various ways of supporting teacher learning. The framework, in turn, reflects Shulman's (1986) model of pedagogical reasoning and action. As discussed in Chapter 2, any act of teaching is cyclical. A teacher must comprehend the material to be taught, which then must be transformed into a form that can be taught. Then, instruction takes place and is accompanied by reflection on the effectiveness in fostering student learning.

What is clear from this schema is the developmental nature of teacher learning. Other developmental models have been used by professional developers to select, combine, and sequence the strategies they use to support teacher learning. For example, the Concerns-Based Adoption Model (CBAM), discussed in Chapter 1, describes the emerging questions or concerns that educators have as they are introduced to and take on a new program, practice, or process (Hall & Hord, 2001). These concerns develop from questions that are more self-oriented (e.g., "What is it?" "How will it affect me?" and "What will I have to do?") to those that are task-oriented (e.g., "How can I get more organized?" "Why is it taking so much time?" and "How can I best manage the materials and schedules?"), and finally, when these concerns begin to be resolved, to more impact-oriented concerns (e.g., "How is this affecting students?" and "How can I improve what I'm doing so all students can learn?").

This model suggests that teacher questions can guide the selection of strategies for professional development. For example, an immersion experience in science or mathematics—that is, actually engaging in science inquiry or mathematics problem solving as learners—helps teachers see (and feel) what new teaching practices look like in action. They get a sense of new roles teachers must play, strategies for grouping and questioning, and the flow of instruction. Curriculum implementation helps teachers with their questions about the teaching task because it guides their use of materials, time management, and classroom management techniques. Teachers' more impact-oriented questions can be addressed through opportunities for them to examine student work and score student assessments or conduct action research into their own questions about student learning.

As noted previously, designers combine different strategies to meet multiple goals and to address the particular needs of the learner at a particular time. For example, over the course of a year teachers might participate in a workshop focused on teaching them to use new curriculum, have a coach who helps them implement a unit from the curriculum, and meet in a study group to review videos of their own or others' teaching and examine student work. This combination of strategies can nurture teacher learning through several stages of development and changes in teaching practice and address multiple goals—for example, improved pedagogical content knowledge and increased professional culture.

We invite professional developers to become familiar with the 18 strategies for teacher learning in this chapter and to reflect on how to best combine them to address local goals, needs, and other contextual factors.

ALIGNING AND IMPLEMENTING CURRICULUM

The strategies described in this section emphasize using quality mathematics or science curriculum as the focus for teachers' professional learning—curriculum alignment and selection, curriculum implementation, and curriculum replacement units. In districts across the country, curriculum selection, adoption, and implementation are such common practices in science and mathematics that focusing teachers' professional learning around the curriculum is a great way to embed professional development within the real work of teachers. This section describes three strategies that

Figure 5.2. Strategies for Professional Learning:
Aligning and Implementing Curriculum

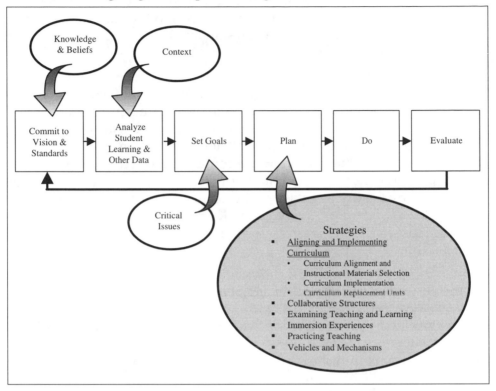

link curriculum improvements and professional learning opportunities for science and mathematics teachers. (See Figure 5.2.) Each of the strategies is based on several underlying assumptions about teaching, learning, and professional development.

Underlying Assumptions

Quality curriculum materials are designed to support students' learning of concepts and content as identified in the national science and mathematics standards. In an era of standards-based teaching and learning, educators are acutely aware of the need and the mandate to provide quality learning opportunities for all students. In many cases, states have developed statewide content standards aligned with the national standards and, often, school districts create their own districtwide standards. These adaptations and interpretations of the national standards vary greatly in their quality. It is critical that those involved in curriculum-based professional development develop an understanding of the national standards and other research that documents what content students should learn and how they can best learn it. They need to consider the extent to which any state's or district's standards align with national standards and the extent to which the curriculum they use provides opportunities for all students to develop the skills, knowledge, and abilities articulated in the national standards.

Teachers become clearer about the goals for student learning and increase their own understanding of the subject matter by learning to use quality curriculum materials. For teachers, going through the process of selecting and implementing new curriculum that is standards based, well organized, and accurate can clarify (a) the nature of the content itself and assumptions about what students bring to the content, (b) how the content can be taught (e.g., what is hard and what is easy for students as provided in the curriculum and as determined by the teacher's use of the curriculum), and (c) the nature of student knowledge—how students work and talk—and the nature of the discourse that teachers orchestrate to give them access to information about what and how students are learning.

Supporting teachers to learn science and mathematics content and pedagogical content knowledge that is directly connected to their curriculum materials increases the likelihood of changes in classroom teaching. Numerous studies report that when teachers engage in professional development that is directly connected to curriculum materials, teaching behaviors change. For example, Cohen and Hill (1998) conducted a study of mathematics teachers in California, studying the effects of varied professional development experiences on teaching and student learning. They found that "student curriculum-centered learning opportunities seem to increase Framework practice and to decrease conventional practice. Teachers did not just add new practices to a conventional core, but also changed that core" (pp. 5-6).

Teachers who experience new ways of teaching and have opportunities to reflect on and enhance their use increase their abilities to use and commitment to the new approaches. Using new approaches to teaching (e.g., inquiry) and curriculum materials designed to support such approaches provides teachers with experiences that often raise many questions. Reflecting on and analyzing what they are experiencing in their classrooms and talking with other teachers about what they are learning enhances teachers' understanding of how to best teach the curriculum. Professional development that teaches teachers to use the curriculum is an optimal way to support teachers to learn content and new ways of teaching. Structured discussion following their use of the curriculum allows teachers to reflect on and analyze their own classroom performance. They can articulate their experiences, receive reinforcement for successes and help in understanding and addressing their problems, and then work through challenges.

Curriculum Alignment and Materials Selection

At the request of the superintendent, a group of teachers from four schools and their principals and the science curriculum specialist formed a committee to coordinate selection of curriculum materials. Their first step was to come to consensus on the criteria they would use to select from among the many science texts and kit-based materials available. They each took responsibility for some reading on trends, research, practices, and attitudes in science education and shared findings with each other. They also carefully studied and discussed the expectations for students reflected in their district, state, and national standards. From this they created a rubric for scoring the different elementary science materials they were considering. The rubric would help them measure the extent to which the curriculum materials reflected the content in the standards; engaged students in the kind of work, learning, and assessment activities recommended by research; and were developmentally appropriate. The development of the rubric resulted in substantial learning among the participants. They learned the contents of the standards as well as research on children's ideas in science and developed a shared vision of what the elementary science program for the district needed to include.

The committee obtained copies of commercially available materials to review for consideration, examining the extent to which each set of materials addressed appropriate science content, the intended learning goals for all students, and strategies for teaching, learning, and assessment. They narrowed their choice down to two different products that the committee scored the highest using their rubric. They enlisted teachers at each elementary grade level throughout the district to pilot test the two different sets of curriculum materials in their classrooms. During pilot testing, teachers engaged in short weekly sessions to reflect on what they did and examine the students' work to better understand what the students were learning and how the instructional materials supported learning. Pilot-testing teachers also met monthly with the curriculum committee to share what they, as teachers implementing the new materials, needed to enhance their ability to use the materials effectively, including science content knowledge and better understanding of inquiry-based learning. The curriculum committee responded to these needs during the pilot testing and used what they had learned to inform plans for large-scale implementation.

Based on the results, the committee and pilot-testing teachers selected one of the instructional materials for use in the coming school year and a long-term plan for implementing the new curriculum materials.

In many districts, the process of selecting curriculum materials has been simply to pick something popular with a few teachers or worse have teachers all use their own materials with little coordination. Increasingly, districts are engaging in more thoughtful analysis of the curriculum and its alignment with local and national standards. They use this curriculum analysis in combination with a deliberate materials selection process to select a coherent and focused program for all students. In addition, many districts are capitalizing on this process as an opportunity for teacher learning. The emerging strategy of curriculum alignment and selection of materials develops teachers' understanding of effective curriculum, science and mathematics education standards, content, pedagogy, and assessment.

As the above vignette illustrates, the selection committee engaged in various activities to increase teachers' knowledge including the following:

- Studying the local and national standards to identify the meaning and intent of student learning goals

- Developing a clear picture of what curriculum was needed based on the standards and student learning goals and how concepts and skills would develop in a coherent fashion through the grades

- Developing a common vision of standards-based teaching and learning

- Identifying local needs based on analysis of student learning and other data

- Using a process for selecting curriculum materials that was guided by a systematic approach to gathering evidence

- Selecting the materials, pilot testing them, and developing a plan for implementation.

Key Elements

Teachers are essential participants in the process of aligning, selecting, and implementing curriculum materials. Many districts appoint a selection committee composed of content area coordinators and classroom teachers to conduct the initial identification of curriculum to consider for adoption. The involvement of teachers, however, often ends once the instructional materials are adopted and added to the approved district or state list. For this strategy to maximize professional learning, teachers need to stay involved throughout the whole process—from establishing learning goals to implementing instructional materials. Their involvement in studying standards

---

KEY ELEMENTS OF CURRICULUM ALIGNMENT AND MATERIALS SELECTION

- Teachers are essential participants in the process of aligning curriculum, selecting instructional materials, and implementing those materials.

- Teachers undertake a process of examining curriculum and instructional materials that leads to a new product and learning.

- Aligning curriculum and selecting instructional materials require a clearly articulated procedure that addresses all aspects of the process.

- Curriculum alignment and instructional materials selection is a collaborative activity.

and setting learning goals increases their understanding of the relationship between the curriculum and the learning goals or standards, giving them insight into the intent of the curriculum. Their active participation in pilot testing the instructional materials helps them see how the curriculum works with children, and this can inform the professional development needed to support the implementation of the materials by other teachers. Helping to shape professional development plans and monitor and support implementation is another learning opportunity for teachers.

Teachers undertake a process of examining curriculum materials that leads to a new product and learning. The outcome of alignment and selection of curriculum materials is the identification of a new or modified curriculum program aligned with standards. The selection process itself provides the opportunity for professional development. As teachers explore the standards and develop a content matrix or adopt one from commercial curriculum materials, they learn what science or mathematics content is valued in the standards, collaborate with peers and experts, examine the extent to which assessments match the content, reexamine their own classroom practices, work with others to solve problems, and interact with subject matter and pedagogy. All these activities enhance the professional growth of individual teachers and can lead to more effective teaching and learning practices.

Aligning curriculum and selecting instructional materials require a clearly articulated procedure that addresses all aspects of the process. There are numerous tools and guidelines available for curriculum selection (see the Resources section). No matter which process is selected, it is critical that the following components be included:

- The formation of a team or committee with representation from teachers at the appropriate grade levels and content areas, different school sites, and administrators.

- The selection of tools and a comprehensive process to guide the examination of national and local standards, analysis of current performance levels in the appropriate grade levels and content areas, development of a content matrix that identifies student learning goals across grade levels, and the selection of the instructional materials.

- Instructional materials selection should include an analysis of the content, student learning activities, teaching activities, teacher content information, and assessment strategies. These components should be evaluated based on rubrics developed or adapted by the committee members to meet their local contexts and goals.

The selection of instructional materials should include a "prescreening" process to narrow the choices of instructional materials; a paper screen process to gather and analyze evidence from the materials to determine if they meet the established criteria and standards, using a rubric or other scoring device; pilot testing of the materials in classrooms to gather and analyze student work and other data from the classroom; selection of the final instructional materials; and full-scale implementation of the materials with accompanying professional development.

Curriculum alignment and instructional materials selection is a collaborative activity. The process of collaborating with other teachers and curriculum experts enriches the professional development opportunities. Through analysis of curriculum and discussion, teachers build their own knowledge of the content, curriculum organization and design, and content-specific pedagogy. They begin to identify content that they do not understand and plan together to address such gaps in knowledge. Often, as teachers examine the curriculum and see how and why different concepts and lessons are organized the way they are, their attitudes about what constitutes effective science or mathematics teaching and learning change. They return to their classrooms with new views. Also, by collaborating with others, teachers become less isolated in their individual classrooms and develop a broader perspective of science or mathematics education.

Implementation Requirements

District or school administrative support. Administrators encourage the process, provide time and incentives for teachers to participate, ensure access to resources and experts, and support ongoing, long-term improvement of the curriculum and instructional materials that are ultimately implemented.

Process for selection including rubrics, tools, and forms for tracking what was piloted and its results. It is essential that the process be clear to everyone involved. Using resources such as those listed later in this section will keep the team on track and document what was done and why.

Examples

The K–12 Alliance at WestEd has developed an instructional materials selection process called analyzing instructional materials (AIM). In partnership with Biological Sciences Curriculum Study (BSCS), K–12 Alliance staff are using AIM with teams of high school teachers and their school district administrators as part of the core learning experiences in the BSCS SciCenter's National Academy for Curriculum Leadership. These teams use AIM to guide their selection of and planning for implementation of inquiry-oriented, standards-based instructional materials. It is used as a professional development experience for the teams and is based on gathering evidence to analyze and select instructional materials. Leadership teams participate in professional development to help them understand the various components of AIM and to enhance their understanding of inquiry-based teaching and learning and further their common vision of best practice before they begin looking at commercially available textbooks and other materials.

The AIM process itself involves identifying criteria that are based on local, state, and national science standards for analyzing instructional materials and developing rubrics for the criteria. Several sample rubrics are provided for the teams to use to guide the development of rubrics specific to their own contexts and standards. The rubrics are designed to assess the science content, the work students do, assessment, and the work teachers do within the instructional materials. Instructional materials are assessed based on each criterion and scored according to the rubrics. Once all criteria have been assessed, the leadership team has evidence of the extent to which the instructional materials meet their criteria. This initial process, labeled the "paper screen," enables teams to narrow their selection of instructional materials to only those that are quality, inquiry-oriented, standards-based materials that meet their specific criteria. These few instructional materials are then pilot tested in classrooms. Pilot teachers participate in professional development to learn more about inquiry-based teaching and learning and the instructional materials. During pilot testing, data are gathered on the same rubric components, adding further evidence for the leadership team to consider in their selection of the final materials.

The selection process, however, does not end with the identification of one set of instructional materials. Central to the AIM process is the development of a long-term plan for professional development for all teachers who will implement the newly selected instructional materials. Leadership teams learn about the process of designing professional development for supporting curriculum implementation and about many of the strategies most successful in enhancing teachers' learning.

The ARC Center in Lexington, Massachusetts, a collaboration between the Consortium for Mathematics and Its Applications (COMAP) and three of the elementary mathematics curriculum projects supported by the National Science Foundation (NSF), works closely with schools and districts to enhance teaching and learning in mathematics. One of ARC's main strategies is to provide guidance and professional development for curriculum selection teams in districts to enhance their reform efforts in mathematics. One of these sites is the school district in Portage, Wisconsin, a small, rural school district with seven elementary schools. During the 1998–1999 school year, the district's director of instruction convened a committee to find ways that the district could improve mathematics scores on the statewide tests administered in fourth, eighth, and tenth grades. On the committee were second- through sixth-grade teachers from each of the elementary schools, who met twice a month during the academic year. The committee examined data about their own students' test scores and initiated a study to learn from other districts: "They started by looking at test data of other Wisconsin districts with demographic profiles similar to that of Portage. Of the 426 school districts in Wisconsin, they chose ten small-town, rural districts that had better mathematics scores than theirs. Committee members visited these districts, observed classes, and asked teachers questions about their mathematics programs" (COMAP, online at www.comap.com/elementary/projects/arc/stories/portage).

During their visits to other districts, the committee was encouraged to look at some of the NSF-supported mathematics instructional materials. They analyzed the materials and assessed the extent to which each set of materials addressed the state standards. After narrowing their options to two high-quality materials, they pilot tested them in fifth and sixth grade classrooms. By the end of the school year, one of those materials had been selected and adopted.

At that point, the committee took a crucial step—gaining the "buy-in" and support from classroom teachers in each of the schools. "The committee members spoke to other teachers at building meetings. They discussed the data gathering process, described the pilot tests, and shared the [instructional] materials. Their message was that the district needed to make a change, that this was an outstanding curriculum, that it would help teachers improve instruction, and that students would like mathematics and do better. The teachers supported the choice" (COMAP, online at www.comap.com/elementary/projects/arc/stories/portage). At the same time, the director of instruction was sharing identical information with each of the school principals, and parents and the community were informed of the new instructional materials through discussions. By the end of the year, each of the seven schools was supportive of the new emphasis in mathematics teaching and the school board approved the materials.

In the second year of the process, large-scale implementation was begun and classroom teachers attended numerous professional development sessions to help them learn more about the overall program and the instructional materials. By 2002, every teacher in the district was using the new curriculum and they have had positive reactions to the changes in their classrooms.

Commentary

Many of the benefits of using curriculum alignment and instructional materials selection for professional development of science and mathematics teachers have previously been identified in this section. As with any professional development strategy, however, there are challenges and issues to consider.

Time and support. It is difficult for teachers to find the time to devote to the intensive process of examining curriculum and selecting instructional materials. Frequently, teachers are available only after school or during the summer months to devote time to this intensive effort. It is imperative that teachers who volunteer for curriculum committees are given adequate time and support for their efforts, such as reduction of class load or some other duties in exchange for their participation on the committee. It is also critical that administrators recognize that this is a long-term process and necessarily engages teachers for more than one academic year.

Selecting the appropriate procedure. As noted previously, numerous documents, guidelines, and procedures are available to guide the curriculum alignment and instructional materials selection processes. It is important to keep in mind that the main purpose of these processes is the professional learning and growth of the teachers involved—both those on the committee and the pilot teachers—and ultimately the selection of curriculum materials that will improve student learning. Both goals can be accomplished if care is taken in the identification of the guidelines used to facilitate the processes. In some districts, multiple-year efforts may not be feasible and shorter alignment and selection procedures may need to be identified.

Leadership development. In addition to individual professional learning, this strategy lends itself to developing teacher leaders during the pilot testing process who can provide ongoing professional development for other teachers as they begin to implement the instructional materials. Early in the process, district-level leaders should plan for taking advantage of this knowledgeable and experienced pool of new science or mathematics leaders.

Resources

Alternatives for Rebuilding Curricula (ARC) Center. The Consortium for Mathematics and Its Applications (COMAP) (www.arccenter.comap.com).

American Association for the Advancement of Science, Project 2061, Curriculum-Analysis Procedure (www.aaas.org/project2061).

Eisenhower National Clearinghouse (ENC) (www.enc.org).

Eisenhower Regional Consortia (www.mathsciencenetwork.org).

K–12 Alliance, WestEd, California (www.k12alliance.net).

National Research Council. (1999a). *Designing mathematics or science curriculum programs: A guide for using mathematics and science education standards.* Washington, DC: National Academy Press.

National Research Council. (1999b). *Selecting instructional materials: A guide for K-12 science.* Washington, DC: National Academy Press.

National Science Foundation, Science and Mathematics Education Implementation and Dissemination Centers (www.nsf.gov).

WestEd and the WGBH Educational Foundation. (2003). *Teachers as learners: A multi-media kit for professional development in science and mathematics*. Thousand Oaks, CA: Corwin Press. (See Tape 3, Program 5, *Curriculum implementation: Issues and challenges, Institute for Inquiry, Exploratorium, San Francisco*.)

Curriculum Implementation

Sarah Johnson is a sixth-grade teacher in a district that has three middle schools, each with approximately 600 students, Grades 6 through 8. The school board has just voted to implement a new problem-centered mathematics curriculum. Sarah participated with other teachers in a preliminary meeting during the spring that provided an overview of this new curriculum, but she really has little understanding of the total program or of what it will mean for her to actually use it.

The middle school coordinator has asked Sarah to join her, one seventh- and one eighth-grade teacher, and the principal from her school, along with similar teams from each of the other two middle schools in the district to participate in a one-week residential professional development institute that will introduce them to the curriculum. At the institute, she finds 18 other middle-grades teachers and their administrators from two other districts. This will be a good opportunity to learn with teachers who are from very different districts.

At the beginning of the institute, an overview of the structure and organization of the curriculum is provided. Very quickly, the leader moves to engaging participants in doing actual activities from the first module they will teach. Sarah jumps right in, as do the rest of her team members and they work through the various activities. Sarah is particularly attentive to some of the teaching strategies that the leader is using. In particular, she likes the way the leader expects different groups to take responsibility for initiating summary discussions about problems that have been investigated. She also notes that the leader makes a point of highlighting particular learning strategies as a way of pointing out the interaction of the teaching methods used and ways to promote student engagement and problem solving.

That night, participants are given homework problems to complete for the next day. Sarah and her team meet to work together on the problems; they are challenged as they solve problems and talk about the implications for use with their students. When they arrive at the workshop the next day, the leader designates various teams to take responsibility for presenting their solutions, providing a model for a strategy that Sarah plans to use as part of her classroom structure for the next year.

As the week progresses, the participants begin to understand the structure of the curriculum and how to use it with their students. The leader makes building a community of learning seem easy; Sarah wonders how she will develop such a community with her own students but is filled with enthusiasm. As the week draws to a close, the leader focuses on planning to use the curriculum. Using the school calendar and the pacing guide provided with the curriculum, teachers from the same grade levels team up and lay out a schedule to implement the first module. Sarah feels confident about the detail provided in the teacher support materials, particu-

larly because the curriculum has actually been field tested at a number of different sites. There are many things planned when Sarah returns to her district. She knows that the middle school coordinator is counting on her and the other teachers in her district to use the new curriculum in their classrooms this year and then to help introduce the curriculum to other teachers in their schools the following year. The principals and the middle school coordinator intend to be quite proactive in their efforts to support the teachers in developing learning communities that are oriented toward problem solving, and they will provide the teachers with opportunities for peer coaching and support group meetings. Two more one-day workshops are scheduled throughout the year with the institute leader both to provide time for discussion and to gain an understanding of other modules that will be used at each grade level. Also, the institute leader will return to the school district in the spring to conduct several one-day sessions for the other teachers in the schools.

For right now, Sarah is focused on what will happen with her students. For the first time in a long time, Sarah finds she is very excited about teaching mathematics and that the curriculum seems to reflect her beliefs about what constitutes good teaching and learning.

The implementation of new curricula in the classroom can serve as a powerful learning experience for teachers. For curriculum implementation to support professional development, plans must be designed that enable teachers to learn about, try, reflect on, and share information about teaching and learning in the context of implementing the curriculum with their colleagues. Through using curriculum in their classrooms, reporting on what happens, and reflecting with others on the strengths and weakness of different ideas and activities, teachers learn about their own teaching and their students' learning (Ball, 1996).

Curriculum implementation involves using a set of materials that includes both content and instructional guidelines. The "set" of materials may be from one publisher or developer, or it may have been selected from a variety of quality materials available and organized by the school or district for use at particular grade levels in the development of specific concepts. For curriculum implementation to serve as an effective professional development activity, it is important that the curriculum selected or organized for implementation meets quality standards for content and for appropriate teaching strategies.

Curriculum implementation that is designed for professional development focuses teachers on learning about the new curriculum and how to use it and on implementing it—not on researching, designing, testing, or revising curriculum. The teachers' time is devoted to learning the science or mathematics content necessary to teach the new curriculum, learning how to conduct the activities, learning how students learn the new material, and incorporating the new curriculum into their long-term instruction.

The goal of this professional development strategy is not only for teachers to implement a new curriculum but also for them to strengthen their knowledge of the content and pedagogy in the curriculum.

KEY ELEMENTS FOR CURRICULUM IMPLEMENTATION

- Quality curriculum materials that are based on standards.
- Teachers learn about the curriculum by teaching it and reflecting on it.
- Planning and support for the implementation are critical.

Key Elements

Quality curriculum materials that are based on standards. Curriculum is the way content is designed and delivered. It includes the structure, organization, balance, and presentation of the content in the classroom (National Research Council [NRC], 1996a). Curriculum or instructional materials structure and organize the content and lend support for the teaching strategies and learning environments used by teachers to help their students learn. The curriculum implementation strategy relies on quality curriculum materials, carefully developed by people with expertise in content and pedagogy, and sufficiently tested for use in diverse classrooms.

Teachers learn about the curriculum by teaching it and reflecting on it. As teachers become familiar with the curriculum and go through the materials as learners, they see the various teaching strategies they will use with their students. Teachers then try the new instructional materials and teaching practices in their classrooms and regularly assess and discuss their results and progress with colleagues.

Planning and support for the implementation are critical. A plan contains the structure and timeline of the curriculum implementation (National Science Resources Center [NSRC], 1997). Teachers and professional developers work together to decide how and when the curriculum will be implemented and the milestones that will be met at different points in the implementation process. As the curriculum is introduced over a period of time, teachers are given different kinds of help and support that are tailored to their changing needs. Teachers share ideas and insights with one another as they implement the new curriculum. They also coach one another and conduct classroom visits to support implementation. (Usually, curriculum implementation involves using an entire curriculum for all grades in the school that covers all topics of the content area instead of only one topic or one grade level. The implementation process spread over time, however, may introduce units at one grade level at a time or introduce one unit at a time at each grade level.)

Implementation Requirements

Time. Teachers must have protected and structured time to learn about the new curriculum, try it in their classrooms, and reflect with colleagues on their experiences and those of their students.

Teacher development opportunities. Teachers must have supported opportunities to become aware of the new curriculum, learn to manage materials in the classroom, learn any new science or mathematics content, teach the new curriculum, and assess both their own and their students' learning.

Policies. The school and district must anticipate and plan for institutionalization by ensuring that structures are in place for the continued use of the curriculum after the initial phases and ongoing professional development for all teachers and that the curriculum is part of the overall school and district goals and policy.

Ongoing commitment and support. Teachers and school administrators must support the curriculum implementation and accompanying professional development over time (i.e., not just for one year) and avoid becoming distracted by other innovations and competing priorities.

Mechanisms for assessment and evaluation. Teachers must have routine meetings and interactions with other teachers to critique and process what and how they are teaching and data must be collected to assess the extent of implementation and the interim results from the new curriculum.

Examples

Since 1995, the NSF has devoted considerable effort and funding to support curriculum implementation in districts throughout the country. The NSF has funded 87 Local Systemic Change (LSC) Through Teacher Enhancement programs in school districts. The LSC programs are designed to improve the teaching of science, mathematics, and technology by providing classroom teachers with more than 130 hours of professional development. "The LSC initiative is distinguished from previous teacher enhancement efforts by its emphasis on preparing teachers to implement designated exemplary mathematics and science instructional materials in their classrooms" (Weiss, Banilower, Overstreet, & Soar, 2002, p. 1). LSC projects have designed and implemented diverse professional development programs that emphasize increasing teachers' content knowledge and pedagogical content knowledge, deepening teachers' understanding of the ways in which students learn science and mathematics, and expanding teachers' repertoire of assessment practices. Horizon Research, Inc. (HRI) has conducted annual evaluations of all LSC projects and their findings support aligning professional development to the use of instructional materials, as noted in the following:

> Classroom observations show that teachers who participated in LSC professional development were more likely to be using the designated instructional materials, and that the quality of the lessons taught improved with increased participation in LSC activities. Furthermore, lessons taught by teachers who had participated in at least 20 hours of LSC professional development and were using the designated instructional materials were more likely to receive high ratings for their lessons, lending support to the program's focus on professional development aimed at implementing exemplary instructional materials. (Weiss et al., 2002, p. 54)

The NSF has also supported school districts' implementation of science and mathematics curriculum through their funding of eight Implementation and Dissemination Centers in sites across the country. The centers are designed to help school districts improve student achievement in science and mathematics by helping them implement quality instructional materials. The centers work in partnership with academic institutions, corporations, educational organizations, and school districts to design and provide teacher professional development in science, mathematics, and technology.

Commentary

Although virtually all schools implement new curricula at some time, often they do not organize the implementation process around professional development that provides opportunities for teachers to reflect on and learn from their experiences over time.

There are several benefits to using curriculum implementation as a vehicle for professional development. First, such an initiative aligns professional development with three other major dimensions of the system—curriculum, instruction, and assessment. This avoids what is an all too common practice in many districts: professional development that is disconnected from and unrelated to the curriculum that teachers teach. A second and related benefit is the efficiency of teachers learning exactly what they need to teach. This contrasts with the situation in which teachers learn content and teaching strategies, but have no ready-made vehicle to put these together in their classrooms. Finally, curriculum implementation is beneficial because it provides a focus for teacher reflection. Teachers can share issues, concerns, and children's work in the context of discussing the new curriculum.

In addition to its benefits, there are also pitfalls of the curriculum implementation strategy. First, there is a tension between the "mandates" to implement a new curriculum with fidelity and teacher creativity and independence. It is important for teachers to know how much adaptation they can do and still implement the curriculum effectively. Some changes in the new curriculum (e.g., finding and developing appropriate connections to other subject areas) can enhance the materials' effectiveness. Others can be harmful (e.g., when science teachers decide that live organisms are too difficult to manage or that demonstrations work better than each student doing his or her own investigations). The nature of acceptable adaptations requires early and ongoing negotiation.

Schools can ensure continual use of the curriculum by proactively supporting all teachers and providing orientation for new teachers or teachers who change grades. The needs of teachers change over time. Initially, teachers may be focused on the "how to's" for using the new curriculum. Given the nature of problem-centered and inquiry-based curricula, this focus could span the first few years of implementation. Once teachers are comfortable with the tasks, they often become concerned with the impact of the curriculum on students' understanding. At this stage, broader considerations of the nature of the mathematics or science content being addressed and how best to understand students' thinking may surface, requiring a different orientation to professional development. Eventually, teachers may find themselves at points at which they want to "fine-tune" or make modifications in the use of the curriculum to better meet the needs of their students.

A final caveat: With this approach, there is a real danger that professional development support will stop once (or before) the curriculum is fully in place. This disregards the need for continuously increasing teacher knowledge and skills. The mechanisms for teacher reflection, sharing, assessment, and adjustment should become part of the overall school routine. As teachers become more sophisticated in curriculum use, they will want to assess the impact on student learning. Professional development can help them learn about effective ways of gathering and analyzing student learning data.

Resources

National Science Foundation's Local Systemic Change Through Teacher Enhancement Programs (www.nsf.gov).

National Science Foundation's Science and Mathematics Education Implementation and Dissemination Centers (www.nsf.gov).

WestEd. (2003). *Teachers as learners: Professional development in science and mathematics, a video library.* Thousand Oaks, CA: Corwin. (See *Standards-based curriculum implementation: Mathematics curriculum workshop.* Clark County Schools, Las Vegas, NV.)

Curriculum Replacement Units

Tamara was enthusiastic about the school district's decision to adopt the Science and Technology for Children (STC) science units for kindergarten through Grade 6. During the past school year, she had attended a workshop at a regional National Science Teachers Association (NSTA) conference that highlighted one of the units for second grade that focused on balancing and weighing. During the summer before school started, she attended the district-sponsored weeklong institute for all second-grade teachers and was delighted to learn that the unit she had explored at NSTA would be the one implemented in all second-grade classrooms in the district; each grade was implementing one unit each year for the next four years.

During the first few days of the institute, teachers from another district who had already taught the unit for a few years introduced Tamara and colleagues to the overall philosophy and design of the STC curriculum and worked with small groups of teachers as they "walked through" each lesson. At first, Tamara was overwhelmed with the kit of materials and panicked at the thought of having to manage the balance beams, buckets, marbles, plastic cups, and a myriad of objects, from plastic spoons to acrylic cylinders, in a room with 30 second graders. Once she and her group explored the science concepts in the unit, the contents of the kit, and learned about the management tips in the teacher's guide, she felt more comfortable.

In the second half of the institute, Tamara and the other teachers worked through the lessons in the unit, completing the activities, exploring the materials, reading the background sections, hearing about "little glitches" and classroom discoveries from the teachers who had taught the unit, and asking questions about how those teachers had incorporated the integration ideas for other curriculum areas.

When school started, Tamara was nervous about trying to teach a messy, hands-on unit with her students but found that having the other second-grade teachers implementing the unit at the same time provided an opportunity for sharing experiences and solving problems. By the end of the eight weeks, Tamara felt elated by her own success in handling the materials and presenting the activities to her students and by the learning her students had expressed in their journal writing and embedded assessment activities. In particular, she discovered much about what each student had learned as each child described the mobile he or she had designed and built, identifying fulcrum points and how he or she had resolved a "tippy" mobile that was too heavy on one side. Her students were ready for more "fun science" and Tamara was looking forward to teaching a unit next fall that would focus on solids and liquids.

Curriculum replacement units offer a window through which teachers get a glimpse of what new teaching strategies look like in action. They also offer a way for teachers to engage in new and different teaching practices without completely "overhauling" the entire yearlong program. There are two ways in which replacement units are used for professional development. In one approach, it is not the intended outcome for the units to be "adopted" or used over the long term. Rather, the units are used to stimulate teacher reflection and discussion. Through the experience of teaching the units, teachers change how they think about teaching and embrace new approaches that stimulate students to problem solve, reason, investigate, and construct their own meaning for the content. The second approach to using replacement units shares these goals, but it also has an additional goal. The intention here is to replace the entire curriculum over time, one or two units at a time, as in the previous vignette. This strategy helps teachers gradually learn a new way of teaching and new mathematics or science content, leading ultimately to an entirely new curriculum through replacing some units each year.

Many reform initiatives have selected quality replacement units developed by expert curriculum developers. The professional development programs introduce teachers to the units that can be used as replacements in their existing curriculum. The units are well-constructed sets of activities that address specific science or mathematics topics or concepts, with the most effective ones designed to elicit thoughtful, investigative problem solving and inquiry from students. They are not designed as activities to supplement or enhance the existing curriculum; rather, they are coherent chunks of curriculum that are used to provide an alternative experience with traditional topics or to introduce new topics that are not currently part of the curriculum. They embody and thus illustrate what standards documents say should be taught.

Key Elements

Teachers must have access to quality replacement units. Replacement units focus on appropriate concepts and skills, present content that is based on standards and frameworks, and provide assessment that is aligned with what is learned and how it is learned. As Burns (1994) notes, quality replacement units in mathematics

> **KEY ELEMENTS FOR CURRICULUM REPLACEMENT UNITS**
>
> - Teachers must have access to quality replacement units.
> - Teachers must learn how to implement replacement units.
> - Teachers must have opportunities to use the units and then reflect on their experiences.

integrate important mathematical topics and help students make sense of mathematics; appeal to students because the activities stimulate their thinking and imaginations and make mathematics interesting; appeal to teachers because they have been tested in classrooms and reflect input from teachers with experience teaching them; offer clear teaching plans, yet are broad enough to accommodate teachers veering from the plans to follow leads from students or add their own ideas; provide direction for assessing student understanding; allow for a span of abilities and interests; encourage students to communicate about mathematics, both orally and in writing; and provide opportunities for students to work individually and cooperatively. (p. 2)

The best replacement units are carefully and thoughtfully designed by expert curriculum developers.

Teachers must learn how to implement replacement units. Teachers are grounded in the theoretical and practical aspects of the new teaching approach. They have opportunities to read and reflect on the units, try the activities as learners, attend workshops where they can explore the rationale and learn from teachers experienced in the units, and practice new techniques.

Teachers must have opportunities to use the units and then reflect on their experiences. Teachers try out the units in their own classrooms, providing them with the opportunity to increase their understanding of and ownership for the new content or teaching strategies. Merely practicing new behaviors is not sufficient, however; teachers need opportunities for debriefing their experiences, discussing the implications for change in their teaching, and evaluating the impact that these practices have on students. Opportunities for reflection and dialogue increase understanding and can motivate teachers to broaden their application of the new approach to other parts of their curriculum.

Implementation Requirements

Access to the replacement units and materials. Criteria for the selection of replacement units include the following: The units must teach important mathematics or science concepts in ways recommended by the national standards, stand alone and require only equipment and materials readily available or accessible to the teacher, and be grade-level appropriate and accessible to a wide range of students.

Preparation for using the replacement units. Teachers need to understand the purposes of the units as well as how to manage materials, allot time for presenting the materials, and manage classroom behaviors, such as providing guidance to their students in how to work together effectively.

Agreement to depart from the standard curriculum. If teachers are expected to try new teaching practices in their classrooms—usually with content that deviates from the required textbook curriculum—they need assurances that they are supported by administration and parents. Teachers cannot be expected to add a new unit to their overloaded existing curriculum.

Time, resources, and support for teachers to reflect on their classroom experiences. Once teachers have begun teaching the units, it is essential that they have time to discuss and analyze what they and their students are experiencing and learning.

Examples

The California Mathematics Renaissance Network used replacement units to improve the teaching and learning of mathematics in middle schools throughout the state. During the 1994 and 1995 school year, more than 1,500 teachers from more than 400 middle schools engaged in the program's year-round professional development, which focused on discussing mathematics reform, experiencing hands-on mathematics, learning how to teach new state-of-the-art curriculum replacement units, and exploring the conditions that create opportunities for learning. Inherent in the professional development strategy of using replacement units is the following belief of the Mathematics Renaissance leadership (Acquarelli & Mumme, 1996):

> Teachers must experience reform in their own classrooms and have opportunities to grapple with the difficulties that arise. Focusing the talk on [replacement units] has been particularly helpful to the process. Teachers have attended unit workshops and then taught the units while cluster leaders observed them. They've brought questions, concerns, and successes to their cluster meetings and shared their students' work with their colleagues. Their experience with alternative curricula has prompted examination, inquiry, and collaboration. This approach has allowed teachers to be exposed to big mathematical ideas in coherent, practical-sized chunks—pieces small enough to seem manageable to even the most reticent. (p. 482)

The Great Explorations in Mathematics and Science (GEMS) program, from the Lawrence Hall of Science, is a series of teacher's guides to hands-on, minds-on science. GEMS units are often used as replacement units because they provide step-by-step instructions for teachers unfamiliar with the curriculum and guidance in using a constructivist approach. Activities generally begin with questions so the teacher can find out what his or her students already know about a topic. Then, they progress into engaging activities, followed by students' discussion of their results and guidance for the teacher in helping the students to construct useful concepts in light of their recent activities.

The GEMS guides have been used as the focus for a number of teacher institutes in which teacher leaders are expected to bring new ideas back to their home districts. The following is a letter from one of the participants—a mentor teacher for science in her elementary school—that was written a few months after returning home (Sneider, 1996):

> When I returned from the institute I worked with Ms. Carter, the fifth-grade teacher. Ms. Carter was a traditional teacher, she had worked predominately out of textbooks but was very open to new ideas. We were able to sit down once a week and plan our weekly class activities. I started out by sharing the GEMS guides, and after doing a weeklong Oobleck unit with four classes in our wing, she was hooked. After working with her closely through three GEMS guides, I found she began to instigate further hands-on science activities. Ms. Carter is now very enthusiastic and is going to be part of the NTEP program this summer with Los Alamos Labs. I really believe that participating in the institute allowed me to expand my personal and professional horizons and expand that excitement not only to Ms. Carter, but to many other teachers who I have since contacted. (p. 21)

Commentary

One of the benefits of the replacement unit strategy is that it helps teachers move at their own pace toward changing the ways they think about teaching and learning. Teachers are not expected to completely change their teaching practices throughout the school day or with the entire curriculum. Instead, replacement units provide an opportunity for teachers to "try on" a new teaching style within one specific area of the content. This helps teachers who prefer to develop their skills slowly become comfortable with new practices. An added benefit is that because new ways of teaching are actually practiced in the classroom, teachers' typical early concerns about "What is it?" "What does it look like?" and "What will it feel like to do it?" are addressed by the firsthand experience.

One of the key elements of this strategy, providing time and opportunities for "debriefing" experiences in the classroom, is also one of its greatest advantages. Teachers are not expected to attend a workshop and go back into their classrooms and simply implement the new teaching practices. Instead, they receive ample exposure to, training in, and discussion regarding both the management and theoretical underpinnings of the replacement units; they then have ongoing opportunities to discuss what they are learning. It is this chance to openly share the problems they encounter and receive support and guidance in how to address them that enhances teachers' professional growth and development. Too often, professional development strategies fail simply because teachers do not have this essential opportunity to reflect on their practices.

In addition, replacement units are a cost-effective approach to providing professional development. Often, schools and districts cannot afford to completely overhaul the existing curriculum and purchase new materials and curriculum units. Investing in replacement units offers a less costly alternative. For example, in several school districts reforming their elementary science program, teachers are introducing into their curriculum one new science unit per year or semester. It is important, however, to ensure that coherence of the curriculum is maintained and most districts develop a content matrix to show what concepts or topics will be taught at each grade level.

No professional development strategy is without its disadvantages. One disadvantage of replacement units is that teachers place too much emphasis on the units and not enough on the learning experiences—both theirs and their students'—that come from using them. They often view the units as pieces of the curriculum that can be taught every year and begin to teach them without examining how to make the new content an integral part of their curriculum and the new practices more a part of their teaching repertoire. This was a struggle that Mathematics Renaissance faced: Acquarelli and Mumme (1996) stated, "How do you develop a deep understanding of the issues in mathematics education when teachers have a strong desire for things to take back, for recipes to add to their files?" (p. 480). To address this, Renaissance teachers selected student work from specific sections of a unit and used this work to examine how students from different settings approached challenging tasks. They "revisited" replacement units a second year, thus allowing them to delve deeper into student understanding and focus less on the mechanics of the unit.

Another disadvantage of replacement units arises out of teachers' enthusiasm for the units. Because teachers like the units, they often look for other pieces to add to their units or to other parts of their curriculum. They end up creating an incoherent, nonarticulated group of activities that do not build conceptual understanding. Sometimes, the replacement units become simply supplemental activities to the existing curriculum and do not have the intended outcome of helping teachers learn new ways of teaching. In fact, teachers who want or feel pressed to implement a new way of teaching may use the units to do so and at other times teach the "old way," arguing that students need both. In some cases, teachers attempt to combine a series of replacement units to create a whole curriculum. This well-intentioned effort often results in a curriculum that lacks a scope and sequence, a conceptual flow, and any coherence.

Teachers who do begin to change their teaching practices through using replacement units and move toward integrating them into the rest of their practice often experience a major stumbling block: finding quality instructional materials that incorporate the new teaching practices. In the absence of new materials, individual teachers seek to modify and adapt the existing curriculum. This creates two additional professional development challenges: (a) how to help teachers ensure that appropriate skills and concepts are still presented to the students, and (b) how to evaluate commercially produced materials to select those that are appropriate for their students and incorporate coherent and important content and effective teaching practices. Several resources are available to assist teachers and others in evaluating instructional materials aligned with standards (National Research Council, 1999a, 1999b; NSRC, 1997; Roseman, Kesidou, & Stern, 1996).

Resources

GEMS, Great Explorations in Mathematics and Science, Lawrence Hall of Science, Berkeley, CA.

National Science Foundation, Science and Mathematics Education Implementation and Dissemination Centers (www.nsf.gov).

COLLABORATIVE STRUCTURES

The three professional development strategies described in this section—partnerships, professional networks, and study groups—are grouped together because they are ways of organizing collaboration for professional learning. (See Figure 5.3.) Collaboration is a goal of all professional learning; these strategies provide a structure through which individuals come together to pursue a variety of different kinds of learning that is dependent on collaborative interaction with others. Collaborative structures provide the mechanism for convening groups for professional learning around goals and procedures that the participants' determine. This distinguishes them from other collaborative strategies such as case discussions or lesson study that have as part of the strategy a specific set of goals and procedures. Study groups, for example, can come together around any topic and are, in fact, often the venue for other professional development strategies, such as when a study group focuses on examining student work. Collaborative structures also differ from other structures such as workshops or technology for professional learning, which can or cannot be designed to be collaborative. Collaborative structures are designed around a group of individuals working together toward a common learning goal.

Underlying Assumptions

The context within which teachers work provides worthwhile content for their collaboration. Addressing issues related to their own practices allows teachers to develop new practices that are directly related to their local contexts. Unlike professional development experiences designed by others or ones that provide teachers with an innovation to implement, study groups, partnerships, and networks provide a forum in which teachers can address issues that embody central values and principles relevant to their own situations.

Figure 5.3. Strategies for Professional Learning: Collaborative Structures

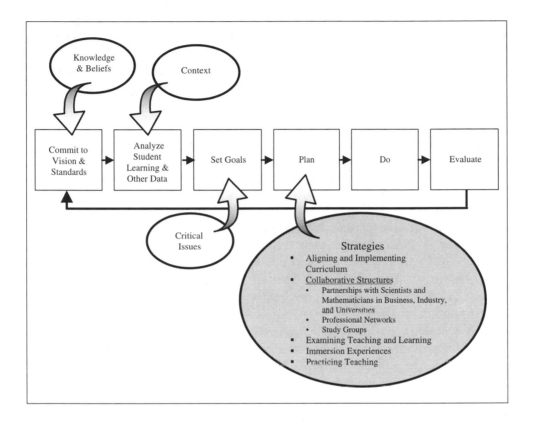

Collegiality, cooperation, and communication among teachers are valued by the school and extended communities. Given the belief that teachers are respected as self-directed, adult learners, the school and extended communities encourage teachers to work collaboratively with each other, other professionals, and in partnership with scientists and mathematicians. Moving out of the isolation of working individually in a classroom to sharing ideas and new learnings with peers and content experts in a supportive group fosters a sense of collegiality and professionalism among teachers.

Quality science and mathematics education is a community responsibility requiring collaboration and input from all. Collaborative structures for professional development are based on the assumption that the quality and effectiveness of science and mathematics teaching and learning are the responsibility of the larger community, not just teachers in the K–12 schools. Both education for students and professional development for teachers can be enhanced by collaborating with science and mathematics resource people and other professionals from the community, region, or state (National Commission on Mathematics and Science Teaching for the 21st Century, 2000).

Learning is a social activity, and adults benefit from interacting with other individuals who have similar purposes and interests as they learn. Collaboration can nurture a professional community, developing norms of collegiality, continuous improvement, and experimentation. Common interests, experiences, and frequent interaction result in a common language regarding issues in science and mathematics that encourages frequent communication about improvement. Teachers are no longer isolated in their classrooms, struggling alone with issues of teaching and learning.

Partnerships With Scientists and Mathematicians in Business, Industry, and Universities

Julie, a fifth-grade teacher, is struggling to understand the concepts underlying why large, heavy boats float. She is working with a group of other teachers and scientists to improve the school's curriculum unit on buoyancy and density. Julie has taught the unit to her students once and recognized many of the misconceptions her students held as they started the unit. She also watched her students' understanding grow as they progressed through the unit. She and the other teachers have found, however, that the science background information in the teachers' guide is incomplete and often misleading.

The teachers are working with scientists from the local university to clearly understand the concepts and then supplement the science content information that is provided to teachers in the guide. Julie thought she understood the concepts of buoyant force and displacement but as she tried to articulate her understanding she found that her understanding was not as clear as she thought. Right now, she is listening intently as one of the scientists asks her to explain why the plastic spoon is floating in the tub of water on the table in front of her. She is confident that when she stumbles over her words, the scientist will encourage her to continue and will guide her through a thought process based on what she is observing to help her fully understand the concepts and not simply "give" her the answer. The next challenge will be to put her understanding of the concepts into words so that other teachers will also begin to grasp them.

The types of collaborative partnerships between teachers and scientists and mathematicians in business, industry, museums, science centers, and universities are as diverse as the individuals involved in the partnerships. One form of partnership—teachers immersing themselves in the world of scientists and mathematicians—is a professional development strategy that is described elsewhere in this chapter (see Immersion Strategies). The partnerships discussed in this section focus on teachers and scientists and mathematicians working together: scientists and mathematicians serving as mentors; teachers and science and mathematics faculty in universities working side by side to improve teaching strategies K–16; and involving scientists and mathematicians in school-based activities, such as participating in the design and evaluation of curriculum materials, or sitting at the table during strategic planning and decision making. An important characteristic of the partnerships discussed here is that both partners bring expertise to their endeavors, with the ultimate goal of improving teaching and learning of science and mathematics in classrooms. As stated by the National Commission on Mathematics and Science Teaching for the 21st Century (2000), "Business/district partnerships must focus on mechanisms for sharing knowledge, expertise, and resources. Together, they must define the best match between the needs and capabilities of the two partners" (p. 34).

Key Elements

Partners are equal. Partnerships, to be effective, must truly be a two-way exchange of resources and knowledge. Scientists, mathematicians, and teachers have equal but different roles to play. Their joint efforts are based on a mutual belief that each has expertise to share and can make important contributions to the effort (McCullum, 2000).

> **KEY ELEMENTS**
> **FOR PARTNERSHIPS**
>
> - **Partners are equal.**
> - **Roles for scientists and mathematicians are clearly defined.**
> - **Consistent values, goals, and objectives are shared by all partners.**
> - **There are benefits to teachers.**
> - **There are benefits to scientists and mathematicians.**

Roles for scientists and mathematicians are clearly defined. Often, collaborative partnerships take the form of scientists and mathematicians working directly with teachers as part of a professional development program, institute, or initiative. In their roles as content experts, scientists and mathematicians strive to help teachers build confidence in teaching science and mathematics by modeling inquiry and providing them with new insights and experiences. Some of the roles they play include presenting at workshops, exploring inquiry-based or problem-solving activities with teachers to increase their content knowledge, being on-site resources, evaluating the scientific and mathematical accuracy of teaching materials, working with teachers to develop goals and classroom-based activities to achieve those goals, assisting in writing grant proposals, providing teachers access to equipment and materials, and inviting teachers into research labs for special seminars and demonstrations or to participate in experiments (National Commission on Mathematics and Science Teaching for the 21st Century, 2000). Teachers also collaborate with science or mathematics educators in museums, aquariums, zoos, nature centers, and other science or mathematics centers to improve both education in the schools and the educational programs offered by the institutions.

Consistent values, goals, and objectives are shared by all partners. Regardless of the specific activities, both partners need to ensure that their involvement is guided by a shared vision that is consistent with the values, goals, and objectives of the science or mathematics program; responds to a clearly understood educational need; supports and does not undermine either implicitly or explicitly an existing curriculum and instruction message; and has been considered and assessed by groups with different views.

There are benefits to teachers. For teachers, working closely with scientists and mathematicians provides exposure to role models and brings real-world application of subject matter into perspective. They have the opportunity to learn more about how the scientific and mathematics processes work—what scientists and mathematicians do and how and why they do it. Teachers are exposed to new perspectives and a different professional culture, and the partnership keeps them in touch with a broader knowledge base.

There are benefits to scientists and mathematicians. For scientists and mathematicians, benefits include the opportunity to become familiar with the needs and realities of a school system and to become advocates for quality science and mathematics education. If they are from a university setting, they can examine their own teaching and become aware of how they model teaching strategies, especially whether they promote active learning and quality process and content teaching. If they are from informal science or mathematics centers, they can benefit from learning more about the needs of teachers and students in schools. And truly collaborative partnerships move scientists and mathematicians away from the traditional roles they have played in public education—as science fair judges, expert speakers, and hosts for field trips—and into more interactive and authentic roles of sharing the enterprises in which they work with learners.

Implementation Requirements

Realistic expectations. Scientists, mathematicians, and teachers must have realistic expectations about what kind of relationship they want to have, how long it will take to develop, and what is required to be successful. They must develop a history of shared experiences that, over time, build the trust and respect necessary for the high levels of involvement and commitment required by collaboration to improve science and mathematics teaching and learning (Fazio, Levine, & Merry, 2000).

Orientation and knowledge building. Given that the worlds of scientists and mathematicians are dramatically different from that of the teachers, an "introduction" to and understanding of both worlds is essential. Teachers are often intimidated by the experts, and the experts sometimes enter the education environment ready to bestow their knowledge and "fix" the problems. A successful partnership between scientists or mathematicians and teachers requires that each value the knowledge and expertise of the other, recognize the importance of the roles played by each person, and begin to learn about each other's work.

Involvement. Scientists, mathematicians, and teachers must all feel an equal stake in the success of the partnership, and they must be invested in quality professional development tied to improved student learning. Both partners must break out of their traditional roles and relationships (e.g., scientists and mathematicians as knowledge producers and teachers as translators of that knowledge) and develop new ones. During the process, each person's roles and expectations should be clarified. To remain interested and committed, partners must see significant results and some important benefits of being involved. When they do see results, they take credit as a team and celebrate joint efforts (Ridgway & Bowyer, 2000).

Commitment. A high level of commitment from all involved in the partnership is necessary to enable a partnership to be collaborative. Commitment involves significant allotments of time and energy. People often underestimate the amount of energy it takes to work with other people, especially in activities as complex as professional development. Thus, there must be administrative and organizational support for the partners. If the school and the teachers are to be more than the passive receivers of someone else's professional development program, school personnel must commit significant time and energy to planning, delivering, and following up on activities. Scientists and mathematicians also need flexibility in their schedules and their own professional responsibilities to devote the time and energy to the partnership (Ridgway & Bowyer, 2000).

Leadership. Partnerships do not form, nor do they thrive, without strong, visionary leadership. Because partnerships often feel above and beyond the call of duty to participants who already have a full work life, the motivating force of a leader (or leaders) is vital. In addition to motivation, good leadership keeps activities moving—coordinating people, timelines, and tasks so that everyone knows what is happening and the benefits are visible. In addition, within the partnership, leadership must be shared by the scientists or mathematicians and the teachers to ensure effective collaboration (McCullum, 2000).

Examples

Partnerships between individual schools, school districts, local institutes of higher education, businesses, industry, science centers, and museums are becoming more prevalent. In fact, many projects that are funded through the NSF require and are designed around partnerships that support the reform of kindergarten through university-level learning, such as the Mathematics and Science Partnerships program (see NSF Web site: www.nsf.gov). Other NSF-funded projects also rely on partnerships to support their school and district science and mathematics reform efforts. For example, most of the LSC projects have developed relationships with professionals outside of school or district personnel. One typical partnership activity is to invite scientists and mathematicians to facilitate or cofacilitate professional development sessions. According to Horizon Research, Inc. (Weiss et al., 2002, p. 8), 32% of all LSC professional development sessions are led by university faculty, 23% are led by scientists or mathematicians, 11% are led by science or mathematics university faculty, and 3% are led by mathematicians or scientists from business and industry. These numbers continue to increase each year in these, and other, projects.

Other instances of partnership are characterized by university science or mathematics education staff serving as coaches, mentors, study group facilitators, or lesson study observers. In addition, most LSC projects collaborate with local science or mathematics education centers, museums, zoos, or planetariums to provide appropriate learning experiences for district teachers. Many local universities have education outreach departments that also codesign teacher learning sessions with LSC leaders. Another form of partnership is the sponsorship of events (e.g., welcome dinners at the beginning of summer institutes) or provision of materials (e.g., supplemental lessons on environmental issues).

In addition to the resources identified in this section (see the Resources section below), an online resource, TE-MAT (Teacher Education Materials), is a source of information to guide district efforts to develop and sustain partnerships. One such resource, *The Role of Scientists in the Professional Development of Science Teachers* (NRC, 1996b), provides specific guidelines and suggestions. It includes descriptions of almost 200 programs throughout the country that use partnerships with scientists and science educators to enhance teachers' learning. There are guidelines for everyone involved in the partnership, including recommended roles for scientists, ways in which universities and industries can recruit and reward their scientists for participation in teachers' learning, and guidelines for districts embarking on establishing partnerships. In addition, the resource provides scientists and their organizations with a better understanding of school environments, ways in which to develop and implement appropriate adult learning sessions, and how to merge science content and processes into workshops and other sessions.

Commentary

Partnerships between teachers and scientists or mathematicians can be powerful learning experiences for all involved; however, there are often challenges to face and obstacles to overcome.

As noted previously, participants in the partnership face cultural and communication differences. Teachers, scientists, and mathematicians live in different worlds and have their own languages unique to their disciplines. As highlighted earlier, it is imperative that all involved have opportunities to appreciate and recognize the value of each partner's discipline. Scientists and mathematicians must understand the needs in science and mathematics education and know about student competencies and developmental learning. They must develop an understanding of how they can bring a piece of what they do in their own world to their interactions with the teachers and to give and receive feedback from teachers.

Sometimes, issues arise regarding the expectations that scientists and mathematicians have when entering into the partnership: that they are there to "fix" the situation, believing the educational problems can be solved if only the teachers will know more content. If they have this perspective, they may want to take control and have difficulty treating teachers as equals with their own valid expertise. Also, some scientists and mathematicians only see their role as working with a handful of people interested in moving into their fields rather than a place where the knowledge of all can be increased. These views affect the ways in which they approach the professional development of teachers: If teachers' main purpose is to educate the selected few, scientists and mathematicians tend to be less cognizant of the need to enhance the teachers' overall knowledge base but, instead, focus more on specific content. Also, if these scientists and mathematicians teach through lecture, they will be less likely to value the inquiring or problem-solving nature of learning science and mathematics.

Scientists and mathematicians often face the obstacle of not receiving support, recognition, or encouragement from their organizations, institutions, or universities to pursue relationships and partnerships in settings outside of their normal working environments. They have conflicting demands to continue with research in the laboratory, publish journal articles and books, and make significant contributions to their fields. Although the values and priorities in many institutions are beginning to shift toward the value of scientists and mathematicians working with teachers, there is still a long way to go.

Finally, teachers sometimes fear intrusion by outsiders, especially those whom teachers view as the ultimate experts. They can feel intimidated by the presence of scientists and mathematicians and not recognize that they bring their own expertise to the partnership. Feeling the respect of scientists and mathematicians for their work as teachers goes a long way toward solidifying and enhancing the relationship and ultimately benefiting students.

Resources

Eisenhower National Clearinghouse, *ENC Focus*, 8(1), 2001 issue: *Partnerships With Business and the Community.*

National Clearinghouse for Comprehensive School Reform (www.goodschools. gwu.edu/).

National Research Council. (1996). *The role of scientists in the professional development of science teachers.* Washington, DC: National Academy Press.

National Staff Development Council (NSDC). (2000). *Journal of Staff Development 21*(2), Partners teaming up to improve adult learning.

Sussman, A. (Ed.). (1993). *Science education partnerships: Manual for scientists and K-12 teachers.* San Francisco: University of California Press.

TE-MAT (www.TE-MAT.org).

U.S. Department of Education. *A guide to promising practices in educational partnerships* (ed.gov/pubs/prompract/index.html/).

Professional Networks

When Christine Moore applied to be a local coordinator for her state's science and mathematics reform initiative, she never dreamed how it would benefit her own teaching and increase her knowledge and skills. As a local coordinator, she became actively involved in two networks of teachers. The first was statewide and involved all of the 30 teachers who were selected as local coordinators. The second was the network of teachers Christine created in her own local district. The statewide network meets once every other month to demonstrate use of new classroom materials, discuss developments from research and practice in the fields of science and mathematics teaching, and respond to one another's questions and issues. Between meetings, the state network members keep in touch through e-mail and phone calls. Several times each month, Christine replicates the state network meetings with teachers in her own district. In after-school meetings, teachers in her district demonstrate lessons, discuss student learning, and present issues and problems for discussion.

Christine has been amazed at the insight many of her district colleagues have offered, and she takes these ideas and information back to her state network for wider consumption. The district network teachers are working together on cross-grade projects and are generating enthusiasm among other teachers. All of the teachers participating in the network report changes in their teaching and greater comfort asking other teachers in their buildings for help and ideas.

A network is an organized professional community that has a common theme or purpose. Individuals join networks to share their own knowledge and experience with other network members and learn from other network participants. Networks appear through school-university collaborations; teacher-to-teacher or school-to-school linkages; partnerships with neighborhood organizations, teacher unions, or subject-matter associations; and local or national groups. In education, these communities are often organized to improve teaching of a particular subject matter, to address pedagogy for teaching certain content or grade-level students, or in support of particular school reforms.

Networks often articulate specific goals and purposes, recruit their members, and have scheduled activities, such as summer institutes, regular meetings, electronic discussions, newsletters, or chat rooms. In addition to drawing on the expertise of network members, many formal networks also involve individuals who are experts in areas of interest to the network participants. For example, a network of scientists and science educators who participated in writing the *National Science Education Standards* (NRC, 1996a) might provide guidance to teachers as they implement the standards. A network that is focused on making high school curriculum and instruction relevant to students' futures might involve employers who can share information about the knowledge and skills needed in the workplace.

One of the most important elements of maintaining a network is to keep people engaged and connected; electronic communication helps with this enormously. Effective networks have means to update members when they miss a meeting or other networking event. Mechanisms such as a buddy system or publishing minutes of discussions help to ensure continuity among participants.

Not all networks are structured formally; informal networks can also provide opportunities for exchanging information and obtaining professional support. For example, teachers in a city or region involved in implementing an innovation such as a new curriculum or trying to create more student-centered instruction might decide to talk regularly to discuss what they are learning, share resources, and identify and solve problems. Likewise, physics teachers from a district or region who are often alone in their schools may, through an informal network, share teaching materials and ideas and information about resources or learning opportunities. These informal networks can often benefit from being recognized by the teachers' schools or districts as legitimate professional development activities.

Key Elements

Interactions among members are ongoing. Interactions within a network are ongoing and are focused on a particular subject or purpose. Networks are "discourse communities" that enable teachers to meet regularly (either in person or electronically, e.g., through e-mail) to solve problems, consider new ideas, evaluate alternatives, or reflect on specific issues in science and mathematics (Lieberman & McLaughlin, 1992). Sometimes they are self-directed with the

KEY ELEMENTS FOR PROFESSIONAL NETWORKS

- **Interactions among members are ongoing.**
- **Membership is voluntary.**
- **Effective communication is essential.**
- **Members' perspectives are broadened.**
- **Facilitation and leadership are necessary.**

participants defining their own agendas; sometimes they are moderated by experienced facilitators who encourage the exchange of ideas within the community. Having a facilitator or moderator, especially if the interaction happens online, increases the quality and participation levels of the network. In defining the focus, teachers build an agenda that is relevant for their contexts and concerns and commit themselves to goals that are broader and more inclusive than their initial concerns. Learning networks must have a high level of trust among participants so that people feel free to disclose information about what they think, how they teach, and what they need and to take personal risks, such as being a critical friend to other members. Achieving the level of trust needed to support direct communication takes time but is useful as a ground rule from the very beginning of the network.

Membership is voluntary. Membership in most networks is voluntary. Members are committed to a new idea or philosophy and develop loyalty to each other. Networks maintain an atmosphere of openness and sharing that helps fellow members see each other as problem solvers. In creating this atmosphere, members demonstrate trust, flexibility, and informality in their contacts with other network members.

Effective communication is essential. A network is not a network without ongoing communication. The more varied the interactions, the more likely the participants are to remain involved and committed to the efforts. Good communications allow all network members to benefit from one another's input and create records that are accessible by members who may have missed a particular meeting or interaction or want to review information. Ground rules encourage everyone to participate equally and to respect the ideas of others.

Members' perspectives are broadened. Networks help members develop perspectives that stretch beyond the walls of their classroom or school. Through interactions in the network, teachers gain new knowledge and access to research-based resources beyond their schools or districts. Effective networks promote sharing of information and ideas with other professionals in different environments and help teachers broaden their perspective of and exposure to issues. Creating an essentially new structure for teachers' involvement and learning outside of their workplaces results in new norms of collegiality, a broadened view of leadership, enhanced perspectives on students' needs, opportunities to be both learners and partners in the construction of knowledge, and an authentic professional voice for teachers.

Facilitation and leadership are necessary. Effective networks require the clear assignment of responsibility for managing the network, orchestrating its activities, brokering resources from diverse segments of the community, and promoting and sustaining the involvement of teachers and others. In some formal networks, the designated leader(s) may be in an organization that has funding for network support. In informal networks, leadership is more emergent, or it may rotate, but it is nonetheless critical to maintain momentum. Capable network leaders are visionary, effective in a variety of contexts (e.g., schools, universities, private sector, and community), comfortable with ambiguity and willing to be flexible, knowledgeable about the focus of the network and its communication mechanisms, organized, action oriented, and able to nurture leadership in participants.

Implementation Requirements

Clear focus of activity. Networks need a purpose. As networks recruit participants, these new recruits need to know why they are joining and what they can expect from their investment of time. The focus of the network might be broadly defined at first giving members the opportunity to fine-tune the purpose to address their common interests and objectives. For example, a state's Presidential Awardee teachers might form a network to share effective practice. New interests and more complex relationships may emerge through networking; there is, however, a need to retain the initial focus or declare that the purpose is shifting in response to a new condition. If the intent of the network becomes unclear, there is a greater chance that the network will become irrelevant for many participants.

Size and logistical requirements. The strength, endurance, and effectiveness of a network are often directly related to its lack of complexity and the low cost of active participation. Although some electronic networks may be able to handle large numbers of participants, networks that rely on in-person interactions and prompting from a trained facilitator must be a reasonable size to allow for adequate interaction among all participants. With adequate resources, strategies such as tiered or multiple leadership can allow for larger membership.

Communication mechanisms. Whether network members have in-person meetings, attend local or regional association meetings, or meet electronically, their networks must have effective mechanisms for promoting communication. Mechanisms such as a collaborative calendar, newsletter, classroom visits among members, topic-specific discussion groups, or a resource book or other means for sharing new information and materials can expand the network and help members to make better use of the new knowledge and ideas they gain.

Monitoring progress and impact. Effective networks pay attention to how they meet the needs of members and how they can improve. They assign responsibility for monitoring the progress of the network. Because participants' needs change over time, it is important to keep tabs on whether the network is keeping pace. Asking members to comment regularly on their satisfaction with the network and suggest ideas for improvement can keep a network strong and vital.

Examples

The purpose of the Urban Mathematics Collaborative (UMC) was to support teachers of mathematics, and at some sites science, to address and resolve poor mathematics performance of inner-city students. Initiated by the Ford Foundation and involving some of the largest school districts in the nation, the network connected urban teachers with one another, other users of mathematics, and individuals involved in mathematics education reform. The UMC exposed teachers to new ideas, providing them with information about how students learn mathematics and what mathematics should be taught in the curriculum. The network focused considerable resources on the development of teacher leaders. Teachers learned mathematics content and pedagogy and group facilitation skills, which enabled them to lead presentations and support reforms in their schools.

The success of the collaboratives at sites throughout the country rested on many of the important assumptions and key elements noted in this chapter: Teachers joined the network voluntarily with a commitment to improving their teaching; the network provided support for teachers' experimentation in their classrooms through collegial support and feedback; the collaboratives created a community of learners sharing a common vision of mathematics education reform; and they existed independently of the school district within which they functioned, with the goals and agenda of the interactions determined by the teachers themselves.

Elementary school teachers in California have had the opportunity to become part of a statewide network, California Science Implementation Network (CSIN). CSIN actually began in 1988, prior to the NSF funding of the Statewide Systemic Initiative, as a fledgling teacher-leader network with one statewide director, 25 teacher trainers (science staff developers), and 50 schools. During its 14-year history, CSIN has grown to include full-time regional directors and hundreds of staff developers. In the process, CSIN has assisted more than 2,800 elementary schools to plan and implement quality science programs, and it has influenced how schools operate—from finances to teacher collaboration and student learning.

The network has a strong leadership structure that provides assistance to its members (schools and teachers) and a clear purpose: to provide in-depth professional development for entire school staffs on the content and pedagogy of science instructional materials; to build site and district leadership capacity by creating an infrastructure for systemic change; to continue to develop staffs who are knowledgeable about science reform and who teach with confidence and content strength toward that effort; and to create an ongoing, living network that maintains an advocacy for elementary science as a basic and core subject, while assisting elementary schools in holistic systemic reform of the elementary school program.

Four levels of interacting networks enable the "inside-out systemic reform strategies" to react to and advocate for programs and policies to meet the needs of the schools. At each school, the implementation team, science staff developer, and scientist cadre, with the assistance from the regional director, plan for and implement 50 hours of on-site professional development for the entire staff. On the local level, clusters of three to five schools meet monthly with their staff developer to share common concerns, successes, content knowledge, and strategies for implementation in the classroom. Three times a year, regional meetings bring together clusters, their science staff developers, and the regional directors to articulate common efforts and discuss issues related to content, pedagogy, and implementation. The meetings are for K through 12th-grade teachers and enable participants to network with other reform efforts. Statewide, the science staff developers, cadres, and regional directors meet twice yearly to determine implementation goals and strategies for improving science education. These meetings are devoted to enhancing the leadership skills, content knowledge, and teaching experiences of all CSIN professional development providers.

Commentary

Networks can be successful strategies for providing professional development for individual teachers and are especially effective in reducing isolation among teachers. Frequently, networks provide a forum for interaction with peers from other parts of the community and throughout the country or internationally. In the process, individual teachers gain access to new resources and perspectives and become part of a collegial, cohesive professional community that examines and reflects on issues related to teaching and learning. In addition to engaging teachers in collective work on issues that emerge out of their own efforts, networks provide support, encouragement, motivation, and intellectual stimulation. For those involved in the process of change, networks provide a venue for teachers to recognize that they are part of a profession that is also in the process of change. This can help legitimize local reform efforts and increase the communication between and among levels of the system.

Sustaining effective networks, however, can be difficult. Lieberman and McLaughlin (1992) discuss the following issues that network organizers and participants must address:

- *Application.* Although networks provide a forum for teachers to explore and discuss issues of teaching and learning, the intention is that the new practices and perspectives they acquire will influence their instruction with students. One challenge that networks face is that the network may draw teachers' loyalty and interest away from the school to the network itself. Consciously addressing this issue in discussions and activities within the network can help increase the likelihood that teachers will apply and implement their new learnings in their classrooms.

- *Stability.* Network participants and organizers must secure long-term funding and support. This includes not only financial support but also the establishment of structures and resources to help ensure the long-term sustainability for the network, such as legitimate time for teacher participation, internet access, and access to other equipment that is needed to participate in the network.

- *Overextension.* Managing a network is a fundamental problem for both networks and their sponsors. The more popular the network, the greater the demand on its limited resources. It is easy to underestimate what it will take to maintain and then to "scale up" a network. It requires new leaders to facilitate interactions and nurture the new members. This challenge may require restricting membership to a size appropriate to both resources and capacity to serve members well.

- *Ownership.* Some networks that are initiated by foundations, by schools and university partnerships, or by national or local reform efforts have their own agendas. This can result in a problem regarding who controls the agenda. Because the power of networks lies in their flexibility, their agendas are in a constant state of refinement rather than irrevocably fixed in time or place. Sometimes, however, the partners with the money or status become uncomfortable as teachers take more control.

- *Expanding objectives.* Most networks are formed around specific goals, but as new responsibilities and roles emerge teachers often find themselves in roles they are unaccustomed to playing: political strategist, negotiator, policymaker, or conflict mediator. Networks must address the issue of emerging roles and how to provide teachers with opportunities for taking advantage of and learning from these new roles.

- *Evaluation.* Networks need constant evaluation to gather information on results and how well they meet the needs of members. The success of networks relies on teachers' perceptions that their own goals are being served. Modifications in network practice should address deficiencies and maintain quality. This will help the network stay true to its purpose and avoid being influenced solely by issues of funding or political pressures.

Resources

Ruopp, R., Gal, S., Drayton, B., & Pfister, M. (1993). *LabNet: Toward a community of practice*. Hillsdale, NJ: Lawrence Erlbaum.

Webb, N., Tate, B., & Heck, D. (1995, February). *The Urban Mathematics Collaborative Project: A study of teacher, community, and reform.* Unpublished draft.

Study Groups

After several years in a project focused on mathematics education reform, the teachers at McKinley Middle School were still fine-tuning their practice. Their instructional tasks were good, their curriculum sound, and their organizational and management skills honed. Somehow, however, they felt that things still were not going as well as they could. They decided that they needed to focus on the instructional tasks they were using in their classrooms. In particular, they thought that the tasks did not always seem to play out in the ways they intended. They had attended a session at a recent NCTM conference in which a framework was presented that described ways in which the cognitive demands of tasks sometimes declined as students implemented them. The teachers wanted to explore this framework further to determine if it might offer some insight into how and why their lessons sometimes did not seem to deliver their potential.

They decided to meet biweekly after school to share videotapes of their teaching and use the framework to reflect on whether or not the cognitive-demanding tasks that they usually set up in their lessons were indeed being carried out by students in a way that maintained their high-level demands. Each week, a teacher would volunteer to show a 20- to 30-minute clip of instruction that would then be discussed using the framework as a guide. A McKinley teacher commented later that year, "This sustained attention to practice was absolutely what was needed to take us over the top." Another commented that the regular group sessions were the motivating force that pushed everyone to be more critical and reflective.

Study groups are collegial, collaborative groups of problem solvers who convene to mutually examine issues of teaching and learning. They are conducted within a safe, nonjudgmental environment in which all participants engage in reflection and learning and develop a common language and vision of science and mathematics education. Study groups are not teachers gathering for informal, social, or unstructured discussions. Rather, study groups offer teachers the opportunity to come together to focus on issues of teaching and learning. The topics addressed in these groups vary from current issues in mathematics and science education to whole-school reform. Groups may be composed of small numbers of teachers interested in pursuing a topic together or subgroups of the entire school faculty addressing whole-school reform issues. Regardless of the topic or issue being addressed, study groups provide a forum in which teachers can be inquirers and ask questions that matter to them, and are based on improving student learning, over a period of time, and in a collaborative and support-ive environment.

KEY ELEMENTS OF STUDY GROUPS
KEY ELEMENTS OF STUDY GROUPS • **Study groups are organized around a specific topic or issues of importance to the participants.** • **Study groups have varied structures.** • **Self-direction and self-governance contribute to the success of study groups.**

Key Elements

Study groups are organized around a specific topic or issues of importance to the participants. One of the primary elements of this strategy is that groups are organized around a specific topic or issue of impor-tance to the participating teachers. These topics range from school-based concerns to curriculum and instructional issues. For example, grade-level teachers might form a study group to learn more about assessing their students' understanding of science concepts. Over a period of time, they might meet to discuss research they have read, share examples of assessments and critique the appropriateness of the assessments, or invite school or district personnel to join the group to discuss other assessment requirements and how these influence classroom practice. Other study groups might be composed of entire school faculties or departments that focus on, for example, implementing specific school improvement initia-tives or increasing parental support and participation in the mathematics program.

Study groups have varied structures. Depending on the nature of topics dis-cussed or issues addressed, the form study groups take varies. Makibbin and Sprague (1991) suggest four models for structuring study groups. The *implementation model* is designed to support teachers' implementation of strategies recently learned in workshops or other short-term sessions. The goal is to provide teachers with an ongoing system for discussing, reflecting on, and analyzing their implementation of strategies after the workshop has concluded. The *institutionalization model* is used once teachers have already implemented new practices in the classroom and want to continue refin-ing and improving these practices. *Research-sharing groups* are organized around discussions of recent research and how it relates to classroom prac-tice. *Investigation study groups* are a way for teachers to identify a topic or practice about which they would like to learn. In this model, teachers read about, discuss, and implement new strategies that are relevant in their own contexts—their teaching practices and their students' learning. These mod-els have been successfully implemented by teachers of mathematics and science as they investigate content, instructional practices, and student learning.

Self-direction and self-governance contribute to the success of study groups. Teachers should join and form study groups voluntarily and determine their own focus for learning and the format for the sessions. Although teachers' professional learning is the goal of study groups, increasing student learning is the end result of teachers' collaboratively examining their own knowledge, skills, and abilities. Carlene Murphy and Dale Lick (2001) suggest a problem-solving cycle that can help teachers effectively structure their study groups around specific goals and needs for student achievement.

- Data analysis: Analyze a wide range of data and indicators describing the status of student learning and the conditions of the learning environment.

- Student needs: From the data, generate a list of student needs.

- Categorize and set priorities: Categorize student needs and prioritize categories or clusters, stating what the "problem" is.

- Organization: Organize study groups around the prioritized needs and specify the intended results that will indicate that the "problem" is lessened or solved.

- Plan of action: Create a study group plan of action that includes specific activities or strategies to implement that will reach the intended results.

- Implementation: Implement the study group action plan, including data collection and tracking changes through logs or journals, and specify procedures for organizing and sustaining the group.

- Evaluation: Evaluate the impact of the study group effort on student performance and teacher learning, and determine plans for institutionalizing the changes.

Implementation Requirements

Time. Like most other strategies for professional development, participating in a study group requires time not only to meet and address the issues but also to do so over a long period. Some suggest a minimum of at least once a week over a period of several months (LaBonte, Leighty, Mills, & True, 1995; Murphy, 1995; Murphy & Lick, 2001). Regardless of how frequently the group meets, it is critical that groups maintain a regular schedule of consistent contact with the expectation that their work is ongoing.

Support from administrators. The formation and success of study groups require direct support from school administrators not only for the time for the group to meet but also for support for the endeavor itself. Administrators send a clear message of the importance of professional development for teachers if time is set aside during the school day for study groups to convene. Administrators can also offer support by providing access to resources, technology, or experts when teachers request assistance in meeting their goals. In instances where whole-faculty study groups are formed, administrator support *and* participation is critical.

Membership and substantive topics. Teachers forming study groups must identify their members (by grade level, across grade levels, schoolwide, or department-wide) and identify a topic or issue that is "complex and substantive enough to hold the group together while individuals are developing the skills of working together as a cohesive group and developing trust and rapport" (Murphy, 1995, p. 41). For teachers just embarking on collaboration with their peers, this new format for sharing knowledge and ideas will require that they become comfortable with the process and make adjustments as they progress. In addition, if the topic selected is too narrow or can be addressed in a very few sessions, the group may find itself moving from topic to topic without really reflecting on what they are learning.

Study group activities. Study group participants must identify a process for how to address the issues or topics. Most study groups use a variety of activities including reading, examining school data, viewing videotapes, and discussing research; learning about new teaching and learning approaches through reading, attending workshops or other sessions, or inviting experts to work with the group; and implementing new practices in their classrooms and using the study group time to reflect on and analyze the experience both for themselves and their students. In fact, many of the other professional development strategies described in this book are often combined with study groups: examining student work and thinking, examining standards to inform curriculum alignment and selection of instructional materials, conducting action research, engaging in case discussions, partnering with scientists or mathematicians to increase content knowledge, and engaging in peer coaching and debriefing.

Group interaction skills. As with other strategies organized around cooperative group work, group interaction skills are critical. Successful groups have members who share a common goal and are committed to accomplishing the goal, work to create an environment of trust and openness and foster communication, believe that diversity is an asset and that each member brings something unique to the group, value risk taking and creativity, are able to plan and implement strategies, share leadership and facilitation of group processes, are comfortable with consensus decision-making procedures, and are committed to building a team that reflects deeply on their learnings.

Examples

The Maine Mathematics and Science Alliance's Governor's Academy for Science Education Leadership, modeled after WestEd's National Academy for Science and Mathematics Education Leadership, uses electronic study groups between face-to-face academy meetings, to enhance the learning of the academy's teacher leaders and to develop a learning community among the staff and participants. The Governor's Academy leaders initiated an "electronic book study group" focused on discussing and learning more about science teaching and learning by reading and discussing professional literature. One of the books for discussion was *The Teaching Gap* by James Stigler and James Hiebert (1999). The director of the Governor's Academy has extensive experience in moderating and evaluating online discussions and applied a rubric and strategies developed for the Maine LabNet to "improve the quality of thinking and discussion that goes on in online courses and electronic study groups" (P. Keeley, personal communication, June 2002).

One of the strategies was the development of reflective questioning guides, posted online, and developed by the book study facilitator prior to the start of the electronic book discussion. These reflective questions greatly enhanced the learning of the participants by focusing their thinking and online discussion on specific sections of the book and encouraged participants to connect their reading and discussion with the issues they were examining and learning about in the academy. The online discourse community took on a character of its own as participants took the responsibility for leading the discussions, keeping them lively and focused, inviting inquiry, and encouraging others to interact. When the academy participants convene in person, they debrief the entire book and reflect on the study group. Participants are then introduced to the next book and the cycle continues again between meetings. A book study has a designated timeframe and usually lasts from six to eight weeks, depending on the book, and each week a new set of reflective questions is posted. In this way, the Governor's Academy has developed an effective combination of professional development strategies for supporting and maintaining the learning of an established group of teachers that is separated geographically.

One participant's electronic contribution to the study group on the preface and Chapter 1 of *The Teaching Gap* illustrates the depth of thinking and reflection that characterizes the success of this study group in probing science teachers' thinking about issues in education and teaching.

The authors of "The Teaching Gap" tell us that learning won't improve markedly until we help teachers increase the effectiveness of their methodology. What a simple yet profound statement! Can you IMAGINE what it would be like to have the time and support to collaborate with others on the way you teach a unit? To have it be seen as a sign of a "strong" teacher to bounce ideas for ways to teach off of your colleagues? To have the time to really evaluate the effectiveness of a lesson after you deliver it? To have the time to put the results of that evaluation to good use to improve the lesson when it is still fresh in your mind, rather than just before you have to teach the concept again the next year?

Whenever I think about practice, I always think about how I would teach someone if I weren't in a school. When I am trying to teach my son how to change a tire, or my daughters how to tell a red fox track from a bobcat's, I do it very differently than I would if teaching it as part of a science course in my school. I wonder WHY I teach it differently; usually, it comes down to one basic thing: It is easier to teach "school" using traditional educational methods. The entire system resists anything else. I genuinely desire to improve the effectiveness of my teaching. I constantly critique my lesson plans. But without support (from somewhere) I am often blocked from using truly experiential, relevant, non-traditional methods. . . . We need to change the climate in schools to be more supportive. (P. Keeley, personal communication, June 2002).

The science study group at Averill Elementary School in East Lansing, Michigan, is a good example of a professional development program that has helped to strengthen the collaborative culture at the school. Combining the strategies of university partnerships, coaching, examining student thinking, and study groups, the program focuses on improving teaching and learning in science. A science education professor from Michigan State University observes science classrooms and scripts students' dialogue. Then she meets with teachers in a study group format to share her observations. In the study group, teachers reflect on students' thinking, the science content, and their own teaching practices. Initially, participants reported that they were intimidated by having a university professor in their classroom, but transformed their fears into excitement and powerful learning as the university partner and teachers together created a safe environment for learning. The science study group sustained itself for many years and is now being used as the mechanism for engaging teachers in a collaborative process for selecting a new science curriculum.

Commentary

Study groups require the participation of teachers who are committed to reflecting on their work and taking initiative for their own learning. It is not a strategy that lends itself to raising awareness about a topic in a short period of time but rather one that encourages teachers to "go deep" and question and reflect on their practices and their students' learning.

Because study groups necessarily involve teachers in reflection outside of the classroom, it is difficult to sustain study groups in traditional school cultures. Although they may be slow to get started in such environments, once study groups "take hold" in a school, teachers enthusiastically support their continuation. Often, administrators come to recognize their benefit and realize that study groups lend themselves well to investigations and inquiries into numerous topics and issues of concern to both teachers and the entire school community. For example, study groups concerned with finding time for professional development, using national and state standards to improve teaching and learning, or developing community support for science or mathematics reform, can benefit teachers and students while building ownership and commitment by a broader school community.

Resources

Annenberg Institute for School Reform. (n.d.). *Critical Friends Groups in Action video series: Making Teaching Public, A Community of Learners* (www. annenberginstitute. org/publications/videos.html).

Murphy, C. U. (1999). Study groups. *Journal of Staff Development, 20*(3), 49-51.

Murphy, C. U., & Lick, D. W. (2001). *Whole-faculty study groups: Creating student-based professional development.* Thousand Oaks, CA: Corwin.

EXAMINING TEACHING AND LEARNING

The four strategies described in this section—action research, case discussions, examining student work and thinking and scoring assessments, and lesson study—emphasize teachers engaging in collaborative professional learning experiences to examine their teaching practices and their students' learning. (See Figure 5.4.) These strategies provide opportunities for *practice-based* learning—the opportunity to solve and grapple with authentic issues encountered in classrooms and schools (Hawley & Valli, 2000; Mumme & Seago, 2002). Practice-based professional development allows teachers to examine the "artifacts" of their work (Ball & Cohen, 1999; Driscoll, 2001). For example, by watching videos or observing in classrooms, teachers are able to examine and reflect on their and others' teaching practices, examining student work and thinking provides an opportunity to explore what students are and are not understanding in science and mathematics, and by uncovering the conceptual development addressed in instructional materials and designing lessons to enhance that development, teachers increase their own science and mathematics content and pedagogical knowledge. In addition, discussion of other forms of "artifacts," such as cases of classroom-based experiences, provides an opportunity to engage in in-depth analysis and reflection on answering some of the most critical

Figure 5.4. Strategies for Professional Learning: Examining Teaching and Learning

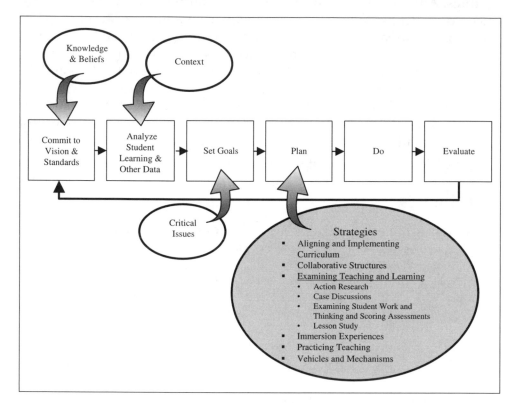

questions that teachers face in their work: What is good teaching? What concepts in science and mathematics are difficult for students to understand?

The four practice-based strategies described in this section are grounded in several assumptions about teaching, learning, and professional development.

Teachers are intelligent, inquiring individuals with important expertise and experiences that are central to the improvement of education practice. Practice-based professional development begins with what a teacher knows and relies on that knowledge to explore and formulate new understandings. The strategies assume that significance and meaning are inherent in the actual situations of teaching and learning and that knowledge about teaching and learning should be determined in part by what teachers and learners actually do (Ball & Cohen, 1999; Miller & Pine, 1990).

The opportunity to carefully observe and analyze actual teaching and learning situations leads to changes in teachers' beliefs, attitudes, convictions, and, ultimately, practice. Advocates of practice-based professional development that focuses on examining teaching and learning believe that teachers will not implement real reform unless their basic beliefs about teaching and learning are confronted and changed. Examining teaching and learning raises teachers' awareness of important issues and causes them to rethink their attitudes and beliefs, and, perhaps, change their classroom practice. As Thompson and Zeuli (1999) advocate, providing an experience that creates "disequilibrium" for teachers can be a catalyst for transformational thinking. For example, seeing the achievement gaps that might exist for students based on standards and current student performance by examining student work or engaging in lesson study can demonstrate to teachers discrepancies between what they believed they were teaching and what students appear to have learned (Driscoll & Bryant, 1998).

The learning of all students is a shared responsibility of all teachers. In Japan, the culture of education and schools reflects a deeply held belief that the education and growth of all students are a shared responsibility among teachers, parents, and the community. In fact, the entire educational system, including policy and standards, advocates teachers as the source of interpretation of national goals for student learning into teaching activities and the accompanying curriculum. In the United States, educational systems vary by states and school districts, as do the cultures within those schools. In schools bringing examination of teaching and learning strategies to the repertoire of teachers' learning, it is imperative that all involved believe that teaching students is a process that is enhanced through a collaborative endeavor and not one that is achieved in isolation.

Improving teaching and learning is a long-term, gradual process. Too often, the educational system seeks quick fixes to solve deep-seated, complicated problems. At the core of examining teaching and practice is the implicit belief that change takes time and improving student and teacher learning evolves over time. These strategies are characterized by engaging in collaborative examination of practice over time and will require a shift in the educational system's approach to and perceptions of what is involved in improving teaching and learning.

Action Research

After attending a workshop on equity issues in the classroom, Pat and Linda, two tenth-grade geometry teachers, were inspired to examine whether they treated boys and girls differently during their classes. In particular, they decided to focus on how many times they called on boys versus girls to answer questions and whether they responded differently to answers offered by boys versus girls. In addition, they wanted to examine the types of questions that they asked all students: To what extent are we asking procedural questions or higher-order questions that promote reflection and discussion? After reading some additional research on gender issues and consulting their school's psychologist, Pat and Linda developed their research design, which included audiotaping several of their classes and keeping running logs of how many boys versus girls were called on during those lessons and documenting the types of questions they asked. Analyzing the audiotapes proved to be a significant challenge for the teachers, but after discussions with an educational researcher from a local college they developed a coding scheme that allowed them to characterize four different types of teacher responses to student comments and to apply a rubric to their questioning strategies.

As they had suspected at the start of the project, they discovered a fair amount of gender bias in their approaches to teaching geometry and that they frequently asked more procedural questions than reflective questions. Through discussing the audiotapes and observing each other's teaching, they were able to work at increasing their awareness of gender equity and develop strategies to address it in their classrooms. One of those strategies was to strive to ask all students probing, reflective questions. As a result of sharing their research findings with other mathematics teachers in their department, three other teachers joined Pat and Linda to form an ongoing action research group, which continued to conduct classroom research on issues and concerns relevant to mathematics teaching and learning.

Action research has a long and varied history. First introduced by Kurt Lewin in the 1940s, action research has evolved in the education community into an ongoing process of systematic study in which teachers examine their own teaching and students' learning through descriptive reporting, purposeful conversation, collegial sharing, and critical reflection for the purpose of improving classroom practice (Miller & Pine, 1990). Action research is also emerging as a form of whole-school collaborative inquiry into improving student learning in science and mathematics (Love, 2002) and a districtwide practice to enhance the knowledge and skills of teachers (National Commission on Mathematics and Science Teaching for the 21st Century, 2000).

Through action research, teachers reflect on their practices and student results by studying teaching and learning. When teachers conduct action research, the emphasis is on practice-based professional inquiry. Its main tenet is that practical reasoning and problem solving are adequate for generating scientific knowledge, and the natural language of practitioners is just as suitable for creating scientific understanding as empirically derived statements framed in technical language (Duckworth, 1986). This form of knowing comes from experience and direct interaction with students.

Holly (1991) notes that "action research as a major form of professional development is now seen as central to the restructuring of schools" (p. 133). The strength of action research as a professional development strategy is that teachers either define the research questions or contribute to their definition in a meaningful way. Therefore, they have ownership over the process and are committed to promoting changes in practice indicated by the findings.

The form of the action research can vary, with teachers working together in collaborative teams of inquiry or with other researchers who are often from universities or research centers. Individual teachers may also pursue their own research studies, with opportunities to discuss their progress and findings with fellow teachers or researchers. In another variation, teachers examine relevant research, which is then used as a basis for collecting and analyzing data from their own classrooms (Loucks-Horsley et al., 1987).

The characteristics of any particular action research project will depend on the goals emphasized, the degree of collaboration between teachers and outside researchers, the process used in carrying out the research, the relationship of the project to the school, and the project outcomes. For example, in some action research projects, the goal is to improve teaching through teacher-led research and reflection on teaching and other classroom strategies. If outside researchers are involved, their role is to help build teachers' skills in research methodology and pedagogical content knowledge and guide teachers in the reflective process.

In some instances of action research, the goal is to not only contribute to teachers' professional growth but also add to the education knowledge base. In these projects, teachers engage in the action and reflection process on a practical issue of classroom teaching, and their findings also contribute to answering larger questions that may be under investigation by the school district, a university, or another research organization.

In still other instances of action research, whole schools engage in collaborative inquiry into improving science or mathematics teaching and learning. At the core of these efforts is teachers and administrators using data collected about their schools to inquire into how to improve student learning. As Love (2002) states,

> The same process of inquiry that invigorates classrooms also breathes life into school reform. In inquiry-based schools, teachers and administrators continually ask questions about how to improve student learning, experiment with new ideas, and rigorously use data to uncover problems and monitor results. (p. 7)

Whichever goal is being pursued, action research supports teachers to examine their teaching practices in a systematic, ongoing way with the purpose of changing those practices. It is not simply about identifying a problem to be solved but rather is more a process based on a vision of creating "learner-centered classrooms and building knowledge through inquiry" (Watkins, 1992, p. 4). Although this can apply to any area of education, it is especially relevant to mathematics and science, whose national standards encourage this vision explicitly. In fact, the National Commission on Mathematics and Science Teaching for the 21st Century (2000) published a report, *Before It's Too Late*, that calls for inquiry groups to be established at the school and district levels to address the specific challenges that science and mathematics educators face. The goals and purposes of the inquiry groups should provide teachers with "continuing, collegial contacts, peer reinforcement and input from experts to sharpen their skills and deepen their subject knowledge" (p. 20). Central to the collaborative work of these inquiry groups is the opportunity for "teachers to share ideas, gain the benefit of one another's teaching experience, engage in common study to enrich their subject knowledge, learn more about technology, and design ways to incorporate local, state, and national educational developments (e.g., subject-matter learning standards) into their teaching" (p. 20). Action research as a strategy for inquiry into teaching and learning in science and mathematics is a professional learning strategy that can further each of these National Commission goals.

> ## KEY ELEMENTS FOR ACTION RESEARCH
>
> - Teachers contribute to or formulate their own questions, and collect the data to answer these questions.
> - Teachers use an action research cycle.
> - Teachers are linked with sources of knowledge and stimulation from outside their schools.
> - Teachers work collaboratively.
> - Learning from research is documented and shared.

Key Elements

Teachers contribute to or formulate their own questions, and collect the data to answer these questions. Educational research has typically been done "on" or "to" teachers and not "with" or "by" them. Researchers have assumed that research relevant to teachers would be picked up by them and used. The action research strategy assumes that a more intense teacher involvement with research will increase the likelihood that they will learn from their practice and use research results, thus contributing to their growth as teachers. It assumes that meaning can be constructed through action and reflection. It gives teachers the power to make decisions and puts the teacher in the position of accepting responsibility for his or her own professional growth (Miller & Pine, 1990; Sparks & Simmons, 1989; Wood, 1988). Several researchers have studied the ways in which teachers' practices, beliefs, perceptions, and knowledge change as a result of engaging in action research. For example, Koba, Clarke, and Mitchell (2000) found that after one year of facilitated action research, teachers in Omaha, Nebraska, school districts changed their perceptions of students, themselves as teachers, and their conceptions of teaching and learning. The changes were the result of "reflection that promoted shifts in belief systems about teachers and learning; collaborative relationships with teachers and students that evolved when teachers listened to student voice; and the knowledge necessary to implement effective change and to empower both students and teachers" (pp. 99-100).

Teachers use an action research cycle. Action research involves a cycle of planning, acting, observing, and reflecting. Teachers identify a subject of research and develop a plan of action, often in collaboration with others. The questions pursued through action research are usually focused on the behaviors and processes of teaching and learning. Data are collected by observation, anecdotal records, checklists, videotaping, logging, collections of children's work, interviewing, and surveying, among other techniques. Data are analyzed, reflected upon, and used to inform further planning and subsequent action.

Teachers are linked with sources of knowledge and stimulation from outside their schools. Action research projects are often informed by others' research and resources. Effective projects draw on available knowledge and build on it rather than re-create it. Furthermore, individuals and resources that offer expertise on research methodology help teachers to ensure the quality of their methods (Holly, 1991).

Teachers work collaboratively. Action researchers typically work together on all aspects of the project—setting common goals, mutually planning the research design, collecting and analyzing data, and reporting the results. The collaborative nature of the interactions allows for mutual understanding and democratic decision making and requires all participants to communicate openly and freely. For all participants, this requires an openness to discussing problems and limitations, to the ideas of others, and to learning new skills and behaviors needed for the research process (Oja & Smulyan, 1989).

Learning from research is documented and shared. Sharing learnings from action research can make a significant contribution to professional development. Opportunities to write about a project, to present findings to various audiences, to participate in discussions of the implications of findings for teaching and schools, and to develop materials that other teachers can use are just some of the ways that teachers can increase their skills and knowledge beyond what they learn from their own action research (Loucks-Horsley et al., 1987).

Implementation Requirements

Access to research resources. If teachers have never conducted action research, they need access to an experienced researcher as a member of the research team or as a consultant who assists teachers with data collection and analysis, ensuring that the results of the research are valid.

Time. Teachers need legitimate time to conduct action research and to do so over time and they need an environment with limited interruptions for discussion, investigation, collaboration with the research team, and reflection.

Administrative support and an atmosphere conducive to experimentation. Administrators who support action research as a professional development activity make material and financial support available to teachers, recognize and reward collegial interaction, ensure that teachers feel that they can try various strategies within their classrooms, and support teachers in making decisions that influence their teaching.

Opportunities to share the results of their research. Once the findings of the research project have been obtained and analyzed, teachers need opportunities to share their results through in-house publications, professional conferences, workshops, journals, or other means.

Examples

The Continuous Assessment in Science Project (CASP) at WestEd offers a model of professional development in science that is based on inquiry and action research. While elementary school teachers use hands-on, inquiry-based science teaching in the classroom, they also collect data about how and what students are learning. The teachers determine areas of focus for their research, gather data, and write cases describing their observations and findings. They use strategies such as observation, questioning, listening, and documentation through videotape and audiotape recording and still photography to gather and analyze data.

Through this program, teachers learn to observe the behavior of students at work and to use their observations to adjust learning activities to better meet learners' developmental needs. By aligning everyday assessment with good instructional strategies, teachers help children reach the goals of science learning the project espouses—that is, understanding science concepts through engaging in the processes and habits of mind of science.

Action research is also a component of the Colorado College Integrated Science Teacher Enhancement Project. Teachers who participate in this three-year master's of arts in teaching program attend six-week, science-rich, summer institutes; develop and build teaching units that they implement during the school year; attend academic year seminars; and formulate and conduct an action research project. One elementary school teacher participant, for example, decided to experiment with teaching science at the beginning of the day rather than at the end, and she documented what happened. She learned that science permeated the day, often became a focus for language learning and mathematics, and encouraged students to inquire more in their learning across the curriculum. A journal article and permanent change in her teaching day resulted (Strycker, 1995).

Commentary

Science and mathematics teachers interested in continuous assessment and improvement can benefit greatly from action research projects. Benefits are generated by both the process and the products of the action research. For example, in the process of conducting an action research project, teachers gain knowledge and skill in research methods and applications (Lieberman, 1986; Miller & Pine, 1990; Oja & Smulyan, 1989). They can become more flexible in their thinking, more receptive to new ideas, and better able to solve problems as they arise. They can change their definitions of professional skills and roles, feel more valued and confident, increase their awareness of classroom issues, become more reflective, change educational beliefs and align their theories and practice, and broaden their views of teaching and learning. Teachers gain new knowledge that helps them solve immediate problems, broaden their knowledge base, and learn skills that can be applied to future interests and concerns (Koba et al., 2000; Oja & Smulyan, 1989).

Action research can also support overall change efforts in schools because findings can help prepare the school staff for needed improvements (Love, 2002). The school culture can also shift positively. The action research team unites teachers and encourages collegial interaction. The collaborative nature of action research has the potential to encourage greater professional talk and action related to teaching, learning, and school problems. In addition, a collaborative team provides possibilities for teachers to assume new roles and exhibit leadership, with feelings of powerlessness transformed into a greater sense of empowerment (Lieberman, 1986).

Another benefit of action research is its contribution to narrowing the gap between research and practice. This occurs when researchers work closely with teachers to define and conduct research. New educational theory and knowledge are generated. As a result of learning more about research and research methods, teachers make more informed decisions about when and how to apply the research findings of others.

With its many benefits, action research can be a powerful professional development activity. As teachers and schools engage in action research, however, some of the implementation requirements discussed previously are often not addressed. Some of the issues that arise are discussed in the following sections.

Time. Action research requires a great deal of time and focus. Research involves many steps, and it takes time to observe how different strategies work with different students and in different circumstances. Teachers should be recognized for the time spent in action research projects and have it count toward district or state professional development or recertification credit. Teachers and administrators can examine the school schedule to find common time, during the day if possible, for teachers to work together on a research project.

Legitimacy of the action research. Often, professional development that is not in the form of institutes or workshops does not receive legitimate recognition in schools. This calls for both administrators and participating teachers to communicate more frequently and publicly acknowledge the value of the research. Teachers can help convey the importance of action research by providing regular updates and presentations of findings to all staff, resulting in other teachers' awareness of the purpose of the action research project and how its findings could be used to benefit all teachers.

Readiness of action research participants. This approach for professional development may not be for all teachers at the same time. Teachers differ widely in their priorities and interests, and these change over time. Teachers who are struggling to get new practices working may not be ready to collect data and then step back and reflect on the data. Teachers who are less concerned with trying to master new practices in the classroom and more concerned about the effectiveness of their teaching and its impact on student learning may be in the best position to benefit from action research projects.

Resources

Colorado College Integrated Science Teacher Enhancement Project (CC: ISTEP), Colorado Springs, CO. For more information contact Paul Kuerbis, Director, 719-389-6726.

Continuous Assessment in Science Project, WestEd, VT (www.wested.org).

Case Discussions

Sharon Friedman is a fourth-grade teacher, case writer, case discussion facilitator, and researcher involved with the Mathematics Case Methods Project. In her reflections on her involvement in case discussions, she writes the following (Barnett & Friedman, 1997):

"When I first participated in a math case discussion, I thought that I would be examining instructional practice. I thought that I would share what I do in the classroom and hear about alternatives, which would lead to better informed decisions for my mathematics program. I was right, except for my understanding of what it means to 'examine' instructional practice. I quickly learned that the 'examination' entailed more than merely acquainting myself with various instructional methods. Through the discussions we looked deeply into the way instructional practice influenced and responded to student thinking. Any teaching practice, it seemed, had a consequence in terms of its effect on student thinking. Some curricula

even led to confusion. We delved into the thoughts and misconceptions that students carry with them to our math classes, derived from past instruction, experience, and intuition. Good instructional practice, I was to discover, is an interaction between what the teacher says and the experiences he or she provides, and what the students do with it. Good practice is not, as teachers are often led to believe, a preset formula that does what it is supposed to do because the curriculum writers say so. I learned the importance of focusing the impact of my words and actions on children, on framing instruction that could anticipate student thinking as much as possible, and on responding effectively to the results. In planning, I learned to consider an interaction rather than simply a teaching method that does not take student thinking into account."

Case discussions offer groups of teachers the opportunity to reflect on teaching and learning by examining narrative stories or videotapes that depict school, classroom, teaching, or learning situations. Cases are narratives (whether in print form or on videotape) that offer a picture of a teaching or learning event and are specifically designed to provoke discussion and reflection. They are not simply stories about teaching or learning but are, as Shulman (1992) notes, focused on events such as a teaching dilemma, students engaged in mathematics or science investigations, images of student thought processes, or teaching strategies in action.

Case discussions are used in a variety of ways with different goals and purposes. For example, educators and researchers promote the use of case discussions to examine student thinking and learning as a means of professional development. In these instances, cases are used as a window into children's thinking within a specific context. Teachers listen to students' ideas about mathematics and science and examine students' responses. By analyzing children's thinking and how their ideas are developing and by identifying what they understand and where their confusions lie, teachers become aware of how children construct their mathematical and scientific ideas. Being able to see mathematics and science through the child's eyes helps teachers know and anticipate how students may misunderstand certain concepts and enables them to choose instructional experiences that can capitalize on the child's thinking. Teachers develop a greater recognition that student misunderstandings can be a valuable teaching tool. These activities promote professional development when they cause teachers to reexamine their perceptions of students' capabilities and their own assumptions about what "understanding mathematics and science" really means (Schifter, Russell, & Bastable, 1999).

The process of reflecting on students' thinking and learning through case discussions often results in teachers "trying out" the ideas or activities contained in the cases in their own classrooms (Barnett, 1991; Davenport & Sassi, 1995; Schifter, 1994). The powerful images of students in the cases prompt teachers to wonder about the thinking of their own students, how they might pose similar problems in their classes, and what might happen as a consequence. Teachers discover that they are better able to provide their students with experiences to help them articulate their confusion and with activities that help them resolve those confusions.

In addition, when teachers confront mathematics and science issues through the lens of students' perspectives, they often increase their own mathematics and science knowledge (Heller, Kaskowitz, Daehler, & Shinohara, 2001; Schifter & Bastable, 1995). As teachers reflect on students' thinking and approaches to solving problems, and assess the reasoning of students' responses, they begin to think through the mathematics or science again for themselves, often seeing new aspects of familiar content and expanding their own understanding (Russell et al., 1995). Case discussions can also be a powerful tool for helping teachers examine their own teaching practices. In these instances, cases typically convey a contextual problem, dilemma, or issue in teaching as well as the thoughts, feelings, and internal struggles of the case teacher (Schifter, 1996b).

Cases can present "whole stories" that include an ending describing how the case teacher addressed the dilemma (Shifter, 1996b). Others stop short of describing how the case teacher handled the problem and instead end with a series of open-ended questions to be addressed by the case discussants. Some are "packed full" of information to convey the complexity of teaching (Merseth, 1991), whereas others focus on discrete instances of teaching. Finally, some cases are grouped into clusters based on cases that have one or two similar dominant themes or that illustrate different aspects of the same principle. Examining clusters of cases requires teachers to retrieve, understand, and grapple with the domain or theme in different contexts and under different conditions (Barnett & Friedman, 1997).

Whatever the focus of a case, case discussions share common goals: to increase and enrich teachers' fundamental beliefs and understanding about teaching and learning; to provide opportunities for teachers to become involved in critical discussions of actual teaching situations; and to encourage teachers to become problem solvers who pose questions, explore multiple perspectives, and examine alternative solutions (Barnett & Sather, 1992; Shulman & Kepner, 1994).

Not only is participating in case discussions a powerful professional development strategy, but also the process of writing and developing cases enhances teachers' growth and development. The act of writing cases and then discussing them with colleagues helps teachers analyze their own instructional practice.

Usually, teacher writers follow a structured case development process that progresses from identifying a topic or issue of concern to collaborative work with an editor or facilitator who helps turn the narrative into a case that has benefits for a larger audience. Most teachers who have written cases report that the writing process has a strong impact on their professional life, how they think about their teaching and students, their strategies and modes of instruction, and the ways in which they interact with colleagues regarding their experiences (Shulman & Kepner, 1994).

Key Elements

Case materials present a focused view of a specific aspect of teaching or learning. Often, observers in a classroom focus on management behaviors and miss opportunities to focus carefully on specific teaching or learning episodes. By using cases, all participants are examining the same experience of the case teacher and students and have the immediate opportunity to reflect on those experiences during the case discussion.

Case materials illustrate theory in practice. Case discussions create a context for teachers to integrate their research-based knowledge into their view of children's learning and their own teaching and to apply this to their instructional practice. Vivid descriptions of classroom process provide grounding for theoretical principles where contexts for interpreting these abstractions are lacking (Schifter, 1994) and help teachers tie abstract learning to the complexities of real world application (Filby, 1995).

> **KEY ELEMENTS FOR CASE DISCUSSIONS**
>
> - Case materials present a focused picture of a specific aspect of teaching or learning.
> - Case materials illustrate theory in practice.
> - Case materials provide images of reform-oriented mathematics and science teaching and learning.
> - Teachers interact and learn through discussions.
> - Cases are facilitated by a knowledgeable and experienced facilitator who promotes reflection by case discussants.
> - Case discussions necessarily involve effective group dynamics.
> - The cases are relevant and recognizable.

Case materials provide images of reform-oriented mathematics and science teaching and learning. Standards-based teaching in mathematics and science requires teachers to change their beliefs about the nature of knowledge and learning and how knowledge is derived, increase their knowledge of content, and reinvent their classroom practice (Nelson, 1995). Translating the ideals of these ways of teaching and learning into actual classroom practice, however, is often the most complex and challenging task teachers face. Some cases offer an image of what reform-oriented classrooms look like and how teachers implement the principles of reform. Far from being examples of the "unattainable," teachers have found that they can identify with many of the struggles faced by teachers and students in the cases and have found them motivating and inspiring (Schifter, 1996b).

Teachers interact and learn through discussions. Through verbalization and interaction, teachers formulate ideas, learn from each other, become aware of alternative strategies and perspectives, internalize theory, critique their own and others' ideas, become aware of their own assumptions and beliefs, increase their pedagogical content knowledge, and engage in "collaborative reflection" on real problems faced by teachers (Barnett & Sather, 1992; Far West Laboratory, 1990; Filby, 1995).

When reflecting on cases that promote discussion about teacher actions, discussants may focus on what the case teacher should do next or evaluate the action that was taken. This process engages teachers in an analysis of why and how to use certain teaching strategies, challenges some of their assumptions and beliefs about the appropriate use of strategies, and broadens their repertoire of strategies for planning and implementing instruction (Shulman & Kepner, 1994). A goal of case discussions focused on teacher action is to develop in teachers an attitude of inquiry toward and strategies for inquiring about classroom practice.

Cases are facilitated by a knowledgeable and experienced facilitator who promotes reflection by case discussants. The facilitator helps participants tease out the facts of the case, identify and understand the problem or issues it raises, inquire into the approach taken or examine the source of students' confusion, discuss alternative actions, and reflect on the theoretical underpinnings of the action taken and discuss the consequences for learning.

Facilitation notes are often developed and published in a facilitator's guide that accompanies a casebook or video. These notes help the facilitator shape the discussions so that the richness of a case is fully explored.

Case discussions necessarily involve effective group dynamics. Case discussion groups establish supporting norms for interaction and commit to the long-term nature of the process. Together they establish ground rules and group norms that enhance an atmosphere of learning and trust. Participants demonstrate their commitment to improving their teaching practice and willingness to help others explore their teaching practices (Filby, 1995). (Note that groups do not always establish effective ways of working together, and this can seriously influence what participants learn.)

The cases are relevant and recognizable. Although some cases depict teaching or learning situations that reflect the "ideal image" of what teaching and learning can look like, teachers need, at least initially, to be able to identify aspects of their own teaching within a case. Ideally, teachers encounter situations similar to the cases in their own teaching and can draw on their experiences during the discussion. Once teachers feel a sense of connection with a case, they can delve deeper into how the case is either similar or dissimilar to their own teaching approaches and beliefs. For example, some cases will parallel a teacher's own approaches or philosophy and can provide opportunities to examine and evaluate the consequences of specific decisions based on those ideas. Other cases will present notions that conflict with the beliefs of the teachers and can provoke critical analysis of the perspectives presented; "wrestling with the resulting disequilibrium" is what leads to changes in teachers' thinking about teaching and learning (Barnett & Sather, 1992; Thompson & Zeuli, 1999).

Implementation Requirements

Attitudes of participants and facilitators. Participants must have a commitment to improving their teaching practice, a willingness to share and critically discuss aspects of practice and explore and learn the science and mathematics content addressed in cases, and be curious about important assumptions that underlie teaching and learning (Davenport & Sassi, 1995).

Skills of facilitators. Facilitators must have an understanding of the science or mathematics being taught or learned in the case and must have the skills and experience to manage discussions that are at once intellectually stimulating, challenging, and supportive, at times confrontational, and, ultimately, useful. (See the Resources section.)

Time. Thoughtful discussions require time to unfold and become meaningful; frequently, study groups incorporate case discussions as one of the approaches to increasing their learning.

Access to quality cases. Cases must be clear, thorough, and well developed. (See the Resources section.)

Examples

Cases and their discussion are the focus of the Mathematics Case Methods Project at WestEd. The project aims to build the capacity of teachers to make informed strategic decisions that draw upon and anticipate student thinking through the development and analysis of mathematics cases. The cases are accounts of classroom experiences written by teachers and describe an instructional sequence in which the teacher is surprised or perplexed by students' responses or by the results of an assessment task (Barnett & Friedman, 1997). Included in the cases are descriptions or samples of student work or dialogues. The approach to examining and studying cases follows a structured format to ensure the most in-depth discussions. As Barnett (1999) outlines:

- Before beginning the discussion, group members work on a mathematics problem related to the case to help teachers, as adult learners, understand the problem.

- As they work, teachers are also asked to think about what might be confusing or difficult from the students' point of view.

- Teachers note their insights so they can be discussed.

- Teachers pair up to identify issues from the case and frame them as questions that stimulate discussion by inviting multiple points of view.

- The issues are posted on chart paper and used to focus the discussion.

Guided by the facilitator, the teachers then discuss the questions and issues raised by the case. The facilitator is a teacher with case discussion experience who has chosen to take on a leadership role and has been formally prepared to facilitate the sessions. In each case discussion, a different case is read and discussed. Barnett and Friedman identify many outcomes from teachers' participation in case discussions: The case discussions provide a powerful stimulus for changes in teachers' beliefs about how children learn and how mathematics should be taught, they lead to improvement in teachers' mathematical content knowledge, they increase the complexity of teachers' pedagogical content knowledge, and they lead to changes in teachers' classroom teaching practices.

Science Cases for Teacher Learning, a project at WestEd, develops case-based materials designed to help teachers make sense of the major ideas of kindergarten through eighth-grade physical science and examine the ways in which children think about and sometimes misunderstand those ideas. The materials combine teaching cases with facilitated hands-on explorations, structured discussion, and reflection. They are designed for flexible use: as individual cases, as multicase modules, or as a comprehensive curriculum. The professional development materials are aligned with the *National Science Education Standards,* support the implementation of standards-based curriculum, and focus on common misconceptions in science.

The cases are intentionally designed for use in conjunction with existing professional development programs and ongoing study groups. The typical unit for teacher professional learning is a discussion group of 8 to 12 teachers from the same district or project. The program takes place over one academic year and typically consists of a 24-hour curriculum (eight or more three-hour discussions, each centering on a different case). During the course of a discussion, participants examine the case from an analytic frame, thinking and reasoning aloud as they grapple with the problem at the heart of the case. Purposeful hands-on exploration and structured reflection are used to challenge ideas, causing teachers to articulate the science content they themselves do not know and reexamine their theories of science teaching. Through evidence and collaborative reasoning, teachers gain a deeper understanding of core concepts and what makes them hard to teach and hard to learn.

The facilitator has a critical role in guiding the group's inquiry process. Facilitators focus and deepen the discussion of the science, often asking teachers to draw diagrams and use hands-on materials to illustrate ideas, or use other resources to help "unpack" the core concepts. They also push the group to analyze student work and dialogue, eliciting careful consideration of what is valid *and* incorrect in students' thinking.

To optimize facilitators' use of the case-based curricula and allow for national scale up and broad impact, the project provides extensive training that builds facilitators' knowledge of science, pedagogical content, and case facilitation, thus preparing them to conduct discussions in their local areas. The typical unit for facilitator training is a cohort of 20 to 50 teacher leaders and professional development providers from multiple school districts and projects. The training takes place over one academic year and typically consists of an 80-hour curriculum. Major activities include discussion of a six- to ten-case sequence, additional science coursework, practice of case facilitation techniques, and analysis of videotaped discussions.

Commentary

Case discussions create a stimulating environment in which teachers use their expertise and professional judgment to consider underlying assumptions, analyze situations, and draw conclusions about teaching and learning. As a professional development strategy, it has many benefits. Teachers' ideas and insights are valued and challenged, leading them to reflect on and change their beliefs about how children learn and how and what they teach. Case discussions lead to increased teachers' content knowledge. They situate learning in actual practice and draw upon teachers' expertise. They provide teachers with opportunities to have in-depth conversations about teaching and learning.

Several issues surround the use of case discussions as a professional development strategy. For example, one issue is whether case discussions must be conducted face-to-face or whether they can be facilitated electronically. Bank Street College has conducted very successful electronic case discussions as part of its online courses. Outside evaluations have shown this approach to be highly valued by and beneficial to participants. There is good reason to argue, however, that because they often challenge teachers' deeply held beliefs about teaching and learning, case discussions are best conducted in person. The interpersonal, face-to-face dimension can be critical to establishing rapport and trust and to communicating disagreements in respectful and constructive ways. Preserving these benefits from the interpersonal dimension via electronic means presents a considerable challenge.

Another similar issue that has been raised is whether teachers can benefit from reading cases on their own and addressing key issues in solitary reflection. Because a serious time commitment may be required to be part of a case discussion group, it is sometimes tempting for teachers to cut the recommended corners and read about, rather than participate in, case discussions. Although teachers can certainly learn many things from reading cases, the real benefits of this strategy derive from the group process itself. It is difficult, if not impossible, to throw oneself into the kind of disequilibrium that Thompson and Zeuli (1999) have shown to be the essential step in changing beliefs and practices. In addition, the diverse contributions of the group are what determine the unique nature of each case discussion and even cause discussions of the same case to have a distinctive character.

The question of whether unfacilitated discussions are as effective as those that are facilitated is at the heart of another issue. A small group of teachers who are committed to using this approach or who are reluctant to designate a facilitator may still benefit from case discussions, but they would need very effective communication skills and would need to have at least some organized method of recording and tracking the group's progress.

The role of the facilitator in many case approaches is more than that of a guide. Particularly in those instances where the approach includes published case facilitation guides or notes, the facilitator can be responsible for encouraging the group to address certain issues raised in the guides. Without a facilitator, some of these issues might be left unexamined.

Another danger inherent in unfacilitated case discussions is that they may become more like informal discussions and lose the essence that characterizes case discussions as a professional development strategy.

Finally, people who use case discussions, and especially those who write their own cases, must be concerned about the confidentiality and ethics involved in this strategy. Case discussions must be treated like cases in other professions, such as health, law, and social services. Participants must ensure that materials such as videotape, print descriptions, and pictures are used with consent and that all materials viewed are kept confidential by the group (Kleinfeld, n.d.). This sets up the right climate as well for those interested in writing, and then sharing, their own cases.

Resources

Barnett, C., & Friedman, S. (1997). Mathematics case discussions: Nothing is sacred. In E. Fennema & B. Scott-Nelson (Eds.), *Mathematics teachers in transition.* Hillsdale, NJ: Lawrence Erlbaum.

Barnett, C., Goldstein, D., & Jackson, B. (Eds.). (1994). *Mathematics teaching cases: Fractions, decimals, ratios, and percents: Hard to teach and hard to learn? Facilitator's discussion guide.* Portsmouth, NH: Heinemann.

Barnett, C., & Ramirez, A. (1996). Fostering critical analysis and reflection through mathematics case discussions. In J. Colbert, P. Desberg, & K. Trimble (Eds.), *The case for education: Contemporary approaches for using case methods.* Needham Heights, MA: Allyn & Bacon.

Casebooks from WestEd, San Francisco: Shulman, J., & Mesa-Bains, A. (1993). *Diversity in the classroom: A casebook for teachers and teacher educators*; Barnett, C., & Tyson, P. (1994). *Enhancing mathematics teaching through case discussions*; Barnett, C., Goldstein, D., & Jackson, B. (1994). *Mathematics teaching cases: Fractions, decimals, ratios and percents—Hard to teach and hard to learn?* WestEd Eisenhower Regional Consortium for Science and Mathematics Education & Distance Learning Resource network. (1996). *Tales from the electronic frontier.*

Cases Institute. (D. Schifter, Director), Education Development Center, Newton, MA. (phone: 617-969-7100)

Center for Case Studies in Education. (R. Silverman and W. Welty, Co-Directors), Pace University, Pleasantville, NY. (phone: 914-773-3879)

Mathematics Case Methods Project, WestEd, San Francisco (www.wested. org).

Miller, B., & Kantrov, I. *A guide to facilitating cases in education.* Portsmouth, NH: Heinemann.

Miller, B., Moon, J., & Elko, S. (2000). *Teacher leadership in mathematics and science: Casebook and facilitator's guide.* Portsmouth, NH: Heinemann.

Science Case Methods Project, WestEd, San Francisco (www.wested.org).

WestEd and the WGBH Educational Foundation. (2003). *Teachers as learners: A multimedia kit for professional development in science and mathematics.* Thousand Oaks, CA: Corwin Press. (See Tape 3, Program 4, *Exploring science through cases*, WestEd, Oakland, CA; Tape 2, Program 1, *Exploring mathematics through Cases I, Mt. Holyoke College, South Hadley, MA*; and Tape 2, Program 2, *Exploring mathematics through cases II, WestEd, Oakland, CA.*)

Examining Student Work and Thinking and Scoring Assessments

Teachers from two middle schools were distressed because their students did not do well on the new state performance assessment. Wanting to help them do better, the teachers decided to look carefully at their students' work to uncover where the problems might lie. They selected ten students in different classrooms and then gathered and studied the students' portfolios, scoring sheets, and other records. The teachers did the assessment tasks themselves and explored several questions: What were the tasks asking? How were the responses scored? What does one need to know and be able to do to complete the task? How did the students interpret and approach the task? As a result of their discussions, the teachers were better able to "see" the students' work and understand their thinking. They listed the kinds of understandings that the assessment seemed to tap and the kinds of problems they saw in students' work. This guided subsequent discussions of how they could help students improve their performance on the state assessment and their understanding of important mathematical ideas (Ball & Cohen, 1995).

In recent years, examining student work and thinking and scoring assessments as strategies for professional learning have exponentially grown in the educational community. Numerous articles have been written describing the process as it is carried out in schools throughout the country. A quick browse on the Web reveals dozens of new sites devoted to looking at student work. Several organizations have developed protocols and guidelines for helping teachers look at student work in meaningful ways.

As Anne Lewis (1998) notes, the increase in teachers collaboratively examining student work seems to have been influenced by three education "events":

- Reform efforts that target schools as well as districts, and which encourage teachers to share responsibility for student success

- A political and policy climate that wants proof that students are learning to higher standards

- The emergence of a research base that is giving teachers better clues on how to move to higher levels of learning (p. 25)

As teachers and entire faculties turn to examining student work as a means of enhancing their own and their students' learning, collaborative learning communities are developing and teachers are becoming more reflective of their practice. The benefits that are emerging from this approach to professional learning are only beginning to be studied and documented, although teachers throughout the country are submitting articles for publication in journals describing the changes in their beliefs, perceptions, approaches to teaching, and the ways in which their students are learning.

KEY ELEMENTS FOR EXAMINING STUDENT WORK AND THINKING AND SCORING ASSESSMENTS

- **Teachers confront real problems that they face in their classrooms on a daily basis.**
- **This strategy engages teachers in examining what they have plenty of: student work.**
- **This strategy provides a focused goal and purpose for the discussions and examination of student work.**
- **Teachers' learning is a result of the shared, collaborative discussions.**
- **Structured protocols enhance the learning experience for participating teachers.**

Key Elements

Teachers confront real problems that they face in their classrooms on a daily basis. The use of real student work situates teachers' learning in actual practice as they examine if their students are meeting local and national standards. Translating standards into classroom practice is a challenge and one that teachers face on a daily basis. As Graham and Fahey (1999) note, "Unless teachers and administrators can come to some fundamental understanding of how their students' work relates to a standard, they will be unable to create the conditions that will raise the work to the level of state standards."

This strategy engages teachers in examining what they have plenty of: student work. The richest discussions are stimulated by work samples that are varied in their nature and quality, require more than short answers, and include students' explanations of their thinking (e.g., why they answered the way they did and what made them do what they did). Student work can include written responses, drawings, graphs, journals, portfolios, or videotapes of interviews with students. Some facilitators of examining student work suggest various collections of student work, including "written work from several students in response to the same assignment; several pieces of work from one student in response to different assignments; one piece of work from a student who completed the assignment successfully and one piece from a student who was not able to complete the assignment successfully; work done by students working in groups; or videotape, audio tape, or photographs of students working, performing, or presenting their work" (Looking at Student Work Web site, www.lasw.org). The type of student work and the collection gathered to examine should depend on the goals and intended outcomes of the process of looking at the work.

This strategy provides a focused goal and purpose for the discussions and examination of student work. The focus of discussion may vary. In the opening vignette to this strategy, for example, teachers had a compelling reason to examine student assessments and did so using the actual test that had been given. At other times, teachers might bring to open-ended discussion groups examples of student work that puzzle them. In some situations, teachers may begin with a rubric supplied by others to apply to a set of student work (e.g., the contents of portfolios or the results of performance tasks) or may take the opportunity to develop their own rubric through examining student work. Also, the focus for a discussion may be a videotape of children's explanations of their understanding of a problem or situation. Teachers also benefit from examining student work as they implement new curriculum. This helps to pinpoint concepts that students are finding difficult and may uncover areas of the curriculum that are not yet being fully implemented.

Teachers' learning is a result of the shared, collaborative discussions. Although an individual teacher can certainly examine student work or reflect on student thinking in isolation, there is power in examining student work as a team. As elementary school teacher Christine Evans (1993) points out, working together greatly enhances what is possible to consider and to learn. Among her teaching group, their ideas differed about the mathematics, the tasks, and particular students. Their discussions broadened what any one person could do. Together, they began to develop shared ideas and standards that could guide their collective efforts. Creating a supportive environment in which teachers can work with each other and examine their own values about teaching and learning enhances the process, as noted by Rebecca

Corwin (1997): "Doing mathematics together in a responsive group creates a safe professional community in which to explore issues and raise questions about both mathematics and pedagogy" (p. 187).

Structured protocols enhance the learning experience for participating teachers. As we are learning more about the most effective ways to examine student work and engage teachers in scoring assessments, it has become evident that structured protocols enhance the learning experience for participating teachers. Numerous protocols and guidelines have been developed (see the Resources section) that describe focusing questions to guide teachers as they look at student work or assessment responses and most describe processes for looking for evidence of learning in the student work, listening to colleagues' thinking and perceptions, reflecting on individual thinking, and applying what is learned and discussed to teaching practices.

Although there are numerous protocols and guidelines, they all reflect a similar structured format for engaging in the study of student work. This format includes the following:

- Identifying a focus or goal by answering the questions: What do we want to learn from the student work? What outcomes do we expect from the process? What data do we have to support our goal? How is our goal related to student performance and schoolwide goals and standards?

- Selecting student work that relates directly to the identified goal and outcomes. It is important that documentation be brought to the session that provides information on the objectives of the task the student responded to, the learning strategy or assessment strategies associated with the student work, and any other information that helps all participants better understand the context within which the student completed the work. Who brings student work to the sessions varies according to the goals, but most groups rotate among the teachers, asking each to share responsibility for bringing student work for all to examine. Many projects refer to this teacher as the "presenting teacher" and there are specific roles in the discussions for the presenting teacher.

- Facilitated discussion of the participants' interpretations and understanding of the student work samples. This facilitation varies among projects, with some more regimented and structured than others. All of the projects, however, emphasize that it is critical to have a facilitator guide the discussions in order to ensure in-depth analysis of student learning and teacher practice. Often, this facilitation rotates among the teachers.

- Reflecting on the implications and applications of what is learned to teaching. This facilitated discussion highlights the ways in which the teachers can enhance their teaching based on what they have learned about student understanding of important concepts.

Implementation Requirements

Focused time for discussion and reflection. Like many professional development opportunities, this strategy requires a focused period of time without distractions to study the material and reflect on what it suggests about students' thinking and learning needs.

The guidance of an experienced content expert. Delving deeply into understanding what students are thinking by analyzing their written work or responses on assessments requires substantial knowledge of the science or mathematics content and, in the case of examining assessments, a facilitator with expertise in assessment is helpful.

Examples

Examining student work is at the core of the Fostering Algebraic Thinking Toolkit (2000), a set of professional development materials for middle school mathematics teachers designed by staff at the Education Development Center (EDC). As lead author Mark Driscoll (2002) states, the purpose of the materials is to "focus on important mathematics; focus on mathematics as learning, as a foundation for teaching mathematics; focus on evidence-based judgment; and establish structures/norms/ expectations for similar evidence-based, collegial professional development" (www.TE-MAT.org).

Teachers engaged in using the toolkit solve, discuss, and grapple with mathematical problems; introduce the problem to their students; and then bring student work to the next professional learning session. The process is designed around a conceptual framework that emphasizes the interaction between teachers reflecting on their own thinking, analyzing student thinking, and discussing with colleagues. Through this triangulation of engagement, teachers' in-depth understanding of their own mathematical knowledge is increased and they gain a more in-depth understanding of the ways in which students explore and conceptualize mathematical ideas.

The toolkit is organized around four modules that engage teachers in varied structures for deepening mathematical and pedagogical understanding: analyzing student work, listening to students, questioning in the classroom, and understanding patterns of student thinking. Teachers read interviews with small groups of students conducted by other teachers, view videotapes of students working on mathematics problems, and analyze students' responses to assessments and examine how to align instruction and assessment. Through all of these explorations, teachers have the opportunity to use data to develop evidence-based understandings of teaching and learning mathematics.

The focus on student work and thinking immerses teachers in exploring students' mathematical understandings, provides an opportunity for them to discuss what constitutes "quality work" and develop and then practice questioning strategies that extend students' thinking. This approach to practice-based professional learning incorporates many of the principles of effective professional development. As Driscoll notes, "We believe that mathematics teachers will grow professionally and become more effective to the extent that their typical experience [when using the toolkit] in professional development engages them with evidence from their practice and challenges them to refine their judgments about mathematics, learning, and teaching" (www.TE-MAT.org).

In another example, middle-school teachers worked with a mathematics educator from a nearby university to discuss the in-depth analysis of students' responses to specific performance tasks. In one task, students were asked to circle the number that has the greatest value: .08, .8, .080, or 008000. Students were to choose the number and explain their answer. Many students could select the correct answer, but they could not successfully explain how they arrived at it. For their part, teachers differed in how important they thought it was to have an explanation at all. The group examined several examples in which students had the right answer but did not understand why. One student gave an intricate, illustrated explanation; one simply noted, "it has the greatest value"; and another wrote, "the .8 is the greatest because it has no zeros before the number or after the number. The more zeros the lesser it is." With regard to this experience, Parke and Lane (1996/1997) noted the following:

> When the teachers compared the explanations, they began to see how much insight those explanations could provide into a student's level of understanding. This discussion was one of the first meaningful interactions these teachers had about their students' conceptual understandings and what they were learning in the classroom. (p. 27)

For elementary school teachers in California, examining student responses to assessment tasks has helped deepen their appreciation of the value of this activity as a professional development strategy. Assessment comes alive for them when they examine a range of student responses to the challenge to create a "Critter Museum." The teachers learn a complex scoring rubric and procedure to assist them in their scoring task. At the same time, they enhance their own understandings of important science concepts and how students exhibit what they know and are able to do (DiRanna, Osterfeld, Cerwin, Topps, & Tucker, 1995).

Commentary

There are many who see this strategy as the most powerful way to help teachers improve their practice. Clearly, it is totally "authentic" in that teachers work with products of student thinking and study closely the very thing they are responsible for improving. As professional development becomes more results oriented, there is no better way to focus on learning.

It is useful to think about how this strategy can be combined with others to optimize professional learning. For example, teachers implementing a new curriculum can bring examples of student work to follow-up sessions. Case discussions can (and often do) relate to student work, discussing in some depth what students did and what teachers can learn from that. In their action research and peer coaching, teachers can pay special attention to students who are talking to each other or working on problems or investigations and teachers can question students about what they are doing and why. Video cases of teaching, including CDs, can be accompanied by student work so that teachers viewing and discussing them can get a clearer picture of what students are learning.

When scoring assessments, teachers benefit from collaborating to develop a common rubric for scoring. They review standards and come to consensus about how they will score student work or assessment items. They practice scoring to obtain interrater reliability and discuss why they scored individual items on assessments in certain ways. This leads them to a shared view of the standards for students learning.

The most important aspect of this strategy is that teachers have access to and then develop for themselves the ability to understand the content students are struggling with and ways that they, the teachers, can help. Pedagogical content knowledge—that special province of excellent teachers—is absolutely necessary for teachers to maximize their learning as they examine and discuss what students demonstrate what they know and do not know.

Resources

Driscoll, M. (1999). *Fostering algebraic thinking: A guide for teachers in Grades 6-10.* Portsmouth, NH: Heinemann.

Driscoll, M., with Goldsmith, L., Hammerman, J., Zawojewski, J., Humez, A., & Nikula, J. (2000). *The fostering algebraic thinking toolkit.* Newton, MA: Education Development Center.

Education Development Center's Schools Around the World Web site (www.edc.org/CCT/saw2000/).

Harvard Project Zero, Collaborative Assessment Conference protocol (learnweb.harvard.edu).

Looking at Student Work Web site (www.lasw.org).

Schools Around the World (SAW) (www.edc.org/CCT/saw).

Standards in Practice (SIP), Education Trust (www.edtrust.org).

STAR Science Assessment professional development (www.maincenter.org/star. html).

Strengthening Science Inquiry Assessment and Teaching Project. WestEd (www. wested.org).

WestEd and the WGBH Educational Foundation. (2003). *Teachers as learners: A multimedia kit for professional development in science and mathematics*. Thousand Oaks, CA: Corwin Press. (See Tape 3, Program 3, *Assessing student work, Arizona State University East, Mesa, AZ*, and Tape 4, Program 5, *Examining content and student thinking, Urban Calculus Initiative, TERC, Cambridge, MA*.)

Lesson Study

Katie, Aiden, and Leah, three third-grade teachers, wanted to start lesson study as a professional learning strategy in their school. They, and almost all of the other teachers and the principal, were already conducting cross-grade and content-alike study groups, had an effective mentoring program in place for new and experienced teachers, and spent numerous hours weekly examining their students' work and thinking to better meet the learning needs of all students. Given the diversity of learning experiences at the school and the collegial culture in place, they believed they were ready—as individuals and a faculty—to embark on lesson study.

They started by first learning more about lesson study by reading The Teaching Gap *and better understanding the contextual issues that influenced the success of lesson study in Japan. They also read numerous articles and studies done by researchers at Teachers College at Columbia University and visited a myriad of Web sites on lesson study. By the end of the semester, they felt ready to try lesson study.*

Katie took the lead on compiling the data they had from their classrooms and from the state test in mathematics to help them identify specific learning goals that needed to be addressed. After they analyzed the data and saw patterns in their students' ability to reason and problem solve, they decided to focus their first lesson on improving their students' abilities in these areas. Throughout the year, and into the next year, Katie, Aiden, and Leah studied the NCTM standards and TIMSS mathematics videos and developed a lesson aimed at increasing students' ability to use proportional reasoning. They followed the eight-step structural design for lesson study as outlined in The Teaching Gap, *including defining the problem, planning the lesson, teaching the lesson, evaluating the lesson and reflecting on its effect, revising the lesson, teaching the revised lesson, evaluating and reflecting again, and sharing the results. They identified a terrific mathematics educator from the state college nearby who provided feedback and helped them think through why some parts of the lesson were not effective. During the next two years, additional teachers joined Katie, Aiden, and Leah and a group of four teachers decided to begin focusing their lesson study experiences on science lessons.*

The Third International Mathematics and Science Study (TIMSS) has shed light on the extent to which education in the United States supports the learning of all students, provides teachers with opportunities for professional learning, and translates national standards into policy and practice. Since TIMSS data were released, discussions have continued concerning ways in which to improve the U.S. educational system. Given the contrasts between the TIMSS results from the United States and Japan, many educators in the United States have analyzed and discussed what can be learned from the Japanese education system to improve education in our own country. Japanese lesson study is a professional learning strategy that has received much of the attention.

In Japan, lesson study is a structured process through which teachers' develop lessons to enhance student learning in all subject areas. Use of lesson study results in teachers developing a thorough understanding of how a particular lesson should be conducted and why. Groups of teachers meet regularly over long periods of time (e.g., several months to several years) to work on the design, implementation, testing, and improvement of one or several lessons (Stigler & Hiebert, 1999). Research lessons are at the core of lesson study—groups of teachers discussing, teaching, observing, and revising specific lessons that are designed to enhance student learning of specific concepts and content. Lesson study and the accompanying research lessons are supported and advocated by all educators and seen as an inherent part of being a teacher. As one Japanese teacher noted, "Why do we do research lessons? I don't think there are any laws [requiring it]. But if we didn't do research lessons, we wouldn't be teachers" (Lewis, 2002b, p. 60).

Increasingly, educators in the United States are exploring ways in which to transfer lesson study as a strategy for professional development, especially in science and mathematics, into schools in the United States.

Key Elements

Teachers collaborate on the development and refinement of lessons. In lesson study, teachers collaborate with each other in every aspect of the teaching process, from planning lessons to assessing student outcomes. Engaging in lesson study requires that teachers voluntarily participate with a motivation to learn from each other

KEY ELEMENTS FOR LESSON STUDY

- Teachers collaborate on the development and refinement of lessons.
- The results of lesson study benefit all teachers and students.
- The focus of the lesson studied and researched is directly related to standards and school goals.
- Critical feedback is on the effectiveness of the lesson and not the teachers' performance while teaching.
- Enhancing teacher and student learning is grounded in practice.
- There is a structured process for guiding the lesson study.

toward the goal of improving student learning. Inherent in the process of researching a lesson is the belief that discussing others' points of view enhances the learning process and the final product, the lesson itself. In addition, teachers' reflection on their own teaching practices and their students' learning comprises a major emphasis of the lesson study process. Engaging in lesson study presumes that participating teachers have the desire to enhance their own learning and their students' learning through interactions with their colleagues and self-reflection.

The results of lesson study benefit all teachers and students. Not only does engagement in researching lessons result in the individual learning and growth of teachers, but also the product developed enhances the learning of students in participating teachers' classrooms. The concrete product of lesson study is well-researched, conceptually grounded lessons that promote students' learning of science or mathematics concepts. The participating teachers incorporate the lessons into their overall curriculum and, often, the new lessons are shared with teachers at other schools. In this way, the benefits extend to numerous teachers and students. Teachers who have engaged in lesson study also relate that they transfer the skills and knowledge that they learn during the study of specific lessons into other content areas.

The focus of the lesson studied and researched is directly related to standards and school goals. To benefit students and teachers beyond those directly involved in the lesson study experience, the themes or concepts being addressed in the lessons must be a reflection of school, district, or national standards and goals for student learning in science or mathematics. In addition, identifying the concepts to explore through lesson study should be based on data that indicate there is a need for improvement in current student achievement or learning.

Critical feedback is on the effectiveness of the lesson and not the teachers' performance while teaching. Although this is a subtle distinction, it is a critical one. The focus of lesson study is on the lessons and the ways in which the teaching and learning strategies enhance student learning. The individual teacher conducting the lessons, who is observed by the other teachers, is not at the center of improvement. Individual teachers do, however, often relate that they gain immense knowledge about ways in which to improve their teaching through reflecting on the feedback from their peers. Keeping the critical feedback discussions focused on the lessons and the student learning that results enhances teachers' comfort level with engaging in a discussion of the strengths and weaknesses of the collaboratively designed lessons.

Enhancing teacher and student learning is grounded in practice. Lesson study is not a professional development strategy that occurs devoid of context. It is firmly grounded in the work of teachers and students. As noted in other strategy descriptions, research continues to emerge that demonstrates that when professional development is directly connected to what teachers teach and what students learn, teachers' understanding and implementation of best practice increase (e.g., Cohen & Hill, 1998).

There is a structured process for guiding the lesson study. Numerous resources have been published describing varied approaches to conducting lesson study, both as it occurs within schools in Japan and how it has been adapted to meet the cultural and contextual issues within schools in the United States (see the Resources section). Most researchers and educators, however, outline a similar process (Lewis, 2002a; Stigler & Hiebert, 1999), which includes the following:

- Defining the theme or concept to guide the lesson study: The theme, topic, or concept to be studied should be based on data indicating a need to improve student learning as determined by local, state, or national standards and goals.

- Designing the lesson: Teachers research the topic or concept of the study, including examining what the research says about how students learn the concept and what common misconceptions students hold, and then collaborate to develop a lesson plan, which is then shared with a larger group of teachers for additional feedback and revision. Although individual lessons are developed and studied, several lessons relating to the defined concept or goal are designed and studied over time.

- Teaching the lesson: One teacher teaches the lesson, although all teachers participate in the preparation of the lesson and, sometimes, teachers role-play the lesson prior to teaching it in the classroom with students.

- Observing the lesson: While the lesson is being taught, the other teachers observe and take notes on what the students and presenting teacher do and say, following the "storyline" of the lesson, and document the questions the presenting teacher asks and the student responses.

- Reflecting and evaluating: Critical, in-depth discussions focus on what was observed during the teaching of the lesson.

- Revising the lesson: Based on their reflections and evaluation, the lesson is collaboratively revised and, frequently, examining student work is used to guide decisions regarding how to enhance the lesson to increase student understanding and learning.

- Teaching the revised lesson: The revised lesson is taught and observed; the same teacher may teach the lesson again, to either the same or a different group of students, or another teacher may conduct the lesson, and, often, additional faculty members are invited to observe when the revised lesson is taught.

- Reflecting and evaluating: This second debriefing is attended not only by the lesson study teachers but also by a larger group of the faculty, the principal, and a "knowledgeable other"—a content expert, university faculty, or other outside professional. As Stigler and Hiebert (1999) note, the discussions in this second debriefing often extend to larger issues: "Not only is the lesson discussed with respect to what these students learned and understood, but also with respect to more general issues raised by the hypothesis that guided the design of the research lesson. What about teaching and learning, more generally, was learned from the lesson and its implementation?" (p. 115).

- Sharing the results: The lesson that has been researched and developed is shared with a broader audience of teachers and other educators. Articles might be published, and many schools and districts have established Web sites to share lessons that result from the process.

Implementation Requirements

Administrator support. As is evident from the procedure outlined above, lesson study can involve all teachers in the school, as well as teachers from other schools and knowledgeable others, and building supervisors must support the intense process of lesson study and structure the school day in ways that provide opportunities for teachers to plan, design, teach, and reflect together.

Access to resources and knowledgeable others. Lesson study teachers need readily available access to the resources required to study and research the theme or concept that they are exploring through the research lesson and have appropriate resource people who can serve in the "knowledgeable other" role.

Examples

Since 2000, Paterson Public School 2, a kindergarten through eighth-grade school in New Jersey, has been using lesson study as a schoolwide strategy for professional development. The school started using lesson study as a means of improving teaching and learning in 1997 after a TIMSS seminar motivated teachers to change the way they taught mathematics. With strong support and involvement of the school's principal, schedules were rearranged and teachers began study of student learning through lesson study. They did not, however, embark on their efforts without guidance. They collaborated with educators from Columbia University, the principal and teachers from the Greenwich Japanese School, and the Mid-Atlantic Eisenhower Regional Consortium for Mathematics and Science Education. With structures in place, a culture in the school supporting reflective risk taking and partners, mentors, and coaches ready to collaborate, some of the Paterson teachers initiated lesson study in mathematics. By the end of 2002, "all mathematics teachers (with the exception of one who opted not to participate) are scheduled from 80–105 minutes per week for lesson study" (Liptak, 2002). A few science and special education teachers are also involved and a schoolwide focus on science lesson study will begin in 2003.

One of the unique aspects of Paterson's implementation of lesson study is their collaboration with the principal and teachers from the Greenwich Japanese School. These teachers were experienced in using lesson study and served as close mentors and coaches during Paterson's first year of exploring lesson study in their own school. Greenwich teachers facilitated the process of identifying a specific area of need in mathematics, designing and writing the research lessons, observing lessons, and modeling the focused critique following observations of the lesson being taught.

Paterson School now has lesson plans and curriculum in mathematics for two grade levels. It is, however, already documenting improvements in students' performance on state mathematics tests and is learning that there has been an increase in the number of students who go on to high school in their enrollment in Honors Algebra and Algebra II (Hoff, 2000).

Another district, Bellevue School District in Washington, uses lesson study to enhance and refine the district's overall curriculum. Because it is an "instituted" professional learning strategy, several organizational and support strategies were put in place by the district's superintendent. Since 2000, all students in the district are released early once a week to provide time for teachers to meet and examine lessons. Lesson study leaders receive stipends and their own professional development and training. Teachers have time during the academic day to observe in each other's classrooms, and principals actively support and are involved in all aspects of designing, observing, and discussing the lessons. Lessons are then posted on the district Web site for all teachers to use in their classrooms.

Because it is a districtwide process based on district curriculum, teachers in separate schools can benefit from the lessons developed in another school. Common curriculum that all teachers teach is one of the critical elements that results in the success of lesson study in Japan and one that has posed challenges in the United States (see the Commentary section below). As Bellevue Superintendent Mike Riley stated, "It's not so much reinventing the wheel, it's more like here's a picture of a wheel, now create one that will actually fit your car" ("A Superintendent's View," 2001).

Although lesson study is implemented throughout the Bellevue district, its use still requires in-depth shifts in the cultures in individual schools. The schools in Bellevue vary in the extent to which they engage in lesson study and those that are most actively involved describe schoolwide efforts to create more collegial environments. For example, the principal of an elementary school in Bellevue reflected on her school's implementation: "My school was ripe for lesson study. I had already spent a lot of time getting the staff together. We were in the habit of talking collaboratively about teaching and learning objectives. Now when we meet as a lesson study team, people feel free to suggest ideas. It's a safe place. It helps to have that teamwork in place. For a school that is less cohesive, lesson study could be the thing you use to bring people together" (Boss, 2001).

Commentary

It is tempting to jump on the bandwagon and import a strategy that clearly works so effectively in one setting into another setting. Several issues arise, however, when schools consider using lesson study as a strategy for professional development. First, as noted previously, the contextual and cultural environments differ vastly between Japanese and American schools as well as within American schools. For example, in Japan there is a national Course of Study that determines the content to be taught at each grade level and the curriculum addresses a few conceptual topics each year. In the United States, there are local, state, and national standards in science and mathematics and the curriculum addresses numerous topics each year. In fact, TIMSS revealed that for eighth-grade mathematics, the Japanese curriculum focuses on only eight topics while U.S. curriculum includes more than 65 topics (Schmidt et al., 2001). This difference between the two countries has implications for how teachers spend their valuable time. In Japan, they do not need to examine standards, translate those standards into curriculum, or select instructional materials to address the different concepts included in the curriculum. Rather, they can focus on enhancing the individual lessons they teach in their classrooms, with lesson study being the strategy to guide their planning and designing. In the United States, on the other hand, teachers often do not have the opportunity or time to focus on the lessons they teach; they are often overwhelmed by testing schedules, an overexhaustive curriculum, and limited opportunities within the school day to focus on their own teaching and learning.

Second, the culture of learning and the perceptions of the roles of teachers vary dramatically between the two countries. In the United States, there is also the issue of vast differences between the culture of learning in individual schools and districts. Lesson study requires a collaborative, critical examination of teaching and learning, and schools need to determine whether such a community exists before attempting a lesson study approach.

Lesson study is much more involved than simply organizing and conducting demonstration lessons with observation. The eight-step process of lesson study distinguishes it from this, and it requires real collaboration among teachers and ideally with external resources—people and research—to expand views. Furthermore, lesson study must be an ongoing process and should be approached this way as one considers it as part of the professional development design for a school district. It involves more than the study of just one lesson.

Lesson study can be a catalyst for schoolwide reflection on the goals and vision for developing a more collegial faculty and encourage teachers and administrators to take steps toward achieving those goals.

U.S. educators and policymakers often turn to the quick fixes to solve the educational system's complex problems. Lesson study is based on the assumption that learning and change are gradual and intensive endeavors. As Stigler and Hiebert (1999) state, "Lesson study is a process of improvement that is expected to produce small, incremental improvements in teaching over long periods of time" (p. 121). Teachers and schools must necessarily consider the political climate that most directly influences their school and the parental and community perceptions of what reforming and changing teaching should entail. If the beliefs inherent in lesson study conflict with those critical factors, it is important to address them prior to implementing lesson study.

Finally, there is the overarching issue of how professional development is viewed. Although there have been significant shifts in recent years in the view of professional development as one-shot, short-term experiences disconnected from student learning, many educators still do not conceive of professional learning experiences, such as those described in this book, as effective strategies. Strategies like lesson study require a paradigm shift in thinking about what best-practice professional development looks like and is an issue that should be addressed prior to implementing a long-term, job-embedded learning experience for teachers.

Catherine Lewis has written extensively about lesson study in Japan and the United States. She raises several additional questions regarding the transfer of lesson study into schools in the United States, including the following:

- What are the essential features of lesson study that must be honored when lesson study is conducted in the United States (and what are the nonessential features that can be changed)?

- How do educators improve instruction through lesson study?

- What supports will be needed for lesson study in the United States, given its educational system and culture? (Lewis, 2002a, pp. 6-7).

Continued research and experience with implementing lesson study in this country will greatly enhance the education community's ability to answer the questions Lewis raises and increase the effectiveness of this strategy in the United States. As illustrated in the two examples above, there are schools that have successfully adapted lesson study to meet their specific school cultures and contexts. It is crucial to consider the specific contexts within a school before moving forward toward implementing lesson study. For example, teachers and administrators need to ask themselves: Does our learning culture support collaborative learning? How will we restructure time constraints to provide the necessary learning opportunities for teachers? Will the parents and community support this long-term, gradual approach to improving science and mathematics teaching and learning? Reflecting on these and other questions can guide a school or district to determine whether and when lesson study is the best strategy for teacher learning in their site.

Resources

Lesson Study Research Group, Columbia University (www.tc.edu/lessonstudy).
Lewis, C. (in press). *Lesson study: A handbook of teacher-led instructional improvement.* Philadelphia: Research for Better Schools.
Lewis, C., & Tsuchida, I. (1997). Planned educational change in Japan: The shift to student-centered elementary science. *Journal of Educational Policy, 12*(5), 313-331.
Northwest Regional Education Laboratory (www.nwrel.org/msec/nwteacher).
Paterson, New Jersey School 2 (www.paterson.k12.nj.us/~school2).
Stigler, J. W., & Hiebert, J. (1999). *The teaching gap: Best ideas from the world's teachers for improving education in the classroom.* New York: Free Press.
Yashida, M., & Fernandez, C. CD on lesson study. Available through Columbia University's Web site (www.tc.columbia.edu).

IMMERSION EXPERIENCES

The two professional learning strategies described in this section reflect approaches to teacher learning that engage teachers in doing science and mathematics: immersion in inquiry in science and problem solving in mathematics, and immersion in the world of scientists and mathematicians. (See Figure 5.5.) Both strategies are grounded in adult learning research indicating that learning is enhanced through direct experience of science and mathematics content and the processes of inquiry and problem solving.

Immersion experiences for teachers of science and mathematics are based on several assumptions about the disciplines of science and mathematics, teachers, learning, and professional development. These assumptions form the foundation for the design and implementation of all science and mathematics immersion experiences.

Figure 5.5. Strategies for Professional Learning: Immersion Experiences

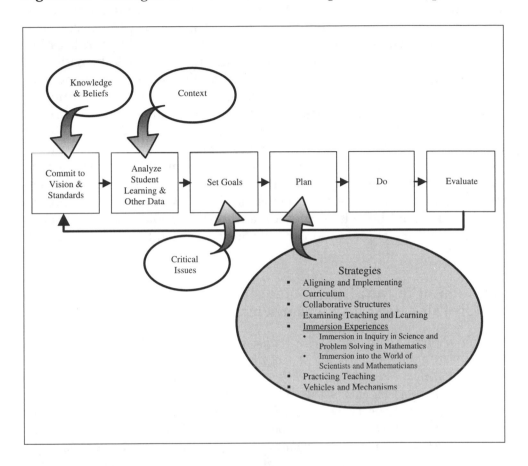

Underlying Assumptions

Science and mathematics comprise process and content. The content of science and mathematics is the understandings, meanings, and models that have been created and continue to be created by scientists and mathematicians. Science and mathematics as inquiry and problem solving encompass the methodologies used to develop scientific and mathematics knowledge and understanding.

Teachers benefit from experiences as learners that are based on the same principles that they are expected to implement with students. As discussed in Chapter 2, the principles of human learning apply equally well to adults and children; they both learn through direct experience and by constructing their own meanings from those experiences using previous knowledge. Immersion experiences provide opportunities for teachers to learn science and mathematics content and processes at their own level of learning.

Teachers must have an in-depth understanding of science and mathematics content and processes. By becoming a scientist or mathematician through immersion in scientific inquiry or mathematical problem solving, teachers necessarily learn both content and the skills necessary for investigating and learning the science or mathematics. This is necessary for teachers to provide students with in-depth learning of science and mathematics content and processes. For example, a teacher with an understanding of the interconnected concepts of buoyancy and density is better able to guide students' learning during inquiry-based activities when students ask, "Why does the cork float and the marble sink?" In mathematics, a teacher who has a firm understanding of fractions would "hear a student's comment that 'the larger the number on the bottom, the smaller the fraction'" as being "true only when the numerator remains constant (1/5 is less than 1/3, but 3/5 is not less than 2/4)" and would be able to provide additional problem-solving experiences to help the student refine his or her understanding (Cohen & Ball, 1999, p. 8)

Immersion in Inquiry in Science and Problem Solving in Mathematics

Elaine, Teri, Kevin, and Shelly, mathematics teacher colleagues at Riverside School, were attending a seminar at a local university. As a prelude to a discussion on open-ended investigations, the teachers were presented with and asked to explore the following problem: How many 1 ft. × 1 ft. square floor tiles would you need to make a border on the floor around the edge of a rectangular room? The group began by trying to decide what the smallest room could be that would have a tile border as described. After some discussion of the meaning of "border," they agreed that a 3 ft. × 3 ft. room would be the smallest and that it would have one tile in the interior. The group proceeded to build a model of the situation and concluded that the border would require eight tiles. At this point, Teri suggested that they look at a room that was 7 ft. × 8 ft. (She had drawn a sketch of the tile border for a 7 ft. × 8 ft. room while the other three members of the group were determining the smallest case.) Kevin suggested that they subtract the area of a 6 ft. × 5 ft. rectangle from the area of the 7 ft. × 8 ft. rectangle because this difference would result in the number of tiles on the border of the 7 ft. × 8 ft. rectangle. He used Teri's diagram to explain this solution method to the members of the group.

The teachers continued to explore different cases and to make conjectures regarding the number of square tiles in the borders of rooms with different dimensions. After much discussion and exploration, Kevin suggested an approach that seemed to "work" for rooms of any dimension. They then tested the suggested generalization and concluded that it did indeed work for any case.

Immersion in inquiry in science or problem solving in mathematics is the structured opportunity to experience, firsthand, science or mathematics content and processes. By becoming a learner of the content, teachers broaden their own understanding and knowledge of the content that they are addressing with their students. By learning through inquiry and problem solving—putting the principles of science or mathematics teaching and learning into practice and experiencing the processes for themselves—teachers are better prepared to implement the practices in their classrooms. The goal is to help teachers become competent in their content and reflective about how to best teach it. Immersion experiences are usually guided by knowledgeable and experienced facilitators with expertise in science or mathematics. The curriculum is designed specifically to highlight the processes of inquiry and mathematical problem-solving approaches to learning mathematics and science content.

Key Elements

Immersion in an intensive learning experience. Teachers are immersed in an intensive experience in which they focus on learning science or mathematics and are able to pursue content in-depth. In science, they participate fully in the generation of investigable questions, plan and conduct investigations that allow them to make meaning out of the inquiry activities, collect and organize data, make predictions, and gain a broader view of the science concepts they are investigating. In mathematics, they "generate compelling questions, conduct investigations to make meaning out of mathematical activities, collect and organize data, make predictions, measure and graph, and gain a broader view of the mathematics concepts they are investigating" (Eisenhower National Clearinghouse, 1998, p. 11).

> **KEY ELEMENTS FOR IMMERSION IN INQUIRY IN SCIENCE AND PROBLEM SOLVING IN MATHEMATICS**
>
> - Immersion in an intensive learning experience.
> - One goal is learning how students learn science and mathematics.
> - Teachers' conceptions about science, mathematics, and teaching change as a result of these experiences.

One goal is learning how students learn science and mathematics. One goal of these experiences is to engage teachers in firsthand learning of what they are expected to practice in their classrooms—guiding students through inquiry-based science or mathematical problem solving.

Teachers' conceptions about science, mathematics, and teaching change. One outcome from in-depth immersion in the processes of learning science and mathematics is a change in teachers' conceptions of the nature of science or mathematics learning and teaching. For example, as teachers begin to see science or mathematics teaching as less a matter of knowledge transfer and more an activity in which knowledge is generated through making sense of or understanding the content, they begin to see their own role as teacher changing from a direct conveyor of knowledge to a guide helping students develop their own meaning from experiences. As Schmidt (2001) proposes, "A teacher's understanding and conception of subject matter is one of the major aspects that defines teacher quality. The key is that the conceptual problem-solving aspect, together with the attendant pedagogical approaches, must be embedded in real science content" (p. 162).

Implementation Requirement

Qualified facilitators. Guiding teachers through the inquiry process and solving challenging mathematical problems must be a specified goal of the immersion experience and one that is carried out by someone with expertise in content and process.

Long-term experiences. Immersion in science inquiry and mathematical problem solving require in-depth, over-time learning that cannot be accomplished in one-shot workshops.

Examples

PROMYS is an immersion-in-mathematics experience conducted by Boston University's mathematics department and the EDC. The program is designed to enhance problem solving and open-ended exploration in high school mathematics classrooms throughout Massachusetts through immersing teachers in adult-level mathematical explorations. According to the PROMYS Web site, "The program fosters new insights into the nature of mathematical investigations and participants practice the habits of mind that are at the core of creative mathematics. Academic year workshops help teachers translate the summer experience into fundamental change in their own classrooms."

The program includes three components: the six-week summer institute focuses on immersing high school teachers in mathematical ideas, five workshops throughout the academic year translate the teacher's learning into classroom experiences for students, and a second summer institute for engagement with more advanced mathematical ideas. During the summer immersion experiences, teachers work with counselors, graduate students, research mathematicians, and previous PROMYS teachers as they solve problem sets focused on number theory. The in-depth examination of individual problem sets is enhanced through weekly "problems sessions" at which PROMYS staff help participants understand themes and ideas that connect the problem sets and focuses them on the conceptual understandings and "big ideas."

A unique aspect of PROMYS for teachers is the parallel program for students. Each participating teacher is asked to recommend a high school student to participate in the PROMYS for student program. That program engages high school students in age-appropriate experiences similar to those of the teachers—exploration of "unusually challenging problems in number theory."

At the Exploratorium's Institute for Inquiry, the professional development is deeply rooted in the belief that human beings are natural inquirers and that inquiry is at the heart of all learning. Educators personally experience the process of learning science through inquiry to stimulate thinking about how to create classrooms that are supportive environments for children's inquiry. Scientists and other educators guide teachers through the inquiry process. As teachers engage in investigations, they develop a deeper understanding of science content and the inquiry process. They also work collaboratively with other teachers to explore the application of their new knowledge and skills in the classroom.

Commentary

Even with extensive coursework in their preservice programs, many teachers come to the teaching of science or mathematics without having had opportunities to engage in science inquiry or mathematical problem solving themselves. Immersion strategies can provide an opportunity to help teachers address this gap in their learning. Immersion experiences are beneficial, but they have their drawbacks as well. Teachers with limited time and programs with limited resources may not be able to afford the time required for in-depth investigation and may opt for shorter-term experiences with, for example, the student learning materials.

Another interesting issue is where immersion in science inquiry or problem solving in mathematics best fits into a teacher's learning sequence. For example, at the City College Workshop Center in New York (see Chapter 6), Hubert Dyasi uses immersion in science inquiry to initiate teachers into a new view of science. Others may choose immersion as a more in-depth enrichment, once teachers learn to use and are comfortable with a set of materials for their students. They then gain a better understanding of how to help students explore important ideas, follow their own lines of investigation, generate alternative solutions to problems, or all three. For example, teachers implementing standards-based mathematics programs such as Investigations or Everyday Math often experience the need to increase their own content knowledge through immersion experiences.

One additional issue related to immersion experiences is the critical need to directly connect teacher learning of science and mathematics to what is taught in the classroom. For example, although an elementary school teacher might personally benefit from learning calculus, unless there is an emphasis in the immersion experience to help teachers translate the new knowledge into direct application in the classroom, the professional development aspect of the experience may be lost.

Resources

Education Development Center (EDC). Newton, MA (www.edc.org).

Exploratorium's Institute for Inquiry. San Francisco (www.exploratorium.edu/IFI).

PROMYS for Teachers, Boston University and Educational Development Center, Boston (math.bu.edu/people/promys).

WestEd and the WGBH Educational Foundation. (2003). *Teachers as learners: A multimedia kit for professional development in science and mathematics.* Thousand Oaks, CA: Corwin Press. (See Tape 4, Program 4, *Immersion in biotechnology, Biological Sciences Curriculum Study, Colorado Springs, CO;* Tape 3, Program 1, *Scientific inquiry, Institute for Inquiry at the Exploratorium, San Francisco;* Tape 4, Program 3, *Immersion in number theory, PROMYS, Boston University, Boston;* and Tape 2, Program 4, *Immersion in spatial reasoning, San Diego State University, San Diego, CA.*)

Immersion in the World of Scientists and Mathematicians

As part of an eight-week immersion experience coordinated by the Department of Energy's Teacher Research Associates (TRAC) program in the 1990s, at the Superconducting Super Collider Laboratory (SSCL), Robert, a high school physics teacher, participated in a research study. He measured properties of scintillating tiles and fibers to understand the production and transportation of light in the tile and fiber assemblies for the Solenoidal Detector Collaboration (SDC) calorimeter. These data were used to understand how to optimize the light output of these assemblies and how to design a calibration system for the SDC calorimeter. His work included exciting tiles with an ultraviolet laser and measuring the light output with a photomultiplier tube under various conditions, measuring the transmission properties of samples of scintillators using a spectrophotometer, measuring the spectrum of the scintillation light in various samples using a fluorescence detector, and using a cosmic ray test station to study the response of a tower constructed from the tile and fiber assemblies.

At the end of his research experience, Robert designed a transfer plan identifying ways he wanted to share his experiences with other physics teachers; he participated in workshops and attended presentations at which he shared his research, in a paper titled "Correlation of Photoluminescence Spectra of Plastic Scintillator Tiles and Wavelength-Shifting Fibers With Light Output From Tile-Fiber Combinations."

The vast majority of science and mathematics teachers have never had an opportunity to actually "do" science or mathematics in a real-world setting. This situation perpetuates certain myths about the nature of science and mathematics because most teachers do not have practical experience in the fields they are teaching. Immersion in the world of scientists and mathematicians is one way to resolve this and provides an opportunity for teachers to strengthen their knowledge base in content areas by becoming active participants in a mathematics or scientific community.

This strategy differs from immersion described previously in one significant aspect—frequently, the setting for immersion in the world of scientists and mathematicians is a research environment, such as a scientific laboratory or a mathematics research group or a museum research department. In other words, teachers are immersed in scientists' or mathematicians' environments and teachers join them in their work and fully participate in research activities. The purpose of this approach to immersion is for teachers to learn science and mathematics content; to learn elements of the research process, such as designing experiments, creating mathematical models, and collecting, analyzing, and synthesizing data; and to develop a broader and increased understanding of the scientific and mathematics approaches to building knowledge and solving problems.

Key Elements

The experiences are designed as mentored research opportunities for teachers, as apprentice researchers, to learn the content, process, culture, and ethos of scientific or mathematics research and development work. Teachers benefit from authentic experiences outside of the classroom. Most teachers find that becoming an active member of a research team allows them to explore and develop their role as leader, equal partner, and contributing member of an interdisciplinary team, and it provides them with the opportunity to share their experiences beyond both the laboratory and classroom (e.g., at national conferences). For example, programs such as the National Aeronautics and Space Administration (NASA) immersion projects develop online

---

KEY ELEMENTS FOR IMMERSION IN THE WORLD OF SCIENTISTS AND MATHEMATICIANS

- The experiences are designed as mentored research opportunities for teachers, as apprentice researchers, to learn the content, process, culture, and ethos of scientific or mathematics research and development work.

- Teachers attend lectures and seminars and read materials on the science or mathematics topics related to the research.

- Teachers actively participate as members of research teams, which include scientists or mathematicians or university faculty.

- The program includes planning for how to connect learning to teachers' classrooms.

- There are opportunities for follow-through with implementation and dissemination at local, regional, and national levels, as well as opportunities for ongoing communication.

- Teachers document their learning and reflect on their experiences.

communities to enable teachers to stay involved electronically once they return to their classrooms.

Teachers attend lectures and seminars and read materials on the science or mathematics topics related to the research. As part of their immersion in the science or mathematics community, teachers participate in activities outside of their research that enhance their experiences and contribute to their knowledge base.

Teachers actively participate as members of research teams, which include scientists or mathematicians or university faculty. As part of their research experience, teachers contribute to the ongoing work of the research team by presenting oral reports on what they are learning, critically reviewing their own and others' work, and participating in team meetings.

The program includes planning for how to connect learning to teachers' classrooms. Teachers create action plans or instructional activities to transfer what they have learned to their classrooms. Although the main objective of immersion experiences is the professional development of teachers, one outcome is that as teachers obtain greater content and process knowledge, understanding of the research community, and experience in "being" a scientist or mathematician they are better able to devise methods for sharing this learning with their students.

There are opportunities for follow-through with implementation and dissemination at local, regional, and national levels, as well as opportunities for ongoing communication. Most immersion programs encourage all members of research teams to both individually and jointly present their findings and their experiences at meetings and in journal articles. Programs also encourage research team members to maintain communication with each other, either through in-person meetings or electronically, view their scientist or mathematician mentors as resources, and, in some cases, invite them to visit classrooms throughout the school year. Other programs offer "class reunions" at regional or national conferences, newsletters, and electronic networks for "graduates."

Teachers document their learning and reflect on their experiences. Many immersion programs incorporate keeping a journal or writing about the immersion experience. Teachers find that writing about their experiences as they progress over time helps deepen the experience itself and helps them recognize that they have "become" a scientist or mathematician. The gaining of this perspective during the immersion program encourages teachers to return to the classroom with a different view of themselves.

Implementation Requirements

Funding. Because this is a "one teacher at a time" professional development experience, it can be expensive.

Access. Teachers need access to a research setting in which scientists and mathematicians are willing and able to serve as mentors.

Shared expectations and goals. All involved in the immersion experience need to have open, frequent communication and establish shared goals and expectations for the assignments and experiences of the teachers.

Resources and support. Teachers need support from their school administrators to return to the classroom and use what they have learned.

Examples

Perhaps the single largest professional development program that enables teachers and scientists to work together is the Teacher Research Associates (TRAC) program located at many of the nation's 28 National Energy Laboratories. One TRAC location is Brookhaven National Laboratory (BNL) in New York. This TRAC program is conducted in close cooperation with New York University (NYU). It began in response to a needs assessment of New York City teachers indicating that 90% of those surveyed felt uncomfortable with their science background, with many interested in personal interaction with a scientist in a laboratory setting. Teachers participate as interns at Brookhaven as part of a master's program for inservice teachers at NYU. As Leonhardt and Fraser-Abder (1996) state,

> Teacher interns arrive at BNL during the second week of July and quickly immerse themselves in their research. The interns perform laboratory and library research under the supervision of their scientist/advisors. Throughout the experience interns are treated as members of the scientific community. They have access to BNL resources and are encouraged to request assistance as needed and perform research as assigned. The interns live on-site for the duration of the internship. They participate in all programmatic and social activities, including weekly lunchtime discussions that focus on transferring the research experience to the classroom. The teachers form a cohesive group and share their laboratory successes, difficulties, and classroom strategies. Toward the end of their internships, teachers apply for small grants to support the transfer of their lab experience into their classrooms. At this time teachers also begin making preliminary plans to have either their scientist/advisor visit their

classes during the fall semester or to have their classes visit BNL. (p. 33)

The University Research Expeditions Program (UREP) of the University of California, Davis, offers opportunities for teachers to work with faculty in the sciences and social sciences on their current field research projects. UREP subsidizes teachers' field expeditions and provides campus workshops at which teachers develop curriculum based on the research performed on an expedition. The mission of the program is to provide teachers with the opportunity to engage in real science so that they can go back to their classrooms and perform similar activities, to teach the process of science rather than accumulating facts, and to open up channels of communication between scientists and educators. One teacher who conducted a wetlands research project in Belize summarized her experiences as follows (WestEd, 1996):

> I've seen teachers make incredible leaps in terms of their confidence. Even if we've had training in science, we've rarely had opportunities to participate in real scientific research. What we do when we are isolated in classrooms is very different than what happens in universities, and UREP gives us a real understanding of how a scientist approaches a problem. (p. 9)

Commentary

Immersion experiences can be extremely rewarding for teachers and result in changes in classroom practices. There are, however, several "pitfalls." First, scientists and mathematicians sometimes prefer "helpers" who already have degrees in science or mathematics; those who fill the bill are commonly high school teachers. This somewhat limits the pool of teachers who can benefit from this kind of experience. There are, however, locations and assignments that welcome teachers with less experience.

Second is the question of the degree to which teachers are able to translate important aspects of their internship experience into the classroom. Staff at one program confronted this problem when past participants told them that, when they returned to their schools, they were frustrated by a lack of equipment and by colleagues and administrators who were unwilling to make changes in the school setting to accommodate an improved science program. Program sponsors addressed the problem by limiting admission to teachers whose administrators promised to provide support to maximize the teachers' effectiveness when they returned to the classroom. Other programs include partnership agreements with school districts or individual schools to implement changes that would use the teachers' research experience during the academic year. Many of these programs also provide structures for continued contact and support for teachers with their mentors, project staff, and fellow participants. Although imposing these types of contracts and partnership agreements on teachers and their administrators addresses the problems identified, it also limits the number of teachers who are able to participate in research opportunities to those with local support.

Third is the issue of whether teachers actually need to bring something back to the classroom other than a renewed interest in and commitment to their field and an increased understanding of the content. Some believe that it is enough for teachers to develop this interest and knowledge and that this will lead them to share their enthusiasm and new knowledge with students. Others believe that it is important to incorporate into the immersion experience strategic plans for implementing new learning in the classroom.

A fourth issue concerns the relationship between scientists and mathematicians and teachers in the research environment. At best, it is collegial, and the scientist or mathematician has sufficient time to work with the teacher to involve him or her in the research process. There is the danger, however, that teachers will be given repetitive tasks with little explanation or that they will be asked to read and attend lectures with advanced scientific or mathematics content and might then try to pass on the knowledge in a similar manner to their students. This problem can be addressed through careful orientation of mentors and guidance in selecting teacher research assignments. It arises less frequently with internship programs connected with museums, where teachers work closely with museum experts in developing exhibits, planetarium programs, or other activities for the general public. Because the main goal of museums is education, museum staff members are frequently more effective coaches for how to translate learning to the classroom than are many scientists and mathematicians.

Finally, the cost of providing this strategy for teachers has led many to dismiss it as a viable opportunity for teacher professional development. Many believe that the money can be better spent in ways that reach more teachers. Some corporations and businesses are working with universities and research facilities to create sponsored internships for teachers. Many provide money for scholarships to purchase equipment and supplies for the classroom, pay for fellows' substitute teachers when they attend conferences and inservice workshops, and reproduce the materials they might develop during the internship (e.g., videos or software). Sponsored internships can help defray the costs associated with this professional learning strategy.

Resources

Teacher Research Associates (TRAC) program, Brookhaven National Laboratory, New York (www.bnl.gov/dtra).

University Research Expeditions Program (UREP), University of California, Davis (www.urep.ucdavis.edu).

Figure 5.6. Strategies for Professional Learning: Practicing Teaching

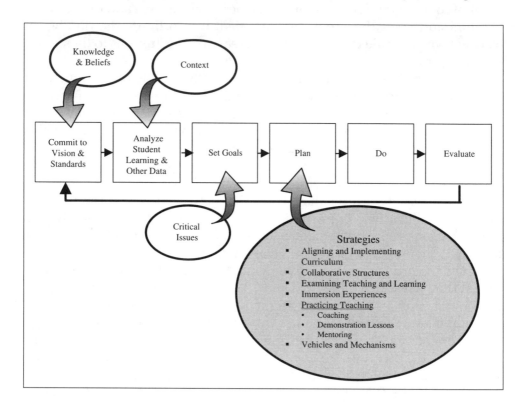

PRACTICING TEACHING

Many professionals use practice sessions as a means to enhance their knowledge, skills, and performance. For example, musicians, lawyers, athletes,
and medical personnel are called on to practice through demonstration and
gain tips and feedback from colleagues and coaches. The three professional
learning strategies in this section—coaching, demonstration lessons, and
mentoring—are the strategies educators use as "practice sessions." (See Figure 5.6.) The strategies emphasize practicing teaching in classrooms with
the purpose of improving science and mathematics teaching and learning.
They are used to induct new teachers or to support the use of new practices
by experienced teachers. Coaching and mentoring are usually conducted in
one-on-one situations—one coach or mentor working with one teacher; the
purpose is to enhance the knowledge, learning, and practice of one teacher.
In demonstration lessons, groups of teachers work together observing and
learning from demonstration lessons. The purpose is to enhance the performance of many teachers.

Underlying Assumptions

Teachers are competent professionals whose experience, expertise, and observations are valuable sources of knowledge, skill development, and inspiration for other teachers. This is a critical assumption to which professional developers must subscribe to consider using these strategies in their professional development programs. Some people believe that what science and mathematics teachers need is assistance from an outside expert. The critical and specialized knowledge that experienced teachers have—pedagogical content knowledge (Shulman, 1986)—is not acknowledged as worth sharing. It is this very knowledge, however, that helps teachers understand what their students need, how they come to understand certain concepts and principles of the content, and what they need to increase that understanding.

Stepping outside of the teaching moment is a valuable way of examining teaching and learning. When teachers are engaged in interactions with students in their classrooms, they are constantly making decisions, gauging the appropriate next steps, and anticipating questions to ask of students. Being in the "teaching moment" does not provide an opportunity for teachers to reflect on their teaching moves or students' interactions. It is a valuable experience for teachers to observe others teaching with the explicit purpose of examining teaching strategies and questioning, listening to student discussions, and seeing a lesson in action.

When teachers objectively observe positive learning results with students, they are more likely to sustain and implement changes in their own teaching. For most teachers it is the enhanced learning by students that leads to commitment to teaching in new ways or using a new set of instructional materials. Observing others teach a lesson with students allows teachers to carefully attend to the questions students ask, the struggles they have with understanding the content, and the ways in which they interact with each other and the demonstration teacher. When student learning is evident, observing teachers are more likely to see the value of the strategies used and be willing to try them in their own classrooms.

Translating new learning into practice is best accomplished in collaboration rather than in isolation. Rather than participate in professional development and simply return to the classroom to implement that new learning, these strategies provide an opportunity for teacher practice, reflection, and continued improvement. Teachers receive support to try new practices in the classroom, are observed and receive critical feedback, and engage in reflective thinking concerning their teaching and their students learning. Research continually shows that changes are more likely to be sustained when there is continuous support for adapting teaching practices than when teachers return to their classrooms without support (Cohen & Hill, 1998; Garet et al., 1999).

The school culture supports and encourages continuous improvement for all teachers. Both new and experienced teachers need opportunities to continue learning and growing. Effective schools routinely provide opportunities for teachers to learn in collegial and collaborative ways. New teachers have access to ongoing support as they learn to manage classrooms and enhance student learning. More experienced teachers also have opportunities for continual growth, moving into leadership roles within the school.

Coaching

Reviewing the schedule for Thursday, Renata sees that Julia, her teacher leader, will come in as usual for a weekly observation during her reading lesson. She reminds herself to review her action plan before their meeting and to make sure that Carol, the paraprofessional, has been scheduled to cover her classroom while she meets with Julia after the observation.

When they meet to talk about a lesson, they focus on Renata's action plan—the one she made for herself—and talk about how it played out in the lesson. One thing they don't talk about is how to "fix" the lesson. Referring to specific things she observes, Julia often asks, "Why do you think that happened?" Sometimes they agree, sometimes they don't. But if they don't, they explore further, and that's when it's really the most fun. Julia also recommends some articles about questioning strategies that she and Renata could read and discuss. In fact, Renata had built one of those new strategies into the lesson Julia would see on Thursday. (WestEd, 2000)

Coaching is a professional development strategy that provides one-on-one learning opportunities for teachers focused on improving science and mathematics teaching by reflecting on one's own and/or another's practice. It takes advantage of the knowledge and skills of experienced teachers, giving them and those with less experience opportunities to learn from each other.

Over the years, particular forms of coaching have emerged with different purposes and correspondingly different techniques, as suggested by the labels of *technical coaching, collegial coaching, challenge coaching, team coaching, cognitive coaching, linguistic coaching,* and *peer coaching* (see the Resources section). All incorporate a traditional supervisory model focused on classroom observations and use a preconference-observation-postconference cycle.

More recently, coaching as a form of professional learning has shifted to focus less on the supervisory model and more toward collaborative, peer learning. In this model, the goal of coaching is to enhance the learning of both the coach and the teacher being coached and the role is characterized by facilitation of learning and not on evaluation of practice. Coaching is most effective when the coach is able to match the coaching style with the level of structure needed by the teacher being coached. For example, teachers who are just learning a new curriculum model have a high need for structure. In these cases, the coach may use a *direct informational style of coaching* where the coach directs the conversation by providing pertinent information. When the teacher has a low need for structure and is simply needing to "talk through" which of several strategies he or she might use in the classroom, a *nondirect style* of coaching is most appropriate. When using a nondirect style, coaches listen, clarify, and encourage the other teacher to present their ideas. A *collaborative style* of coaching is one where the coach and the teacher engage in a collegial exchange of ideas and coplan/problem solve. When teachers have a moderate need for structure, that is, they have some ideas and some challenges to work through, this approach works best.

The purpose of most coaching is to enhance the use of specific curriculum, instructional materials, or teaching strategies. For example, many school districts combine the use of coaching with science or mathematics curriculum implementation (see description of Curriculum Implementation in this chapter). Teachers new to the science or mathematics curriculum have a coach who helps them understand the conceptual ideas in the lessons and who provides feedback on their teaching. Coaching is a teacher-to-teacher professional learning strategy that helps teachers embed new learning into their classroom practices.

Key Elements

Teachers focus on learning or improvement. Coaching is most successful when teachers agree that they will work on examining particular teaching techniques, student interactions, perplexing problems, or learning strategies. Sometimes, this is as focused as tallying the number and kinds of questions teachers ask of different students

> **KEY ELEMENTS OF COACHING**
>
> - **Teachers focus on learning or improvement.**
> - **Mechanisms for practice and feedback are critical.**
> - **Coaching requires that teachers have opportunities for interaction.**

to understand any gender or cultural biases, which is of great importance in teaching science and mathematics. Other times, it is more general, such as techniques used to manage materials. Although being supportive in general is an important role for coaches, when coaches observe in classrooms they need a predetermined focus that they agree on with the teacher being observed.

Mechanisms for practice and feedback are critical. For classroom observations, preconferences typically are opportunities for the coach and the teacher being observed to agree on the focus and set ground rules about the kind of feedback that will be helpful. Postconferences, then, are guided by these agreements. Different approaches to coaching suggest different forms of sharing and feedback, some structured by classroom observation instruments and others as open as sharing detailed, but unstructured, observations of the flow of the lesson. Likewise, forms of feedback vary from simple description to particular forms of questioning. Critical feedback provided in a nonthreatening manner is essential in all reflective sessions. Teachers often are not experienced in challenging each other's ideas, and in a coaching relationship it is essential that both participants be willing to be a "critical friend" (Costa & Kallick, 1993).

Coaching requires that teachers have opportunities for interaction. It almost goes without saying that for coaching to be successful, teachers need opportunities to interact with each other. For example, just having time for classroom observations without protected time to talk before and after defeats the purpose of careful and shared examination and understanding of teaching practice. Although a less experienced teacher may pick up some tips from sitting in on a lesson taught by a more experienced teacher, a follow-up discussion of what was done, why, and with what impact is critical to understanding teaching.

Implementation Requirements

A climate of trust, collegiality, and continuous growth. Coaching relationships are strengthened by a willingness to take risks and learn from failures, acknowledgment of strengths and weaknesses and desire to build improvement strategies on both, welcoming the role of a critical friend (Costa & Kallick, 1993), and accepting learning as a continuous process.

Long-term commitment to interaction. Coaching requires building trust, which takes time. Teachers in coaching relationships also must build an understanding about what each knows about teaching, learning, and content. As this understanding increases, they become more helpful to each other. This can happen only if their interaction occurs with some regularity, so that suggestions and insights can be tried and reflections on their impact shared.

Skill building in coaching. Coaching requires special skills in communication (e.g., clarifying, paraphrasing, conflict management, and listening), observation, and giving feedback. Training programs are available for this purpose (see the Association for Supervision and Curriculum Development and the National Staff Development Council in the Resources section and Learning Innovations at WestEd). Coaches need their own professional development to learn how best to translate their own knowledge and experience to others. Coaches also benefit from understanding principles of adult learning and the change process (see Chapter 2). In addition, the more a coach understands about the content being taught and knows from experience how students learn it (and how to teach it), the better. Good coaches help teachers become more reflective in their practice and better inquirers into problems and dilemmas of teaching. They can be of much greater assistance when they know the specific science or mathematics content being taught by the teachers with whom they are working.

Administrative support. Coaching requires that teachers form ongoing relationships. Administrators must recognize and articulate the importance of coaching relationships and activities, allocate or reallocate time in ways that pairs have time to observe each other and work together, and nurture and support the building of a learning community in the school that has these teacher partnerships at its core (Garmston, 1987; Showers & Joyce, 1996).

Examples

In school districts throughout the United States, Critical Friends Groups (CFGs) are working with teachers to increase student learning and enhance collegial interactions among school faculty. CFGs—teachers from schools who want to develop leadership and coaching skills—attend professional development and training conducted by the National School Reform Faculty, located, since 2000, at Harmony School Education Center in Bloomington, Indiana. The training program is "practitioner-driven and highly collaborative" and trains coaches to help their schools "identify learning goals that make sense in their schools, look reflectively at practices intended to achieve those goals, and collaboratively examine teacher and student work in order to meet their objectives" (Dunne, Nave, & Lewis, 2000). Coaches facilitate several different professional learning strategies to move teachers and schools toward collaborative learning communities, including examining student work, study groups, peer observation, and helping teachers build portfolios. By 2000 in the United States, 1,000 coaches in 700 schools had attended CFG professional training sessions.

During 1996–1998, a study was conducted of the CFG training and the impact of CFGs in their schools. The researchers found that the most frequently cited reasons for the effectiveness of the professional development and training were that it is ongoing, it is practice based, and it is implemented in their own schools (Dunne et al., 2000). The researchers also found that seemingly long-lasting changes were occurring in CFG classrooms and schools. For example, CFG classrooms had shifted from more teacher-centered environments to student-centered ones focused on instruction aimed only at learning and not at passing standardized tests. They also reported that teachers in CFG schools were more "thoughtful about the connections among curriculum, assessment and pedagogy" (Dunne et al.,

2000). The impact in the classrooms is also having an impact on students: Mathematics scores on standardized test increased in CFG classrooms.

In the Boston public schools, coaches are supporting schoolwide changes in leadership, culture, and content areas. Since 1999, the 132 schools have benefited from the sustained support of a coach—either a content coach in literacy or a change coach. In 2000, mathematics coaches joined the literacy coaches.

Although somewhat different from one-on-one teacher coaching situations, Boston's schoolwide coaches engage in many of the same professional development activities with many of the same goals and benefits. For example, change coaches work with whole faculties in schools to develop instructional leadership teams, lead teachers in examining student work, and guide schools in analyses of data to drive their reform efforts. Content coaches work one-on-one with individual teachers, facilitate demonstration lessons during six- to eight-week sessions with different grade level teachers, and lead study groups.

Behind all coaching in Boston schools is the idea that coaching needs to address the specific learning needs of teachers and schools and that to reduce isolation and increase collaboration teachers need opportunities to observe in each other's classes and reflect on their own teaching in collegial environments. Coaches are helping schools develop these collegial environments.

The other tenet driving the use of coaches is that to build capacity, teacher leadership needs to be expanded. Schools establish instructional leadership teams with the guidance of their coach, and teachers in schools throughout the city are taking on more diverse leadership roles.

The practice-based, school-based nature of coaching in Boston has resulted in changed cultures in schools, increases in student learning, and individual teacher growth and learning (Guiney, 2001).

Commentary

Several issues arise when coaching is introduced to teachers, whether in a department, as a schoolwide effort, or as a part of a professional development program or initiative. First, norms of isolation and privacy work against many teachers' willingness to open their classrooms and their teaching to observation and scrutiny. Going slowly, developing trusting, building relationships before classroom observations occur, and having a very specific focus that is nonthreatening but challenging are some ways to overcome teachers' hesitancy.

Time for making and discussing classroom observations is a challenge within a typical school schedule. Creative solutions include rearranging planning times, using team teaching, and having substitutes and volunteers work with students on independent projects during demonstration time.

It is important that before coaching is initiated the school or district decides on the coaching methods it will use and plans for the training coaches will receive. As noted at the beginning of this section, not only does coaching have many labels, but also each type has a different purpose, technique, and outcome. Studying and then learning the techniques, through reading or focused professional development, can maximize the impact of coaching as a professional learning strategy. (See the Resources section for materials for review.)

Resources

Association for Supervision and Curriculum Development (ASCD), Alexandria, VA (www.ascd.org). Consult the Web site for information on professional development in peer coaching and mentoring.

Caccia, P. F. (1996). Linguistic coaching: Helping beginning teachers defeat discouragement. *Educational Leadership, 53*(6), 17-20.

Costa, A., & Garmston, R. (2002). *Cognitive coaching: A foundation for renaissance schools* (2nd ed.). Norwood, MA: Christopher Gordon.

Glickman, C. D. (2002). *Leadership for learning: How to help teachers succeed.* Alexandria, VA: ASCD. (Contains peer coaching forms.)

National School Reform Faculty. Harmony School Education Center (www.harmonyschool.org).

National Staff Development Council (NSDC), Oxford, OH. Consult the Web site for information on professional development in peer coaching.

Phillips, M. D., & Glickman, C. D. (1991). Peer coaching: Developmental approach to enhancing teacher thinking. *Journal of Staff Development, 12*(2), 20-25.

WestEd and the WGBH Educational Foundation. (2003). *Teachers as learners: A multimedia kit for professional development in science and mathematics.* Thousand Oaks, CA: Corwin Press. (See Tape 4, Program 2, *Content-based coaching: Belmont public schools, Belmont, MA;* and Tape 4, Program 1, *Curriculum-focused coaching, City On A Hill Charter School, Boston.*)

Demonstration Lessons

Kendra, a second-grade teacher, and Jamika, a third-grade teacher, are participating in a demonstration lesson study group as part of their district's approach to supporting teachers as they implement the new mathematics curriculum. They are both experienced teachers but are new to the curriculum being introduced. As part of the demonstration lesson group, they have requested that they spend some time looking at how the curriculum in second grade supports the content in third grade. In response to their request, the teachers in the group, all second- and third-grade teachers, are observing the teacher leader who has been working with them all year coteach lessons in two classrooms. During the preobservation conference, they discuss their questions about how the lesson in second grade and its underlying concepts can be built on in the lesson being taught in third grade. They also decide that they want to make sure to watch for how the teacher leader asks questions to probe for student thinking and talk with him during the postobservation conference about any "teaching decisions" he makes based on what he thinks students understand.

After observing both lessons, the teachers gather for the postobservation conference. Kendra starts the conversation by noting, "I really saw how the mathematical concepts in my class are transferred to third grade." The discussion quickly moves into sharing how they think the curriculum aligns with the school goals and what they know from their student data about the gaps in students' mathematical learning and understanding. They raise and discuss in-depth such questions as "How do I address errors in thinking when I notice them? What are the concepts behind each of the activities in the curriculum in second and third grades? What are the mathematical ideas that are built on from first through fifth grades?" The teacher leader provides great insight for the other teachers by sharing his own thinking about the specific teaching moves and the minute-by-minute decisions that he made based on his understanding of the purpose and learning intent of the lesson. In particular, hearing the reasons why the teacher leader chose the strategies he did helps the other teachers to become more conscious of the need to connect teaching moves to purpose. By the end of the conference, more questions than answers have been raised, but all of the teachers are ready for their next demonstration lesson study and the chance to continue exploring.

Demonstration lessons are professional learning opportunities that are practice based and provide an opportunity for enhancing teacher practice and reflection. The learning is grounded in teachers' daily work and directly connected to the content and curriculum that they teach in their classrooms. Teachers' expertise and knowledge are brought to the learning situation, and through collegial reflection, their perceptions and understandings are increased.

Many school districts have been using demonstration lessons as a key component of reform. Often, the term refers to a master, experienced teacher or facilitator presenting an exemplary model of teaching that other teachers observe and then discuss. Observing teachers are expected to gain insights and ideas for use in their own classrooms and often to implement what they observe. Groups of teachers meet ahead of time to discuss the goals and intent of observing one teacher in the group conduct a classroom lesson. All others in the group observe the lesson and then debrief their experience. Unlike lesson study that is focused on fine-tuning a lesson (as described in the Lesson Study section), demonstration lessons aim to help teachers actually see what it looks like to teach in particular ways. They may focus on how the teacher identifies and addresses students' prior conceptions or on the questions a teacher asks of students as they explain how they solved a mathematics problem.

The purpose of demonstration lessons is not always to teach an exemplary, model lesson to other teachers but rather to use a "prelesson, classroom demonstration lesson observation, and postlesson debrief" cycle as a catalyst for in-depth reflection on science and mathematics teaching and learning. In the same way that teachers use student work as a means for increasing their understanding of student understanding, teacher work—in this case, classroom teaching—is used as a means for increasing understanding of teaching practices specific to mathematics and science education.

For example, in the previous vignette, the demonstration lesson observation and accompanying pre- and postlesson discussions focused on enhancing second- and third-grade teachers' implementation of a mathematics curriculum and understanding the mathematical concepts common to both second- and third-grade student learning. The teachers were all either second- or third-grade teachers, and the explicit purpose of the demonstration lesson and discussion was on increasing understanding of the concepts addressed at each grade and to enhance implementation of the curriculum. The new learning in this vignette does not come from the observation alone. The prelesson and postlesson discussions are critical in raising the teachers' awareness of the larger mathematical concepts, increasing their understanding of the overall curriculum, and providing them with specific "teaching moves" related to implementing the lessons in the curriculum. In addition, their discussions highlight several issues frequently asked by science and mathematics teachers, including "How do I know if the students are learning?" and "What are the key concepts behind the activities?" Through collegial discussion they share their ideas and develop greater understanding.

Demonstration lessons are often used as a strategy in combination with other professional learning strategies, such as with curriculum implementation, action research, study groups, lesson study, or case discussions. As the previous vignette illustrated, demonstration lessons can provide a vision of learning and teaching associated with the implementation of a set of instructional materials for numerous teachers within one school. Or, in another case, teachers who are participating in a study group might decide to use demonstration lessons to enhance their understanding of questioning strategies that lead to increased student understanding of science or mathematics concepts. Demonstration lessons—whether implemented alone or in combination with other strategies—are an effective way to increase collegial and reflective interactions on science and mathematics teaching and learning.

Key Elements

Groups of teachers observe each other. Unlike coaching or mentor-

> ### KEY ELEMENTS FOR DEMONSTRATION LESSONS
>
> - **Groups of teachers observe each other.**
> - **There is a cycle of prediscussion, observation, postdiscussion.**
> - **Observations and discussions are facilitated.**
> - **A clear purpose and intent focus the discussions and observations.**

ing—that can occur in one-on-one situations—demonstration lessons usually involve groups of teachers working together. One of the underlying principles girding the strategy is that the interactions of a group of teachers lead to more diverse discussions, bring varied perspectives to the discussions, and provide an opportunity to observe different teaching approaches. Together, they develop a shared vision of what teaching and learning should look like.

There is a cycle of prediscussion, observation, postdiscussion. During the prediscussion, teachers learn about the goal and purposes of the specific lesson they will observe, become familiar with the instructional materials used in the lesson, and hear from the teacher whose classroom the lesson will be taught in about what students have done prior to this lesson to build conceptual understanding of the content. The lesson is then taught by a teacher leader in one of the teacher's classrooms, cotaught by the teacher leader and teacher, or taught by the teacher himself or herself with his or her own students. The observing teachers take notes and attend to specific classroom practices identified during the prediscussion. The postdiscussion engages teachers in a dialogue regarding what was observed—usually after the demonstration teacher reflects on what he or she experienced and perceived—and the facilitator raises issues related to content, pedagogy, instruction, or assessment that were related to the teaching of the lesson. Many groups also ask teachers to reflect in a journal at the end of the postdiscussion on their insights or perceptions. Thus, the common experience of discussing and observing the same lesson provides a basis for grounding science and mathematics issues within a context.

Observations and discussions are facilitated. Although demonstration lessons can be conducted without a "trained expert," it is essential that the prediscussion, the demonstration lesson itself, the teachers' observations, and the postdiscussion are facilitated by an experienced teacher or leader. The teachers as a group need a clear focus and purpose for their discussions and observations, and a facilitator enhances the dialogue among the teachers, raising important issues in science and mathematics content and teaching.

A clear purpose and intent focus the discussions and observations. As just noted, a clear purpose and intent are needed for this strategy to be successful. Often, the implementation of instructional materials and the accompanying teaching strategies are the goal for teachers engaged in demonstration lessons. Teachers benefit from observing another teacher conduct a lesson that they themselves will then teach in their own classrooms. They agree in the prediscussion on a focus for the observation (e.g., the demonstration teacher's questioning strategies or student interactions and discussions). The postdiscussion is guided by reflections on and discussions of what was observed using specific evidence from notes taken during the observation. This enables participants to replay a moment and ask the demonstration teacher, "What were you thinking when you said. . . ."

Implementation Requirements

Time and structure. As with all professional learning strategies, but especially those that are job embedded and occur during the school day, teachers need protected time to interact with each other. Demonstration lessons necessarily include numerous teachers being released from their classrooms to observe lessons being taught and to reflect on their observations.

Critical reflection in a risk-free environment. For many teachers, it can be intimidating to have others observe their teaching and to then engage in critical reflection on what was observed. It is essential for this strategy that teachers feel comfortable with each other and have experience critiquing teaching practices in a nonthreatening environment before engaging in observation. Often, teachers will use videotapes of other teachers' classrooms as practice for learning to observe demonstration lessons. In many cases, the teacher leader teaches or coteaches the lesson in one of the participating teacher's classrooms to build trust and to reduce anxiety. This strategy requires an attitude of self-reflection on the part of all involved with the goal of improving each teacher's understanding and practice.

A process of examining lessons. Demonstration lessons require that teachers agree on and use a common structure and process for documenting their observations. This can include note taking, scripting of observations, or videotaping of lessons.

Examples

Demonstration lessons are part of the Clark County, Las Vegas, Nevada, professional development design for supporting teachers' implementation of the FOSS science curriculum. Teachers are guided through discussions and observations by teacher leaders who have experience with the FOSS curriculum and have received their own professional development to enhance their understanding of adult learning and effective professional development.

Each demonstration lesson session begins with a preobservation discussion during which the teacher leader (who usually teaches the lesson) describes the lesson to be taught, the hands-on activity the lesson uses, the purposes and goals of the lesson, and the student learning outcomes. Teachers raise questions and discuss issues related to teaching the unit and they identify a focus for their observation of the demonstration lesson.

As a group, teachers then observe the lesson being taught, documenting their observations by, for example, noting specific questioning strategies the teacher leader uses or writing down comments the students make during their conversations. After the lesson, the postconference debriefing provides an opportunity to discuss their observations and ask questions of the demonstration teacher.

The use of demonstration lessons to support curriculum implementation has met with success in Clark County. Teachers benefit from the varied perspectives that are brought to conversations and discussions. They are able to observe how others teach the FOSS units and share their ideas for teaching with each other. Teachers are supported as they begin to implement the units and are challenged once they have gained more experience with individual units. The discussions before and after observations stay focused on teaching strategies and the resulting student learning, helping teachers avoid the "open the kit and teach the activity" that is sometimes common with hands-on science curriculum. As one teacher in Clark County remarked, "The collaboration among a group of teachers promotes a dialogue of reflection. It gets us out of our own classes and lets us see others teaching, which makes us reflect on our own teaching."

The previous vignette is based on another example of demonstration lessons being used to support curriculum, in this case, mathematics curriculum. In Bracken Elementary School in Nevada, teacher leaders work with other teachers to help them implement the Investigations curriculum in elementary school. What is not captured in the vignette is the extent to which teachers in this image engage in in-depth discussion regarding the teaching moves that the teacher leader made to ensure that all students in the class understood the underlying concepts in the lesson. For example, when it was evident to the teacher leader that students were having difficulty skip counting to 100 by 4's, he stopped the activity and posed questions to help students refocus on the purpose, directed their attention to a visual representation of skip counting by 4's, and asked individual students to explain their thinking. During the postobservation conference, the teacher leader described how he knew students were experiencing confusion, what he did about it, and why. It is conversations like this that enhanced both the understanding of the teachers in the demonstration lesson group and their ability to make similar teaching moves in their own classrooms.

Commentary

As noted previously, one of the changes in professional development in recent years has been an increased focus on embedding teachers' learning in their practice. Demonstration lessons are an example of such practice-based learning. For example, the focus for learning and observations during the teaching of a demonstration lesson is often on the interaction between the science or mathematics content, the students, and the teacher. Judith Mumme and Nanette Seago (2002) have adapted the work of Deborah Ball

Figure 5.7. Teaching Interactions

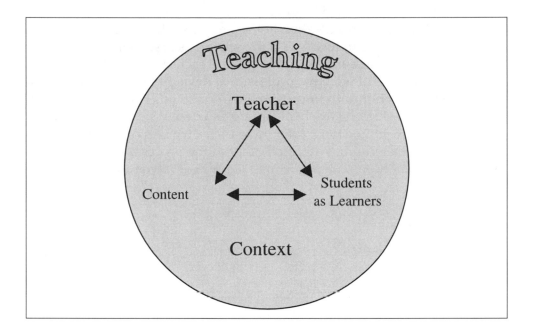

and David Cohen (2000) to reflect this interaction (see Figure 5.7). Mumme and Seago define teaching as "a set of relationships between teacher and student, student and content, and teacher and content" (p. 3). Teachers must have an in-depth understanding of the science or mathematics content, knowledge of their students' needs and prior experiences and how students learn the content, and the teaching strategies and activities that will lead to student learning. In demonstration lessons, observing teachers often identify this interactive relationship as the focus of their observations, attending to the ways in which the demonstration teacher guides and facilitates learning based on her knowledge and understanding of the content, students, and teaching strategies. Through postobservation discussions, observing teachers can further question the demonstration teacher to surface her thinking about how she approached the lesson and why she engaged in certain activities, behaviors, or questioning at certain times during the lesson.

In addition, by focusing on the dynamic interactions in teaching, demonstration lessons raise the level of in-depth discussions and learning. For example, during the postobservation discussion, the focus stays on understanding what the students learned and understood, why the teacher asked certain questions or guided the students in certain directions, and what was significant about the content being presented. Keeping the observations and discussions focused on these interactions helps avoid discussions that emphasize only the most obvious actions and behaviors in a classroom, such as the ways in which students are grouped or the hands-on activity itself. Rather, the increased learning comes from examining the thoughts and perceptions regarding *why* students were grouped the way they were or what content was learned by engaging in the hands-on activity.

Finally, because demonstration lessons require administrative support and structural changes in teachers' daily schedules, a school that routinely uses demonstration lessons as a strategy for teachers' learning embodies one of the principles of effective professional development: lifelong learning for teachers. Continuous improvement in knowledge, skills, and understandings is key to lifelong teacher learning and demonstration lessons provide teachers with a model for examining their own and others' practice, a structure for collaborating with each other in the process, and convey the message that reflection on teaching and learning is important.

Resources

Glickman, C. D. (2002). *Leadership for learning: How to help teachers succeed.* Alexandria, VA: ASCD.

Joyce, B., & Showers, B. (1988). *Student achievement through staff development.* New York: Longman.

WestEd and the WGBH Educational Foundation. (2003). *Teachers as learners: A multimedia kit for professional development in science and mathematics.* Thousand Oaks, CA: Corwin Press. (See Tape 2, Program 5, *Observing mathematics teaching, Clark County Schools, Las Vegas, NV;* and Tape 3, Program 2, *Observing science teaching, Clark County Schools, Las Vegas, NV.*)

Mentoring

Jacob was anxious about starting his first week as a fifth-grade teacher at the local elementary school. He had done his student teaching and practicum experiences in elementary schools and had some sense of what to expect, but was not sure about how he would be received by the other teachers. Some of his anxiety was lessened by the summer meetings he had with his mentor, Wesley. They met for coffee a few times and spent a day at the school helping Jacob learn his way around. It was a relief just to know where the supply closet was located!

When Jacob arrived at school on Monday morning, Wesley was already waiting for him in Jacob's classroom. The students weren't scheduled to start school for another three days so Jacob knew he had some time to adjust. Wesley welcomed him and let him know that they would spend the day together walking through the school to meet all of the other teachers, reviewing the curriculum and lessons Jacob would teach his first few weeks, and working with Elisabeth, the technology specialist, to orient him to the computers in his classroom and the school networking system.

At the end of the day, Jacob was feeling welcomed and more comfortable about joining an already cohesive faculty; they had organized a pitch-in lunch to give him a chance to be with the entire faculty and the principal in an informal setting. He admired the friendly and collegial interactions and knew he would have several "mentor buddies" in addition to Wesley. Before Jacob left for the day, he met with Wesley to debrief on how the day went and to discuss any unanswered questions. They reviewed the schedule for the next day when Jacob would meet with teachers from other grades to discuss the mathematics curriculum and with the school's instructional leadership team to discuss some schoolwide issues, such as "What is expected of us here at this school? How are we evaluated? How do we know if students are learning what we are teaching?" Wesley assured Jacob that this was not going to be a crash course in teaching, but only the beginning to his immersion into teaching.

Mentoring, like coaching, is a teacher-to-teacher professional development strategy that sustains long-term, ongoing professional learning embedded within the school culture. Coaching, however, can and often does involve two experienced teachers, although one of the teachers might have more expertise in a certain area, such as with a specific teaching approach or with a set of instructional materials. Mentoring, on the other hand, usually occurs between a teacher new to the field and a more experienced teacher or an experienced teacher taking on a new role or new teaching approach. That said, effective mentors also serve as a coach to the new teacher. It is within the coaching role that mentors assist new teachers in becoming more deliberate about effective teaching, learning, and assessing.

In mentoring, a primary purpose is to provide support for the new teacher and to enhance the leadership roles of the mentor. A mentor is an experienced teacher who serves as content specialist, guide, provider of resources, advocate, facilitator, coach, and collaborator with the goal of enhancing science and mathematics teaching practices of a less experienced teacher. Mentors in science and mathematics programs are typically teachers with more content knowledge or experience in using a particular curricular program or teaching practices. Sometimes, scientists and mathematicians are mentors for teachers, helping them to develop an increased understanding of the content they are teaching and to incorporate discussions of real-world applications in their teaching of science or mathematics content. They also take on the role of "problem-solvers for instructional dilemmas" to help teachers address many of the challenges in their first years of teaching (Robbins, 1999, p. 40).

Mentoring as a strategy for professional learning has expanded in recent years to focus on the retention of practicing teachers and, specifically, the support of new teachers in their first years. Of new teachers, 30% to 50% leave the profession during their first few years of teaching with the highest attrition rates occurring in urban settings (National Commission on Teaching and America's Future, 1996). A recent online survey by the National Science Teachers Association (NSTA, 2001) found that 33% of those teachers with one to three years of experience are considering leaving the profession. Beginning teachers who are not provided with adequate support and help with their transition feel isolated and begin to question their competence and their career choice, leading them to leave within their first three years of teaching. Effective mentoring programs have shown a significant increase of teacher retention ranging from 85% to 90% (Newton et al., 1994; Villani, 2002). The National Commission on Mathematics and Science Teaching for the 21st Century (2000) report calls for induction programs that will bring new teachers into the culture and practices of the school. Such programs would provide formal mentoring, collegial learning groups, and classroom observation and critique.

In addition, demanding standards and changing demographics present challenges for new and experienced teachers. Educating highly diverse students to meet much higher science and mathematics standards requires tremendous skills on the part of teachers. Teachers today need to provide a wide range of learning experiences connected to what a diverse student body knows, how they learn, and the content and structure of the disciplines (Ball & Cohen, 1999; Darling-Hammond & McLaughlin, 1999). Teachers need opportunities over time to deepen their understanding of how children learn science and mathematics and to stay abreast of emerging research. Veteran and novice teachers alike need collegial arrangements, like mentoring, that provide a structure through which they continually develop their expertise as teachers (Bransford, Brown, & Cocking, 1999).

Key Elements

The mentoring relationship focuses on science and mathematics content and pedagogical content knowledge. If mentoring only addresses the generic teaching strategies of new teachers or how to manage the classroom, there is little opportunity for science or mathematics content knowledge to be increased. Mentors need in-depth science or mathematics content and pedagogical content knowledge to provide the most effective help to new teachers who are learning to teach or use new strategies.

> ### KEY ELEMENTS FOR MENTORING
>
> - **The mentoring relationship focuses on science and mathematics content and pedagogical content knowledge.**
> - **New teachers and mentors have valuable expertise to share with each other.**
> - **It is essential to have mutual agreement and understanding on the goal and purpose of the mentoring relationship.**

New teachers and mentors have valuable expertise to share with each other. Although the intent of mentoring relationships is for the mentor to enhance the learning and growth of the new teacher, teachers new to teaching bring their own level of expertise and learning to the relationship. For example, new teachers often have a wealth of information on new research and learning in their content area, how students learn the content, and awareness of curricular goals and standards. The mentor's role is to facilitate the translation of the new teachers' knowledge into classroom practices. When working with experienced teachers, mentors can help them build on their existing expertise and knowledge as they, for example, try new teaching strategies or implement a new curriculum.

It is essential to have mutual agreement and understanding on the goal and purpose of the mentoring relationship. For individuals pursuing mentoring as a structure for continual learning, both the new teacher and the mentor must have common goals and intended outcomes. In situations in which a mentoring program has been instituted schoolwide, it is critical that the school goals (e.g., orientation to a new curriculum, instructional improvement, or changing the culture of the school) align with the goals of the individuals engaging in the mentoring relationship.

Implementation Requirements

Mentor competencies. Mentors need their own professional development and orientation to their roles. Although a mentor may have extensive experience as a teacher of students, mentoring adults requires additional knowledge, skills, and abilities including the following:

- *Establish a climate of peer support.* Mentors need to know how to nurture a supportive environment and relationship with the new teacher by communicating an attitude of support rather than one of an expert with all of the answers (Denmark & Podsen, 2000, p. 21).

- *Model reflective teaching practices.* One of the most valuable aspects of mentoring relationships is the opportunity for the new teacher to learn about the ways in which the mentor thinks about teaching and learning—"getting inside the mentor's head." In addition, by modeling reflection, mentors provide new teachers with a valuable skill and attitude for continuous learning that is part of the teaching profession. "Mentors can assist novices in translating content knowledge and skills into successful instructional behaviors . . . by demonstrating a reflective approach to teaching, self evaluation, and implementation of new ideas" (Denmark & Podsen, 2000, p. 21).

- *Stay current on research.* Mentors can model best practice professional learning by reading recent research and sharing articles, books, and other resources with novice teachers. Accompanying discussions and reflections enhance the learning of both.

Structure for assignments. Given the interpersonal nature of mentoring relationships, it is critical that the mentor and new teacher develop a collaborative, mutually rewarding environment for learning. Careful attention must be given to "matching" mentors and new teachers. Criteria are often used in making these matches and include alignment of content areas, grade levels, or even personal interests. If mentoring "matches" are not effective, however, structures need to be in place to allow either the new teacher or mentor to withdraw from the relationship and identify another mentor or new teacher.

Time. Time is a key component for implementation of mentoring as a professional learning strategy. Time must be allocated to building the mentoring relationship, for observing in classrooms, and for informal and formal interactions. Not only is structured daily or weekly time essential, but the mentoring relationship necessarily evolves over time and often requires several years to develop its full benefits for the mentor, the novice teacher, and the students in both teachers' classrooms.

Examples

The Dover-Sherborn regional school district located in Dover, Massachusetts, is in the fifth year of a comprehensive teacher leader mentoring model that supports science and mathematics teachers as well as teachers in other disciplines. In this model, two teacher leaders are identified in each of four schools who provide mentor training for mentors in each building, serve as liaisons to the administrative council and school committee, and manage the logistics of scheduling release time for mentors and new teachers to observe one another's classrooms. Learning and leading happen at multiple levels in the Dover-Sherborn model—for teacher leaders, mentor teachers, and new teachers.

Teacher leaders work with an outside consultant and meet four to six times per year to deepen their communication and leadership skills as they are developing a multiyear strategy to mentor new teachers within their district. Several professional development strategies are combined to provide continued support to new teachers. In the first year, the primary strategies are coaching, mentoring, and classroom observation. In preparation for the 2002-2003 school year, teacher leaders and administrators have agreed to expand support to new teachers through a focused use of examining student work.

Mentor teachers are provided with initial mentor training during the summer workshops. The focus of this training is on the needs of new teachers, communication skills, conferencing and coaching skills, and data gathering strategies. Throughout the school year, teacher leaders work with mentor teachers one-on-one to problem solve around challenges that may arise when working with new teachers. In addition, mentor teachers participate in three to four afterschool seminars with their new teachers. Topics for these sessions are based on an assessment of the new teachers' needs and their concerns at different points during the school year.

New teachers participate in a summer orientation session where they learn about the "nuts and bolts" of their school and classroom responsibilities, meet their mentor teacher, and learn about the ongoing learning opportunities available to them throughout the school year. New teachers and mentors engage in four classroom conferencing and observation cycles throughout the school year. The Dover-Sherborn teacher leaders have created and utilized videotapes of colleagues within their district to provide examples/models of "strategies in action" for new teachers. For example, tapes have provided examples of how to start class, manage difficult behavior, deal with the "paper chase," conduct a concept attainment lesson, and assess how students are understanding "in the moment."

Overall, the key features of the Dover-Sherborn model include strong and ongoing teacher leadership, building of professional culture that supports and expects opportunities for teachers to observe one another and talk about what they are learning, enhancing internal capacity to design and implement professional development, utilization of financial and other resources from multiple sources that continue to provide formal support, and administrator involvement and commitment.

The Northern New England CoMentoring Network (NNECN) is a collaboration among organizations in three states, New Hampshire, Maine, and Vermont, that is designed to provide mentoring and leadership professional development for teachers throughout the three states. The goal is to support and retain middle and high school new or transitional teachers in mathematics and science and to increase the professional learning of experienced teachers. Through the three-year content-focused program, mentors develop skills and knowledge to help them build schools' capacity for supporting novice teachers in their first three years of science or mathematics teaching.

The tiered support that mentors provide is aligned with the professional development experiences they have during the three years and is designed to allow mentors the necessary time and commitment to support several teachers. In the first year, mentors focus in-depth on developing their own mentoring and leadership skills and knowledge and work with one new teacher helping him or her problem solve their most immediate needs as a new teacher. In the second year, mentors continue their own learning and begin to address the needs of teachers entering their second year of teaching—implementing strategies for curriculum, instruction, and assessment that are standards based. In the third year, mentors add another new teacher to work with while decreasing the dependence of their first-year teachers by helping them focus on their own self-assessment, reflection, and teaching. During the three years, mentors and new teachers engage in a variety of learning situations, including study groups, collaborative action research,

research literature circles, national standards studies, attending conferences together, peer observations, and electronic networks. All of these activities provide opportunities for both the mentor and new teacher to learn and continually grow as professionals.

Commentary

In recent years, mentoring as a formal structure for providing professional learning has grown into a strategy used with novice teachers, experienced teachers, principals, and administrators. Its influence on enhancing practice and learning appears to be largely positive. For example, according to the National Center for Education Statistics (2001) report, 66% of teachers responded that collaborating with a mentor improved their teaching and 52% of mentor teachers responded that the relationship improved their teaching.

As mentoring becomes more prevalent, there are, however, issues that impact the successful implementation of formal structures for mentoring. First, many projects are learning that simply matching a mentor with a new teacher is often not successful. As noted previously, careful consideration and thought must go into pairing teachers in a mentoring relationship. For example, mentors should volunteer to serve in mentor roles, be committed to the time and interpersonal requirements of the role, and recognize that they too can benefit from the relationship. In addition, structures should be in place that allow mentors and new teachers to "select" alternate partners should there be major obstacles to an effective relationship. Some programs anticipate the critical need for the "authentic" development of a mentoring relationship and pair teachers with a team of mentors, resulting in individual relationships developing at a more authentic level.

Second, the school culture must support collegial interactions among teachers. Instituting a mentoring program in a school in which time is not provided for collegial interactions or in which teachers' continual learning is not valued often results in failure of the mentoring program. A related issue noted previously is ensuring that the goals and intended outcomes of the individual mentoring relationships align with the overall school goals. For example, one initial activity for a newly developing mentoring relationship is to examine the school vision and mission concerning science and mathematics teaching and learning and identify specific teaching practices (e.g., implementing a specific set of instructional materials designed to address specific student learning goals) to focus on in the mentoring situation. It is also important to balance the individual needs of the new teacher with the goals of the mentor and the school's goals.

Finally, it is critical for professional developers and administrators who are considering mentoring programs as a strategy for inducting new teachers or supporting veteran teachers to use new teaching strategies to consider the overall professional development provided for both new and experienced teachers. Mentoring alone cannot address all of the learning needs of all teachers in the school. Teachers also need opportunities to increase their understanding of science and mathematics content, interact with a larger professional community outside of the school, and attend sessions off-site that enhance their learning.

Resources

Fiedler, E. F., & Haselkorn, D. (1999). *Learning the ropes: Urban teacher induction programs and practices in the United States.* Belmont, MA: Recruiting New Teachers.

Ganser, T. (1996). Preparing mentors of beginning teachers: An overview for staff developers. *Journal of Staff Development, 17*(4), 8-11.

Lipton, L., & Wellman, B., with Humbard, C. (2001). *Mentoring matters: A practical guide to learning-focused relationships.* Sherman, CT: Mira Via.

Mathematics, Science, and Technology Coalition, and the Vermont Institute of Science, Mathematics, and Technology (www.vismt.org).

Mentoring Leadership and Resource Network. An affiliate of ASCD supporting mentoring and mentoring programs (www.mentors.net).

Newton, A., Bergstrom, K., Brennan, N., Dunne, K., Gilbert, C., Ibarguen, N., Perez-Selles, M., & Thomas, E. (1994). *Mentoring: A resource and training guide for educators.* Andover, MA: Regional Laboratory for Educational Improvement of the Northeast and Islands.

Northern New England CoMentoring Network. A collaboration between three partners: Maine Mathematics and Science Alliance (www.mmsa.org).

Reiman, A. J., & Thies-Spingthall, L. (1998). *Mentoring and supervision for teacher development.* New York: Addison-Wesley/Longman.

Rowley, J. B. (1999). The good mentor. *Educational Leadership, 56*(8).

Shulman, J. H., & Colbert, J. A. (Eds.). (1987). *The mentor teacher casebook.* Eugene, OR: ERIC Clearinghouse on Educational Management, University of Oregon, and San Francisco: Far West Laboratory for Educational Research and Development.

Villani, S. (2002). *Mentoring programs for new teachers: Models of induction and support.* Thousand Oaks, CA: Corwin.

VEHICLES AND MECHANISMS

This section describes three professional development strategies that are used as structures through which teacher learning is provided. The content and experiences included in these structures vary widely and often include other strategies described in this chapter. The vehicles or mechanisms for professional learning are developing professional developers; technology for professional development; and workshops, institutes, courses, and seminars. (See Figure 5.8.) Each is based on several underlying assumptions about teaching, learning, and professional development.

Figure 5.8. Strategies for Professional Learning: Vehicles and Mechanisms

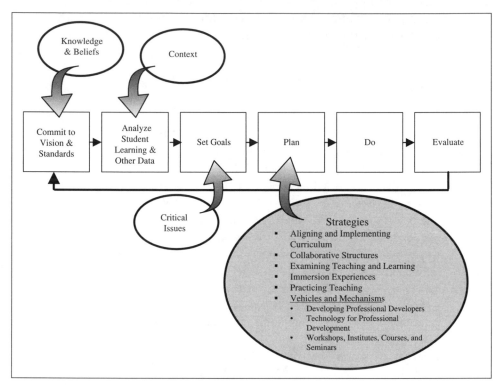

Underlying Assumptions

External knowledge is valuable. Educators must constantly expand their knowledge of both their teaching fields and how to teach them. The structures of the strategies described in this section provide teachers with opportunities to connect with outside sources of knowledge in a focused, direct, and intense way.

Learning outside of the work environment allows in-depth study and practice needed for success. Time away from their classrooms and the opportunity to reflect, think deeply, argue alternative explanations, interact with other educators, and practice new ideas and techniques in safe settings are valuable learning opportunities for teachers. Adults benefit from time spent as focused learners being guided through new material and helped to make meaning of it for their own growth and experience.

Teachers take responsibility for their own learning. Increasingly, individual teachers are taking the initiative to design their own professional development plans and to seek resources and avenues for their ongoing learning, such as through the structures described in this section. One resource for individual teachers is a CD produced by the Eisenhower National Clearinghouse in collaboration with the National Staff Development Council, *By Your Own Design* (2002). The CD provides frameworks for planning effective professional development, resources, and links to other sites and organizations. Similarly, the NSTA and other professional organizations have Web sites that include information on resources and access to online courses. They also provide formats for networking with other teachers in the same content area.

Developing leadership strengthens schoolwide and districtwide reform efforts. Developing the leadership skills and knowledge of teachers not only benefits individual teachers but also the schools and districts within which they work. Science and mathematics education programs rely on the expertise of teacher leaders and professional developers to sustain the efforts and continual learning of teachers and students.

Developing Professional Developers

Sandra Hart had taught fourth grade for five years when her school became a pilot site for the district's new science program. She and her colleagues received the new set of instructional materials and participated in three days of workshops for each of the next two years. When the district recruited teachers to help prepare and support other teachers to use the program, she readily volunteered because she loved using it with her students and had observed an increase in student learning during the time she taught using the new materials, and she wanted to share the many strategies she had developed to make it work well in her classroom.

Sandra and nine other teachers became the staff developers for the program. They attended a two-week leadership academy during the summer, at which they increased their understanding and skills in the program; learned to conduct workshops; practiced skills in coaching, consultation, and collaboration; and learned about the change process. Released half time to be staff developers for two schools each, the ten teachers met weekly and, with the support and assistance of the district's curriculum coordinator, designed and implemented a plan for districtwide program change.

The strategy of identifying and developing professional developers has been used widely in mathematics and science improvement. When professional development was narrowly construed as training, this strategy was more commonly called "train the trainer." Now, however, as professional development has broadened to include a variety of strategies to support professional learning, so too have the roles and attendant skills of those who help professionals learn. Train the trainer has become "professionally develop the professional developer."

This strategy has two distinct benefits to the individuals involved. First, individuals who serve as professional developers increase their own knowledge and skills in mathematics and science, learning, and teaching. The following adage applies: There is no better way to learn something than to have to teach it. Second, the new professional developers acquire skills and knowledge well beyond what they need to teach students—those required to support change.

These additional abilities help schools, departments, and districts build the capacity to collaborate, experiment, and continuously improve. Increasingly, schools are implementing job-embedded, practice-based professional learning experiences for teachers. Developing a cadre of experienced school-based or district-based leaders and professional developers who engage in these types of ongoing learning opportunities with teachers enhances the capacity of schools to meet the needs of all teachers, both those new to the field and those with extensive experience. This can result in more learning for all students and for all members of the school community. Given the critical need in mathematics and science to retain new teachers and support more experienced teachers (National Commission on Mathematics and Science Teaching for the 21st Century, 2000), developing teacher leaders and professional developers can renew and challenge teachers and contribute to the cultural shift in schools toward learning communities. As Katzenmeyer and Moller (1996) note, "Restructuring the school as a workplace for teacher leaders to have collegial interactions is one initiative that can encourage talented teachers to remain in the profession. Teacher leadership opportunities can promote teaching as a more desirable career and help to retain outstanding teachers who can assist in the complex tasks of school change" (p. 93).

The strategy of developing professional developers designates teachers, administrators, or other school personnel and local service providers as leaders of other teachers, often in regard to a particular program or change initiative. These individuals are responsible for preparing others to use new programs or approaches or to induct new teachers into effective use of existing methods. The preparation and support of these new professional developers are critical to their success and require careful planning for effective recruitment, training, incentives, and support.

Professional developers need a broad range of knowledge and skills. Depending on the roles they play—for example, trainer, mentor, coach, and consultant—they must develop expertise in the content and pedagogical content of mathematics and science education, organizational change, adult learning and development, coaching, evaluation, and many of the professional development strategies described in this chapter.

As an organization or project considers its long-term professional development plan, there are many benefits to using local professionals to assume professional development roles. It provides accessible local "talent" who can implement new programs and professional development. It builds local capacity for ongoing development and can serve as a reward for teachers and other professionals who have the requisite skills, attitudes, and interest. Investing in professional developers also provides the school, district, or project with individuals who can connect those in the organization to innovations occurring outside through national and regional networking. As discussed previously, developing leadership is both a critical issue (see Chapter 4) to consider in a professional development design and a guiding goal or purpose for any professional development program. Developing professional developers can serve as one strategy for enhancing the capacity of programs to support continual learning and sustain the program.

The processes for preparing professional developers have been evolving during the past two decades. Fifteen years ago, there were few formal programs for professional developers. Most people grew into their roles by implementing new instructional practices and sharing the good ones with colleagues and sometimes they attended "train the trainer" workshops. Many graduate programs now provide coursework and even majors in staff development and, increasingly, school districts are identifying and supporting staff to provide learning opportunities for their colleagues in the district.

The content of programs for developing professional developers can be guided by a conceptual framework from Judith Mumme and Nanette Seago (2002), based on work conceptualized by Ball and Cohen (2000). This framework suggests that there are three major areas of knowledge professional developers must understand and be able to support teachers to know. These include science or mathematics content, students' thinking and learning, and a repertoire of teaching strategies. These three areas of knowledge interact with one another to bring learning into the classroom. They form the content of what professional developers must know and be able to do. As Figure 5.9 shows, in the classroom (the innermost circle), the teaching of mathematics or science is the complex interaction between the teacher implementing teaching strategies, the content of mathematics or science, and the students' thinking and learning. In a professional development setting (the middle circle), the content becomes the triangular interaction of these three factors, with the learner now the teacher participating in the professional development, and the teacher now the professional developer implementing professional development strategies. These relationships expand further when the focus is on leadership development and developing professional developers (the outermost circle): The content becomes professional development to enhance classroom learning and teaching, the learner is now the professional developer learning new skills and knowledge, and the teacher is the trainer implementing and teaching effective professional development strategies. This model has been used in numerous professional development experiences to help new professional developers remain focused on and attentive to the specific, and ultimate, content

Figure 5.9. A Taxonomy of Teaching and Learning

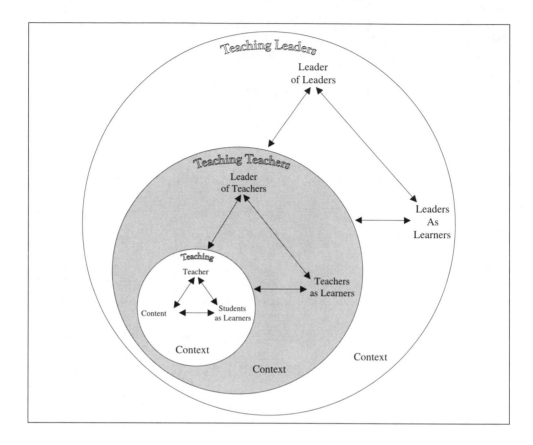

and purpose of their work—student learning in science and mathematics classrooms—by examining the interactions among students, learners, and their content.

<table>
<tr><td>

KEY ELEMENTS FOR DEVELOPING PROFESSIONAL DEVELOPERS

- **Effective professional developers have diverse knowledge and skills.**
- **Professional developers use a repertoire of professional development strategies.**
- **Professional developers have their own learner community.**

</td><td>

Key Elements

Effective professional developers have diverse knowledge and skills. Local professional developers develop in-depth understanding of science and mathematics content; a thorough knowledge of the best practices in teaching, learning, and school organization; self-awareness and an ability to be self-critical; willingness to learn from mistakes and successes; knowledge of schools, both

</td></tr>
</table>

the learning and teaching processes and the political structures and culture; knowledge of how adults learn; and an understanding of the process of implementing and evaluating changes. Professional developers must also be skillful organizers and coordinators, networkers and relationship builders, and fundraisers. Effective professional developers are flexible, adaptable, and creative. They value the knowledge adults bring to their learning experiences and are willing to take risks and experiment with new approaches and ideas.

Professional developers use a repertoire of professional development strategies. The work of the professional developer is varied depending on the goals of teacher learning. For example, when new curriculum is being implemented, professional developers conduct workshops and in-class demonstrations, coach teachers, facilitate problem-solving or trouble-shooting sessions, brief and consult with administrators, and possibly organize material support systems. When teachers' content knowledge is being enriched, professional developers may teach content courses, lead study groups focused on science or mathematics content, or select and introduce replacement units rich in new content not previously taught by teachers.

Professional developers have their own learner community. Collegiality and collaboration among professional developers leads to many positive outcomes. Professional developers need access to many resources—the latest findings from research and information about effective programs—and an awareness of the quality of training programs and curriculum. Professional developers cannot work in isolation; they must continually expand their knowledge and stay current in the field. Through national and regional networking, they gain access to these important resources and continue their own development.

Implementation Requirements

Ongoing training and support for professional developers. To build the capacity within a system, new professional developers need to be continually recruited, trained, coached, and supported. Just as new teachers need support, so too do new professional developers. There is no one prescription, however, for developing the requisite skills and knowledge of professional developers. Many colleges and universities offer courses that address inservice education, coaching, collaboration, and change management in schools. Some institutions offer doctoral-level training in staff development. More commonly, school-based professional developers develop the necessary skills through workshops on effective training, team development, and change management (many of which are offered by the Association for Supervision and Curriculum Development and the National Staff

Development Council) and by continuing their development in their particular area of expertise (e.g., science or mathematics education, assessment practice, or action research). They are involved in self-study and networks and are mentored by more experienced staff developers. They read journal articles, attend training or conferences, and join online networks.

Allocate time to do the work. Designing and conducting learning experiences for others is not a job that can be done after school and on weekends if it is to be done correctly. When local professional developers are used well, they have time released from student responsibilities to do their work.

Communicate clear expectations for professional developers. One way the school administration supports local professional developers is to communicate clear expectations for performance, time requirements, and available resources. In addition, issues that can create problems or signal a lack of support are anticipated, such as how the new professional developers will be introduced to their peers and what, if any, benefits or rewards the professional developer will receive for taking on the new role.

Conduct ongoing evaluation of programs and performance to ensure quality. The professional developer and school staff should gather formal and informal data on all professional development activities through a variety of mechanisms (e.g., surveys, observations, and interviews). (See the Resources section.) Data should be analyzed to determine what, if any, changes are needed in the programs. Similarly, the performance of professional developers can be monitored on an ongoing basis, with opportunities to discuss strengths and weaknesses and areas that can be improved.

Examples

The Leadership Curriculum for Mathematics Professional Development (LCMPD) project is developing leadership curriculum materials to use for professional development of mathematics teachers and leaders. The project is firmly grounded in the content of mathematics—mathematical concepts and problem-solving experiences are at the core of the curriculum. The project uses immersion in mathematical learning to develop the "skills, sensibilities, and long-term capacity of teacher leaders, enabling them to design and implement quality mathematics professional development" (J. Mumme, personal communication, June 14, 2002).

The curriculum contains three-hour videocases that teacher leaders observe, discuss, read about, and reflect on, focusing on the issues that are critical for mathematics professional developers. The videocases highlight six leadership principles: designing for learning; building a professional community; knowing the mathematics used in practice; understanding how to manage discourse; knowing how to select, adapt, and create strategies; and using a lens of equity (J. Mumme, personal communication, June 14, 2002). The curriculum materials include the videocases, mathematics activities, interviews, commentaries, research papers, articles, references to the literature, assignments designed to help apply learnings to practice, and facilitator guides. The curriculum is being developed to support Web-based formats and will also include a CD, extending the capacity of the project to distance learning. The curriculum materials are designed to be used as a "case method, lesson study approach" to help leaders inquire into K–12 mathematics professional development practices, in much the same way that teachers use videotapes to inquire into teaching practices.

The Mathematics Case Project at WestEd focuses on recruiting, identifying, and supporting new teacher leaders. Project leaders strongly believe that all teachers can lead their colleagues in examining student ideas and can come to new understanding about the content and how students think about the mathematical ideas. One of the project's main strategies is to encourage case discussants to take on roles as case facilitators and professional developers. (See Chapter 4, Ensuring Equity section, for a more thorough description of this project.) Carne Barnett Clarke, the director of the project, describes what she has learned in the process of becoming an effective facilitator of case discussions as follows (Barnett & Friedman, 1997):

> As a facilitator, I also had to learn to depend on case discussion participants to modify their own opinions and ideas as their pedagogical content knowledge grew. However, it was not a laissez-faire approach. I learned ways to evoke deeper analysis of student thinking, to elicit alternative points of view by playing devil's advocate, and to press for justifications and consequences of various ideas. I learned to "pull" ideas from the group and ways to reflect them back for further analysis. I continue to grapple with the balance between taking an active role in the discussion process, sharing authority with the group, and maintaining my neutrality toward the ideas brought up.

Even though Barnett Clarke is an experienced professional developer, her comments reflect the need for continual growth and refinement of skills and abilities, no matter how experienced the professional developer. She and her colleagues have used their reflections on their own development as case facilitators to mentor and develop new facilitators and leaders.

Commentary

Becoming a professional developer is a process that includes developing expertise as a teacher, as a coach and supporter of other teachers' learning in a particular content area or program, and as a leader, facilitator, evaluator, and negotiator. Effective professional developers, like effective teachers, are continuous learners who are constantly seeking new ideas, trying them, and making adjustments to meet the needs of their clients and colleagues. They require time and a commitment to ongoing learning. This combination is often hard to find in schools. Teachers are busy people who face many demands and pressures. Some people believe that professional development would be better left to consultants and outside experts. They argue that teachers should focus on good teaching and that professional developers require a different set of skills from those of good teachers. Because teachers are expected to align their practices with one another and collaborate on new initiatives, however, they need the skills of good professional developers. As Katzenmeyer and Moller (1996) state, "Teachers who are leaders lead within and beyond the classroom, influence others toward improved educational practices, and identify with and contribute to a community of teacher leaders" (p. 6). Schools and districts must create the opportunity for teachers to take on these roles and create communities of learners.

Quality control is a key concern as schools and projects develop professional developers from among the teaching staff. New professional developers need ongoing coaching, networking, and support to develop their expertise. Pairing a developing professional developer with a veteran is one strategy for ensuring quality. Engaging professional developers in debriefing sessions after they conduct workshops, model lessons, or work with a team helps professional developers learn from their experience and increase their effectiveness. Feedback from participants in professional development activities can be used to assess quality and make continuous improvements in the professional development.

As teachers and others become professional developers, they also must establish their "credentials" so that they have the respect and support of their colleagues. It is said that it is difficult to be a prophet in your own land. Effective professional developers demonstrate their skills, are a source of useful information and resources, and value and respect the contributions of their colleagues. They share the credit for the programs they support. Their success comes from building support among their colleagues and sharing the credit when they reach key milestones.

The role of professional developer is demanding and often thankless. The professional developer must juggle schedules, negotiate with school administrators and the community for resources and support, and stay current in areas of expertise. These demands, coupled with a teaching or administrative position, can lead to the professional developer becoming overextended and overwhelmed. Although developing local staff who have the expertise and abilities of professional developers is a beneficial strategy, these individuals need support to balance their multiple roles.

Resources

Guskey, T. R. (2000). *Evaluating professional development.* Thousand Oaks, CA: Corwin.

Illinois Mathematics and Science Academy & Teachers Academy of Mathematics and Science. (2000). *Quality criteria for selecting or designing school-wide professional development in mathematics and science: Tools you can use.* Chicago: Author.

Lambert, L. (1998). *Building leadership capacity in schools.* Alexandria, VA: ASCD.

Miller, B., Moon, J., & Elko, S. (2000). *Teacher leadership in mathematics and science: Casebook and facilitator's guide.* Portsmouth, NH: Heinemann.

Technology for Professional Learning

Jessica and Hannah, two teachers in a rural elementary school, had each read The Teaching Gap *and engaged in many afterschool discussions regarding the book. They were intrigued with the ways in which classrooms differed around the world and wanted to learn more about how teachers in other countries taught science. Through the district's e-mail and listserv system, they started a chat room to share their thoughts and questions with other teachers in the district. By the end of the semester, 15 additional teachers had read the book and were routinely discussing ideas and sharing experiences from their own classrooms. Jessica and Hannah rotated the role of facilitator for the threaded discussions, but realized that they needed more knowledge about effective online moderation. Through the state university— located 200 miles away—they were able to recruit a science educator with online experience to facilitate their chat room discussions. By the end of the school year, the teachers, with the guidance of the university facilitator, had read and discussed several books and articles devoted to examining student work and thinking to expand their understanding of the ways in which different teaching approaches impact student learning.*

Through an Internet search, Jessica learned about an online workshop offered by a national learning center for science teachers from around the world to examine student work online. The rest of the teachers were eager to join the workshop and they spent six weeks during the summer engaged in discussions with teachers from Japan, Australia, and throughout the United States. Each teacher posted a selection of student work on an online database and a description of the context (the students, the school, the curriculum), the assignment that resulted in the student work, and their own questions about the student thinking based on the work. For example, Hannah posted an assessment item from one of her students and posed the question, "How do I know if the student's response reflects real understanding of the concept of electric circuitry or just rote memorization?" Her question elicited a response from a Japanese teacher who asked about how Hannah taught the content of electric circuits. Others joined in the analysis of the student's assessment response, and the dialogue focused on teaching strategies, student thinking, and assessment.

By the end of the six weeks, Hannah and Jessica decided to extend their examination of student work to include looking at mathematics with other teachers in their school. In the fall, many of the teachers in the school joined an in-person study group to focus on the mathematics concepts they taught across the grade levels. They continued their chat room discussions and added video footage of classrooms to their repertoire of online discussions.

Technology could be considered everything from paper and pencil to elaborate communication devices. Here, *technology for professional development* is defined as using electronic means of communication and delivery to support and expand on in-person professional development or provide distance learning with or without facilitation.

In the past decade, the use of the Internet, e-mail, online courses, CDs, chat rooms, real-time electronic conversations, bulletin boards, listservs, video- and audiotapes, and videoconferencing has exploded. Many of these are now used instead of face-to-face interactions and to provide follow up support after in-person learning events. Individual learning that comes from seeing background reading and resources has never been easier. Technology has put the world's libraries and databases at the fingertips of all who have access to the World Wide Web.

To use any technology for teacher professional learning, a first step should be to clearly examine the purposes and goals. For example, if a mathematics teacher is searching for an avenue to communicate and learn with others online, accessing one of the various electronic networks is a natural choice. If a school wants to provide an opportunity for the entire staff to participate in an awareness presentation being made off-site, investigating the possibility of linking the school to the presenter through a videoconference may be the best choice. A small study group of elementary science teachers wanting to expand their knowledge might choose to enroll in an online course. Like all professional development, the goals and purposes should drive the selection of the strategy.

In whatever ways technology-based professional development formats are utilized, it is critical to keep the guiding principles of effective professional development (see Chapter 2) firmly in the foreground as professional developers design programs. As NSDC's Joellen Killion (quoted in Richardson, 2001) reminds professional developers, "E-learning also has the potential to accentuate the worst parts of traditional staff development—the fragmentation and the isolation—without any monitoring of the rigor of the work that teachers are doing" (p. 1). Furthermore, she wonders how professional developers will incorporate "e-learning" into the overall professional development program and not simply enhance individual teachers' learning: "Extending learning into educators' personal time increases the likelihood that learning will be isolated from the needs of the whole learning community, focus on the individual rather than collaborative needs, and fail to contribute to the improvement of the whole community" (Killion, 2002, p. 14).

When carefully selected as the most appropriate strategy for professional learning, the benefits of using technology are numerous. The "just-in-time, technology-mediated environment" (NSDC, 2001a) for teacher learning provides ample opportunity for teachers to participate from home on one's own schedule, attend online workshops or courses from a university located across the country, engage in electronic networking with other teachers, or increase their content knowledge in science or mathematics through videoconference courses. Additional benefits are identified in the National Staff Development Council document, *E-Learning for Educators* (2001a, p. iv), including the following:

- Job-embedded learning opportunities
- Content-rich learning opportunities
- Personalized professional development
- Increased access to professional learning experiences
- Reduction of the costs of professional development

Key Elements

Technology-based professional development should meet participants' learning needs. The use of technology for professional development must live up to the rigorous standards for effective, ongoing professional learning. In fact, in recent years, standards and other documents for technology in professional development have emerged to guide designers and users of technology-based professional development (International Society for Technology in Education, 2000; NSDC, 2001a). These guides should be used by teachers to evaluate the extent to which any technology-mediated learning provides quality experiences to meet their needs.

> **KEY ELEMENTS FOR TECHNOLOGY FOR PROFESSIONAL DEVELOPMENT**
>
> - **Technology-based professional development should meet participants' learning needs.**
> - **Skilled facilitators or moderators are essential for learning.**
> - **The content connects with teachers' practice.**
> - **A learning community is developed and nurtured.**
> - **Mechanisms for reflection are established.**

Skilled facilitators or moderators are essential for learning. Whether participating in an electronic network, an online course, or an in-person session, the skill of the moderator or facilitator can "make or break" the professional learning experience. Simply viewing and discussing videos is not necessarily a learning experience. Although "surfing the Internet" to obtain information or taking part in discussions in chat rooms can be beneficial, for the use of technology in professional development to be effective, it is often the skill and expertise of the facilitator or moderator that can lead to deeper and more reflective learning on the part of the teachers. Facilitators of online courses or workshops include varied formats and structures for learning, including threaded discussions and streaming video or audio in addition to text-based content. Numerous resources have been produced in recent years to provide guidance and training for facilitators of online learning for teachers, such as the North Central Regional Educational Laboratory's CD, *Blueprints: A Practical Toolkit for Designing and Facilitating Professional Development* (2000). Maine's very successful electronic learning community, LabNet, has developed a moderator's guide to provide guidance for online facilitators of adult learning and professional development (see the Resources section).

The content connects with teachers' practice. In addition to meeting standards for technology-provided professional development (International Society for Technology in Education, 2000), this form of learning must also live up to the rigorous standards for effective, ongoing professional development. Implicit in that statement is that the learning is focused on increasing science and mathematics content knowledge and pedagogical content knowledge, deepening understanding of student thinking and learning, and enhancing teachers' use of varied teaching strategies.

A learning community is developed and nurtured. Technology expands teachers' access to a larger community of learners. As noted by NSDC (2001a), "Teachers can exchange ideas with leading experts in their content areas, visit classrooms of exemplary teachers, receive coaching from their mentors via web conferencing, and access online virtual libraries" (p. v). In addition, the most effective technology-mediated professional learning opportunities incorporate numerous avenues for participants' development of a "cyber-community" (NSDC, 2001a), including small group activities, personal side-bar conversations, probing and challenging of ideas, and in-depth discussions regarding issues in science and mathematics teaching and learning.

Mechanisms for reflection are established. One drawback of technology for professional learning is that it has the potential to isolate participants and provide one-way learning—e-lectures delivered through written text without accompanying discussions. To successfully utilize this approach to professional development, the structure and format need to incorporate numerous opportunities for learners to reflect on their own and others' ideas and practices, including real-time discussions or journal entries posted online.

Implementation Requirements

Participants. The number of teachers involved plays a critical role in selecting a technology for professional development. If the purpose is to provide a large number of teachers spread out over a great distance with access to information, then videoconferencing, online courses, or e-mail networks may be the most logical choice. Small groups of teachers at one school interested in examining their own teaching and their students' learning may want to use videotaping technology.

Quality of available technology. If the cameras and audio equipment used during a videoconference are of poor quality, the endeavor is rarely worth the effort. Like a live but poor presenter or instructor, participants are distracted from learning. Similarly, an e-mail system or online course that is only accessible 50% of the time undermines the advantage of easy, anytime access and frustrates communication. For teachers to benefit from any use of technology, the available tools must be of high enough quality to ensure that the investment of both money and time is beneficial for all involved.

Training to use technology. Looking at videos or CDs of classroom activities or engaging in discussions during a videoconferencing session are rarely uncomfortable or difficult activities for the participants. If teachers are expected to access electronic networks, e-mail, or online courses, however, they must have time at the beginning to learn how to use the technology and become comfortable and confident with using it before they can move forward in meeting the goals of the experience. Ongoing technical assistance is critical because it allows teachers who encounter difficulties to have access to help when they need it (NSDC, 2001a). In addition, technological advances require that users stay up to speed and familiar with new ways of learning electronically.

Examples

Maine LabNet, started in 1997, is an electronic network that connects science and mathematics teachers throughout Maine. The network is supported, moderated, and sustained by the Maine Mathematics and Alliance (MMSA). In a rural state, the opportunity to interact with other teachers from different schools enhances the sense of a collegial learning community. The network incorporates various structures for online learning, including content-specific listservs to access information, online courses to support content learning, virtual academies to support participants between in-person learning sessions, and conversation networks that engage teachers in facilitated, threaded discussions on issues of importance in science and mathematics education.

Maine LabNet moderators are one of the main reasons this network has been so successful and continues to meet the needs of hundreds of teachers. Moderators are trained and receive their own professional development to enhance their skills as facilitators of online learning and reflection. For example, a moderator's guidebook notes that there are three basic levels of participation: (1) teachers who read posted information and conversations but do not themselves participate, (2) teachers who respond only to individuals and not the larger learning community, and (3) teachers who are actively engaged in reading, discussion, and posting messages. Moderators are given strategies and ideas for ways to encourage each type of participant to best take advantage of what Maine LabNet offers. Furthermore, Maine LabNet provides its moderators with an understanding of the Concerns-Based Adoption Model and Stages of Concern (see Chapter 1) to help them gauge how to respond to the types of messages that teachers post (e.g., seeking information, responding to other postings, or reflections on discussions). The goal of all moderators' facilitation is to encourage teachers to "engage in discourse that invites inquiry, stimulates others to respond, and encourages reflection on teachers' own practice" (ENC, 1999, p. 36).

The Teacher Leaders in Research-Based Science Education (TLRBSE) project in Tucson, Arizona, funded by the NSF, provides content-based learning in astronomy, and leadership and mentorship development through both an online course and in-person summer institutes. TLRBSE incorporates into the online course print materials, videotapes, small group and collaborative activities, and electronic threaded discussions. Videotapes provide images of teaching practice and allow teachers to analyze and then discuss online the learning processes of students engaged in research-based science inquiry. Print materials that are sent to participants prior to the online course provide them with astronomy content and research, research-based science investigations to try in their classrooms with students, and are a source for online discussions and posting of assignments. Teachers share and reflect on their learning about astronomy and leadership through online dialogues that are facilitated by TLRBSE scientists and educators who raise questions, guide discussions, probe for more in-depth thinking, challenge ideas, and provide reflective commentary on assignments. These learning experiences are conducted prior to the summer institute at which teachers are immersed in research-based astronomy learning and spend a week at either a solar or lunar observatory. During the summer institute, teachers also attend one week of sessions focused on increasing their science content knowledge and understanding of leadership and mentoring. Technology provides a means for the follow-up support after the institute as well: TLRBSE staff continue moderating online discussions and learning and provide one-on-one assistance to each participant on a monthly basis according to the science content or leadership/mentoring needs of the participant.

Commentary

For many teachers, access to learning with others who are separated by distance is one of the greatest advantages of using technology to enhance professional learning. Teachers in separate schools or from throughout the country have access to each other and to resources not available locally. Teachers in isolated rural areas can enroll in courses given at a major university hundreds of miles away or enroll in one of the many "virtual universities." Scientists and mathematicians in universities or laboratories are accessible for sharing information, and presentations given in one city can be viewed in another. Technology has given teachers access to information and people that were previously unavailable to them.

Another advantage, noted repeatedly by providers of e-mail, networks, and online courses, is that technology is largely neutral in regard to race, status, age, income, and disability (Schmidt & Faulkner, 1989; Smith, 1996; Taylor & Smith, 1995). When communicating online, the only personal characteristic that is identifiable is gender, which is typically given away by a name. Technology also meets the needs of learners who are homebound due to health, family responsibilities, or personal preferences because it can accommodate individual schedules and time constraints.

Teachers have found that learning to use a certain technology, originally as a way of communicating with others regarding a topic of interest, acts as a catalyst to open the door to more extensive computer knowledge and use. Once teachers begin using these technologies and sustain ongoing conversations, they feel less isolated and begin to create a community of learners committed to each other's growth. Many of the technologies also help teachers move away from the traditional model of learning in which an expert presents information; instead, teachers begin to learn from each other, especially with the guidance of a skilled facilitator.

The use of technology can be effective in providing follow-up or enhancing other professional learning experiences. Workshop attendees can create an electronic network to continue discussing the ideas and information shared during the workshop. They can develop online study groups to collectively examine student work and engage in threaded discussions. Viewing a videotape or CD of another teacher's practices before implementing the same practices in their classrooms can help expand teachers' perspectives on their own teaching and provide an example of the practice "in action." If the video-viewing experience is offered during the school year, teachers then have the opportunity to apply what they learn in their classrooms.

Electronic communication has benefits for the professional developer as well. A facilitator or monitor of an online course or electronic network can take advantage of built-in "management functions," such as monitoring participation, collating answers, and posting assignments. Because communication is conducted electronically, there is a complete record of all interactions and exchanges.

The lack of face-to-face interactions is the most commonly noted disadvantage of the use of technology. "A leading cause of dropping out in e-learning is isolation among learners and a lack of direction and motivation. Increased interactivity among participants and the instructor through immediate feedback, frequent assessments, shared assignments, and small study teams will create a cyber-community among learners" (Killion, 2002, p. 15). Creating this motivation and community of collaborative learners focused on specific and clearly identified goals is crucial to the success of technology-based learning. E-mail and other electronic communication, such as chat rooms or listservs, however, often lack the goals of other formats, such as online courses. Without a competent facilitator or guided instruction, these electronic forms of communication can become little more than places to converse, with limited learning taking place. Facilitators help initiate, contribute to, moderate, and sustain dialogues carried out online and assist in linking teacher reflection with practices in the classroom.

There are disadvantages to using technology for professional learning. Lack of appropriate hardware, software, or technology can impede teachers' access to the medium. This is an important equity issue. Although technology improves access for those who are geographically dispersed, such as teachers in rural areas, the economically disadvantaged have less access than those with technology already in their homes and schools. This is no different from non-technology-based professional development opportunities—those who are the "haves" receive more opportunities, whereas those who are the "have nots" receive fewer opportunities.

For those teachers who "fall behind" in an online course, it is often more difficult to catch up without face-to-face interactions and guidance. For some teachers, technology is simply not an effective means of learning or communicating. They suffer from a lack of social and visual cues that normally accompany personal interactions, and this can interfere with learning. In addition to anticipating teachers' individual learning styles, it is important to consider their individual perceptions. For example, the Professional Development Laboratory (PDL) at New York University's School of Education found that when it incorporated electronic networking into its mentoring program, the results were not as expected. The main reason for the lack of success was that "the project hadn't taken into account the teachers' feelings about technology, a fear of writing, or the pull of existing networks, such as school-based teacher communities or memberships in national organizations" (Goldenberg & Outsen, 2002, p. 29).

To address some of the disadvantages noted here, many programs have learned the value of combining technology-based learning with in-person learning in which participants have the opportunity to develop relationships face-to-face, engage in activities and discussions at their leisure through online formats, and conduct collaborative study, such as examining student work in real-time, online formats. The description of the TLRBSE program described previously is one example.

For some forms of technology, there is a limit to the number of people that can effectively interact at any one time. For example, many online courses have found that they must limit their course enrollment to 30 or fewer participants if both the participants and the facilitators are to benefit from the interactions. This can make it difficult to scale up online courses to reach more teachers. This is especially true when one of the main goals of a technology-based professional learning experience is to develop a learning community with in-depth discussions.

Technology is being touted by many as a critical ingredient in education for the future. Although it clearly holds great potential, professional developers must think carefully about when and where it is most appropriate and how it can extend the ability to create effective professional learning experiences for teachers. According to NSDC's Dennis Sparks, "The ultimate test is whether the achievement of all students is increased because the electronic learning deepens teachers' content knowledge, broadens the range of research-based instructional strategies available to them, and helps them use classroom assessment more effectively" (quoted in Richardson, 2001, p. 6).

Resources

Eisenhower National Clearinghouse (ENC) and National Staff Development Council (NSDC). (2002). *By your own design: A teacher's professional learning guide* [CD]. Columbus, OH: NSDC.

Maine LabNet, a Web-based professional development forum support by the Maine Mathematics and Science Alliance (MMSA) (www.mmsa.org).

National Staff Development Council (NSDC). (2001) *E-Learning for educators: Implementing the standards for staff development.* Oxford, OH: Author (www.nsdc.org/standards_tech.html).

North Central Regional Educational Laboratory (NCREL). (2000). *Blueprints: A practical toolkit for designing and facilitating professional development* [CD]. Oak Brook, IL: Author.

Schools Around the World (SAW). A professional development program designed by the Council for Basic Education (CBE) in collaboration with EDC's Center for Children and Technology (CCT) in New York. SAW Web site (www.edc.org/CCT/saw2000/). CBE Web site (www.c-b-e.org).

Workshops, Institutes, Courses, and Seminars

In the summer of 1992, Tony Sanchez and the other mathematics teachers at his school participated in a two-week summer institute held at the school. The institute was intended to help them develop their knowledge of algebra. The instructor, in this case a teacher educator who would be available to teachers during the following school year, regularly used the algebra pieces, which were available in each algebra classroom, to engage teachers in exploration of traditional algebraic concepts and procedures from new perspectives. The teachers often worked in small groups and then shared their solution strategies with the whole group. Following an activity, the instructor and teachers would discuss both what the teachers had done and what the instructor had done to support their learning. They would talk about how the algebra pieces had been used, the kinds of questions that arose, and the decisions the instructor had made.

Workshops, courses, institutes, and seminars are structured opportunities for educators to learn from facilitators or leaders with specialized expertise as well as from peers. They bring together educators from the same school or district or from different locations in a region or the country for common experiences and learning. They provide opportunities for participants to focus intensely on topics of interest for weeks (e.g., institutes) or for an extended period of time (e.g., courses). Workshops and seminars tend to be offered for shorter periods of time and address more discrete learning goals, such as learning to use a particular set of lessons or try a new assessment strategy. Workshops typically include more experiential or hands-on activities through which participants engage with new ideas and materials. Seminars tend to be more oriented to sharing knowledge and experiences through discussions and reactions to others' practice or research results. Depending on the learning goals for a particular group, a professional developer might choose to combine one or more of these strategies, such as combining a multiweek institute with a quarterly seminar series.

Whether implementing a workshop, institute, course, or seminar, it is critical that each be designed to include principles of effective professional development. Too often, they are characterized by passive learning or "sit and get" approaches that do not meet the needs or the interests of the participants. In the book *Designing Successful Professional Meetings and Conferences in Education* (Mundry, Britton, Raizen, & Loucks-Horsley, 2000, pp. 6-8), the authors identify features of effective learning sessions like workshops, institutes, courses, and seminars. These are:

- Clear purpose and outcomes: Participants know the goals, expectations, purposes, and benefits of the session(s).

- Value: The session offers value to the participants by addressing their goals for learning and growth.

- Variety: A variety of learning activities are combined that engage participants and appeal to different learning styles.

- Networking: Session(s) provide time for participants to interact with each other and build relationships with new colleagues.

- Effective use of time: Effective sessions make "every minute count." For example, lunch discussions can be tailored to help participants process the content of the morning and to network.

- Quality of leaders and facilitators: The facilitators know their content well and are skilled in effective adult learning methods. They understand and respond to the goals of the participants.

- Ongoing evaluation: Sessions are evaluated daily and feedback is used to make adjustments and enhance future sessions.

- Quality of content and design: The content is "credible, sound, current, and interesting."

- Resources: Participants get access to print or electronic resources that extend their learning and provide them with reference material to use in the future.

- Products: Participants are guided to develop artifacts or products that reflect what they are learning. These include plans, conceptual frameworks, assessments, or maps of their progress or thinking.

- Right audience: The session communicates clearly about its goals and purposes to target the right people for participation.

Optimal workshops, institutes, courses, and seminars also reflect what is known about effective adult learning (Mundry, 2003; Regional Educational Laboratories, 1995), including the following:

- Opportunities for learners to provide input to the content of the workshop, institutes, courses, or seminars and understand the purpose for learning the content that will be addressed

- Time for reflection, predictions, and explorations

- Multiple modes of presentations and information processing and opportunity to address real problems or challenges

- A respect for the expertise adults bring and activities that encourage all to share their knowledge

- Support and feedback from people with expertise

- Connections between new concepts and information and current knowledge and experience

- A safe environment to try new ideas and approaches

Designers should keep these features, as well as the principles of effective professional development discussed in Chapter 2, in mind as they develop workshops, institutes, courses, and seminars that meet the intended goals of the designers and the learning needs of the participants.

> **KEY ELEMENTS FOR WORKSHOPS, INSTITUTES, SEMINARS, AND COURSES**
>
> - Clearly stated goals are communicated to the participants.
> - A leader or facilitator guides the participants' learning.
> - Group structures necessitate a collegial learning environment.

Key Elements

Clearly stated goals are communicated to the participants. Leaders of effective workshops, institutes, seminars, and courses communicate with participants about the goals of the learning experience prior to and during the sessions. They receive input from learners before setting goals so that the learning experience addresses the learners' needs.

A leader or facilitator guides the participants' learning. The leader or facilitator also guides and supports the participants' learning, often by being a primary source of expertise or bringing in other information through readings, consultants, the participants' experiences and knowledge, and structured experiences.

Group structures necessitate a collegial learning environment. Because these strategies are intended for groups of people, the learning environment should be designed so that it is collegial for participants to learn from one another and from the leader of the session.

Often disparaged as the "traditional form of professional development," workshops, courses, institutes, and seminars, like other professional development strategies, can range in quality, depending on the extent to which they reflect the principles of effective professional development and incorporate effective adult learning strategies. At their best, they provide adult learners with important and relevant new knowledge and opportunities to try new ideas, practice new behaviors, and interact with others as they learn. The following paragraphs describe what these strategies look like "at their best."

Workshops, courses, seminars, and institutes can use the "training" model, which has a strong research base for helping teachers learn new behaviors that contribute to improved student learning (Joyce & Showers, 1988). This model includes the following steps: explanation of theory, demonstration or modeling of a skill, practice of the skill under simulated conditions, feedback about performance, and coaching in the workplace. An example of the application of this model would be training in cooperative learning strategies for use in science and mathematics teaching.

These structures also lend themselves to a teaching or learning model for developing conceptual understandings, such as those on which many science curricula are based. For example, a model developed by the

National Center for Improving Science Education (NCISE) suggests the following four stages: invite, explore, explain, and apply (Loucks-Horsley et al., 1990). These stages can help structure a multiday institute, a workshop or seminar series, or a course. Table 5.2 indicates how professional developers can structure appropriate activities at each stage.

For example, during a five-day professional development institute on inquiry in environmental education, participants might engage in a two-day inquiry into participant-generated questions about a beach area (invite); two days of analysis and limited tryout of activities from different environmental education curriculum materials (explore); discussion of that analysis with regard to questions of congruence with the *National Science Education Standards* (NRC, 1996a), clarification of the scientific concepts and processes embedded in the activities, and an opportunity to share insights (explain); planning for tryout in participant classrooms (apply); and follow-up, in-classroom coaching and support group meetings to review, revise, and retry (apply and recycle).

Another conceptual model for learning goals, the "5 Es Model" (Bybee, 1997), reflects a similar flow of learning phases that includes engagement, exploration, explanation, elaboration, and evaluation. Either the NCISE or 5 Es Model can be used by professional developers to guide the design and implementation of effective sessions that incorporate what is known from research and practice about effective workshops and seminars as strategies for adult learning.

By nature, courses are ongoing, which provides time for teachers to practice new ideas and behaviors and return to the course setting to reflect together on problems and successes. Effective course instructors provide time for these important reflections and help participants generate clear ideas about how they will apply what they learn. Likewise, the best workshops, seminars, and institutes are designed to include a variety of modes through which learners can process information. These include journal writing, analysis of case studies, role playing, small group discussions, modeling lessons, engaging in problem solving, and exploring questions. Learners have ample time for follow-up opportunities to discuss the application of their learning, solve problems, and generate new ideas for teaching.

In addition, the most effective workshops, institutes, seminars, and courses are designed to include a variety of learning and engaging activities. As Mundry and associates (2000, pp. 29-40) describe, there are diverse learning activities that engage participants in active learning, including break-out sessions, carousel brainstorming, case study, commitment statements, consensus decision making, demonstration, dialogue and discussion, ground rules, fishbowl, group reflection, ice breakers, interviews, observers, panel presentations, poster sessions or exhibits, product development, questionnaires, readings, review or reflection worksheets, "sea-

TABLE 5.2   What the Professional Developer or Designer Does

Stage	Consistent With the Model	Inconsistent With the Model
Invitation	Creates interest Generates curiosity Stimulates dialogue Raises questions Elicits responses that uncover what the teachers/learners know or think about the concepts/topics	Explains concepts Provides definitions and answers States conclusions Provides closure Lectures
Exploration, discovery, and creativity	Encourages the teachers/learners to work together without direct instruction from the professional developer Provides or stimulates multiple opportunities or experiences to explore an idea, strategy, or concept Observes and listens to the teachers/learners as they interact Asks probing questions to redirect teachers'/learners' investigations and dialogues when necessary Provides time for teachers/learners to grapple with problems and challenges Acts as a consultant to teachers/learners	Provides answers Tells or explains how to work through the problem Provides closure Tells the teachers/learners that they are wrong Gives information or facts that solve the problem Leads teachers/learners step by step to solutions
Proposing explanations and solutions	Encourages teachers/learners to explain concepts and definitions in their own words Asks for justification (evidence) and clarification from teachers/learners Formally provides definitions, explanations, and new labels (e.g., through lectures) Uses teachers'/learners' previous experience as the basis for explaining concepts	Accepts explanations that have no justification Neglects to solicit teachers'/learners' explanations Introduces unrelated concepts or skills

SOURCE: Loucks-Horsley (1996, p. 88). Adapted from the National Center for Improving Science Education, *The High Stakes of High School Science*, 1991.

sonal partners," simulations, small group activities or exercises, speeches or formal presentations, video viewing, and writing a "think piece."

Implementation Requirements

Expert knowledge. Knowledgeable people must be available to provide or facilitate access to the knowledge that learners will gain during the sessions.

Time away from the workplace, with arrangements for substitutes or stipends. Most workshops and seminars meet during regular school hours and require that a teacher have a substitute for the classroom and teachers usually participate in courses and institutes during nonteaching time (such as the summer or evenings and weekends).

Curriculum or syllabus. Learners should know what content they will learn through the professional development experience.

Access to resources and materials. Depending on the content of the course, workshop, institute, or seminar, classroom materials, student work, texts, or articles are needed.

Incentives. There are a variety of incentives that can be offered for participation, such as teachers being given stipends when time is taken beyond regular school hours or graduate or professional development credit.

Examples

The Math Learning Center at Portland State University offers a series of courses related to the Visual Mathematics curriculum. The courses are designed to help teachers become familiar with visual thinking (a hallmark of the curriculum) and its role in the teaching of mathematics. They include readings related to philosophy of the curriculum and current mathematics reform and considerable exploration of mathematical content based on a constructivist approach to learning. The courses put teachers in the role of learner and give them opportunities to explore mathematics concepts and connections, discuss solutions and strategies with their colleagues in a manner similar to that which they would use with their own students, and develop powerful representations or mathematical abstractions. The courses are offered nationwide by workshop leaders (often classroom teachers) who have considerable personal experience using the curricular materials.

In San Diego, California, at a five-day workshop conducted by a mathematics educator from San Diego State University, elementary school teachers learn geometry through immersion in mathematical problem solving. The workshops are designed to increase teachers' understanding of geometry by exploring two- and three-dimensional shapes. The mathematics educator has designed the explorations so that teachers engage in learning in the ways in which they will teach in their classrooms. They engage in a variety of learning situations, including small group discussions and sharing of ideas between groups.

At the beginning of the workshops, the facilitator asks teachers to respond to the questions, "What is a cube? What are the characteristics of a cube?" The responses reflect what individual teachers and the group as whole already know and understand about the content. Based on the responses, the facilitator has a better understanding of how to guide their subsequent learning. The facilitator then asks the teachers to find all of the combinations of "nets"—the cube laid flat. Using manipulatives, small groups begin exploring and creating tables and charts to document the nets that they identify.

As the teachers work, the facilitator moves to each table and asks probing and clarifying questions. When groups claim that they have identified all of the possible nets, the facilitator asks, "How do you know that you are done? What is the proof that you are done?" Often, this leads into discussions concerning how to respond to students who claim they are done. Teachers delve into assessing students' understanding and discuss how to determine when students are simply applying an algorithm or are grappling with the underlying concepts.

Throughout the five-day workshop, teachers explore important mathematical content, develop their own ideas and solutions to problems, and interact with each other and with the facilitator in a collegial environment. These workshops immerse teachers in effective adult learning strategies and help them apply their new learning to their teaching of geometry in their own classrooms.

Commentary

One-time workshops or seminars are unlikely to result in significant, long-term change in teacher practice (Fullan, 1991; Joyce & Showers, 1988; Little, 1993). Change requires multiple opportunities to learn, to practice, and to reinforce the use of new behaviors. In addition, the sessions should incorporate opportunities for teachers to surface and challenge their existing beliefs and assumptions and resolve conflicts that result when new ideas and practices do not fit with existing beliefs. Too often workshops, institutes, and courses focus only on adding new skills and methods without helping teachers to understand underlying beliefs that support their use or help them know what practices they should discard as they take on new approaches. Although a single workshop may be a good kick-off for learning and can result in new knowledge or awareness on the part of participants, additional opportunities are needed for producing meaningful change in beliefs and teaching behaviors.

As stand-alone strategies, workshops, institutes, courses, and seminars fall short of providing a well-rounded professional development experience. It is wiser to combine workshops and courses with other strategies to enhance the learning experiences of the participants. For example, one workshop on mathematical pedagogy is insufficient for teachers to alter their practices. They also need opportunities that help them to translate their learning into practice (e.g., by modifying their curriculum), to actually use their new knowledge (e.g., with support from coaching), and to reflect on their practices (e.g., through examining student work resulting from the use of the new practices). When the principles of effective professional development are incorporated into the design of workshops, institutes, courses, and seminars and are then combined with other strategies, they yield greater benefits.

Resources

Garmston, R. J., & Wellman, B. M. (1999). *The adaptive school: A sourcebook for developing collaborative groups.* Norwood, MA: Christopher Gordon.

Math Learning Center, Portland State University, Portland, OR (phone: 503-725-4850).

Mundry, S. (2003). *Honoring adult learners: Adult learning theories and implications for professional development.* In J. Rhoten & P. Bowers (Eds.). *Science teacher retention: Mentoring and renewal.* Arlington, VA: National Science Education Leadership Association/National Science Teachers Association..

Mundry, S., Britton, E., Raizen, S., & Loucks-Horsley, S. (2000). *Designing successful professional meetings and conferences in education: Planning, implementation, and evaluation.* Thousand Oaks, CA: Corwin.

WestEd and the WGBH Educational Foundation. (2003). *Teachers as learners: A multimedia kit for professional development in science and mathematics.* Thousand Oaks, CA: Corwin Press. (See Tape 4, Program 3, *Immersion in number theory, PROMYS, Boston University, Boston,* and Tape 2, Program 4, *Immersion in spatial reasoning, San Diego State University, San Diego, CA.*)

6

The Design Framework in Action

W hy did professional development designers in Cambridge, Massa-chusetts, decide to implement a districtwide curriculum implementation strategy while the City College Workshop Center staff in Harlem, New York, opted for immersion? Why did a statewide kindergarten through sixth-grade mathematics reform initiative in North Carolina choose curriculum implementation while California's middle school mathematics effort focused on curriculum replacement and networking? Why did a national high school science program go the route of curriculum development?

This chapter describes the decision-making process of five different professional development programs. It is based on writings by and interviews with program developers. These professional development designers provide us with the rare opportunity to see the "artists" at work. We learn about more than their final products, if there ever are any *final* products. We learn how and why they and their colleagues made the decisions they did. We see the design framework presented in Chapter 1 come alive as these professional developers explain how knowledge and beliefs influenced the design of their programs, how they took into consideration features of the context, and how the planning cycle unfolded from committing to vision and standards to evaluating. And, as we unravel the process, we learn more about the complexities and realities of planning for effective professional development not just in these five unique instances, but, to the extent that they act as mirrors, in the readers' settings as well.

Figure 6.1. Design Framework for Professional Development in Science and Mathematics

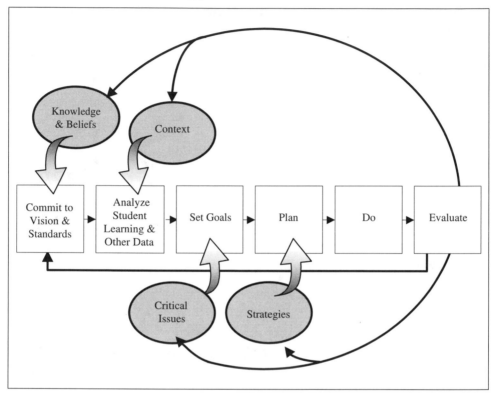

In Figure 6.1, we repeat the design framework to guide our journey through professional development design and implementation.

TAPPING THE KNOWLEDGE BASES, FRAMING BELIEFS: "WE STOOD ON THE SHOULDERS OF GIANTS"

When asked if they consciously drew on the knowledge bases about learning, teaching, and professional development, the five designers unanimously replied, "Of course." "In the first year," said Judy Mumme of the Mathematics Renaissance program, "a team of professional development leaders came together and formulated a set of principles to guide our work. We were pretty conscious of the knowledge base we were drawing on all along the way." Susan Friel of Teach-Stat echoed Mumme's sentiments: "We stood on the shoulders of giants. Our definition grew directly out of the Standards work."

Mumme's and Friel's responses were typical of the other designers. In every case, an important part of the planning process involved calling up the knowledge base and clarifying and articulating a set of beliefs, which influenced virtually every aspect of design. These professional developers could not imagine going about their design in any other way.

That did not mean that their beliefs were adhered to 100% of the time. Inevitably, compromises had to be made. But the designers were aware of the tensions, knew that they were making compromises, and remained committed to having their professional development program reflect, as consistently as possible, the beliefs that they held most dear.

Furthermore, as they carried out their work and reflected on it, the designers' own knowledge grew and some early beliefs gradually changed. "Belief systems are not static," noted Mumme, "they have been subject to ongoing reflection and modification."

What was the particular set of knowledge and beliefs that drove the design process for the developers and how did these influence their goals and plans? Some common themes cut across each of the five cases. All shared a similar view about the nature of mathematics and science learning, a belief that all students and all teachers can be successful learners, and a commitment to principles of effective professional development. Each of these themes and their influences on design are explored below.

KNOWLEDGE AND BELIEFS ABOUT THE NATURE OF LEARNING AND TEACHING MATHEMATICS AND SCIENCE

"How did we want students to engage in mathematics and the learning process? That guided how we would go about our work with teachers," Mumme of Mathematics Renaissance simply stated. Each of the developers asked themselves the same question for mathematics and/or science. How they answered that question had a great deal to do with how their program took shape.

Susan Friel (1996) described the relationship between beliefs and program design for Teach-Stat as follows:

We [developers] spent a number of sessions articulating our beliefs and then framing a coherent curriculum that supported teachers learning statistics in an environment that both modeled and encouraged teachers' eventual use of the key components of teaching as articulated by the *Professional Standards for Teaching Mathematics* (National Council of Teachers of Mathematics [NCTM], 1991). To do this, we worked to get past the notion of putting together a set of activities that addressed selected statistical concepts because developing a list of activities did not address the process of teaching and learning that was believed central to the program. Two theoretical perspectives helped shape this direction. One was the conception of statistics as a process of statistical investigations and the articulation of the process by Graham (1987). The other was the introduction of the use of concept maps (Novak, 1984) as a way of assessing what teachers knew about statistics prior to and following the institute (p. 7).

For Hubert Dyasi and his colleagues at the Workshop Center, a passionate belief about the nature of science as inquiry led to their focus on educating teachers to become "confident science inquirers" by immersing them in the investigation of familiar phenomena:

> At the core of the Center's educational approach is the importance of experience and meaning in learning and the belief that each person is capable of inquiring and observing with meaning and understanding. . . . Concomitant with our beliefs about human capacity to learn and to create knowledge is our view that science encompasses both content and approach. Its contents are in the common materials and phenomena we encounter and the approach is inquiry built around observations and experience and around making meaning of them. Direct experience with phenomena of the world connects the content of science with children's curiosity, experiences, and observations outside the classroom (Dyasi, 1995, p. 1).

Dyasi and his colleagues believe that this approach to learning is as applicable to adults as it is to children:

> Principles of human learning are not different between adults and children; they learn through direct experience and by constructing their own meanings from those experiences and from previous knowledge. Teacher education must faithfully reflect the way you want teachers to teach. They must themselves experience the ways they will guide children.

This belief was shared by all of the developers, who crafted professional development experiences that closely paralleled those to be used in the classroom.

"ALL HUMANS ARE EDUCABLE"

> *We have to select strategies that give both students and teachers the opportunities to demonstrate their educability.*
>
> —Hubert Dyasi

Closely related to their understanding of the nature of mathematics and science learning were strong beliefs about the potential of all humans to master complex mathematical and scientific concepts and procedures. These permeated all the cases, but played out in the design of professional development in different ways. For instance, at the heart of the Workshop Center's work is a commitment to the belief that "all humans are educable." "The ways we were doing education in schools masked that," commented center director Hubert Dyasi. "We were using strategies that were uni-dimensional. We have to select strategies that give both students and teachers the opportunity to demonstrate their educability." This belief is another underpinning of the center's immersion strategy, which makes deep under-standings of science content and process accessible to Harlem's diverse teacher and student populations.

Equity concerns influenced Melanie Barron, director of science in the Cambridge public schools, to choose a different strategy: curriculum implementation. She designed a centralized program to implement science-inquiry-based units of study across the curriculum. Barron explained: "You need clear city-wide goals, objectives and curriculum for what all children are to be taught. Then you need school-based technical assistance and support to the teachers." Karen Worth, who worked with the district from the Education Development Center (EDC), added: "If you don't require science from the center, not all teachers will teach it. If it is not mandated, some students won't get it." These beliefs determined Barron's decision to develop a team of science staff development teachers to provide ongoing support to teachers in every elementary school across the district. The combination of a mandate and a strong network of support, composed of both school and district-based staff developers, was Cambridge's approach to ensure that all students receive quality instruction in science. (Note: Both Barron and Worth speak about the Cambridge program in this chapter.)

The mathematics reform programs mirrored the science programs' commitment to excellence and equity. "None of it [reform] will matter unless it improves learning for all students; regardless of race, gender, or class," writes Judy Mumme and her colleagues from the Mathematics Renaissance (Acquarelli & Mumme, 1996). This belief strongly influenced the initial selection of the grade span for intervention, because the middle grades are often where decisions about a child's future are made. Furthermore, a concern with equity influenced both what strategy was chosen—curriculum replacements units—and how it was implemented.

We used curriculum replacement units to surface issues about equity. Teachers were asked to try the units with all of their classes. We purposely asked teachers from different settings to describe their experience. They were surprised that kids from a learning disabled class and a gifted class were doing similar things.

A principle of the Mathematics Renaissance program is that "issues of equity must permeate the fabric of staff development." Mumme provides two examples of how that looked for participants at all levels of the program:

> As uncomfortable as it often makes participants, meetings of teachers [and] cluster leaders . . . tackle issues of equity head on, sharing information, data and statistics about inequalities, confronting their own beliefs about tracking, or discussing examples of race, gender, and class discrimination in mathematics classrooms.
>
> At a March cluster meeting one teacher reported, "ESL students don't always have the words to write down but they definitely have the ideas. We let them talk about what they're going to write before they write it. Sometimes we let them dictate their words to someone else." Other teachers reacted to her comment, many nodding heads and taking notes. Teachers also learn to identify their own behaviors that can disadvantage females (e.g., calling on males more often and asking males probing questions). They may discuss the implications of the belief that "all children can learn," and probe the inconsistencies that exist between their beliefs and actions. (Acquarelli & Mumme, 1996, p. 481)

KNOWLEDGE AND BELIEFS ABOUT TEACHERS

Developers were inspired by teachers' capacity to learn, lead, and change. "We have strong beliefs that all kids are capable of engaging in quality mathematics," remarked Mumme. "But the temptation is to not believe that about teachers. We knew we could not write off any teachers."

An explicit principle of the Mathematics Renaissance program is that "all teachers are capable of making the changes." As a result, the program targets all teachers at a school, not just the most innovative or eager. It also employs strategies and structures to remove, as much as possible, obstacles to teacher change. This was, in part, the thinking behind the choice of replacement units, which provided teachers with the concrete "stuff" to take back to their classrooms that they were clamoring for, but were also used as a catalyst for teachers to rethink their own practices and beliefs.

Similarly, the City College Workshop Center program was designed explicitly to contradict prevailing opinions that members of minority groups, such as residents of Harlem, lack the intellectual capacity to understand science. Through its approach of firsthand inquiry, teachers generate investigatable questions, plan and conduct investigations that sharpen direct observation, and make meaning out of inquiry experiences. As a result, they become inquirers into school science as well as into their own learning and teaching. These experiences prepare them to implement new approaches in their classrooms, improve their attitudes toward science, and lead professional development workshops for other teachers. "Of course, they can do this because they are humans. Teachers have been incapable only because they have not had the opportunity to do this," argues Dyasi.

A strategy that relies on teachers to develop curriculum has to be rooted in respect for teachers' capabilities, an explicit belief of Global Systems Science (GSS). GSS brings teachers together to codevelop curriculum with staff of the Lawrence Hall of Science. Teachers field test curriculum units first, before ever convening, and come to a summer institute to share their experiences and feedback on the curriculum. Then they create new activities and assessment instruments. "We have a strong belief in the importance of trusting teachers and respecting their craft knowledge. When we do that, we get the best product and the best performance from the teachers," commented developer Cary Sneider.

While GSS relies on teachers as curriculum developers, other cases emphasize developing teachers as staff developers. Teach-Stat trained a cadre of 84 "statistics educators," teachers who serve as resources to other teachers across North Carolina. Cambridge is nurturing school-based liaisons, teachers who have a role supporting other teachers in their building in implementing the curriculum, as well as district-based staff developers, former teachers released full-time to provide training and technical assistance districtwide. Mathematics Renaissance is heavily focused on developing its 70 cluster leaders, who, in turn, provide support to 350 schools. "Teachers are the best leaders of other teachers," Mumme stated, summarizing what each of the developers believe and exemplify in their goals and plans.

KNOWLEDGE OF EFFECTIVE PROFESSIONAL DEVELOPMENT

It is not hard to see how the designers drew heavily on what is known about effective professional development. Principles of effective professional development summarized in Chapter 2 are obvious aspects of all the programs. Clearly, each of the programs was driven by a well-defined image of effective classroom learning and teaching, provided teachers with opportunities to develop knowledge and skills to broaden their teaching approaches, mirrored methods to be used with their students, and prepared teachers for leadership roles. The Workshop Center designed a program that embraced the idea that teachers must experience science learning that reflects the national standards and provides opportunities for all students to learning challenging science content through inquiry. The GSS program grounded teacher learning in their own practice by supporting teachers to try out and reflect on their use of a new curriculum. The Cambridge program explicitly linked their efforts to the overall system by building support for improved science learning and support for adopting and implementing new curriculum. Each of the cases provides evidence of their commitment to building and strengthening the learning community through development of leaders, ongoing dialogue about what is working and why, and a zest for ongoing learning.

How the cases embodied the important principle of continuous assessment is described later in this chapter.

KNOWLEDGE OF THE CHANGE PROCESS

Each of the developers was well schooled in the knowledge base on change. Several reported studying and referring back to Michael Fullan's work like doctors use *Gray's Anatomy*. Knowledge of the change process served as an important touchstone for these developers. It shaped their initial designs, steeled them for the chaos and complexity they faced during implementation, and informed their daily "diagnosis" and problem solving.

Because these professional developers shared a common understanding of change, their program designs had common hallmarks. They were all long-term endeavors. They were clear about the changes they were about. They addressed change at many levels, from the individual to the organizational. They had mechanisms in place for feedback and ongoing improvement. They provided different kinds of supports for learners over time as their needs evolved. However, exactly how the programs embodied a particular change principle varied widely.

Take, for example, the principle that "as individuals go through a change process, their needs for support and assistance change." Each of the programs designed different learning experiences over time to address participants' changing concerns, questions, and experience. Most typically, programs began with some kind of knowledge-building experience like the summer institutes in Teach-Stat, Mathematics Renaissance, or the Workshop Center. These were followed by opportunities for planning for implementation, classroom or clinical practice with coaching and feedback, and reflection with colleagues.

GSS, however, stood conventional wisdom about that sequence of learning experiences on its head. Participants' introduction to the program was not in a workshop, but in their own classrooms. Before ever coming to the summer curriculum development institute, teachers received the materials and taught units to their students. Then they gathered at Lawrence Hall of Science for a summer institute. The first phase of the institute was not knowledge building, as one might expect, but reflection on participants' experience teaching the program, which grounded the teacher learning in their own practice. Cary Sneider explained:

> We focused on experienced teachers and invited them to be creative, teach the material first, and then come back and talk about it. First

they reflected with other teachers and gave us feedback on the units. Then, after that, they were hungry for new knowledge. That's when they were most interested in seeing what earth scientists were doing and in gathering more information. Later, teachers were given the opportunity to plan for how they would adapt materials for use in their classroom when they used them again.

While staying true to the principle that professional development is "developmental," GSS's design capitalized on the questions and concerns teachers would bring to a workshop *after* experiencing a change in their classroom. The change literature, discussed more in Chapter 2, informs us that learners move through a sequence of developmental stages in their feelings and actions as they engage with new approaches. That is predictable. That made the designers sensitive to teachers' needs and questions as they learned. Then, based on the designers' experiences, they found that precisely what kinds of support teachers needed at each stage varied greatly, depending on experience level and the nature of the professional development program itself.

As much as their knowledge about change influenced their initial designs, it served another equally important purpose during implementation. It helped designers understand, cope with, and navigate through the resistance to change and the chaos they encountered as the change process unfolded. As Judy Mumme put it, "It gave us a language for what we were observing."

We saw chaos in classrooms and schools. Teachers were struggling to make sense of what was happening. Change didn't come out in coherent ways. There was a lot of fumbling around. We came to understand this as our version of what Michael Fullan (1991) called "the implementation dip." I'll never forget one teacher who entered the process feeling that he was a good teacher. By all accounts, he was. But his world was being turned upside down. All that he had been doing was called into question. Before, he was clear in his mind what to do. Now it was fuzzy. He lost his sense of efficacy—his ability to say to himself, "I'm a good teacher!"

Without a framework for understanding events like these, staff developers could easily become discouraged. For Mumme and her staff (and each of the developers we interviewed), the change principles they had studied offered them perspective and reassurance. They were able to step back and look at what might seem like a setback as a natural part of the process and possibly a turning point if managed well. From initial design to daily problem solving, change theory was not "book knowledge," but a valued guide and partner in designers' work.

The knowledge bases that the professional developers brought to their programs were indeed important in their design work. However, two themes emerge as we hear their stories. First, their own experiences proved an important source of knowledge. And, second, although they "knew" some things to be true, they were often called on to abandon that knowledge and make compromises. These themes are discussed below.

EXPERIENCE AS A SOURCE OF KNOWLEDGE

In addition to drawing on research and other literature, designers also tapped their own professional development experiences both as learners and staff developers. Hubert Dyasi described the process:

> You build a repertoire of experiences, which you bank. That is your database from which to select a strategy. You think, that approach worked because of this. That one didn't because of that. That takes you beyond guesswork to a more scientific, organized way of thinking.

Teach-Stat's decision to go with curriculum implementation, for example, was based, in part, on developers' analysis of why a previous effort at mathematics education reform they had been involved in had failed. Susan Friel explained:

> I had been involved in another effort where teachers were just trained in approaches to problem solving, but given no curriculum to implement. The results were that teachers went back to a very structured, didactic textbook. They couldn't take what they had learned and translate it into changes in the classroom. That's why I have a bias now toward curriculum implementation. I think you can do a lot of workshops around problem solving. But if teachers don't have something to go back and work with, eventually it won't work. Teachers don't have the time to transform the curriculum.

GSS developers' experience as teachers trying to develop interdisciplinary curriculum was the impetus for the design for GSS, according to Cary Sneider:

> Each of us on staff of the GSS project had considered ourselves "innovative" teachers in the past, and we had all spent many years developing hands-on activities in astronomy, physics, chemistry, and biology. But we reeled from the disorientation of our first experiences in interdisciplinary teaching. Our need to prepare new lessons would take us to unfamiliar territories in libraries and bookstores.

We had to be ready to switch from physics to biology as we went from one chapter to the next, or from science to economics and politics, so that we could follow up the implications of an issue instead of going on to "cover" the next science topic. If that was challenging for us in the supportive environment of a science center like the Lawrence Hall of Science, we realized it would be even more difficult for many teachers in the context of local and state school systems where the resistance to change is likely to be far greater. (Sneider, 1995, p. 5)

This experience informed GSS designers about what knowledge and skills teachers would need to implement an interdisciplinary program in their own classrooms. It also led to their choice of curriculum development as a professional development strategy. "We also hoped that involving teachers as co-developers would engage their commitment to the new program, and help them acquire a deep understanding of the principles on which it is based," Sneider continued.

Just as understanding the underlying principles of GSS was important to participating teachers, so was understanding the underlying principles of mathematics and science teaching and learning and professional development important to each of the professional development designers. They came to their "artist's palette" with knowledge of these principles as well as their own rich experiences as learners and professional developers. These gave rise to a set of beliefs that guided the moves and choices they made. However, staying true to those beliefs turned out to be more of a challenge than designers anticipated.

MAKING COMPROMISES

Tensions are inherent in the work. The challenge
is how to make them live comfortably together.
—Karen Worth

The designers started out with clearly articulated beliefs that influenced their goals and plans. But what happened when beliefs collided with reality or even with each other? The creative tensions around these conflicts made for some interesting dynamics.

The conflict between a belief in inquiry and the necessity to jump-start a change effort quickly was an important one in Cambridge. Designers settled on implementing the same commercial units districtwide, not because they believed that these units represented inquiry at its purest and best; they were simply a good place to start. The considerations were more practical—providing teachers with good materials, coordinating the logistics of materials support, coordinating a support system. Science director Melanie Barron explained:

> What was missing in Cambridge was a curriculum. We needed a way to get teachers engaged in teaching science, to get the kids learning and the teachers teaching. Many of them hadn't been doing it. We didn't have time to immerse them in inquiry. We wanted to get them familiar with a unit and then build in more reflection, inter-action, and autonomy over time.

Another compromise Barron made was to focus more strongly on lead-ership development rather than on broad-based teacher development. One can't do everything at the same time—even though there was a strong belief in developing teachers. Given the constraints of time and money, the Cambridge team decided to put the bulk of the resources into building the capacity of a smaller group—not all the teachers. The goal was to develop a structure to permanently sustain the program over time.

The Cambridge team members simultaneously grappled with the ten-sion between their beliefs about teacher professionalism and their decision to mandate a curriculum. They knew the curriculum needed to be owned by the teachers. At the same time that they were telling the teachers, "We want you to own this curriculum," they were telling them that they had to do these three units.

Furthermore, Cambridge professional developers felt that the system needed to have a centralized system to handle logistics and to maintain the quality and rigor of science for all students. There was a definite tension be-tween the two beliefs of teacher autonomy and centralized decision mak-ing. Barron was trying to balance them by supporting teacher initiative, en-couraging their creativity, and providing professional development for teachers to develop their own strand of the curriculum. They were not mutually exclusive, but they were difficult to reconcile.

Similar conflicts characterized the design of the Mathematics Renais-sance program. Regional director Kris Acquarelli and Renaissance director Judy Mumme (1996) describe the planning as a process of balancing "ten-sions that are inherent in our work" (p. 479). For example, the belief that change needs to be systemic and fundamental often collides with teachers' needs. As they write in their case later in this chapter:

> "I do not want to be gone from my classroom for days where I am not taught a specific unit that I can take back and use. My students lose every time I am gone." This teacher's comment is typical of many. How do you develop a deep understanding of the issues in mathe-matics education when teachers have a strong desire for things to take back, to add recipes to their files? Time spent exploring con-structivism may not feel like a day well spent to some participating

teachers. Short-term gains often limit long-term growth opportunities. (p. 480)

The decision to go with a curriculum replacement unit strategy grew out of this tension. Teachers would leave with "stuff" to try, not as an end but as a tool for their continuous learning. Like in Cambridge, Renaissance developers concede that they chose a strategy as a place to begin, not as their ultimate purpose.

Designers universally seem to struggle with being true to their beliefs. "That's just part of the design process," remarked Karen Worth. "Beliefs can't get played out purely. You have to decide what gets into the foreground, what into the background, and sometimes, what is the most expedient." Balancing beliefs with expediency has a great deal to do with the unique circumstances of a particular program—the community, policies, resources, culture, structure, and history that surrounds it—what is called context in our design framework.

CONTEXT

Design always has to be tempered with reality.
You want to both be realistic and push the
system at the same time.
                                        —Karen Worth

The context of the five cases varied widely—the state of California; Harlem, New York; multiple schools across the state of North Carolina; a national program based at the Lawrence Hall of Science in California; and Cambridge, Massachusetts, a small, urban school district. The different contexts helped to shape very different programs. But some common lessons emerged from their varied experiences: (1) Pay close attention to your context as you design, (2) watch for and respond to changes in context and needs as a program proceeds, and (3) help participants consider their own context as they implement changes. Each of these lessons is discussed in the sections that follow.

Pay Close Attention to Context as You Design

"Design always has to be tempered with reality. You want to both be realistic and push the system at the same time," explained Karen Worth. For example, in Cambridge, science director Barron would have loved to have school-based liaisons freed up from classroom responsibilities full-time or more than five district-based science specialists. The resources just were not there. So, working within the constraints of the resources available (nothing new for educators), she settled on two liaisons per school, who received stipends for their work and professional development time, but were not released from classroom responsibilities, and the five full-time district specialists. "Tempering design with reality," Cambridge ended up with a structure for developing teacher leadership and supporting curriculum implementation that was not perfect, but a real advance for the district nonetheless.

Context was not always constraining. In the case of Teach-Stat in North Carolina, designers were able to capitalize on preexisting infrastructure—the University of North Carolina's Mathematics and Science Education Network, centers across the state housed at ten of the state university system's campuses. Susan Friel explained how this contextual factor facilitated their design:

> The fact that these ten centers were available really influenced our design. The center's job was to be in touch with school districts in their geographic area. This was perfect for what we wanted to do—have university faculty help to prepare statistics educators who would in turn work with teachers in their districts. Using the structure of the centers, we were able to reach 450 teachers across the state and develop wonderful partnerships between teachers and university faculty.

Certain features of context were readily apparent and drove the design from the beginning. This was also true for the Mathematics Renaissance program. As a statewide systemic initiative funded in part by the National Science Foundation (NSF), the Mathematics Renaissance program had a political context that could not be ignored—the expectation of the funder. Its charge was to institute a process that would not just make a difference in schools, but would have a ripple effect, impacting multiple levels of the educational system, including state policy.

Judy Mumme described how that charge propelled their design process:

> As we thought about design, we had to consider those expectations. We had to reach a large number of schools. We had to be visible. We had to be viewed as more than a project. These considerations influenced our decision to go with a large-scale effort.
>
> The theory was that if you get a critical mass of schools heading in a particular direction, that pushes on the system, informs legislators, informs CDE [California Department of Education], and influences policy—"inside-out" systemic reform. We needed a design that had the potential for influencing policy at various levels. That affected how we solicited schools for participation, how we worked through the State Department, why we needed to remain neutral on

issues around specific instructional materials, and lots of other features of our design.

In other cases, designers wished they had been more attuned initially to certain aspects of their context—particularly parental and community concerns. Hubert Dyasi described how those concerns played out in Harlem:

In our context, Harlem, parents thought that anything that looked different was discriminatory. What was this funny thing we were doing—inquiry science? Why were their kids the guinea pigs? Oppressed groups often want what oppressing groups have. We had to find ways of addressing their concerns. We had to bring parents into the discussion.

Mathematics Renaissance initiatives also met with parental objections:

We had to redesign some of the focus of professional development. We paid more attention to helping teachers become more articulate about where basic skills were in the work they were doing. We made the false assumption that people would see that basic skills were getting taken care of. We also realized that our parent outreach component needed to be strengthened. We worked with each school to design activities to engage parents, including initiating Family Math.

While developers underscored the importance of being responsive to context, they also pointed out the danger of being too responsive. Judy Mumme offered an example from Mathematics Renaissance where designers' and teachers' needs were in conflict:

Sometimes we found that what the schools wanted wasn't what we thought was in their best interests. That felt uncomfortable. What we heard was "just give us more curriculum units." We felt what was needed were more philosophical underpinnings. We couldn't be slaves to context. We had to take it into consideration, but also try to reshape it.

Scanning contextual factors such as teacher and student needs, political expectations, parental concerns, policies, structures, and organizational culture helped designers ward off unexpected problems as well as take advantage of potential supports. But, beware, our developers learned. Just when you think you understand your context, it changes!

Watch for and Respond to Changes in Context and Needs as the Program Proceeds

> *Productive educational change, at its core, is not the capacity to implement the latest policy, but rather the ability to survive the vicissitudes of planned and unplanned change while growing and developing.*
>
> —Fullan (1993, p. 5)

Context is slippery. It is constantly changing, sometimes serendipitously, sometimes as a direct result of the professional development programs we design. What was right for one moment in time may not be right for another. The successful designers we talked to found that they had to constantly monitor their context to discern changes that signaled the need for redesign. What happened with the emergence of teacher leadership in the Teach-Stat program illustrated the need to remain flexible and make changes:

> Originally, the pilot teachers were going to be available to help [with the workshop] but not to teach. However, by the second summer, faculty and teachers had developed such a good working relationship that the model of a "professional development team"—faculty and teachers coteaching—naturally emerged and was very successful. This forced us to realize that you could back off and be flexible.

Cambridge science staff development teachers also found that teacher leaders' needs and capabilities changed over time. Melanie Barron explained:

> The more experience the liaisons had, the more they became rigorous determiners of what they do next. They became more reflective and more autonomous and were looking for different kinds of support, like small study groups. We couldn't have started there. The context wouldn't permit it. But we had to be ready when they were.

Context could be as close to home as the individual teachers you were working with or as removed as the national education scene. Hubert Dyasi noted that the momentum for mathematics and science education reform nationally had a dramatic effect on the Workshop Center's approach. As the national reform movement developed, so did the Workshop Center's approach to inquiry:

> What we are disseminating is not so strange now. Initially, we didn't want to scare people. Now we are more up-front. We have matured, too. Before, we were satisfied with having students uncover a phe-

nomenon. We didn't push much on conceptualization. Now we are getting more to the heart of the matter . . . the real nature of doing science. People think that hands-on is science. It's not just a set of steps. Science is a great intellectual activity. Our work now is truer to that.

Other contextual changes were less intentional or desirable, such as the school personnel changes encountered in the Mathematics Renaissance program. "Superintendents left. Principals were transferred. Key people kept changing. We had to invest a lot more time in relationship building," commented Mumme.

As California's state system discontinued its newly developed statewide assessment, the Mathematics Renaissance found itself missing one of the central elements it thought was in place to support reform. Mumme and her team were required once more to "regroup." Surviving the "vicissitudes of planned and unplanned change" was an essential skill for these designers of staff development. It was also important for their teachers, who faced the challenge of implementing change in the context of their own classrooms and schools. The programs found ways to help teachers meet this challenge, as the following example illustrates.

Help Participants Consider Their Own Context as They Implement Changes

Any multischool or multidistrict effort can appreciate the design problem GSS faced. Participants in their national curriculum development institute came from all over the country. GSS literally had to consider as many different contexts as participants. How could GSS make the program as relevant as possible to a variety of contexts and help participants successfully implement the program? Designers had some creative answers to that question, as they write in their case later in this chapter:

> *Principal:* Diane, I understand that you're excited about this new integrated program called Global Systems Science, but I'm concerned that some of our parents will worry that their children will do poorly on standardized tests if it replaces the usual science curriculum.

> *Diane:* Then it's about time we educate some of our parents about the need for science literacy concerning environmental issues. *National Science Education Standards* and our State Science Framework say we should spend less time teaching science vocabulary and more time helping our students relate science to the real world.

> *Jim:* I'm not convinced that students who take integrated science will miss out on chemistry, physics, and biology. We plan to present the same concepts we taught before, but in a meaningful context.

Students will still have labs, but they'll also debate the social implications of science and technology.

Principal: Now I didn't say I was against it, but I'll be the one to take the heat if our community is not convinced it's a good idea. Are you willing to present your ideas at the Parent-Teacher Association next Thursday evening? (Sneider, 1995, p. 1)

The above conversation did not take place in a real principal's office. It was a role play from the GSS summer institute, where teachers thought about what might actually happen when they went back to their school districts to implement the GSS curriculum. At the GSS summer institute, participants did not just learn about the curriculum. They studied principles of change and thought about how the principles would apply to their own particular school context.

This was one of several ways that GSS honored participants' different contexts at the national institute, as former director Cary Sneider explained:

Because we had as many contexts as school districts, we had to look at commonalities. We discovered that there were four different ways in which GSS was fitting in to the schools. The implementation strategy depended on which one was at play. For some schools, the first year of science was wide open and GSS easily slid in. Other schools were starting it as an experimental program with the expectation that students would like it. Students demanding the program would bring about the change. In other districts, there was enough top-down pressure to have non-track science, and they needed a program like GSS. At the other extreme, the teachers taught in a traditional school and they would sneak GSS into a traditional course. We addressed each of these realities at the institute.

Most important, participants came to the summer institute having already implemented units from the curriculum in their own classrooms. Discussions about GSS did not happen in a vacuum, but were grounded in the teachers' experiences. Participants gave feedback to the developers and designed their own activities and assessments based on what they knew from their experience would work best with their own students. In these ways, GSS was able to tailor their program to a diverse national audience.

The section above described how knowledge and beliefs and context influenced the professional development design process. But many questions about professional development design remain unanswered. What did that process look like? Who was sitting at the table? How much time did it take? What was the implementation of the program like and how did that fuel reflection and redesign? These are the focus of the next section, which takes a closer look at the four steps involved in program design as they played out in the five cases.

THE PROFESSIONAL DEVELOPMENT DESIGN PROCESS

Commit to Vision and Standards

Each of these designs was motivated by a vision of mathematics and science teaching and learning based on national standards. Earlier in this chapter, we discussed how all the designers drew heavily on the multiple knowledge bases and worked with their colleagues to articulate and clarify the commitments and vision on which their programs rested. The designers were themselves pathfinders and visionaries, who strengthened and spread their vision through their professional development programs.

For example, Hubert Dyasi is sometimes called the "founding father of inquiry," so far ahead of his time was he in envisioning teachers and students as confident science inquirers and, with his collaborators, devising learning opportunities for teachers to achieve that end. In his case later in this chapter, he notes that "the present focus of the center's work is on educating teachers to be confident science inquirers who understand the potential for science learning in the common everyday phenomena that capture children's interests." Many participants in the program came to embrace that vision as well. As one teacher wrote, "The center's modeling of what we were learning in the classes about classroom organization, social interaction, curricular inquiry, and observation gave me more confidence in the practicability of the ideas and allowed me to raise deeper questions about them and to try them in my classroom."

The Teach-Stat program was designed to enact the vision statistics teaching articulated in the *Professional Standards for Teaching Mathematics*. One of the early projects in this particular strand of standards-based mathematics, Teach-Stat was committed to teachers' learning statistics through a process of investigation and relevant hands-on applications and activities. Its success served as proof-of-concept that when teachers learned statistics in these "new" ways, they deepened their content knowledge and changed their classroom practice.

Judy Mumme articulated the central commitment of the Mathematics Renaissance in this way: "At its core was the commitment to increase access and success for students historically underrepresented, while holding high expectations for improving performance for all students." That commitment, along with a set of guiding principles, became the touchstone for all the design elements of the program and was ultimately realized in achievement gains for students.

Extending access and student success was also central to the vision of GSS. By engaging teachers as codevelopers of this new science program, the project enlisted 125 teachers in its mission to "change the current emphasis of high school science departments from preparing a small segment of the population for college to providing all of the nation's students with the skills they will need to thrive in the modern world." In the same vein, the Cambridge public schools initiative rested on its commitment to the *National Science Education Standards* and their local framework, based on the Massachusetts framework, for science in the elementary years. As teachers became involved in developing the local framework, implementing a standards-based curriculum, and leading the science reform effort, the commitment to this vision spread beyond the small cadre of project staff to many teachers throughout the elementary system.

Collect and Analyze Student Learning and Other Data

Each of these programs relied on analyses of students' and teachers' learning needs to frame program goals. For example, the Mathematics Renaissance made a decision to target middle school mathematics because of its role as the gatekeeper to high-level mathematics. They analyzed demographic and student achievement data to document a compelling need for mathematics improvement at these grade levels. They also knew that "curriculum at this level was a wasteland, and this area seemed ripe for development and exploration."

National standards placed a new emphasis on statistics as a content strand for elementary mathematics. At the same time, students performed poorly in this strand on national, state, and local assessments. Many students were not being taught statistics at all, and teachers were often poorly prepared in this content strand. These factors were influential in establishing goals of the Teach-Stat program. See also the City On A Hill example of a data-driven professional development design in Chapter 7.

Set Goals

You've got to know what you are going to do,
make a map, define end points and mileposts
along the way. Then you meander toward them.
—Karen Worth

Setting goals was an important launch point for the five programs, but not a process that bogged designers down. They agreed that without clear goals, they would have had no place to start and no reason to get involved. Also important was that goals were grounded in the expressed needs of participants and not just in the imagination of the designers. While all the designers engaged in some kind of process for figuring out what their vision was and then how to get from "here to there," they also warned against getting too caught up in the initial goal setting. As Cary Sneider explained, "You've got to start out with some goals. But goals evolve. The ones you start out with aren't the ones you end up with."

Plan

While planning for each of the five programs looked very different, three common themes emerged. Planning was collaborative, time-consuming and ongoing and often involved the use of external consultants. These themes are elaborated below.

Collaborative

Each of the developers described a collaborative planning process with a small, clearly designated core group that expanded when necessary to take in more input. Developers consistently involved participants in the decision making.

At the Workshop Center, the idea for the immersion program was developed by three professors at the college. They immediately brought in school people to see if there was a possibility of doing something. From then on, "we shaped the program together."

The planning group for Mathematics Renaissance was the regional directors. Judy Mumme recalled:

> They came together in several meetings with staff development folks. The first year of the SSI [Statewide Systemic Initiative] we brought cluster leaders in to the planning process. They put flesh on the model and advised us about what needed to happen. They were encouraged to talk to teachers about what they needed. It was an ongoing process of listening to teachers, administrators, and teacher leaders.

In the Cambridge public schools, reported Melanie Barron,

> The program began slowly. It was the decision to write a proposal that pushed the design process to the next stage. The original planning team was me, the director of science from the district, and the science staff development teachers, with assistance from consultants from EDC and others from MIT [Massachusetts Institute of Technology]. Once the proposal was funded and the liaison teachers became a reality, a number of them became involved with the ongoing planning.

Time-Consuming and Ongoing

Planning was time-consuming, sometimes painfully so. Susan Friel described the process for Teach-Stat:

> The first year was a planning year. We met as a group of five to seven in long sessions—two to three days. We drafted some material. I was intent on getting everyone's input. That was hard. I was criticized. People said I let things drag on too long. But it was worth it in the end, because we all "owned" the result.

Not only was planning time-consuming, it never stopped. Even when the programs were being implemented, they were simultaneously being redesigned. Mathematics Renaissance is a good example of the iterative planning process. "The regional directors went out and did the work. Then we would debrief and figure out what to do next," Mumme explained. Similarly, in Cambridge, Barron added, "The detailed planning was a constant back and forth among the science staff development teachers, the liaisons, the EDC consultant, and others from MIT."

Involving Outside Expertise

In Cambridge, Melanie Barron was convinced of the need for external partners. She brought to the job in Cambridge years of experience in collaborative work and was convinced of its importance at the institutional level, the professional level, and the personal level as well. "You can't do it alone. You need expertise and support internally and externally. A system cannot close its doors to the outside world. Any project is a combination of building internal capacity and injecting external expertise." In the case of Cambridge, Barron developed a relationship with nearby MIT. She also contracted with EDC for technical assistance. The resulting partnership between her and EDC has been a critical component of the program.

Involving stakeholders, taking time, and bringing in outside expertise were important aspects of developing a well-conceived plan for staff development. While planning was an ongoing process that continued after the programs were implemented, the staff developers' focus eventually shifted from planning to doing. Designers settled on a plan and set it into motion. Their plans were now ready to meet the test of implementation.

Do

What happened to professional development plans as they were implemented, how they unfolded over time as programs matured, and what new decisions were made and why is as rich a story as the initial design process. In every case, programs looked very different two to five years (or in the case of the Workshop Center, 30 years) into their implementation than they did on the drawing board. Over the 30-year history of the Workshop Center, the approach to professional development changed dramatically as staff developed and refined their immersion approach and added significant, new components to the program. In Cambridge, the basic program components remained the same, but took on new qualities as the staff and program matured. Finally, as the Mathematics Renaissance scaled up from 78 to 420 schools in five years, some program elements stretched and grew as the program grew while others, including replacement units, were abandoned as core strategies. The lives of these programs parallel survival in the natural world. Their capacity to adapt and respond to change was their greatest asset, enabling them to weather the inevitable storms of implementation. Their evolution over time is traced in the section that follows, as professional development designers describe key elements of their programs' implementation.

Workshop Center: Inquiring Into Inquiry

The Workshop Center actually did not start off with what is now its trademark—immersing teachers in scientific inquiry. It began in 1972 with Workshop Center staff engaging children in active learning strategies for language development in the corridors of Harlem's schools. The one condition center staff put on their work was that teachers keep the classroom doors open so other students and teachers could see what was going on in the hallways. The idea was that teachers would see change happening and want to try it themselves. It worked. Curiosity mounted as teachers heard children's busy chatter and saw the hallways cluttered with high-quality work. Many teachers were inspired and motivated to learn new strategies. But Workshop Center staff quickly learned that watching them work with children was not enough. Teachers needed experiences that would help them develop the capacity to do what they saw staff doing.

When the center moved into science education, center staff members drew on what they had learned—good and bad—from the early corridor program. Workshop Center director Hubert Dyasi elaborated:

> We knew we had to educate teachers directly to become inquirers. They would learn how to learn by using materials themselves at their own level. For a long time, that is what we did. After a while, however, we realized that teachers weren't implementing inquiry science in the ways they were experiencing it with us. They were tied to using the materials in exactly the ways we had used them. They weren't really engaging students in asking their own questions. Their mind-set hadn't changed.
>
> Then we remembered the corridor program. Teachers changed because they were following their kids. That's how they got won

over. This led us to add a series of Saturday sessions during the academic year with children. Sessions were taught by teachers with support from center staff. Following that, we had the teacher study groups to talk about what was happening with their kids.

The addition of two new strategies, teachers practicing with children and study groups, helped the program in two ways. First, it offered the teachers important professional development experiences that they needed to successfully implement inquiry-based learning. They had the opportunity to practice new techniques with feedback from center staff and reflect on their practice and classroom experiences. Second, the addition of the practice and study groups gave center staff more information about what teachers were doing and thinking so staff could become more effective at supporting teachers.

As center staff members observed and listened to teachers, they discovered another important stumbling block to successful implementation of inquiry science.

Teachers were often just giving the students materials and letting them go. They had difficulty raising questions that would draw children's curiosity to the important science. It seemed that the teachers weren't able to distinguish between what was valuable in the children's explorations and build on it and what was just play. Take the example of heating up water until it boils, and then continuing to apply heat. That is trivial until you begin exploring what it really means. You keep on supplying heat but the temperature of the boiling water doesn't change. Why not? What does it mean to "supply heat"? Is it the same as providing energy? If yes, is energy then different from temperature? What else can we do to find out about heat and temperature?

Teachers themselves did not necessarily know the science content. And, even if they did, the issue was not that they should tell it to the students, but rather that they should think about whether the students were ready to learn it. This observation led Workshop Center staff to another modification in the program—not a new strategy, but a change in how staff worked with teachers.

We needed to be more overt in pulling out what we were doing with the teachers. As we were doing the science with the teachers, we needed to say out loud, "The reason this is interesting is . . ." or to talk explicitly about the strands of inquiry from firsthand experience with phenomena, from asking questions, to collecting data, to making sense out of all this.

We also needed to help them see what the children were doing. For example, when children put materials in a certain way, we asked, "Why did you do that that way?" and refused the answer, "I was just doing it." Then we asked, "What did you see as a result?" Children often do not raise questions verbally; they act their questions out through what they do. The change for us was to be much more explicit about both the important science and the scientific process. When we did this, teachers began to open up about what their difficulties were. They started to raise questions about themselves. That's when we could open up the doors.

The Workshop Center has opened up many doors for students and teachers over its long history. And it is not only teachers and students who have been immersed in inquiry. It is the program staff members themselves, who have been engaged for the past 30 years in investigating and improving their own practice. As they learned more about what it really takes to "change mind-sets," they moved from the corridors to the classrooms and to New York City's living laboratory, improving on their workshops and adding new strategies to their professional development program.

Cambridge: Building Capacity

The professional development program in Cambridge developed quite differently and over a much shorter period of time. In contrast to the Workshop Center, the basic strategy of the program remained the same—the development of local leadership through a structure of district-based staff developers and school-based liaisons. However, as these leaders developed, their needs changed and so did the nature of the support provided for them. Five years into the project, the EDC consultant to the project, Karen Worth, reflected:

The five district-level staff developers' skills and knowledge have increased by leaps and bounds. We still meet once a week. But those meetings look very different now. I don't lead every meeting. The staff developers are more and more in charge of their own structure. Other kinds of interactions have been very important, like their intensive e-mail conversations. They are also more and more in charge of pieces of the program as a whole—the resource center, volunteers, the national gardening program, the bilingual program. And they are doing all the staff development and training for teachers; we are using no more consultants.

It is no surprise that the character of the training for teachers changed as district-based staff developers took it over and made it their own.

The summer institute has been greatly enriched. Trainers are not marching straight through the units now. As units are becoming more a part of the science program, staff developers are more interested in embellishing them. Every unit now has a field trip to a local resource. All the professional development is now delivered on site.

The school-based leaders, the liaisons, also moved in the direction of taking more control over the design of their own learning experiences. They wanted less whole-group activity and more small, diversified groups based on their emerging interests and expertise. By the fourth year, they were pursuing an area of focus through four active study groups on assessment, how to pilot test units, "Cambridgizing" the units through use of local resources, and peer coaching. The annual liaison institute was scrapped and the time and money were reallocated to group meetings and classroom visits throughout the school year.

It isn't that the topics the leaders were interested in changed over time. They just moved along a continuum from novice to expert in a whole variety of topics ranging from science content and pedagogy to leadership skills.

As liaisons and district staff developers in Cambridge moved along that continuum, structures for their own learning changed to accommodate them, offering them increasingly more autonomy and choice.

Mathematics Renaissance: Scaling Up

Scaling up from 78 to 420 California schools over a five-year period brought about inevitable changes in strategy for the Mathematics Renaissance. Teacher academies, for instance, the initial foundation for the work, disappeared after the first year despite their apparent success. The academies brought teachers together from across the state to work with students in the morning and debrief the experience in the afternoon. The teachers involved were enthusiastic about the opportunity to experience new curriculum with their own students and receive direct support in the process. So, why were they dropped? Judy Mumme explained:

They were a nightmare to administer. The first year, we involved 78 schools in eight to ten academies. The negotiations for stipends, time, locations were monumental. When we grew to 210 schools, we knew that we couldn't pull it off. We continued to have academies whenever we could, but they were dropped as a primary strategy. Instead, we relied on two-week summer institutes and one- to two-day workshops during the school year.

Growing from 78 to 210 schools in one year resulted in other changes as well. The original support structure of seven regional directors (one for every 11 of the first cohort of schools) could not possibly meet the needs of an additional 132 schools. Three more regional directors were added in the second year. But even ten regional directors could not make frequent enough visits to all the schools and build the necessary personal relationships with the teachers. So, a whole new structure was instituted—the cluster leaders.

> Out of the initial 78 schools, we took 57 promising teachers who showed leadership potential and created a cadre of cluster leaders. They were released from the classroom for 35 days to provide direct support for other teachers. That meant one cluster leader for every five schools. This move was based on the belief that personal relationships were critical.

With the emergence of cluster leaders and the expansion of regional directors, another need arose, which helped to shape the program for the next four years.

> The need for ongoing professional development for leaders cannot be understated. This is perhaps one of the central lessons we have learned thus far. Leaders must have opportunities to reflect on their work, learning from one another the crucial lessons of leadership for reform. They constantly need to be challenged as learners, expanding their own understanding of mathematics, teaching, and learning. The initial design of the Renaissance failed to take this into account and much of the statewide professional growth opportunities have been funded catch-as-catch-can. (Acquarelli & Mumme, 1996)

In the third year, the project did not grow in numbers of schools (although the number of teachers involved doubled). It was an opportunity to refine the work more and respond to problems that emerged.

> One of the problems we observed was that much of teachers' time and attention was focused on management issues. This distracted from getting at meatier issues about how kids were learning and experiencing mathematics. So, we developed workshops on setting up classroom environment, cooperative learning, managing extended tasks, and writing in mathematics. We asked all continuing teachers, instead of doing new replacement units, to do the same unit, only this time to focus more on kids' learning. There was a lot of resistance to this. They wanted more replacement units. They wanted to cobble together a whole curriculum. Their intent was to permanently replace their curriculum. Our intent was to provide more in-depth professional development experiences.

In the fourth year, the project grew in breadth and depth. As more schools were added and new teachers joined from participating schools, project staff had a pleasant surprise:

We thought new schools and new teachers from old schools were going to be less sophisticated and require more intensive work. That didn't bear out. The new teachers were quite sophisticated partly because of the spreading effect of our work beyond those who directly experienced it.

By the fifth year, the Renaissance faced the monumental challenge of maintaining the quality of an effort that had grown to 420 schools—with about the same number of cluster leaders and regional directors. A key strategy was continuing to emphasize the professional development of the cluster leaders, despite their limited time on the project.

The professional development of the cluster leaders grew more important over time. It was critical that they had professional growth opportunities, which we continually had to balance with their classroom teacher role. They were now only released from their classrooms for 30 days because of concerns that they were away too much. We also realized that the coaching role was an important one, and provided more professional development for them in cognitive coaching. We asked the cluster leaders to play a coaching role with each other. Here again time got in the way. Because of that, it was the least uniformly effective strategy—one we wished we could have done better. Despite the difficulties of their role, over the life of the project, the cluster leaders grew into a remarkable group of people.

The fifth year brought another major challenge to the project. The state of California adopted instructional materials, rendering the Renaissance's central strategy—the use of replacement units—irrelevant for adopting schools. In response to schools' changing and diverse needs, the Renaissance provided three choices for participation. Schools that adopted instructional materials were clustered and provided with professional development in how to use them effectively. Schools that were still interested in replacement units continued with professional development related to their use. And, in schools that were interested in more site-based activities, cluster leaders focused on supporting a site-based facilitator, who took over some of the functions of the cluster leader.

Over the life of the Mathematics Renaissance, the project made several shifts in strategy. Due to the sheer logistics of scaling up, intensive summer teacher academies gave way to a focus on developing cluster leaders. As context and school needs changed, even the core strategy of the project—the use of replacement units—was replaced with a more flexible, multidimensional approach.

None of the changes in the programs described above would have happened without reflection. While absorbed in the "doing," these staff developers were simultaneously able to step back, gather data, and learn from their experience. How some of them did so is the subject of the next section.

Evaluate

Each of the programs had multiple mechanisms—formal and informal—for gathering data about how the program was going, which fueled a process of continuous reflection and redesign. Formal mechanisms included evaluations of events, teacher surveys, and case studies. Some of the programs had a project evaluator to carry out some of this work.

However, it was often the less formal, more frequent means of collecting data that had the biggest influence on program redesign—the one-legged chats in the hallway, the conversations in the teachers' room, or the visits to the classroom. Many of the programs had structures in place that allowed for a steady flow of information between the leadership and participating teachers. Karen Worth reported on how that worked in the Cambridge public schools:

> Melanie relied on collective observation and the wisdom of the staff development team. She regularly went to the liaisons and asked them what they wanted, what they liked, what their impressions of the staff response were. The staff development teachers were quite rigorous in collecting information from the liaison teachers, who had regular conversations with teachers and were in their classrooms. There was a constant back and forth between the teachers and the liaisons and between the liaisons and the staff development team.

The Mathematics Renaissance's system of 70 cluster leaders helped to ensure that regional directors stayed in close touch with what was happening in the 350 participating schools. Cluster leaders are classroom teachers with experience and credibility among other teachers. They were released from the classroom 35 days during the academic year and worked five weeks during the summer to carry out their role as professional developers. Close to the schools and teachers, these leaders provided regular input to the regional directors about how the work was progressing. In turn, regional directors used their input to reflect and redesign as needed:

> Regional directors meet monthly. Part of that meeting is an assessment of how things are going. We don't look at things at a macro level every time. But we do have an annual retreat for our cluster

leaders, where we take stock. And we have a retreat just for regional directors. We also visit classrooms on a regular basis and debrief among ourselves.

The Mathematics Renaissance also relied on outside reading to help regional directors assess their work. Mumme elaborated:

> We focused mostly on reading about change and the change process. A lot of what we read was validating of what we were observing, but gave us a language to talk about it. For example, Fullan's work on the implementation dip was reassuring. But we also made changes in our program as a result of outside reading. The literature was clear that peer coaching was important, but that was not part of our original design. We have now attempted to institute a cognitive coaching program.

Reflection often spurred developers to go back and redesign. This happened with the Teach-Stat workshops, as Susan Friel explained:

> The first year, we led people through the curriculum. But our experience was that participants had very diverse understandings of statistics. The second year, we decided to do something different. We got a big problem from one of the modules. We found out what teachers' prior knowledge was of the mathematics involved. Then we designed the workshop experience to build on that knowledge. We had to find out more about where people were coming from first.

External evaluators collected valuable information about the quality and results of these programs, enabling the designers to make improvements and enhance program effectiveness along the way.

None of the programs discussed in this chapter moved neatly through the design process. They inevitably met up with the "vicissitudes of planned and unplanned change," discovered design flaws, were temporarily out of synch with teachers' needs, or underestimated what it took to manage change. But two factors led to their eventual success. Because they went about the process systematically, they left the starting gate with good designs—programs that were grounded in sound principles of teaching, learning, and professional development, crafted from combinations of traditional and unconventional strategies, and tailored to their own unique contexts. And they never stopped trying to get better. They were able to "treat problems as their friends" (Fullan, 1993), use data to inform decision making, learn from their mistakes, and improve their initial design. They put the decision-making framework described in this book to work—not as a prescription, but as a map to help them navigate the chaos of improving mathematics and science education.

DESIGN FRAMEWORK IN ACTION CASES

As mentioned several times in this book, the basis for the development of the professional development design framework came from work with five collaborators who conduct teacher learning programs in mathematics or science. The collaborators' complete cases of professional development design and implementation, which are referred to throughout this book, are included in the next section of this chapter. A summary at the beginning of each case highlights the components of the professional development design framework that are addressed by the case. (See Design at a Glance, Tables 6.1–6.5.)

PROFESSIONAL DEVELOPMENT CASE A: THE WORKSHOP CENTER AT CITY COLLEGE OF NEW YORK

Hubert M. Dyasi
Director, Workshop Center
City College of New York

Rebecca E. Dyasi
Professor of Science Education
Long Island University, Brooklyn, New York

The Context

The Workshop Center is an academic unit at the City College, City University of New York. Lillian Weber, who was a professor at the college, founded it in 1972. Its work has always been centered on the professional development of educators to make their classrooms rich and suitable contexts for inquiry-based learning in general and in science education in particular. A major portion of the center's work takes place in Harlem and in the school districts of New York City, drawing teachers from the city's boroughs. In the past, many minority children and teachers from these communities have been described and analyzed as lacking understanding of science, even sometimes the capability to develop it. Staff members of the center do not accept that analysis and assert the capacity of all children for active, quality educational development, and descriptions of the center's work are a record of what it actually does to back up the nonacceptance of that analysis. It is a record of building teachers' understanding and acceptance that difference does not mean incapacity, a record of educating teachers to acquire a deep understanding, through their own experience, of the process of science inquiry in the context of common phenomena of the world, and a record of teachers learning to engage other learners in learning science through inquiry.

TABLE 6.1   Design at a Glance: Workshop Center

Level and content: Elementary science

Knowledge and beliefs highlighted: *National Science Education Standards*—Teachers learn science through inquiry and by constructing understanding through their own experiences; teachers learn in ways they can later use to engage students in science learning in the classroom

Context: University-based program working primarily with teachers in urban school districts

Goal: Educate teachers to be confident "scientific inquirers"

Primary strategies: Immersion in inquiry, workshops, partnerships

Critical issues: Ensuring equity, developing leadership, garnering public support

---

The present focus of the Workshop Center's work is on educating teachers to be confident science inquirers who understand the potential for science learning in the common everyday phenomena that capture children's interests. Three corollary aspects of the focus are teachers learning firsthand how to successfully conduct and make science sense from their inquiries into phenomena of nature, how children construct their knowledge of science as a result of inquiry into everyday phenomena, and how to successfully implement a science inquiry approach in their classrooms.

The teacher is the principal agent in the introduction, guidance, and maintenance of children's many-layered inquiry. To play this role well, teachers need a science education that is faithful to the practice of scientific inquiry and to human ways of learning and that gives them the reassurance that the physical reality of the world is a most legitimate subject of scientific inquiry. They need extended opportunities for sustained engagement with phenomena to see how their own inquiries unfold and to revisit earlier observations and notions in light of their explorations and growing understandings of inquiry. Furthermore, they need to conceptualize the role materials, activity, interaction, and reflection play in the inquiry process. Most important, teachers themselves need to *experience* what they are trying to develop in children—a scientific understanding of phenomena and an experienced-based vision of how they learn.

As part of its work, the center also conducts workshops for school principals and for parents. Workshops for principals introduce them to constructive ways of supervising teachers who use the inquiry approach in their classrooms. Those for parents familiarize them with children's roles as firsthand learners in science inquiry so that they can better support their children's efforts.

The Workshop Center's Approach to Professional Education

At the core of the Workshop Center's educational approach is the use of direct experience in learning through inquiry, generating science knowledge as a consequence, and the belief in each person's capability to inquire with meaning and understanding. In the center's view, science inquiry encompasses both content and approach. The content is derived from the common materials and phenomena learners encounter and from other sources. The approach is inquiry through which the learner is engaged in experiences, observations, and sense making in science. Learners gain scientific knowledge through a continual search for underlying commonalities in apparently disparate phenomena and refinement of their understanding by constructing and reconstructing what they know.

Direct experience with phenomena of nature helps learners to build connections among different phenomena, on the one hand, and between their conceptions of the world and actual events in the world, on the other. They refine their knowledge by asking more and better-focused questions that help them correct the limitations of their first understanding. Conceptual change and refinement by learners are common ingredients in elementary and middle school science practice; they have to be, because children's conceptions of the world undergo change as children grow and gain more direct experience with the physical world and with the worlds of symbols and ideas.

Framework of Professional Development

The Workshop Center's science education programs for middle and elementary school teachers educate teachers to be successful, confident, scientific inquirers in the world of school science. They enable teachers—through carrying out their own science inquiries—to become possessors and interpreters of significant science content and to be adept users of the requisite spoken and written language.

The educational practice adopted in the programs is based on four broad categories: primary or firsthand inquiry, representation, abstraction, and "science research council conference" (Dyasi, 1990).

Primary or firsthand experiential inquiry involves noticing and exploring phenomena and raising questions that can be answered through scientific investigations. It also incorporates designing and carrying out investigations, collecting and organizing data in scientifically reliable ways, and formulating testable scientific conclusions based on evidence.

Representation occurs in all four categories, encompassing as it does both verbal and written descriptions. Depending on the kinds of investigations carried out, it also incorporates use of pictures (e.g., charts, diagrams, graphs, equations), numbers (measurements), and other suitable descriptive mechanisms. Firsthand investigation and representation are necessary but not sufficient; teachers must also make scientific *abstractions* from data; that is, they should see testable patterns and generate possible scientific explanations consistent with evidence.

In a *science research council conference,* science inquiry teams or individual inquirers present comprehensive oral and written reports on their investigations to a critical but friendly community of peers. Reports include investigation question(s) raised and how they arose, designs followed (including equipment used, observations made, and the number of tests conducted), modifications made to the design along the way and why, data collected and scientific ideas they suggest, and unresolved questions. One of the peers or a staff member serves as moderator. After each report, the moderator highlights its scientific achievements, unresolved issues, and possible next steps.

By building teachers' understanding of science inquiry (how to raise questions that can be answered through scientific investigations, how to make meaning from inquiry experiences, and how that process is related to the acquisition of scientific concepts) and by building teachers' personal capacities to internalize the center's learning environments that helped them to develop and internalize scientific knowledge, the center's educational framework supports teachers to educate their students in a similar fashion and to create suitable rich learning environments for that to happen. The framework provides opportunities for teachers to see themselves as capable learners, mobilizing their capabilities, and succeeding in investigating and understanding what they had previously regarded as beyond their capacity.

Utilizing the approach they experience in the Workshop Center programs, teachers also learn to work directly with children, observing and recording how they learn, and responding positively to their inquiries and sense making. They leave the programs equipped with a rich repertoire of knowledge, practice, and resources necessary for an imaginative and educationally sound response to children's inquiries into natural phenomena.

In some of the programs, teachers also acquire knowledge and strategies for providing supportive leadership to their fellow teachers, thus creating communities of inquiring teachers in schools and in school districts.

In all programs, participants engage in science inquiry at their own level, often working in small groups and sometimes individually. In all programs, each participant maintains a written journal of his or her experience in the program. Since the journals include descriptions and reflections on the teachers' experiences in the workshop sessions, they facilitate recall and focus on participants' experiences and on special moments of the experiences that illuminate and further the teachers' investigative efforts. The journals also serve as a means of communication between each participant and the staff. They allow staff to revisit and "hold" for the teacher specific instances that illustrate their evolving understandings. As the staff learns directly from the teachers' or students' journals what they choose to recapitulate and what meanings they attach to events, staff members are better able to confirm insights into what each teacher might use to further his or her efforts. With this process, they are increasingly able to identify problems that might impede growth. Participants also study, write summaries, and reflect on professional literature associated with the learner-focused approach used in the workshops. They relate the readings to possibilities of engaging children in their classes in practical science inquiry.

A very significant component of all the programs is the staff. Staff members model what they wish the teachers to learn in science inquiry, curricular inquiry, social interaction, and classroom organization. They use instructional strategies such as engaging teachers as learners in social contexts characterized by both learning and instruction. Participants and staff work with children and parents and examine and evaluate science curriculum resources.

Staff members work as an integrated unit composed of experienced science educators, scientists, and selected public school teachers with many years of experience at various educational levels. The integrated style of work is exhibited in observable ways: Participants observe faculty relate to other faculty in planning sessions in the morning and they can "listen in" to faculty discussion in review sessions at the end of the day, they see faculty interaction in jointly led workshops and in response to a guest speaker, and they see in action how dialogue among colleagues occurs and what issues faculty continually think about. Participants also have the opportunity to relate to and see faculty members pursuing their own inquiries, and they share in the excitement of continuing professional development and learning. The way staff members interact with the teachers is based on the belief that the restoration of self-worth cannot be achieved through lectures and reasoned analysis, but through active engagement.

Two Illustrative Programs

The Lillian Weber Summer Institute

Open to college graduates regardless of field of study and to selected undergraduates, the Lillian Weber Summer Institute has been held annually since 1971. Its central feature is intensive immersion in a long-term investigation of a phenomenon over a four-week period to develop participants as competent inquirers and analytical students of their own individual learning. Selection of a phenomenon for investigation, the design of investigative activities, collection and organization of data, and construction of science knowledge from collected data are the responsibility of the participant in consultation with staff and with other participants.

During the introductory week, staff members highlight key elements that permeate successful inquiries, for example, an intense curiosity about a phenomenon, close observation and direct manipulation of the phenomenon, raising questions that increase a person's knowledge of the phenomenon, designing and carrying out ways to answer questions, formulation of some tentative generalizations that lead to further questions and perceptions of patterns, and generation of models demonstrating scientific understanding of phenomena. To give participants a general feeling for the elements of inquiry, staff members use a variety of mechanisms such as exploratory field trips on campus and in the neighboring park, visual exploration of portions of New York City from the top floor of one of the college buildings, and study of the total environment inside the Workshop Center. Inquiry activities that require participants to make general and specific observations of phenomena and report on them in small group sessions are assigned regularly, and assigned readings on the Workshop Center approach to inquiry in education, on issues in science learning and teaching, and on the nature of science are discussed.

In the second week, each participant selects an area of investigation, raises questions to pursue, and proceeds to design and to carry out investigations. Two- to three-hour blocks of time per day are devoted to these activities. Many selected areas of investigation are predictable (e.g., leaves, sound, or water), but others are more unusual (e.g., chewing gum or cracks on sidewalks). In addition to carrying out individual investigations, participants meet with staff in small (advisory) groups to share and discuss their individual investigations and to receive feedback from one another and from staff. Occasionally, invited specialists make presentations in general sessions involving all the participants, and at other times films on specific aspects of science inquiry are shown and discussed. Also during this week, a panel presentation by participants from previous summer institutes share their experiences and education they received when they were participants.

The third week is devoted to more intensive individual investigations. In the final week, each participant makes a professional presentation of her or his work during the institute. The audience of other participants contributes by raising questions and quite often by providing additional observations and data related to the investigations. Staff members also raise questions and make comments that highlight the scientific and educational significance of the work presented. At the end of the institute, each participant writes a reflective account of his or her institute experience.

Participants have had interesting reflections on their experiences in the institutes. For example, a former participant wrote:

As the staff talked about getting firsthand experience, I thought about the farm and all the things I had been fortunate enough to try

Figure 6.2. Fall Cycle of Activity

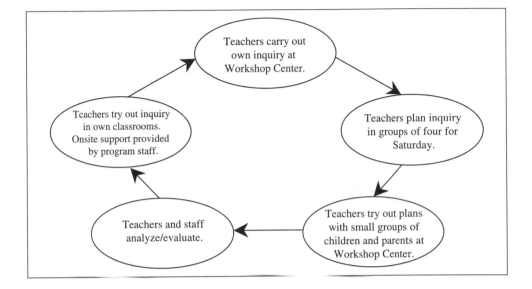

firsthand. . . . Whenever we went to the farm my cousins and I . . . captured frogs and tried to keep them alive, we looked at minnows in the fishpond along with dragonflies. For inner-city kids this was heaven! Little did I know that this was related to science.

Another stated her thoughts this way:

I caught the vision that real learning about the natural world comes out of a combination of inspiration and technique. I saw how much more meaningful and helpful secondary sources are when they are used to support firsthand learning. I learned about myself and about my own learning style. I learned that I could move back and forth between rhythms of action and reflection, that I could take apart my darkest emotions and feelings of frustration, deal with them in the privacy of my thoughts, memories, and writing, and turn them into productive starting points. And perhaps most importantly, I learned how much more there is to learn, and . . . how capable I am of pursuing new knowledge.

Developing Teachers as Science Inquirers and Science Education Restructuring

Collaborative programs with Community School Districts 5 and 8 (Developing Teachers as Science Inquirers), and with Community School

Figure 6.3. Spring Cycle of Activity

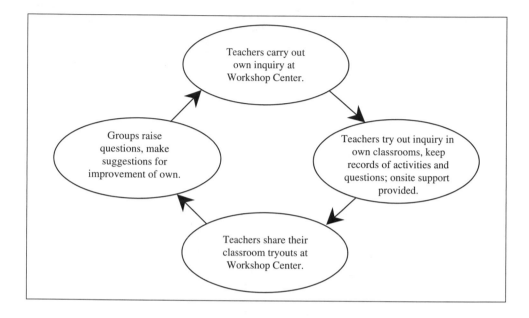

District 6 (School-Based Science Restructuring Program) in New York City, provided contexts for implementation of the center's professional development model, approach, and practice. The model involves reflective teaching applied in a cyclical process, in which staff and teachers continually examined, adapted, and evaluated their practice. (See Figures 6.2, 6.3, and 6.4.) Each program was divided into four phases: (a) development of teachers as learners; (b) teachers' implementation of inquiry learning, first in a clinical setting and later in their own classrooms; (c) planning, implementation, and documentation of classroom inquiry experiences to be used by teachers and administrators; and (d) dissemination of program outcomes throughout the school district. Each phase of the program was planned and sometimes implemented in collaboration with districts' supervisory staff, school principals, and teachers; there was, therefore, a built-in element for enabling school districts to sustain the program with minimal outside assistance.

Each participant in the Districts 5 and 8 program spent two semesters to earn six graduate credits. The program deepened and increased participants' investigation skills, for example, their ability to formulate researchable questions, carry out investigations directly, and collect, organize, and interpret data, while pursuing answers to their own questions about natural phenomena. The program created a critical mass of teachers who were educated in the implementation of inquiry approaches in the teaching and learning of science in the elementary school and in working with parents to support their children's inquiry activities at home.

Figure 6.4. Cycle of Activities for Principals

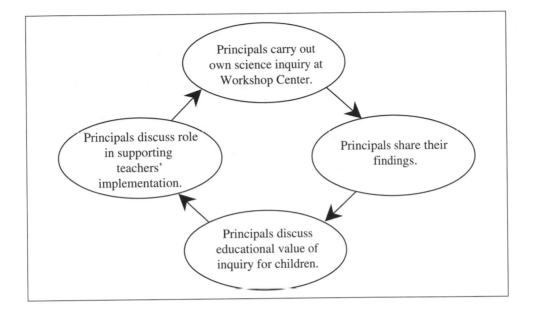

To aid reflection on learning and teaching, each participant read and summarized prescribed science education readings that dealt with children's learning. The readings also provided guidelines for helping children to develop their capacities in planning investigations, developing observation skills, and constructing science knowledge commensurate with their stage of intellectual development. Some of the readings also dealt with the role of questions in stimulating children's thought and action, resources to encourage and engage children's inquiry, and the importance of children's communication in the learning process. In addition to the readings, each teacher kept a journal on workshop investigations, class discussions, and implementation of activities.

Program staff included a science educator, a scientist, a teacher who partnered the science educator, a parent education specialist, a program evaluator, and on-site staff who worked as teachers' coprofessionals. The staff planned together, taught together in a seamless manner, and collaboratively reviewed teachers' work. Occasionally, a steering committee of university scientists, social scientists, science educators, public school personnel, and representatives of professional agencies provided advice and review of the program activities.

Saturday practicums with children facilitated and supported teachers' direct practice of skills acquired during the workshop sessions. Saturday workshops for parents ran concurrently with the teacher/children practicums; these workshops built bases for communication between parents and teachers and helped parents to understand how they could be helpful to their children's learning at home.

The Community School District 6 program had an added component of educating lead teachers and supervisors in science inquiry and in the education of other teachers; each lead teacher was in the program for two academic years and summers. It also substituted Saturday field trips for the Saturday practicums, to help lead teachers generate inquiry ideas for their classrooms and for their work with other teachers. Other additional aspects of the program included workshops for school principals and the development of on-site instructional teams.

As illustration of teachers' reflections on their experience in these programs, two teachers wrote:

> I found the Workshop Center to be a very valuable experience. Too often teachers get caught in a tightly bound mindset. The workshop can provide the teacher with a different way of looking at things. I also gained new insight into structures and how they are built. I hope to utilize the physical knowledge activities in the classroom . . . the center is a marvelous experience for children. It was wonderful to see the kids looking at all the plants, animals, instruments, etc. around the center. A teacher can make the classroom the same sort of place on a smaller scale.

> The center's modeling of what we were learning in classes about classroom organization, social interaction, curricular inquiry, and observation gave me more confidence in the practicability of the ideas and allowed me to raise deeper questions about them and to try them in my classroom. The Workshop Center is a place where I could "try" things I was unfamiliar with or uncertain of and where I could flounder a bit without the risks usually attendant on that. Experiencing the ups and downs of active learning gave me a more solid sense of confidence in my own ability to learn.

Conclusion

The Workshop Center's educational model and practice have been adopted in several educational institutions around the country and modified to suit local circumstances. For example, the model was adopted, refined, and adapted by the San Francisco Exploratorium's Institute for Inquiry, the teacher educators' network of the Association of Science-Technology Centers, and the Clark County (Nevada) School District. It has also been highlighted in national programs through the North Central Regional Education Laboratory in collaboration with the Public Broadcasting System and the Harvard-Smithsonian Center for Astrophysics and the Annenberg Corporation for Public Broadcasting programs. In 2002, its work continued to be supported by the City College, New York City School District/NSF programs, and by the New York State Department of Education.

Resource

Hubert Dyasi first presented the model at the San Francisco Exploratorium in 1987. It was later published in a chapter (Dyasi, 1990).

PROFESSIONAL DEVELOPMENT CASE B: TEACH-STAT—A MODEL FOR PROFESSIONAL DEVELOPMENT IN DATA ANALYSIS AND STATISTICS FOR TEACHERS OF GRADES KINDERGARTEN THROUGH 6[1]

Susan N. Friel
School of Education
University of North Carolina at Chapel Hill

The *Curriculum and Evaluation Standards for School Mathematics* (NCTM, 1989) identifies statistics and probability as a major strand across all grade levels. Since 1989, there has been growing interest in what to teach and how to teach with respect to statistics. Appropriate curricula for teaching statistics (e.g., Used Numbers[2] and Quantitative Literacy Series[3]) are available for use at the kindergarten though 12th-grade levels.

At the elementary level, available curricula are an essential ingredient in helping teachers find ways to integrate the teaching of statistics in a coherent and comprehensive manner. Curricula for use with students are not sufficient, however; using such curricula effectively requires a reasonable knowledge of statistics to pose tasks appropriately and promote and manage classroom discourse successfully. Elementary teachers are in need of professional development opportunities that will support their learning of content and promote the use of an inquiry orientation to help their students learn and use statistical concepts.

Teach-Stat: A Key to Better Mathematics was a project (Friel & Joyner, 1991) designed to plan and implement a program of professional development for elementary teachers, Grades 1 through 6, to help them learn more about statistics and integrate teaching about and teaching with statistics in their instruction. This project included the following three components:

1. The design of professional development curricula for use with teachers and with teacher leaders (here referenced as statistics educators)

2. A large-scale implementation program to provide professional development for both teachers and statistics educators using the professional development curricula

TABLE 6.2   Design at a Glance: Teach-Stat—A Model for Professional
Development in Data Analysis and Statistics Level and
Content: Elementary Mathematics

Level and content: Elementary mathematics

Knowledge and beliefs highlighted: Principles and Standards for School Mathematics

Context: Inputs considered included teacher background, state regional structure,
availability of curriculum

Goal: Help teachers learn statistics and integrate it into their instruction

Primary strategies: Developing professional developers, workshops, and curriculum implementation

Critical issues: Developing leadership, building capacity for sustainability

---

3. A program of research and evaluation to assess the impact of the
   project and to surface research questions related to the agenda of
   the project.

Project Design

The project was funded by the NSF through the University of North
Carolina Mathematics and Science Education Network (MSEN). MSEN
consists of ten centers throughout North Carolina housed at ten of the state
university system's campuses. Each center is directed by a faculty member
in mathematics or science education; one of the main tasks for each center is
providing professional development in mathematics or science or both for
K–12 teachers in its service region. Because of its structure, MSEN is particularly well suited for supporting the implementation of large-scale, statewide projects.

The project involved nine of the ten MSEN centers; one faculty member
(here referenced as site faculty leader) from each of the sites served as the
local coordinator of the project. The nine site faculty leaders, with the addition of a few other university consultants, designed and implemented the
Teach-Stat project. More than 450 teachers throughout North Carolina participated in the project, and, of those, 84 received additional professional
development to prepare them to be statistics educators.

The first fall and spring of the Teach-Stat project were used as a planning time to bring together the site faculty leaders and additional faculty
consultants from across the state. This group met intensively for two- or
three-day meetings several times during the first year. Their tasks were to

design the draft of the professional development curriculum that would be used to teach teachers and then to jointly teach the first three-week summer institute.

The project was designed so that, during the first year, each site faculty leader selected six or seven teachers as a pilot team. The 57 teachers and nine site faculty leaders participated in a three-week summer institute, which was offered as a residential program at a central site. The faculty, working in teams of three, was responsible for various parts of the program. Throughout the following school year, each faculty site leader met with and visited the regional teacher team, jointly exploring with the teachers what it meant for them to teach statistics and integrate statistics with other subject areas.

In the second year, each of the nine sites offered a revised (nonresidential) version of the three-week professional development program to 24 new teachers. Each site faculty leader and the pilot team of six or seven teachers worked together to plan and provide the workshop. Originally, the pilot teachers were going to be available to help but not to teach. By the second summer, however, faculty and teachers had developed such a good working relationship that the model of a "professional development team" naturally emerged and was very successful. The second-year participants were able to hear from teachers who had spent the preceding year teaching statistics and had many actual examples to show them. The first-year pilot teachers received a great deal of support, informal "how to be a staff developer" training, and coaching and mentoring from their respective site faculty leaders.

In the third year, 84 teachers from either the first or second year were selected to become statistics educators to serve as resource people throughout North Carolina to provide professional development programs in statistics education for other elementary teachers. They participated (regionally at the nine sites) in the equivalent of a one-week seminar focused on the "how to's and the why's" of staff development. The statistics educators at each site were responsible for developing and providing a two-week summer institute for an additional set of 24 new teachers at their site. As a result of this program, the statistics educators were equipped to offer the Teach-Stat professional development program to other elementary school teachers and to design variations of this program to meet the needs of the audience with which they happened to be dealing.

The documentation of the project includes the following various materials that permit others to replicate the program of professional development and implementation:

1. *Teach-Stat for Teachers: Professional Development Manual* (Friel & Joyner, 1997) provides a "how-to" discussion for planning and implementing a three-week teacher education institute. It is written in a way that addresses teachers' needs for inservice education, and its audi-

ence is mainly those who provide professional development programs for elementary-grade teachers.

2. *Teach-Stat for Statistics Educators: Staff Developers Manual* (Gleason, Vesilind, Friel, & Joyner, 1996) provides a "how-to" discussion for planning and implementing a one-week Statistics Educators Institute. This institute is designed for teachers who will serve as staff development resource people (statistics educators) who have participated in a three-week program in statistics education and have previously taught statistics to students.

3. *Teach-Stat Activities: Statistics Investigations for Grades 1-3* (Joyner, Pfieffer, Friel, & Vesilind, 1997a) and *Teach-Stat Activities: Statistics Investigations for Grades 3-6* (Joyner, Pfieffer, Friel, & Vesilind, 1997b) provide "how-to" discussions of the planning and implementation of activities for elementary-grade students that promote the learning of statistics using the process of statistical investigation.

Statistics Educators: Developing Leaders

The benefit of a structure such as MSEN is that it provides access to the state's school systems and assists in maintaining a consistent level of quality in the professional development programs it provides. North Carolina, however, still lacks the capacity to provide high-quality opportunities for the majority of elementary school teachers to increase their subject matter knowledge and to continuously examine and modify their teaching practice. The Teach-Stat project sought to address the "capacity question" not only by providing professional development for a large number of teachers on a regional basis but also, more important, by developing teachers (statistics educators) who can work with other elementary school teachers in support of their learning statistics and how to teach statistics and teach using statistics. This is one of the elements needed in building an infrastructure for professional development.

The final teams of statistics educators varied in composition: Some teams included only first-year teachers, some included a balance of first- and second-year teachers, and some included a few or no first-year teachers with the preponderance of second-year teachers. They were selected based on their interest and on their potential ability to provide professional development to their peers. In cases in which first- and second-year teachers were balanced, it was found that teaming of a first-year teacher with a second-year teacher created a mentor-coach arrangement that seemed to support the second-year teachers in their initial experiences teaching other teachers. It was assumed that, in most cases, these teachers would work in teams of two statistics educators to provide such experiences for other teachers once they "graduated" as statistics educators.

Teachers selected for this opportunity participated in an additional week's professional development program that helped them explore staff development issues and ways to conduct a workshop. The Statistics Educators Institutes included content on adult learning, the change process, and statistics pedagogical content knowledge. Statistics educators completed three or four days of work prior to the Teach-Stat workshop they taught for third-year teachers; the remainder of the work was done as part of a "looking back" effort to reflect on what happened during the workshop.

As part of their participation, approximately half the statistics educators participated in a study (Frost, 1995) to investigate the effects of classroom teachers becoming Teach-Stat workshop leaders. They responded to three different instruments, and some also participated in interviews. These were completed at three different times: at the beginning and at the end of the Statistics Educators Institute and after teaching the third-year Teach-Stat summer workshops.

Frost's (1995) study is rich with information. For purposes here, the results suggest that staff development designs built on teachers becoming leaders should provide special assistance to help them develop in this role over time. The following are relevant:

- Opportunities to develop and/or demonstrate strong content knowledge in mathematics before becoming a workshop leader should be an important consideration in staff development.

- Teachers' classroom experiences are valuable assets to their work as workshop leaders. Classroom experiences using teaching activities like those presented in workshops provide the workshop leader with "personal memory tapes" of the practical, as well as the pedagogical, issues related to the activities.

- Teachers who become workshop leaders may need specialized assistance in conceptualizing effective staff development. The study suggests that workshop leaders progress through stages of growth in their conceptions about effective staff development; such stages can be used as "benchmarks" to assess readiness or potential of the teacher to serve as a workshop leader.

- Teachers who become workshop leaders need opportunities to develop their own understanding of the nature of adult learners and of creating a climate conducive for adult learning. Furthermore, there is a need to help workshop leaders explore pedagogical content knowledge related to teaching adults.

What We Learned

When the study of statistics is framed within the context of a process of statistical investigation and involves the use of relevant hands-on applications and activities, teachers and students quickly become engaged. Unlike much of traditional elementary school mathematics, teaching statistics within this framework provides for a much more open learning environment. No longer is there only "one right way" to do mathematics and questioning and exploration are encouraged and promoted. Professional development experiences that model such learning environments can be successful in helping teachers bring similar excitement and engagement in learning to their students. Overall, individuals at all levels of involvement, primary grade teachers to college teachers of statistics, learned from their Teach-Stat experiences and described these experiences as having influenced change in their respective classrooms.

PROFESSIONAL DEVELOPMENT CASE C: THE CALIFORNIA MIDDLE GRADES MATHEMATICS RENAISSANCE

Judy Mumme
Director
Mathematics Renaissance Leadership Alliance

Project Update

The Middle Grades Mathematics Renaissance ended in 1997 and was followed by the Mathematics Renaissance K–12 (MRK–12) from 1997 through 2002. This project was funded by the NSF and the California Department of Education as a systemic change initiative designed to work with a network of schools to create a coherent, articulated program of instruction in mathematics K–12, promoting mathematical excellence for all students. In a collaboration between WestEd and San Diego State University, eight full-time MRK–12 regional directors worked statewide with 28 districts (160 schools K–12) to improve mathematics programs. At its core was the commitment to increase access and success for students historically underrepresented, while holding high expectations for improving performance for all students. The Renaissance received recognition from the U.S. Department of Education as an exemplary mathematics professional development program. It was identified by the National Staff Development Council as meeting the stringent criteria as a model staff development program that increases student achievement.

In its current form, the Renaissance is now working as the Mathematics Renaissance Leadership Alliance (MRLA), which is a leadership development initiative, funded by the California Department of Education, Eisenhower Program. It builds on the ten-year history of the Mathematics Renaissance in California and is designed to help districts build and sustain

TABLE 6.3   Design at a Glance: Mathematics Renaissance

Level and content: Middle school mathematics

Knowledge and beliefs highlighted: Principles and Standards for School Mathematics, effective learning, and understanding of the change process

Context: Teachers' background in mathematics, current practices, student learning levels, state and local policies

Goal: Increase access and success of all students in mathematics

Primary strategies: Curriculum replacement units, professional networks

Critical issues: Ensuring equity, developing leadership, building capacity for sustainability, garnering public support

---

a leadership infrastructure capable of promoting sustained teacher growth. MRLA provides leadership development and support for 14 district-based leadership cadres throughout California. These cadres are composed of four to six teachers and administrators, who take responsibility for leadership and ongoing support for state, district, school site, and/or university-sponsored mathematics initiatives within their respective districts. In addition, districts receive assistance in designing, selecting, supporting, and evaluating effective professional development in mathematics in order to provide high-quality mathematics education programs for all students. MRLA realizes that the building of capacity within districts is necessary but not sufficient for sustaining growth. Therefore, MRLA also provides technical assistance to participating districts to increase their ability to provide ongoing professional development. The nature of this assistance varies depending on local needs.

Context and Desired Outcomes

The Middle Grades Mathematics Renaissance was a component of the California Alliance for Mathematics and Science, an NSF-funded State Systemic Initiative. Using professional development as its central strategy, the Renaissance was designed to help schools transform their mathematics programs so that all students, especially those historically underrepresented in mathematics, become empowered mathematically. During 1995 and 1996, 1,800 teachers from approximately 350 schools participated in the academic year and summer or off-track work, which focused on professional development issues: discussing mathematics reform, experiencing hands-on mathematics, learning how to teach new state-of-the-art curriculum "re-placement" units, and exploring the conditions that create opportunities for learning.

The Renaissance was developed against the backdrop of California, a state with a rich and complex environment for mathematics reform. The state has more than 5 million students, 230,000 teachers (140,000 of which teach mathematics), 7,000 schools, and 1,000 districts. Average class size is approximately 30 and per-pupil spending is $4,874, placing California 38th among states ($1,000 less than the national average). Approximately half of California's students are from Latino, African American, or Asian American backgrounds. There are more than 100 languages spoken, and 22% of the student population speaks limited English. Approximately 2.2 million children live in poverty.

Several critical decisions were made early in the planning. First, a professional development strategy was chosen as the vehicle to achieve goals. Reaching the large numbers of California's teachers and students, however, required resources beyond the available funding (approximately $1.1 million annually). Therefore, a second decision was made: Middle school mathematics was selected because it acts as a gateway to future access to higher-level mathematics courses. Moreover, curriculum at this level has traditionally been a wasteland, and this area seemed ripe for development and exploration. Third, it was decided that the program would use a school-based rather than an individual teacher focus. Collaboratively, work among faculty members can provide a support system that provides opportunities to address the school structures that promote and inhibit reform. It was believed that by working with schools as the unit of change, a process that would sustain the effort beyond program funding could be established.

Designing the Work

With middle grades as the target, schools as the focus, and professional development as the strategy, the Renaissance was born. The challenge became the creation of professional development experiences that would create the fundamental transformation of middle-grade mathematics, helping teachers meet the challenges of reform.

Leveraging Resources

Resources in education are rarely sufficient and are less so in a state the size of California. Consequently, plans were formulated to ensure that efforts not only maximized the available resources but also established an infrastructure designed to sustain and expand the efforts throughout the system.

To maximize the leveraging of resources, the Renaissance asked schools to support their own costs. Indeed, the approximately $1.1 million in funding barely supported the statewide leadership infrastructure (one director and ten regional directors). Schools paid a $3,000 annual participation fee to cover the costs of local teacher leadership. Establishing an expectation that schools annually allot a sizable sum for professional development increased the likelihood that the process will continue once the initiative ceases.

Large numbers of schools were enrolled statewide to take advantage of a "tip-point strategy," which suggests that systemic reform begins with a small vanguard of schools taking the lead in reform and gradually expands to include more schools. Once a critical mass of one fourth to one third of the schools is engaged in the reforms, the argument states, the system will "tip," and the majority of the other schools will follow. During the five years of the Renaissance, more than 500 schools participated, well beyond the one third envisioned.

Teacher Engagement

At the heart of the Renaissance is the belief that such change takes time. The 8 to 12 professional development meetings a year and the summer experience allowed time to deal with a wide range of issues. Teachers discussed current research on learning and effective instructional strategies, the nature of mathematics, and the redefinition of basic skills. Teachers learned how to teach new state-of-the-art curriculum replacement units. They taught these units in their classrooms and returned to debrief their experience with other network members. The replacement strategy provided an opportunity for teachers to have direct, firsthand experience with reform curriculum. Often, teachers engaged in direct mathematical experiences as learners. It is not enough to talk about what can be. Teachers must experience a broader version of mathematics themselves to break their traditional views.

Although there is much that is common about what teachers need to learn, the Renaissance work was also responsive to regional and local demands. In a district near San Diego, the issue of algebra in middle school was a crucial discussion point, whereas another district nearby was grappling with effective methods for engaging parent and community support. Topics of interest ranged from the place of algorithms in the middle grades to cobbling together a whole curriculum from available pieces. Agendas in one cluster included gender bias, portfolio assessment, and the effects of tracking. Regional agendas grew to meet the interests and needs of the cluster participants.

It was also learned that two of the program's commitments—fostering fundamental change and responding to teachers' needs—are sometimes in conflict. There is often a tension between challenging teachers to consider new ideas and being responsive to what teachers want. For example, one teacher commented, "I do not want to be gone from my classroom for days where I am not taught a specific unit that I can take back and use. My students lose every time I am gone." This teacher's comment is typical of many. How does one develop an in-depth understanding of the issues in mathematics education when teachers have a strong desire for things to take back—to add recipes to their files? Time spent exploring constructivism may not feel like a day well spent to some participating teachers. Short-term gains often limit long-term growth opportunities.

Even when teachers take back curriculum units, the opportunities for reflection often begin with managerial issues. These tensions are part of the inherently paradoxical nature of constructivist teaching. How does one respect what teachers want while pushing them to reinvent themselves? Time is part of the answer. Bit by bit, discussion by discussion, clusters begin to become communities of learners, reflecting on practice in critical ways and learning to ask tough questions and to push individual and collective thinking deeper. Over time, teachers' comments shifted to "I appreciate all the time allowed for discussion."

Leadership

The two-tiered structure of the Renaissance provided both statewide and local leadership. The ten full-time regional directors interacted as a statewide team while directing and designing the unique work of the individual regions. Selection criteria for this role was based on experience in teaching middle-grade mathematics and background in leadership for mathematics education. They played the role of a "critical friend," possessing both an understanding of the research and broad experience in schools attempting to change. Monthly three-day regional meetings and constant communications provided an immediate feedback mechanism.

Each regional director worked with a team of teacher leaders called cluster leaders, who were classroom teachers with the personal experience and credibility to help their peers change classroom practice. Typically, a cluster leader was released from the classroom 35 days during the academic year and worked five weeks each summer to serve in this professional development role. The ratio of cluster leaders to teachers was kept small to allow for the crucial development of relationships with the participating teachers. (See Figure 6.5.)

Cluster leaders were key to the quality of the professional development. Their credibility stemmed from the fact that they grappled with the same issues as those of the teachers with whom they worked. It gave them acceptance into the school, cluster, and regional learning communities. These cluster leaders did not simply emerge from the classroom as leaders. California has a long history of leadership development in mathematics. Many cluster leaders came from the California Mathematics Project or other

Figure 6.5. Renaissance Leadership Structure

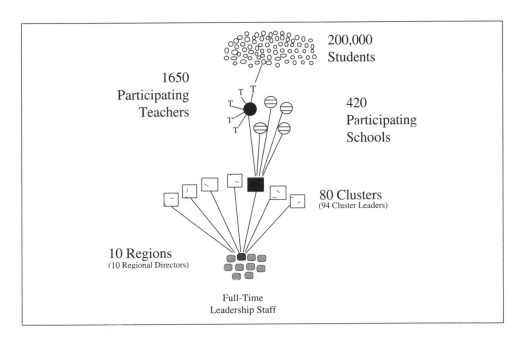

reform projects. A good majority of them came from the ranks of participating Renaissance teachers—many from the first schools to join.

Their work was challenging and demanding, requiring the development of skills beyond those that make one a good teacher. Therefore, another complication arose. The Renaissance design required professional development for both teachers and the teachers who led those teachers. The need for ongoing professional development for leadership cannot be understated. This is perhaps one of the central lessons that was learned. Leaders must have opportunities to reflect on their work, learning from one another the crucial lessons of leadership for reform. They constantly need to be challenged as learners, expanding their own understanding of mathematics, teaching, and learning. The initial design of the Renaissance failed to account for this need, and much of the statewide professional growth opportunities have been funded catch-as-catch-can.

Cluster leaders created their own version of professional development for participating teachers, and regional directors provided guidance, inspiration, and support. Here, another tension emerged. The program's commitment to shared leadership and delegated authority did not always produce results matching its goals. Messages sometimes got distorted as individual cluster leaders constructed their own understanding of the reform and the Renaissance. The program continued to struggle with the degree of control and guidance cluster leaders received. Does one intervene and risk damaging a cluster leader's credibility and opportunity to learn? How is quality maintained while leadership develops?

Supporting Reforms

Other important elements supported the Renaissance efforts. Enlisting parents as partners is one example. Schools throughout the Renaissance pilot tested the middle school version of Family Math, anticipating that more than 500 parent nights would be conducted during the 1995 and 1996 school year. Administrative support offers yet another example. Principals need time with teachers and other principals, and district administrators must understand and support the reforms.

Efforts of the Renaissance also moved beyond the middle school, in part due to conflicts that arose between some Renaissance middle schools and high schools they feed. Middle school teachers expressed concerns that their students went onto high school eager and excited about mathematics only to have their enthusiasm squelched by the high school placement tests and traditional course work. In many districts, these conflicts were seized as opportunities to promote discussions between middle and high schools. As a result of these discussions, some high schools began to revise their programs using new innovative high school curricula.

Guiding Principles

As the Renaissance engaged in this process, much about teacher change and professional development was learned. Principles that guided the Renaissance program, and all future Renaissance programs, are elaborated on in the following sections.

Teachers should be part of a professional learning community. The NCTM's *Professional Standards for Teaching Mathematics* (1991) and *Principles and Standards for School Mathematics* (2000) call for "classrooms as mathematical communities." Likewise, we believe that teachers need to belong to learning communities that place inquiry at their center and focus on building capacity for further learning.

Beliefs and behaviors are interdependent. Belief systems guide behaviors. It is the examination of belief systems that encourages us to rethink our actions. Behavior, however, provides the grist for examination of beliefs. Without concrete experience, discussions of beliefs can remain empty talk untethered to practice.

The pedagogy of professional development must be self-similar to the pedagogy desired in classrooms. Just as students construct their understanding of mathematics, teachers construct their understanding of the processes of teaching and learning mathematics. One's current views of teaching and learning are grounded in one's own experiences as a learner and teacher. Most teachers have learned mathematics in traditional ways. They know of no other recourse. The mold must be broken. People need ample opportunities to construct new understandings of mathematics, teaching, learning, and schooling. As learners, teachers must see firsthand how interaction with others increases opportunities to learn so that they can provide similar opportunities for their students. Unless effective collaborative work has been a personal experience, how can teachers be expected to establish an environment in which collaboration plays a pivotal role in increasing the quality of the classroom discourse?

Issues of equity must permeate the fabric of professional development. At the very heart of the reform is one simple standard: None of it will matter unless it improves learning for all students, regardless of race, gender, or class. Changing beliefs about who can do worthwhile mathematics must be central to the efforts.

Professional development must be grounded in classroom practice. The real hope for making broad-scale change is the ability to tie professional discussions and examinations to what is happening in classrooms. Teachers must experience reform in their own classrooms and have opportunities to grapple with those experiences.

All teachers are capable of making the changes. We believe that the driving force for the majority of teachers is the dream of helping children to become successful, productive adults. They want to do the best for their children. Teachers need opportunities to rethink their practices in light of new information. Given opportunities to share current professional thinking and findings, teachers can begin to make shifts. These changes must occur in all classrooms, not just the classrooms of the innovative teachers. Teachers who are new to the profession and teachers who have taught for 30 years can engage in reflective practice.

Conclusion

The Renaissance leveraged significant resources. It used networks of teachers and created new ones. Teachers engaged in high-quality professional conversations about practice. The program's cadre of teacher leaders demonstrated its capability to support school-based professional development. The Renaissance clearly had an impact, but this is a complex agenda that will take years to assess.

PROFESSIONAL DEVELOPMENT CASE D: GLOBAL SYSTEMS SCIENCE—A PROFESSIONAL DEVELOPMENT PROGRAM FOR HIGH SCHOOL TEACHERS

Cary I. Sneider
Vice President, Museum of Science
Boston, Massachusetts

(Dr. Sneider was formerly the director of Global Systems Science, at the Lawrence Hall of Science, Berkeley, California).[4]

Principal: Diane, I understand that you're excited about this new integrated program called Global Systems Science, but I'm concerned that some of our parents will worry that their children will do poorly on standardized tests if it replaces the usual science curriculum.

Diane: Then it's about time we educate some of our parents about the need for science literacy concerning environmental issues. The *National Science Education Standards* and our State Science Framework say we should spend less time teaching science vocabulary and more time helping our students relate science to the real world.

Jim: I'm not convinced that students who take integrated science will miss out on chemistry, physics, and biology. We plan to present the same concepts we taught before, but in a meaningful context. Students will still have labs, but they'll also debate the social implications of science and technology.

Principal: Now I didn't say I was against it, but I'll be the one to take the heat if our community is not convinced it's a good idea. Are you willing to present your ideas at the Parent-Teacher Association next Thursday evening?

The previous dialogue did not take place in a real principal's office. Zooming our "camera lens" back from the small group seated around the table, one can see at least 20 other teachers listening intently as their colleagues role play scenes that might actually occur when they return from the 1995 Summer Institute in Global Systems Science (GSS). Previously during the institute, the participants met with colleagues from throughout the nation and compared notes with other science and mathematics teachers who field tested the student guides and laboratory activities. Later, they helped to create new activities and assessment instruments that would eventually be used in hundreds of other classrooms.

As codevelopers of this new science program, the 125 teachers who participated in the GSS programs increased their understanding of how studies of the planet are actually conducted and how resulting insights can best be

TABLE 6.4 Design at a Glance: Global Systems Science

Level and content: High school science

Knowledge and beliefs highlighted: National Science Education Standards,
the nature of science

Context inputs: Current practices in science teaching and curriculum, teacher
background, students' access to quality science programs, national audience and
participants

Goal: Enable teachers to carry out science education reforms and implement a
new course of integrated studies

Primary strategies: Curriculum development, curriculum implementation,
workshop

Critical issues: Developing leadership

---

communicated to diverse groups of students. They also returned to their
school districts with a mission to change the current emphasis of high
school science departments from preparing a small segment of the population for college to providing all of the nation's students with the skills that
they will need to thrive in the modern world. The GSS program is one vehicle for accomplishing that, and the GSS professional development strategy,
in which teachers learn to develop, implement, and disseminate new instructional materials, is one way to prepare them to change the course of
science education.

Although the professional development aspects of the GSS program
took place in the 1990s, its genesis can be traced to the context of the 1980s,
when the national agenda began to focus on global change and science education reform.

The Context of Global Environmental Change

The worldwide climatic disturbances of 1988 (no less than an epidemic
of droughts, famines, severe storms, and forest fires) focused attention on
the danger of global warming—the theory that increased carbon dioxide in
the atmosphere, due to the burning of fossil fuels and other human activities, is warming the entire globe. The potential for the industrial revolution
to cause global warming had been predicted more than 100 years ago, but it
was not until 1988 that the prospect was finally taken seriously, although
scientists were by no means in complete agreement about whether global
warming was under way and, if so, what it would mean for the future.

The prospect of global climate change was not the only environmental problem on the horizon at the end of the 1980s. The ever-increasing use of the world's resources to provide energy, food, and housing for a rapidly increasing human population was clearly changing natural environments, resulting in a loss of biodiversity. Also, new developments in technology were found to be influencing the global environment in unexpected ways such as depletion of ozone gas in the stratosphere, exposing all life on the planet to higher levels of ultraviolet radiation from the sun.

Although men and women of every age probably consider themselves to exist at a unique time in history, during our lifetimes we are witness to the transformation of millions of square miles of natural habitats into farms, cities, industrial parks, and malls. The world's growing population and its tendency to become even more urbanized and industrialized is affecting the environment on a global scale. Although these changes have been under way for decades, only recently have a large number of people become aware of the scope of these changes and their implications for future generations.

The Context of Science Education Reform

The 1980s were characterized as the decade of "crisis" in science education and the 1990s were characterized as the decade of "change." Project 2061 from the American Association for the Advancement of Science (1993), the Scope and Sequence Project from the National Science Teachers Association (1993), and the *National Science Education Standards*, created by the National Research Council (1996a), challenged the status quo. Although each of these projects deals with a different aspect of the science education system, they all project a similar image of the ideal science classroom. All three identify similar lists of the most important scientific concepts, theories, and attitudes that should form the core of the school science curriculum. All three emphasize the need to teach fewer topics in greater depth and to teach not only what scientists have learned about the world but also how they have learned it. All three support an inquiry-based approach, recognizing that students bring their own ideas to the classroom, and that students construct new meaning from these prior ideas. Also, all three projects suggest that high school science courses might be more useful and appealing to students if they focus on interdisciplinary issues relevant to the modern world than on the traditional disciplines.

Responding to the call for change, many administrators directed teachers to spend the summer "writing a new course" that integrates the sciences and meets other criteria laid out by the reform documents. Global change has been a popular subject for these courses because relevant topics appear in the news almost every day. Environmental protection is of concern to high school students, and the subject lends itself to an inquiry-based approach in which depth is emphasized over breadth. Although many creative teachers developed excellent activities and assembled useful reading materials, most of these efforts have been conducted in isolation. The problem with developing instructional materials in isolation is that the same work must be repeated by many individuals, the opportunities for testing activities with students are limited, and the potential benefit of teachers working together to share their knowledge and build on each other's ideas and strengths is entirely lost.

Development of the GSS Program

Development of the GSS materials started in 1990, when the Lawrence Hall of Science was awarded grants from the National Institute for Global Environmental Change, with funds from the U.S. Department of Energy and the NSF. The product of the six-year effort is an interdisciplinary course for high school students that emphasizes how scientists from a wide variety of fields work together to understand significant problems of global impact. Big ideas of science are emphasized, such as the concept of an interacting system, the coevolution of the atmosphere and life, the goal of a sustainable world, and the important role that individuals play in both influencing and protecting the vulnerable global environment.

The GSS course materials involve students actively in learning. They perform experiments in the classroom and at home. Students read and discuss background materials. They "meet" a wide variety of men and women who are working to understand global environmental change. They work together to dramatize their ideas for working toward solutions to worldwide environmental problems. They are challenged to make intelligent, informed decisions and to take personal actions, such as conserving energy, recycling, and preparing for their roles as voting citizens in a modern industrialized society.

The GSS Professional Development Program

The goal of the GSS professional development program was not just to implement a new course of integrated studies but also to enable teachers to actively carry out the new educational reforms. The key strategy that was selected to achieve this goal was teacher as curriculum developer. According to nearly all the teachers who attended the institutes, the experience of working intensively with colleagues for three weeks to discuss what to teach and how to teach, within a framework of guiding principles, was a valuable educational experience in itself. In addition, their creative work in helping to shape and improve the program increased their commitment and their understanding of the principles on which it is based. In the GSS program, this strategy played out in five distinct phases, which are discussed in the following sections.

Phase 1: Pilot Testing

Unlike many professional development programs that begin with an institute or workshop, this strategy begins by asking the teachers to help pilot test new course materials. During the four- to six-week period of pilot testing, the teachers do what they usually do—teach science; they substitute, however, a new unit of instructional materials in place of what they normally teach at this time of year. The materials themselves are quite different from the usual textbook, and the accompanying teacher's guide offers suggestions for teaching methods and supplementary activities. During this phase of the program, teachers become familiar with and develop opinions about the new approach.

Phase 2: Summer Institute

Having pilot tested the GSS materials, teachers arrive at the summer institute with a common experience. During the first week, they share their insights about the content and process of teaching the new materials and provide critical feedback to the GSS staff. In the second and third weeks of the institute, the teachers focus their creative energies on making the course better by inventing new activities and assessment tasks. They present these to their colleagues and receive affirmation of their efforts and constructive feedback. They also visit laboratories and meet scientists involved in GSS research. Finally, they learn how the GSS program fits into the context of science education reform, and they participate in activities such as the role-play session described at the beginning of the case.

Phase 3: Assessment of Impact on Students

For teachers to commit to an innovative approach, they need to be convinced that it is making a positive contribution to their students' learning. The teacher's guide provides several ideas for testing student understanding before and after teaching a unit so that it is possible for teachers to see what their students have learned; the guide also provides ideas for maintaining portfolios of student work. Many of the teachers also provide student test data to the GSS staff in Berkeley for analysis and publication of comprehensive evaluation studies.

Phase 4: Networking

Experiences in working with other teachers to develop innovative approaches often lead to a desire for continued contact with the growing community of teachers who share an interest in the program both to find out about new activities developed by others and to share their own innovations. Electronic bulletin boards, newsletters, and reunions at teachers' conferences are used to support the network of teachers using the GSS materials.

Phase 5: Dissemination

It is hoped that the teacher developer strategy will be maintained as new teachers learn about the program and adapt it for use by their own students.

The strategy of teacher as curriculum developer is by no means a new approach to professional development. Federally funded curriculum development projects have traditionally involved teachers both in the early brainstorm phases of materials development and in trial testing experimental activities. Teachers have contributed very important ideas to many of the science programs used in today's schools, and some sets of classroom activities have been entirely developed by teachers. The focus of these programs, however, has generally been on the products of the instructional materials that were developed rather than on the value to the teachers who helped to develop them. Recognizing that teacher as curriculum developer is a strategy for professional development should make it easier to export it to new situations. This strategy is especially effective for experienced teachers who are being asked to expand their capabilities and adopt new approaches and perspectives.[5]

PROFESSIONAL DEVELOPMENT CASE E: PROFESSIONAL DEVELOPMENT FOR ELEMENTARY SCHOOL SCIENCE CURRICULUM IMPLEMENTATION— THE CASE OF CAMBRIDGE, MASSACHUSETTS

Karen Worth
Senior Scientist, Education Development Center
Center for Urban Science Education Reform
Newton, Massachusetts
and Faculty, Wheelock College

Melanie Barron
Director of Science, Cambridge Public School System
Cambridge, Massachusetts

Context

This case describes the professional development components of an effort to reform science education in a district through implementation of a districtwide core of in-depth science inquiry-based units of study. The setting is Cambridge, which is a city of 72,938 people with an elementary student population of 5,725 in kindergarten (K) through sixth grade and an elementary teacher population of 300. Fifty-six percent of the children are minorities and 43% percent come from poor homes. The city has 15 K through eighth-grade schools and one large high school. The program described in this case is for elementary schools only; the district, however, is also implementing reform in Grades 7 through 9 with the goal of having a fully articulated K through ninth-grade program in place within the next several years.

In the early 1990s, the city hired a new science director who came with the charge and mission of reforming science education throughout the district. At the start, she undertook four key initiatives, which laid the foundation for the professional development plan that has been in place since the mid-1990s.

The first initiative was the redeployment of science specialists who had been teaching science classes in the elementary grades. The role of teaching science specialist was eliminated. To support the district reform effort at the classroom and school levels, five teachers were selected to become science staff development teachers. Each works in up to three schools with approximately 50 teachers and provides a wide range of support to individual teachers, groups of teachers, and school-level planning teams.

A second initiative was the development of a conceptual framework for science in the elementary years. This framework, based on a new state framework, the *National Science Education Standards* (National Research Council, 1996a), and the *Project 2061: Benchmarks for Science Literacy* (American Association for the Advancement of Science, 1993), was brief and to the point, providing an outline of basic concepts that students were to have studied by the second and sixth grades. This framework is providing the necessary guidance for the gradual selection of hands-on, inquiry-based science units at every grade level—the curriculum itself.

A third initiative was the decision to require all teachers at each grade level to teach four units of science per year, with three to be determined by the district and the fourth to be selected at the school or classroom level. A plan was set into place in which a wide variety of curriculum units were to be pilot tested in classrooms throughout the district. Out of this process would come a set of criteria for selecting units and information that would lead to the list of required units at each grade level. Teachers would be asked to begin with one unit and then, during a period of three to five years, incorporate all four. This process is currently ongoing.

Finally, a plan for a centralized resource center was initiated to provide teachers with the necessary materials for teaching the science units.

As these efforts were proceeding, the district science director prepared and submitted a proposal to the NSF for an intensive multiyear teacher enhancement program to support the entire elementary teaching staff in the

TABLE 6.5   Design at a Glance: Cambridge, Massachusetts

Level and content: Elementary science

Knowledge and beliefs highlighted: National Science Education Standards, science for all, students learn science through inquiry

Context inputs: Past professional development efforts, teacher background, levels of student learning, national and local standards

Goal: Improve science learning through curriculum implementation

Primary strategies: Curriculum implementation, workshops, study groups, developing professional developers

Critical issues: Developing leadership, building capacity for sustainability, and developing professional culture

---

implementation of this modular, inquiry-based science program. The following were the goals of the plan:

- To improve science learning for all elementary students in the Cambridge public schools
- To implement an inquiry-based, modular science curriculum across the district
- To build teacher leadership and expertise within the system
- To develop a structure that would permanently sustain the science program.

The following assumptions were made as the program was designed:

- Districtwide reform of science education must be systemic with strong support structures at the central and school levels, real support for classroom teachers, and support and engagement from the community.
- District-mandated reform reduces the risk of teachers and administrators at the school level.
- Professional development must support different tiers of teachers, different levels of expertise amongst teachers, and different areas of interest among teachers.
- Implementation of materials-rich, inquiry-based curricula is often a staged process during which teachers move from awareness to mechanical use, to inquiry teaching, and to ownership and adaptation.

- Building capacity for growth and renewal within a system is critical to sustainability.

The professional development plan that was funded followed a structure that, in various guises, is quite common throughout the country where systems are attempting to put into place a centrally determined modular curriculum. It is a three-tiered approach with five science staff development teachers, two liaison teachers acting as point people at each school but with full classroom responsibilities, and the remaining staff teaching in their classrooms. The professional development program had to address the needs of these three different groups of professionals. In addition, the program had to consider the reality that teachers in the district and in each category were very diverse. For some, teaching from an inquiry perspective was unfamiliar; others were already skilled in the instructional strategies of inquiry teaching but did not apply them in science; and still others, although fewer in number, were skilled in teaching inquiry-based science.

Program Description

The following sections present a brief description of each group of teachers, the professional development program for each group, and some of the reasoning behind the design.

The Science Staff Development Teachers

It was clear from the start that the staff development teachers were critical to the success of the reform effort. The district had to develop a cadre of experts from within who could lead the implementation process. The science staff development teachers were the front line professional support people; their skills and knowledge would be critical in helping the district, schools, and teachers implement the district plan. It was important to build an intensive professional development program with and for them from the start so that they would be supported on a continual basis.

The science staff development teachers all came from classroom teaching. All but one had been a science specialist within the district's more traditionally structured program. Each was chosen for his or her experience and interest in teaching science. All were interested in moving from working directly with children to playing a role supporting other teachers.

The professional development program for the staff development teachers needed to address several areas. It had to systematically and continuously enhance their knowledge of inquiry-based science and science teaching. It had to develop their knowledge of the curriculum materials that were under consideration and those being used in the system. It had to provide them with skills in working with others, both individually and in groups; skills in leading workshops, institutes, and presentations; and skills in taking responsibility for the design and implementation of a variety of activities within the district.

The following four professional strategies were selected:

- Weekly meetings: These three-hour meetings provide the opportunity for reflection, communication, sharing, and problem solving. They are facilitated by one of the program consultants.

- Ten professional days: The professional development days provide an opportunity for intensive work in science inquiry and curriculum, peer support and mentoring, and group leadership. These days are facilitated by individual experts but are structured and designed by the five science staff development teachers.

- Apprenticeships and mentoring: Learning to be a staff development teacher also requires clinical experience. Working with more experienced facilitators and workshop leaders allows the staff development teachers to develop the skills they need before assuming the full responsibility for such activities themselves.

- Access to individual professional growth opportunities: The local community offers many opportunities for individual professional growth, including courses, workshops, and conferences. Making the science staff development teachers aware of these and assisting with access and, at times, cost is an important component of this program.

Liaison Teachers

The reform effort in the district could not rely on the work of just five people to support the implementation in every school and every classroom; therefore, school-based liaison teachers were critical. With limited resources, it was impossible to provide release time for the liaison teachers. Therefore, the program planners felt it was critical at the start that the liaison teachers focus their time and development on their own science teaching so as to create exciting science classrooms within each building. At the same time, this plan would begin the process of developing a cadre of classroom experts within the system.

There are two liaison teachers in each building who work with the science staff development teacher to support schoolwide implementation of the reform. They are not released from their classrooms but receive stipends for their work and for their professional development time. To become a liaison teacher, teachers must submit an application. Some do so because of their particular skill and interest in science teaching, some apply because of their interest in something new and in working in a new way, and some apply because they were asked to do so by a building administrator.

The professional development program for this group needed to address the skills of good science teaching. The liaison teachers needed experiences with the concept of inquiry, the teaching of inquiry-based science, and the curriculum units that were being identified by the district. In the long run, they also needed the skills to work as a liaison within the building, supporting colleagues and supporting school-level planning.

The following four professional development strategies were selected:

- Four-day institute: A four-day institute each summer, jointly led by the staff development teachers and selected external consultants, provides the opportunity for the liaison teachers to engage in inquiry, discuss and share ideas about teaching and learning science, and study the Cambridge frameworks and the modules that are under consideration for the Cambridge curriculum. These four days also bring the group together to discuss and reflect on the many demands of their role as liaison.

- Unit workshops: All liaison teachers are given the opportunity to participate in two types of unit workshops: (a) afterschool meetings and (b) mentoring and coaching.

Six afterschool meetings take place during the academic year. These maintain the networking and communication among the members of the group and provide opportunities to familiarize the liaisons with a range of resources for their buildings and particular aspects of science teaching, such as assessment and adaptation of units.

The staff development teachers provide mentoring and coaching to support the liaison teachers in their growth and development. They coach the liaisons in their classrooms, meet with them to discuss school issues, and cofacilitate activities at the school with other teachers.

- Apprenticeships: Some liaisons have begun to apprentice themselves to workshop leaders, engage in leadership in other science projects in the district, and take advantage of resources made available through the district.

- Study groups: During the second year, small study groups of six to ten liaison teachers were formed to allow liaisons to pursue issues of particular interest and to become experts in a particular domain.

Regular Classroom Teachers

For the reform effort in the district to reach the classroom level, support was necessary for every teacher.

All the classroom teachers are being asked to eventually teach four units of study per year. They are, as in any system, a diverse group of people with many different levels of expertise and experience. Some are very knowledgeable in the teaching and learning of inquiry-based science; others are less comfortable with science but teach from a child-centered, inquiry-based philosophy; and some teach form a more traditional belief system.

Because of limited resources, it is not possible to provide intensive professional development experiences for everyone. The decision was made to provide the intensive development support to the leadership cadre—to build the leadership capacity within the district—and limit the program for the rest of the teachers. The program planners, however, feel it is essential to provide teachers with a significant introduction to each of the units. Once familiar with a unit, teachers could turn to the staff development teachers, the liaisons, and one another for ongoing in-school support.

The following professional development strategies were selected:

- Two-day institute: A two-day summer institute was developed for each unit selected for the district. These two-day institutes are designed to take teachers through an entire unit, exploring the materials themselves, the science content, the nature of the inquiry, and the teaching strategies required. In addition, time is spent exploring ways in which each unit might be enriched by local resources and connected to other areas of the curriculum. The institutes are led by the science staff development teachers and external consultants and include scientists from the community for each unit.

- Individual school-based support: This support is available to all teachers through the science staff development teachers who are present in each school at least one day a week. The support they provide varies in response to teacher and school needs and includes model teaching, classroom assistance, leading grade-level discussions, being members on schoolwide science action committees, and helping to access community resources. The liaison teachers are not freed from classroom responsibilities, so they have a limited role in direct classroom support. They are, however, available for such things as answering questions, providing resources, and coordinating meetings.

Neither the overall program in Cambridge nor the individual components have remained static during its years of operation. As the groups have matured, a number of interesting developments have occurred. This growth and development is a powerful sign of success. As each group changes and becomes more diversified in strengths, needs, and interests, the program leaders must reexamine the design and make new decisions to meet a new set of strengths, needs, and interests in a changing context.

Status of the Program in Its Third Year

The staff developers began to broaden their activities, engaging in grantwriting and program management. One coordinated the volunteer students from two local universities, one wrote a successful grant to the National Gardening Association and is coordinating the infusion of this program into the system, and another was responsible for a program of minisabbaticals at the local science museum. Their work in the schools had become increasingly sophisticated. Weekly meetings and professional development days for the science staff development teachers now focused on in-depth issues of teacher change, school reform, and the role of a staff developer. They had become leaders of institutes and workshops and cofacilitators of liaison study groups. There was a trade-off in this change. As they took on new tasks and their roles changed, the staff development teachers spent less time in their schools and in classrooms providing the site-based support for reform. Care needed to be taken so that the shift away from direct classroom support did not move more quickly than the building of capacity of liaison teachers and the overall capacity of the teaching staff.

The liaison teachers had become more comfortable in the classroom and in their roles, and many had begun to develop interests in different areas as well as interest in becoming more involved with the design of their own professional development activities. A uniform professional development plan for them was no longer possible. The study groups described previously reflected one adaptation to their request. In addition, opportunities such as the museum fellowships, courses at local institutions, and intensive institutes provided additional possibilities. Full-group meetings still occurred, although less frequently, to maintain the sense of community deemed critical by the liaisons themselves.

The K through sixth-grade teachers had been introduced to many of the kits. The individualized and small group support they received at the school was, of course, constantly changing to meet their needs as the science staff development teachers became increasingly skilled in their roles. Some teachers were considering the adaptation and enrichment of the kits; others were looking forward to a second institute with the materials to increase their understanding of a particular unit. A number were becoming involved in new initiatives within the district and growing professionally through these. This development was powerful and a sign of success, but it required that program designers reexamine decisions and realign the components to meet a new set of needs and groups within groups.

Many questions confronted the Cambridge team as it moved forward. Much had been accomplished. There was now a foundation that included a framework and a curriculum, a materials center, a growing cadre of teacher leaders, a powerful relationship with the Massachusetts Institute of Technology, and a partnership with several key consultants at the EDC. Every Cambridge school and teacher at the elementary level had been influenced by the work in science. To no one's surprise, however, true inquiry-based science teaching and learning in every classroom was not yet a reality.

As the Cambridge team members moved into their fourth year, they continued to reexamine the progress made, what needed to be done to continue progressing and growing, and how to do so with the resources available. The questions they grappled with included, "Is the decision to focus on leadership development still a good one? What is needed now for the liaison teachers in their work at the school level? Should the balance of efforts be shifted to the classroom teachers? What is the nature of professional development for classroom teachers once the kits are in use? Should building administrators be the target of some of the professional development efforts? Are the efforts at the seventh- through ninth-grade level moving forward so as to support the students as they emerge from the elementary years? What is the long-term picture after the Teacher Enhancement grant is over? How will the progress be sustained? Who will pay for the efforts needed to sustain the work? What will those efforts look like?"

NOTES

1. This section is a shortened version of a chapter by S. N. Friel and G. W. Bright, "Teach-Stat: A Model for Professional Development in Data Analysis and Statistics for Teachers, K-6," in S. P. Lajoie (Ed.), *Reflections on statistics: Agendas for learning, teaching, and assessment in K-12*. Mahwah, NJ: Lawrence Erlbaum (1998).

2. *Used Numbers: Real Data in the Classroom*, a set of six units of study for K–6 students, is published by Dale Seymour Publications (Palo Alto, CA).

3. *Quantitative Literacy Series*, a set of four units of study for Grade 8–12 students, is published by Dale Seymour Publications (Palo Alto, CA).

4. In the first edition of this book, curriculum development was specified as a teacher learning strategy. In the second edition, curriculum work such as that described in this case is discussed in our treatment of curriculum alignment and selection and curriculum implementation.

5. The Global Systems Science course for high school students is now online at www.lhs.berkeley.edu/gas/

7

Putting the Professional Development Design Framework to Work

How schools, districts, and professional development programs design and provide quality learning experiences for teachers has been the subject of this book. In the first chapter, the design framework for professional development was introduced. (See Figure 7.1.) The chapter outlines all of the considerations one must weigh when designing professional development for teachers of mathematics and science. Each of the framework's major inputs is elaborated on in its own chapter. This chapter discusses how to put the design framework to work for you, provides examples of how others have used it to reflect on or design their teacher learning programs, and confronts misconceptions about professional development design.

VERSATILITY OF THE DESIGN FRAMEWORK

Since the introduction of the first edition of this book and the subsequent learning it has produced among many staff developers around the country, there has been an increased level of awareness and skill in the area of professional development design. More people who organize teacher learning programs are thinking strategically, assessing needs, building on strengths,

Figure 7.1.   Design Framework for Professional Development in Science and Mathematics

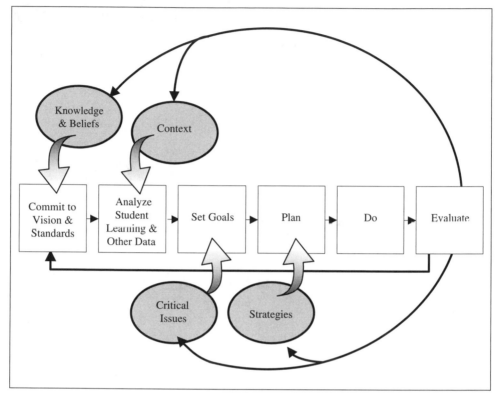

addressing weaknesses, and tying goals to student learning (Sparks, 2002a). As we have used the design framework with educators throughout the United States, we have seen examples of how it can be applied on a large or small scale for assessment and design of professional development. For example, in a Montana school district the science curriculum improvement team members examined their professional development programs for teachers through the lens of the design framework and realized that they had not considered one key *critical issue*—leadership development. The result was that they discovered a missing component in their program—they had no process for building leadership throughout the geographically widespread district to support the implementation of their new curriculum. They identified this gap and redesigned the program to address it. In another example of the use of the design framework, two dozen or so participants in the National Academy for Science and Mathematics Education Leadership talked about how they realized they had been designing and providing professional learning sessions for teachers with little to no knowledge about what the teachers already knew or what they were trying to improve about their teaching. Assessment of the *context* as discussed in

Chapter 3 was not a common practice for them. In both of these examples, professional developers used the design framework to look back at existing designs of teacher learning programs to ask: "What have we missed? What would we change based on a look at all of the inputs suggested by the design framework?"

Starting at the very beginning with the design framework is not always possible. Life is already under way. Schools and districts already have teacher learning programs in place or designed. Using the framework as a reflection or communication tool is a good place to start in these instances. You can use it to assess the design you have in place, asking yourself and your colleagues to take a look at your plan to see how closely it is linked to the needs you have, how well it fits in your context, and whether the strategies you have chosen are a good match for the goals you have set. Use your assessment to suggest changes for the future.

Another way the framework can be used with an existing program is as a communication device. The team or individual responsible for planning professional development can use the framework as a way of organizing and communicating information with teachers about the needs that were identified, the subsequent goals that were set, and how the knowledge and beliefs, context factors, and critical issues were factored into the design. All teachers should be afforded the opportunity to understand the goals for any professional development and the relevance for them. As one teacher wrote to us, "Too often we just don't know why we are attending a particular workshop or conference and what we are supposed to do with it after we attend." Communicating the "big picture"—what you are doing and why—builds teachers' understanding and commitment.

When you *can* start at the very beginning, the design framework can be used on a large scale to develop a multiyear, overall professional development plan for the school or district or on a smaller scale, such as designing a session to examine student work. For example, one district in Virginia prepared its overall professional development plan with a detailed summary of each of the input areas (i.e., their context, critical issues, and the knowledge driving the plan). District planners convened a team to gather data in each of the input areas, discuss the evidence, and identify needs. They used their assessment to come to conclusions about the focus and the strategies for their professional development plan. The plan itself cited the data they used to generate the plan and showed how the professional development design was connected to the needs they identified. The result was a design for ongoing development in the use of new frameworks for teaching matched to the content, and extensive coaching to support all teachers in their use.

The framework can also be used on a smaller scale to address a particular need in a particular school. For example, one school whose students were not meeting expectations on the state's fifth-grade mathematics assessment used the design framework to decide what to do. The teachers started by looking at the *context* input to learn which mathematics concepts the students were understanding and which they were having trouble with, and the practices different teachers were using—areas that are addressed in the framework under *context*. What they discovered was that teachers were implementing the curriculum in a hit-and-miss manner—covering some topics repeatedly and others not at all. They examined the different strategies for teacher learning that might help them address their needs and goals. They decided to initiate a study group of nine teachers representing the three grade levels. The group examined curricula resources and suggested frameworks to become smart about how the curriculum should flow over the three grade levels and the connections that should be made. The use of the design framework helped these educators design the right intervention to address the right purpose. This is especially critical when designers need to combine multiple strategies to address complex goals, as described in the next section.

PROFESSIONAL DEVELOPMENT STRATEGIES ARE CHOSEN AND COMBINED BASED ON GOALS, NEEDS, AND THE LOCAL CONTEXT

After the first edition of this book, many in the education field were anxious to see real images of the kind of professional development advocated for in the book. We embarked on two different projects to document more examples of effective professional development. The first was to convene a group of collaborators who were using innovative or practice-based teacher learning strategies such as case discussions, immersion in inquiry, and examining student work to learn more about the context and conditions for these strategies. Once again, we were surprised by the outcome. The nine collaborators resisted the invitation to simply provide further elaboration on these strategies. Rather, they advocated for understanding how these strategies contribute to a different kind of professional development—teacher learning that is more purpose driven and intentional. As Brown Kovacik (2000) writes:

> The necessity of a shift in mindset, from a view of professional development as bits of training to the creation of a learning environment that values reflection, examination of student thinking, and collegial feedback, is a formidable change in perspective. The recognition that purposeful, focused professional development means depth of consideration and depth means time, is still difficult to assimilate. It makes the phrase "teacher as learner" take on meaning as the starting point for modeling a true learning environment for both educators and students. The resulting learning community serves as a means of continuous focus on the improvement of instructional

practice and makes a statement that establishes an atmosphere receptive to collegial feedback. It envisions the professional teacher as one who learns from teaching. The job of teaching becomes one of inquiry into the effects of teaching and the nature of learning. It requires that professional developers respect theories of learning and incorporate strategies that are consistent with learning theory. (p. 3)

We were reminded once again that there are no "one size fits all" models or a magic purple pill for professional development. Different designers combine different strategies to address their particular purposes, and there are multiple ways to do it well. For example, a school district that is overhauling its middle grades mathematics program might have these three purposes in mind as it designs its professional development program:

1. Enhance the teachers' knowledge of the content and pedagogy in the new curriculum

2. Increase the teachers' abilities to interpret students' ideas and assess learning

3. Build professional community in which teachers support each other to use curriculum

What would the design look like if you were addressing these three purposes? In the old paradigm of professional development, the answer is simple. Professional developers would have designed a summer workshop to address purpose no. 1 and asked teachers how they were doing with goals no. 2 and 3 at a follow-up meeting in the spring. Today, professional developers have better and more options open to them. Here are just a few ways different districts might design a professional development program to address the three purposes above.

In the hypothetical examples shown in Table 7.1, District 1 chose to build teacher leadership as a means to support other teachers. District 2 decided to use an interim strategy of replacement units to see how well the new types of curriculum materials work and what student learning resulted. The district designed coaching into the plan to ensure that all the teachers used the units well. District 3's design takes advantage of a local resource—mathematicians from the nearby university. The district capitalizes on this resource by choosing a partnership strategy through which teachers and mathematics content experts team teach. The teachers use lesson study to assess the quality of teaching and learning and make improvements with support from the mathematicians. Each design addresses the three purposes stated earlier, but they look different from each other because they each base their designs on the context and critical issues at work in their unique districts. This is a basic idea that professional developers need to keep in mind as they design.

Table 7.1   A Variety of Designs

District 1's Design	District 2's Design	District 3's Design
Choose new curriculum and provide structured workshops for all teachers on the use of the new curriculum	Choose curriculum replacement units and provide workshops for all teachers on their use	Establish partnerships with university-based mathematicians
Ten to fifteen percent of teachers develop as leaders through immersion in mathematics and learning to lead case discussions	Convene a year-long study group to examine the results obtained using curriculum replacement units	Teachers and mathematicians work together to review and learn curriculum and team teach lessons.
Teachers engage in case discussions to deepen understanding of how students learn mathematics.	All teachers have coaching in the use of the curriculum replacement units	Teachers conduct lesson study to assess quality of learning and enhance lessons using mathematicians as resources
	Teachers learn to examine student work and use data to make adjustments in teaching	

Another one of our projects has underscored this basic idea about professional development design, the Teachers as Learners project (WestEd, 2003). Our objective for this work was to find and videotape images of professional development. The resulting video collection shows the wide variety of options open to professional development designers as they consider how to combine teacher learning strategies into a coherent and purpose-driven program. Below are three examples from the collection as illustrations of how designs must be tied to purpose as well as local conditions.

Designs Based on Purpose and Other Factors

City On A Hill in Boston, Massachusetts, offers a glimpse into professional development design at a fine-grain size—one department within one school—that is built predominantly on one strategy—examining student work and thinking. Examining student work is a part of the daily life of mathematics teachers at City On A Hill, a public charter high school in Boston, resulting in continuous improvement for students. In the past two years, more students achieved competency in the school's rigorous mathematics exit exams than ever before, and mathematics results on the state assessments have improved dramatically, especially on challenging open-ended items. One hundred percent of the school's graduates, who comprise a very diverse urban population, go on to college.

To understand how the professional development program emerged as it did, one first needs to understand the context of the school. A charter school started by teachers, the school was founded on a commitment to urban education and to the idea they could take any student who walked through the door and get him or her into college. To accomplish this, the school would rely on the expertise of teachers—not individual teachers, but teachers working together to design curriculum, develop a set of core competencies for each course, and take collective responsibility for every student achieving competency. The culture of collegial learning was established early on, and the leadership of the school fully supported it.

It was in this context that the mathematics department went to work to define core competencies in mathematics. Department members set the bar high, considering that many of their students arrive poorly prepared in mathematics. They decided students needed to know a set of key concepts and achieve 70% or better on an end-of-the-year assessment. They needed to be able to "talk mathematics" by doing a mathematics presentation before a jury and be able to "write mathematics," explaining their reasoning and their solution on a complex problem. They needed to have 100% mastery, as freshmen, on a set of basic mathematics skills. The department was united in its commitment to a vision for students' learning in mathematics and a clear set of standards, the starting point of the professional development design process.

Examining student work began as a way to help teachers figure out what competency in mathematics actually looked like. They all needed to be able to look at the same presentation and score it consistently. That meant that they needed to build rubrics, test them out with student work, and score written and oral mathematics work together. "As soon as we started looking at student work together, it was obvious it was a good idea," explained Grace Kelemanik, mathematics team leader. Kelemanik brought considerable expertise in looking at student work, having codirected the K–12 Mathematics Center at the Education Development Center (EDC) and authored a book on looking at student work called *Structured Exploration: New Perspectives on Mathematics Professional Development* with Susan Janssen, Barbara Miller, and Kristi Resnick (1997).

Once department members were hooked on looking at student work, they began using it in other ways. At each grade level, they built common tasks and unit tests. Kelemanik explained:

We couldn't wait until June to find out that students couldn't do their competencies. We needed to know if students were making progress toward, say, generalizing. And what did that mean? How did you know? How good is good enough in 9th grade? 10th grade? What are the variations? We wanted to teach it so they would learn it, really learn it, not so they could do it on a test and then forget it.

After administering the common assessments, teachers in the mathematics department come back and share the student work, looking at scores generally and also at individual work. In department meetings after the teachers have finished a unit and are summarizing what they have learned from the unit and then again at the end of the year, the teachers write their reflections on changes in instruction they each want to make. They compile a list of their ideas then check their lists against the student data to determine if the data bore out what they thought, adjusting the list accordingly. Next year, whoever teaches the unit can look at the lists, so the learning is codified and passed on to the next group of teachers. In this way, they sustained the learning from year to year, even if individual teachers came and went.

Looking at student work and other assessment data to understand student thinking and improve instruction is now the culture in the mathematics department "We very rarely plan anything without looking at some data," Kelemanik went on. "For example, basic skills was a huge issue. The first week of school, we assessed students' basic skills. We had everything from students who got no problems correct to students who got 100% and everything in between. Then we sat down together to figure out how to help kids."

Initially, teachers examined student work during their weekly department meetings, along with completing other work. Since the school went to block scheduling, the mathematics teachers now have a full day a week to work together. While looking at student work is their main form of professional development, they also participate in curriculum implementation workshops and follow-up, have coaching focused on use of the mathematics curriculum, and seek out other learning opportunities outside of the school.

City On A Hill is an excellent example of professional development that is embedded in teachers' work and focused on students' learning. Several design elements made it successful. First, the commitment of the staff to core competencies and high expectations for their students was the essential backdrop along with a culture that supported teacher initiative and collegiality. The expertise that the mathematics team leader brought in mathematics content and pedagogy as well as the process of examining student work and thinking was equally important. From Kelemanik, the department learned a structured process for looking at student work that began with a clear question or purpose for the investigation. In the context of the competency-driven culture and with internal expertise available, the teachers learned to rely on multiple assessments—local and state—to determine the focus for looking at student work and guide instructional improvement.

Another important factor was that the teachers were implementing a common curriculum, the Interactive Mathematics Program, and shared a set of understandings and beliefs about teaching and learning mathematics. New teachers were mentored by more senior teachers. Finally, they grappled with critical issues such as time and building capacity for sustainability by institutionalizing a structure and a time for examining student work and passing on the learning that resulted to next year's teachers.

Curriculum Implementation in the Clark County, Nevada, Schools

Another example is of a large-scale, multischool effort to increase student learning in mathematics and science in kindergarten through fifth grade in the Clark County, Nevada, schools. Such an ambitious undertaking required a comprehensive plan. This district is the sixth largest school district in the country. It is located in an economically diverse community with a population of nearly 1.5 million. The goals they set for their professional development program were to support teacher learning in four areas:

- Use of standards-based curriculum materials
- Content knowledge in mathematics and science
- Effective, standards-based instructional practices
- An understanding of how students learn and the use of assessment practices that measure such learning

The design also took into account several critical issues that were relevant for the district, including a desire to build professional culture and a capacity for professional learning, develop leadership, promote equity, and find time in the school day for teacher learning. Based on these inputs the project's leadership team designed a professional development program that combined the following teacher learning strategies:

- Curriculum implementation: The district selected new curriculum for kindergarten through fifth grade in science (FOSS) and mathematics (Investigations). All teachers participated in multiple workshops and collegial meetings to learn to use and refine their use of new instructional materials. Teachers on special assignment (or teacher leaders) facilitated many of these workshops.

- Content workshops: Teachers participated in structured opportunities outside the classroom to learn mathematics and science content and content-specific teaching and learning approaches reflected in the curriculum.

- Immersion in content and inquiry: Teachers and teacher leaders engaged in immersion experiences in mathematics and science.

- Observing teaching or demonstration lessons: Teachers and teacher leaders conducted formal observations in one another's classrooms and developed and taught demonstration lessons together from the new curriculum.

- Study groups: Teachers and teacher leaders engaged in regular meetings to examine new information, reflect on classroom practice and student work, and analyze outcome data.

- Developing professional developers and leaders of learning: Teacher leaders and administrators participated in professional development programs to prepare them for their leadership roles. Sessions focused on building leaders' understanding of the science and mathematics content and pedagogy needed to create standards-based teaching and strategies for professional development and educational change. Building administrators attend sessions with district science and mathematics leaders to learn to support standards-based teaching in their schools.

The designers of this program said, "The bottom line is a focus on children and teachers examining their practice. The driving force behind both ideas is the issue of access. We're constantly thinking about how to teach in ways that all children have access to being successful in science and mathematics." As they look to the future, they say they are focusing on maintaining a strong component for administrators and refocusing professional development at the site level. "Involving principals and gaining their support is key to what we do, especially as we move toward basing more of our work at individual schools and tailoring it to meet its staff's particular needs. We hope this approach will help sustain the work long into the future" (personal interviews with Mathematics and Science Education (MASE) project staff, May 2002)

Immersion in Content at Biological Sciences and Curriculum Study

A third example of using the design framework to choose professional development strategies comes from curriculum developer Biological Sciences and Curriculum Study (BSCS). Staff there confronted the fact that many high school biology teachers never had the opportunity to learn biotechnology content when they were in school, nor did they have the opportunity to learn this content in relevant and engaging ways that build on what they know. Yet these same teachers are expected to teach this way. From a look at the background and experiences of many of the teachers who use the A Human Approach curriculum, BSCS established the goal of building teachers' content knowledge and capacity to teach challenging biotechnology content.

The emphasis on building content understanding led the BSCS team members to design the professional development as an immersion in content experience. Based on the various inputs they considered, the immersion strategy made a great deal of sense to them. For example, with regard to the knowledge input about the nature of science, the BSCS staff wanted a professional development design that would engage high school biology teachers in learning science in ways that it is used in the real world. They wanted the teachers to use real-life examples, such as how to use biotechnology to solve a crime or decide a paternity case. They also wanted teachers to have access to content knowledge, so a biologist was on hand at the sessions to work with the teachers, raise questions, and help fill in missing content knowledge.

The knowledge of effective professional development also informed this design. The designers paid close attention to building in activities that mirrored those in the classroom and that teachers could later use with their own students. The learning is designed to happen in groups of two to four with some large group discussion, modeling active and cooperative learning. Background information about the teachers is used to pair teachers with some experience using biotechnology with those with less experience. Teachers are engaged in the activities as adult learners and challenged at a high level. Later, they reflect on how to make the activities accessible to their students by reflecting on these questions, "How would your students approach this? What support would they need from you to help them understand?" For many of the participants, this immersion in biotechnology was just one part of a larger professional development experience through which they increased their confidence in using cutting edge content and technology with their students.

These images provide examples of the careful designs that are constructed when professional developers use a systematic design process. Like the professional developers in the examples, you, too, are more likely to design and provide teacher learning experiences that are tied to identified needs and learning goals and reflect best practice when you are guided by the inputs and processes of the design framework.

AVOIDING MYTHS AND MISCONCEPTIONS

We have encountered a number of myths and misconceptions about professional development design that warrant a word of caution as you begin to work with the design framework. This section summarizes some of the common ones that need to be challenged to avoid the pitfalls they bring.

Myth 1: New Strategies Are the Answer

As we have seen with other innovations in education, people grab at new strategies for professional development as the next silver bullet. They aren't. As illustrated above, good professional development is hard work. Simply changing the way it is provided from mandatory workshops to more collegial study groups without changing its content, focus, and duration is not the answer.

Even some of the best-intentioned designers often jump enthusiastically to picking the professional development strategy (e.g., "Let's initiate lesson study!") without thinking through their goals, needs, and the other inputs to design that are described in this book. The major message of this book is to make sure that the strategies you choose to invest in are right for your particular situation and that they include quality content. We know from the recent study of the national Eisenhower program that the form of professional development alone—whether it was a study group, lesson study, or a workshop—did not necessarily contribute to teacher learning (Garet et al., 1999). It is what is designed inside the strategy that counts. Does it help teachers increase content and pedagogical content knowledge? Does it build a professional community? Does it build capacity for leadership? Without a focus on these critical areas, the form of the strategy will not matter a great deal.

Myth 2: You Just Need Collegial Structures for Teacher Learning

Another bandwagon people jump on is the teacher collegiality one. These people say any professional development that promotes collegiality is good. We are big supporters of teachers working with teachers and see learning as a social process enriched by collaboration, but have heard enough horror stories to be cautious. There is the classic example of teachers opening their doors to allow other teachers to observe them, only to hear later that the observers gossiped all around the school about what they saw. There are less hurtful situations, but no more productive, in which teachers are encouraged to meet together without a clear focus or goal. The right conditions need to be in place to make teacher collegiality contribute to teacher learning. First of all, the school leadership needs to set the context for collegial learning in the school as it relates to the mission, vision, and goals for student learning. Within those structures teachers need to establish ground rules for observing and talking with one another and clear goals related to student learning to guide them as they work together. Strategies that require teamwork and collegiality may not work in cultures of distrust or when it is impossible for teachers to find time to get together.

Myth 3: Content for Content's Sake

A major shift in teacher professional development has occurred over the past decade. People know the importance of teachers having extensive content knowledge and the role this plays in facilitating learning. Teachers cannot promote learning beyond their own knowledge (Ma, 1999). There are two cautions here, however. Professional development to improve student learning focuses on helping teachers learn the content they are responsible for teaching. Like many adults, teachers may wish to pursue study of particular content for their own enjoyment, and many teachers have learned to use the inquiry process through immersion in a scientific investigation or learned mathematics through solving challenging mathematics problems in an environment supported by mathematicians and mathematics educators. While these experiences are valuable, teachers need opportunities to learn the content knowledge in ways that are linked to the classroom. Content that is learned disconnected from how to teach it may provide teachers with more scientific or mathematical understanding but will not necessarily result in improved student learning. The content more teachers need to learn is the content they will teach (Cohen & Hill, 1999).

Myth 4: All Teachers Are the Same

Teachers come in all shapes and sizes. One of the biggest crimes of professional developers is lumping together all teachers in a school for the same kind of learning. Teachers have different levels of experience. Those who have mastered the use of the curriculum can be offered the opportunity to serve as mentors and coaches for others who have not. This is an especially promising approach for schools with novice teachers. Experienced teachers can help new teachers in many ways by conducting demonstration lessons, modeling how to interpret student thinking and ideas, and providing insight from examining teaching through the lesson study strategy. Veteran teachers benefit from sophisticated learning that comes from engaging in lesson study or classroom-based action research. Creating the contexts in which teachers with different experiences can work together in meaningful ways is critical. Too often, schools require all teachers to participate in the same professional development each year without helping them see the different roles they can play, nor creating the kinds of structures that would support new teachers.

THE PROMISE OF THE DESIGN FRAMEWORK

As you use the design framework, you can expect to become more strategic about the choices you make regarding teacher learning and literally start to see things differently. As you embrace the knowledge base described in the framework, you come face-to-face with the realization that what is there may not match your past practices and beliefs. Dennis Sparks (2002b) in *Dreaming All That We Might Realize* encourages all of us to actively revisit our beliefs about teachers and teacher learning and calls for adopting more productive beliefs. He writes that holding on to impeding beliefs limits us and we must consider new beliefs such as the following:

- Quality teaching fed by powerful professional learning can make a difference in all schools.

- Teaching is a complex, intellectually demanding task that requires sustained, intellectually rigorous forms of professional development.

- Teachers are contributing their best efforts.

- Professional development that promotes a deep understanding of subject matter and a wide repertoire of research-based teaching strategies is essential if all students are to achieve at high levels.

As you dig into the questions about the context for your professional development, you may find yourself asking whether you really need to consider so much data—that is, until you do it once and see how it changes your perspective of what is needed and what to do. Using the same data to assess changes through your evaluation can be a powerful indicator of your progress. Analyzing context data drives home the realization that professional development is for people—real people with real needs. It helps you to contextualize what you do, strengthening its relevancy and potential utility.

Using the design framework to establish and communicate goals that are connected to a vision of quality learning for all and specific needs creates a sense of purpose and coherence for teachers—they see where they are headed and why. They are involved in professional development *for* them not *done to* them. Finally, the framework opens up a world filled with many different approaches to teacher learning. It suggests that there is no one right way, but many good choices.

SUSTAINABILITY

Our last word on putting the design framework to work for you is a plea that you use it to make professional development a part of the fabric of schools. It should happen every day as teachers gather informally or formally. King and Newmann (2000) examined teacher learning as it interacts with and impacts the advancement of school goals. They contend that professional development will substantially improve teaching when it happens through the specific contexts in which teaching occurs, when there are sustained opportunities to study and obtain feedback in collaboration with peers, and when teachers have control over the process of professional development. In addition, they recognize the importance of building a schoolwide professional community and the need for coherence in the school program.

We all need to see the value of professional development as an ongoing, systematic strategy for enabling staff members to acquire the knowledge and skills they need for teaching science and mathematics. If this were the case, every district and school would have a professional development plan that is tied to student learning goals. Each teacher would feel empowered to set and pursue professional development goals tied to enhancing their and their students' performance.

One principal said that changing practice begins with setting clear expectations. "As the school administrator, I must communicate my expectation that the faculty will actually use what they learn. But then, I've got to make sure they have the chance to become competent with the new practices." Opportunity for practice and feedback and steady pressure to change science and mathematics teaching and learning will support improvements. Professional developers can encourage this by establishing support networks of teachers using new practices and providing local technical assistance to help teachers sustain their use of quality practices.

School leaders say that expectations for teachers to learn new things and implement quality science and mathematics curricula and teaching and assessment strategies must be an explicit part of the teachers' performance expectations. Professional development is an investment in both the teacher and the school. It is reasonable to expect a "payoff" for the investment in the form of new knowledge, improved teaching and learning, or the creation of school cultures that are open to ongoing learning for all.

Teachers and school administrators also need to assess whether the professional development is leading to desired outcomes. They need to know if teachers are using new practices and if there is evidence of student outcomes for science and mathematics. Educators can then use the evaluation data to make adjustments in future professional development (i.e., do more of what is working and less of what is not). Assessment can also tell us whether the professional development is reaching the right people. As one principal said to us, "I believe in voluntary professional development, but at some point I need to push certain people to participate or they never will."

"It takes time for new mathematics and science teaching practices to become part of the fabric of the school organization, but there are many things teachers and principals can do to ensure that they do," writes one seasoned professional developer. Active efforts to sustain new practices include allocating resources to support continued use of new science and mathematics materials or programs; getting all teachers involved; establishing clear expectations and policies that mandate the new approaches; aligning organizational structures such as performance reviews, rewards, and recognition with the desired changes; getting the support of parents and the public; and assessing and communicating results.

We also need to keep in mind that professional development is but one element of a successful reform initiative. It must be aligned and integrated with other efforts. For example, there need to be adequate plans, policies, infrastructures, and community supports in place to support change.

"Professional learning is most powerful when it takes place in a community that is deeply committed to common goals and to sustaining new practices when those methods meet the inevitable challenges of implementation. Principals and teacher leaders play critical roles in this process. Most important among those roles is nurturing in other staff members a belief in their capacity to do what has never before been done—educate all students to high levels of performance" (Sparks, 2002b).

Resource A
Images of Learning and Professional Development

The reform of mathematics and science education rests firmly on a commitment to change the kind of teaching and learning that is currently the norm in our nation's classrooms. Throughout this book, we have presented a new vision for education that embraces learning for all and creates schools as places where teachers are leaders for learning. What do classrooms look like in which the new vision of science and mathematics teaching and learning is playing out? And, following from that question, what do professional development opportunities look like in which teachers learn in that way, and learn to teach in that way? To address these questions, we offer images and some reflection questions. We hope that they create for the reader a vision of where we need to head to achieve the vision of reform.

The first two vignettes illustrate enhanced learning in the classroom. The next three vignettes move the action to professional development, where teachers are learning the pedagogical content knowledge they need to make classrooms with rich learning for all a reality.

Vignette 1: Fair Games

Mr. Luu has been working on probability for a few days with his class of sixth graders. Because his textbook is old, there is little about probability in the book. He has been drawing from a variety of sources as well as making up things himself, based on what he hears in the students' comments. He

SOURCE: National Council of Teachers of Mathematics (1991, pp. 40-42).

began by asking students to decide whether a coin-tossing game he presented was fair or not. He found out that although most of the students did consider the possible outcomes, they did not analyze the ways those outcomes could be obtained. For example, they thought that when you toss two coins, it is equally likely to get two heads, two tails, or heads-and-tails. He also learned that many of his students were inclined to decide if a game was fair by playing it and seeing if the players tied: If someone won, then the game might be biased in their favor, they thought.

He decides to present them with two dice-tossing games—the sum game and the product game.

Sum Game

Two Players

Choose one player to be "even" and the other to be "odd."
Throw two dice.
Add the numbers on the two faces.
If the sum is even, the even player gets 1 point.
If the sum is odd, the odd player gets 1 point.

Product Game

Two Players

Choose one to be the "even" player and the other to be "odd."
Throw two dice.
Multiply the numbers on the two faces.
If the product is even, the even player gets 1 point.
If the product is odd, the odd player gets 1 point.

After explaining how each game is played, Mr. Luu challenges the students to figure out if the games are fair or not. He begins by holding a discussion about what it means for something to be "fair." Then he presents the rules for each game, telling the students simply that they are to report back on whether or not either of the games is fair or not and to include an explanation for their judgment.

The students pair off and work on the problem. Some play each of the games first, recording their results, as a means of investigating the question. Others try to analyze the games based on the possible outcomes. Mr. Luu walks around and listens to what the students are saying and poses questions:

"What did you say were all the possible totals you could get? How did you know?"

"Why did you decide you needed to throw the dice exactly 36 times?"

After they have played the game or worked on their analyses for a while, Mr. Luu directs the students to stop, open their notebooks, and write in their notebooks what they think about the fairness of the two games.

Next, Mr. Luu opens a whole-class discussion about the games. On the basis of what he saw when he was observing, he calls on Kevin and Rania. Rania beams. She explains that they figured out that the sum game is an unfair game "and we didn't even have to play it at all to be sure."

Kevin provides their proof: "only five odd ones—3, 5, 7, 9, and 11. So the game is unfair to the person who gets points for the odd sums."

"What do the rest of you think?" asks Mr. Luu, gazing over the group. Several shake their heads. A few others nod.

"Marcus?" he invites. Marcus's hand was not up, but his face looks up at Mr. Luu. "It don't make sense to me, Mr. Luu. I think that there's more ways to get some of them numbers, like 3—there's two ways to get a 3. But there's only one way to get a 2."

"Huh?" Several children are openly puzzled by this statement.

"Marcus, can you explain what you mean by saying that 3 can be made two ways?" asks Mr. Luu.

"Well, you could get a 1 on one die and a 2 on the other, or you could get a 2 on the first die and 1 on the other. That's two different ways," he explains quietly.

"But how are those different? One plus two equals the same thing as two plus one!" objects a small girl.

"What do you think, Than?" probes Mr. Luu.

Than remains silent. Mr. Luu waits a long time. Finally Than says, "But they are two different dices, so it is not same."

"Hmmm," remarks Mr. Luu. "Where are other people on this?"

After three or four more comments on both sides of the issue, time is almost up. Mr. Luu assigns the students, for homework, to repeat the coin-tossing game they had investigated last week, to record their results, and to decide if it is fair when three people play it:

Coin-Tossing Game

Three Players

One player is "two heads," one player is "two tails," and one player is "mixed."
Toss two coins.
If the result is two heads, the "heads" player gets 1 point.
If the result is two tails, the "tails" player gets 1 point.
If the result is one head and one tail, the "mixed" player gets 1 point.

Mr. Luu thinks that this game may help them with their thinking about the dice games. He asks them to play the game, record their results, and decide if it is fair when three people play it. They are to write about their experiments and explain their conclusion. Mr. Luu suspects that now, if they find out that the "mixed" result person gets about twice as many points as either of the others, they will be able to figure out what is going on and eventually agree with Marcus and Than.

REFLECTION QUESTIONS

What are the learning goals in the classroom activities described in this vignette? What knowledge does Mr. Luu need to facilitate the learning in these activities? In what ways does he tap into what students already know? What difficulties might he encounter in helping these students learn about probability? In what ways could professional development help him to reflect on his use of these activities to promote mathematics learning? What strategies might work best for this?

Vignette 2: Straight-Line Motion

Sister Gertrude's fifth-grade classroom had been working for several weeks on how and why things move. She had given them a circus of 22 examples to consider: a book at rest on a table, a parachute dropping, a toy airplane circling on a string, and so on. They spent time in small groups working on a particular example, observing the motion, and trying to decide what forces were present. A group would present its conclusions to the other students. In time, the students had satisfied themselves, among other things, that when a book was at rest on a table top, they needed two forces to explain it: gravity pulling down and the table pushing up with equal magnitude.

Sister asked for a volunteer to explain another example, and Don presented to the class his explanation of the forces acting on a toy parachute falling from the ceiling to the floor. He had drawn a dot on the white board representing the parachute, and two arrows of equal and opposite magnitude representing forces acting on the parachute. For Don, the parachute was falling in a straight line at a consistent speed, a steady pace. [A physicist would term this constant velocity.]

> Don: I did the parachute and I think that there are [two] equal forces because it's going in a pretty straight line and consistent speed and those two arrows are. One's gravity and the other one is friction.

SOURCE: Adapted from Beeth (1993, pp 126-132).

This statement was followed by a very rapid sequence of questions from a variety of students trying to understand why Don found this idea plausible. All of the students speaking at this time were very confident in asking their questions, and there was a feeling in the classroom that Don's idea was about to be refuted. Most were clear that a book at rest required two equal, opposing forces and that an object speeding up needed an unbalanced force. Don's explanation didn't fit into either category, and they thought that it should.

> Kitt: Why do you have equal arrows? I don't think it would be moving if they had equal arrows.
>
> Don: Well if [one arrow was] smaller they would be speeding up.
>
> Kitt: Well . . . [it] strongly suggests she thought it was speeding up.

Kirsty decided to follow up on the two equal arrows in opposite directions in Don's diagram, assisted by the teacher.

> Kirsty: I'm not sure if this has a lot to do with this but if that parachute was at rest, what would the arrows look like? You don't think that's not at rest?
>
> Don: Well . . . [it's not] at rest.
>
> Kirsty: No, I mean if it was.
>
> Teacher: She's just saying, in your mind, imagine this thing at rest. How would you label it?
>
> Don: Probably nothing [different].
>
> Teacher: Nothing [different]?

Kirsty hadn't bought Don's explanation, and after a while she continued with her argument about things at rest.

> Kirsty: Yeah. How would you label it if it was at rest? Pretend it's sitting on this table, on a station, pretend it was just sitting there. How would you label it at rest? You don't think that's what at rest is [two equal and opposite arrows]?
>
> Don: Well, gravity [is one force] and the table is a force.
>
> Kitt: So it would be exactly like this [two equal and opposite arrows] . . . OK, wouldn't it be going at a consistent speed?
>
> Rob: It is! [said emphatically]

Kitt's reentry to the conversation showed she had reconsidered her earlier position, and things had also clicked for Rob. Don then explicitly stated the commonality he saw between objects at rest and moving at a consistent speed.

Don: At rest is also at a consistent speed.

Stu: So you have two [ideas] for the same sets of arrows?

Don: If a thing is at rest it's still going in a straight line at consistent speed.

This was a significant breakthrough for Don and his fellow students: recognizing that the consistent speed and equal forces explanation was conceptually a more powerful bond than the visually obvious difference between a book at rest and a moving parachute

REFLECTION QUESTIONS

What were the interactions that produced learning in this example? What roles were played by the teacher and students? What classroom culture would be needed to support such learning? What professional development might help other teachers build such a culture in their classrooms? What teacher learning strategies might work well for this?

There are several things to note about these vignettes. First, the tasks presented by the teachers are familiar ones to the students: They have played with dice and tossed coins and have manipulated moving objects such as toy airplanes and parachutes. The tasks, therefore, allow students to mobilize their prior knowledge and to tap into what they already know about probability and forces. The students are set up to build on what they know or challenge it (or have it challenged) in some way. Note that the teachers understand deeply the concepts they are teaching so it is possible for them to know where students are to begin with and build constructively to new understandings.

Second, there is an extraordinary level of engagement by students. They are thinking deeply about the curriculum tasks of the classroom. They are expected and are able to explain what they are doing and why they are doing it. They listen to and expect to understand what their peers are saying. They do not automatically accept what they hear. The solutions to the tasks that they arrive at clearly matter to them.

Third, the tasks students are engaged in are constructed around significant concepts in mathematics and science. These tasks require them to think scientifically and mathematically by making conjectures and hypotheses and marshaling different forms of evidence to support or refute them. The nature of the solutions provided goes deeper than a fixed set of symbols or words to be reproduced exactly.

Fourth, students are communicating constantly with each other and with the teacher, learning by constructing and sharing explanations and having their explanations challenged and elaborated by others. Students are not restricted to consider only the ideas of the teacher and textbook authors. They are unlikely to develop images of mathematics and science as something done in isolation, or facts to be memorized and regurgitated. Their understanding of science and mathematics deepens and develops through communication and community.

Fifth, the teachers in these vignettes are playing a very different role than in typical classrooms. They have chosen curriculum tasks that are important and challenging, but not impossible for their students. They have established a classroom environment that enables students to express themselves, to disagree with their peers (and their teacher), and to feel safe in doing so. The teachers continually monitor classroom interactions, deciding when and how to intervene. They use their deep understanding of the concept they are teaching to help students make sense of their observations and analyze carefully what is going on.

There is reason to believe that the science and mathematics teaching envisioned in these vignettes leads to students who understand these disciplines (whether or not they intend to pursue careers that depend on them), are confident in their own abilities, and are motivated to study further as they see the value of their education. Furthermore, this vision is not a restricted one. It is not confined to a minority of students privileged by a social or a genetic inheritance, and it does not happen only in a few classrooms where "superteachers" create miracles out of reach of others in the profession. On the contrary, it illustrates that all students, regardless of their gender or race, class or culture, are intrinsically curious about and capable of understanding science and mathematics concepts. All teachers have these goals for their students, and they are capable of the quality of teaching needed to achieve them.

Teachers have an essential part to play in achieving this vision in the classroom. While there are many factors in educational environments that present barriers for good teachers, without major change in typical teaching, the vision of an enhanced educational system will evaporate. Throughout this book, a central theme has been that achieving the vision requires a revolution in teachers' professional development.

How does such professional development look "in action?" The next three vignettes illustrate the nature of the professional development we advocate in this book.

Vignette 3: Science Alive

Science Alive is a three-week institute for teachers sponsored by the Pacific Northwest Laboratory in Richland, Washington. Its purpose is to enhance teachers' content knowledge and investigation skills in environmental sciences, with a special emphasis on global environmental change. It emphasizes the use of "scenarios" that immerse learners in problems that require them to use a wide variety of investigative skills and integrate knowledge from a number of scientific disciplines. Over three weeks, teachers participate in four scenarios, work with several science curricula that take a similar approach to learning, learn how to use community resources, and develop their own lessons.

Today is the field component of the environmental geology scenario. Teachers load into two field vehicles, with one geologist per vehicle, and arrive at the scene of a dump site. They learn that the farmer who owns and farms these fields has chosen this location, a ravine that drains down toward the road, to dump many kinds of waste, from diapers to leftover herbicide. The question posed to the teachers is: What is the impact of this kind of dumping? They will address this question after a thorough tour of the area, learn about the geology and topography as they feel the need for information, and have an opportunity to work in the laboratory, doing any tests they feel would be useful.

A geologist asks: "What do you think you would need to know to address the question?" The teachers suggest many questions they have about the soil, water, underlying rock, nature of the waste material, and so on. All then reload in the vehicles to begin to get the "lay of the land."

The geologists have prepared for the teachers a nine-page guide: "Environmental Geology: Travel Log for Ringold/White Bluffs Site Survey." Each teacher has a journal, and the geologists have brought lots of materials along with them, including several road and topographic maps, air photos, soil and water sampling containers, Brunton Compasses, hand lenses, dilute HCl, a Munsell Soil Color Chart, and a fire extinguisher and shovel.

They begin 38 miles from the dump site and learn, through several stops and reading through the guide, about the economy of the area, the rock deposits, and the water diverted for agriculture from the Grand Coulee Dam. They mark several locations on their map: the water tower, the WPPS nuclear power plant, and so forth. They stop near a culvert and are given a handout with a cross-section of the area. A geologist asks: "Why is the water seeping out between the two formations?" The teachers discuss possible explanations, then the geologist talks about the difference in "hydraulic conductivity" between the two formations. They go on to another roadcut through the same formation and a geologist asks the teachers to predict how water applied at the surface might move through the deposits. The teachers discuss this and make some jottings in their journals. More questions are asked by the teachers and the geologists provide information—not too detailed, and they ask as many questions as they answer.

After several more stops, locatings on the maps, and observations about the nature of the rocks and water runoff patterns, the group begins to observe differences in the soils around the formations. A teacher suggests it would be useful to begin to take soil samples. A geologist produces the Munsell color chart and they check for soil color and test for calcium carbonate content with the dilute HCl. More stops and soil sampling, and discussions about what they make of what they are observing.

They have reached the dump site again, and from a distance the geologists ask them to describe the general topography of the land and compare it to the contour lines on the topographic map. What vegetation changes do they observe? What do these changes suggest about water movement in area? What kind of sediment would they predict to occur in this location?

The teachers scatter around the dump site and many of them take both soil and water samples, marking clearly on the map where they were taken from. The geologists suggest that to address the primary question of the impact of the waste dumping, the teachers might want to do several activities. These activities are listed at the back of the guide: (1) site characterization activities (e.g., What is the area underlying the waste debris? What is the slope? What is the direction and distance to the Columbia River?); (2) soil characterization activities (e.g., collect samples from various places, look for evidence of chemical or water movement off site); and (3) water chemistry and movement (e.g., observe vegetation patterns, take water samples from various locations).

As the day ends, the teachers and geologists reload into the vehicles for the trip back home. The discussions range from implications for the nuclear waste site nearby, to the accessibility of these activities to their students, to the variety of considerations scientists have to make to understand the natural world. Tomorrow will be spent in the laboratory, with small groups testing water and soil samples, working with their descriptions, their maps, and their calculations, to address the primary question (as well as many other questions that have arisen over the course of the day). Their activities will be interspersed with input from the geologists and a laboratory chemist helping them understand the scientific ideas behind their observations, analyses, and conclusions.

REFLECTION QUESTIONS

Teachers in this example are engaged in using science to address real world problems. How can that contribute to their learning? What can they take back to their classrooms from such an experience? In what ways can this example of professional development enhance student learning? In what ways were teachers' understanding of science content reflective of inquiry into scientific phenomena? How did the geologists model effective facilitation of learning?

Vignette 4: Computers in Geometry Class

A group of high school mathematics teachers has been meeting in a seminar twice a month at their school with partners who are mathematicians and mathematics educators from a nearby university. These teachers have been using computers in their geometry classes for the past year and a half, and the seminar provides them with opportunities to discuss what is happening in their classrooms as they think about new ways of teaching and learning.

The computer software allows students and their teachers to construct geometric shapes and to make measurements of lengths and angles and computations based on these measurements, thus providing an environment for open-ended exploration and discovery of patterns and relationships.

Although the teachers have been excited about their use of computers in geometry, many have voiced frustration in trying to make decisions about appropriate tasks for their students. Some teachers have been most comfortable focusing student attention on specific relationships, while others are dissatisfied with activities structured to lead students toward a particular "discovery." At times, many of the teachers have felt their own knowledge of geometry inadequate to deal with questions and conjectures that arise from open-ended explorations.

Gloria described a task she assigned her class early in the year: "I wanted my students to learn that the sum of the angle measures in a triangle is 180 degrees, so I had them construct a lot of triangles on the computer and record the angle measures. The software made it possible to collect a lot of data quickly and make a generalization. I thought my students would remember the relationship better if they discovered it themselves."

Rich talked about the same task: "I was really reluctant to use that activity because it didn't seem like exploration. It made me feel that I would be directing the students toward a single result and not really taking advantage of the technology. But when Gloria told me about some of the things her students came up with, I thought it might lead in some interesting directions. I was amazed at what happened. My students didn't just see what I thought they would see; many of them went off in all sorts of directions exploring other shapes. One even asked about a circle! I wasn't quite sure

SOURCE: National Council of Teachers of Mathematics (1991, pp. 141-142).

where to go with that question, but it certainly seemed intriguing—and it took us into lots of other ideas when we discussed it in the seminar."

Constanza remembered a lesson that was especially important to her: "One of my students had constructed a shape on the computer screen that he said looked three-dimensional. We took off on a discussion of geometric models and representations of shapes, something I hadn't really expected them to get into in that lesson. As we were talking about two- and three-dimensional shapes, Jan asked about a line. Well, a lot of the students thought that was boring, but then Raoul held up a paper clip and said he thought it was two-dimensional. And another student said that if you bent the paper clip it would be three-dimensional."

"That sent off a bunch of conjectures, with students coming up with good reasons for why the bent paper clip could be considered one-, two-, or three-dimensions. There was a lot more there than I had anticipated, and I thought it would be a great topic for discussion in the seminar. It made us think a lot about representations and how we describe and define geometric shapes."

The seminar has been a place where teachers can share their struggles with colleagues and university faculty and develop meaningful activities for their students. For many of the teachers, one of the most valuable aspects of the seminar has been the opportunity to extend their own understanding of geometry.

REFLECTION QUESTIONS

How do teachers who increase their own content knowledge increase confidence in the kind of open-ended exploration described in the vignette? What can make such instruction intimidating for those less knowledgeable about the content? How does bringing actual student work and their ideas into the professional development seminar enrich the experience? What are some of the different ways teachers can use real student work in professional learning situations? What professional development strategies work well for examining student ideas and work in the context of teacher learning?

Vignette 5: Plants

Andy Sanchez is a member of a study group that the teachers at his school recently formed to improve their teaching of science. When the district coordinator, Irene Patton, invited the teachers to form this group, she suggested they consider drawing on scientists and science educators from the

SOURCE: Adapted from Raizen and Michelsohn (1994).

local university and teachers from other schools as resources as they learn about ways to enhance science teaching and learning in the school.

At the first meeting, the teachers agreed to find a focus for their initial work. Andy brought a book he had recently read about learning in a constructivist way. He said he became more interested in learning theory after reading about research on the brain. He proposed that the study group learn more about it. He said he was nearly ready to introduce a unit on plants to his fifth-graders, a unit he's never used before, and that he would like to use the study group as a way to clarify what constructivist teaching is and to design the lessons in the new unit to reflect the constructivist learning theory.

Other teachers express interest and the teachers decided to work together in teams with others who are soon to introduce a similar topic (in most cases this turns out to be two or three teachers who teach the same grade level). In subsequent study group meetings, they read articles and presented one another with examples of teaching moves that are designed to help students build their knowledge, such as ways to assess students' prior knowledge. They discussed and agreed that to help them with their lesson planning, they should learn what the students know about the topic, learn more about the topic themselves, and then plan how to teach it to their students.

The teachers interviewed their students and came back to the study group the next week and shared with what they have learned. They realized that they were not always sure how to interpret students' ideas and explanations of what they knew about plants and their life cycles. They decided it was time to draw on a local scientist to help them. A botanist from the local university helped them focus on what they wanted the students to know and understand and helped them narrow their questions about what students already know. Andy and two other fifth-grade teachers decide to ask their students to describe how they think plants make food, and get them to draw their ideas. Other teacher teams agree on other things to focus their students on.

The teachers follow through in their classrooms over the next week. Andy's students drew pictures and diagrams about relationships between plants and the sun and the rain and the soil, and they explained their drawings and Andy took notes. He carefully recorded his data, as well as kept a journal of his reactions and feelings about the information-gathering process.

At the next week's session, the teachers were again joined by the botanist to help them share and make sense of their data. Andy and his team report that they are quite astonished at the range of ideas expressed by their fifth-graders. One of Andy's students told him that plant food was the green stuff his father mixes in water and puts on the plants in the house and garden once every two weeks. This student "knew" that plants need to be fed just like people do. Another student "knew" that the sun makes food for plants, which the plants can then give to animals. On probing, the child admitted that he wasn't quite sure how this works. One girl said she knew how plants make food because she planted carrots and beans in a little garden beside her house last year and then she ate the carrots and the beans. But she wasn't sure how the seeds turned into the vegetables. She guessed it has something to do with the dirt.

The teachers are fascinated by what they are learning from their students about what they know. And it forces them to examine their own understanding of plants. What do they really know? How and where did they get this knowledge? Andy's team is sure photosynthesis is a key process related to plants and their food. But what could they remember about photosynthesis from their own education? They remember some cycle (one teacher calls it the Krebs cycle) and that it was a nightmare memorizing it for a big test. What were all those arrows exiting a circular path, like roads branching from a rotary? What was the point of it all anyway?

At that point the teachers agree that it is time for them to learn more about plant physiology, and the botanist invites them to spend two consecutive Saturdays in the lab with him where they can pursue a "course" designed for adult learning. Once the teachers have more of a grasp on the subject matter, they will need to discuss what is developmentally appropriate for each grade level of student and how they can address the questions the students have in engaging ways. They know from what they've done so far that they'll need more help on this—this time from an experienced teacher who has worked with older students and can help them translate the content they will learn to appropriate teaching strategies for students at different ages.

REFLECTION QUESTIONS

This example of professional development shows how teachers can influence the focus of their own learning and draw on local resources to support them. What are the advantages and disadvantages of this? How did the use of outside resources such as books, new curriculum materials, a local scientist, and an experienced teacher strengthen this study group? What might happen if study groups do not have access to resources to help them with their questions? This book suggests that changing teacher practice can lead to changes in beliefs. How might the focus of this vignette help teachers change their beliefs about learning?

In Vignette 3, the geology field trip, the teachers are students again, but this is different from any learning they experienced in grade school and college. The way they are learning is different: The teachers are investigating an open question that seems simple and clear but that requires a complex, involved answer; they interact with one another and the instructors with interest and frustration; and there is nothing repetitive in what they are doing. The science these teachers are doing is different: They are gathering information, making hypotheses, and arguing about the interplay of various factors. There is no book with the correct answers in the back, but there is opportunity to learn science content from experts on the spot, when it is appropriate. The teaching they are experiencing is different: Their instructors ask as many questions as they answer, many of those questions seem to have many possible answers, and the instructors have set the context for their activity and provided extensive resources for the teachers to use, but they have not shown them what to do.

In Vignette 4, the mathematics seminar group, the teachers are teaching but that is not all there is to it: They are studying their practice in collaboration with colleagues and peers. By sharing their successes and failures with each other, they get new ideas to try, encouragement to keep going when things do not seem to be working, a richer understanding of the students they teach and the geometry they want them to learn, and a greater sense of their involvement in a professional practice and in improving their own competency. What a difference from the isolation of closing their classroom doors on the world outside!

In Vignette 5, preparing to teach their young students about plants, the teachers are again collaborating with their peers, this time to construct new understandings about constructivist learning and the kinds of teaching it implies. They are conducting an investigation into their students' understanding of important science concepts, and in doing so, raising questions about their own understanding of the same ideas. At their own initiative, they combine their expertise about how children learn with the expertise of a scientist and teacher of older children; they pursue deeper understanding of science, to design more effective learning experiences for their students.

These last three vignettes provide a glimpse into the many faces of effective professional development, mirroring the beliefs of the book's authors identified in the Introduction. First, if science and mathematics teachers are to become the teachers envisioned above, they need to experience for themselves the science and mathematics learning they will want their students to do. Hearing about it in a vicarious manner is no substitute at all. Next, professional development takes time, it requires teachers to be reflective about their practice, and it is greatly facilitated by open discourse with professional colleagues. Professional development that is confined to short, discrete events is a wasted effort. Each vignette is part of an ongoing sequence of learning opportunities. Also, professional development happens in a community of learning; just as students increase their knowledge of science and mathematics through communication, so, too, do their teachers learn through formulating, sharing, and challenging what they and their colleagues think they know in order to learn. Finally, professional development needs to be linked to the real context of the local schools to influence teaching and learning. This can occur indirectly through the structures and policies that can help or hinder a teacher's efforts and directly through the nature of professional development that is offered. School systems have a key role in developing leadership in their teachers.

These scenes from classrooms and professional development experiences suggest, but in no way detail, what effective professional development is and needs to be. We invite you to begin building toward a new way of teaching and learning now. Toss away old conceptions of teaching as telling and learning as listening. Put into practice the common knowledge of effective teaching and learning, and you will change the teaching profession for years to come and the quality of living for many children you touch along the way.

References

Acquarelli, K., & Mumme, J. (1996). A renaissance in mathematics education reform. *Phi Delta Kappan, 77*(7), 478-484.

American Association for the Advancement of Science. (1993). *Project 2061: Benchmarks for science literacy.* New York: Oxford University Press.

American Association for the Advancement of Science. (2000). *Atlas of science literacy.* Washington, DC: Author; Arlington, VA: National Science Teachers Association.

Anderson, R. D., & Pratt, H. (1995). *Local leadership for science education reform.* Dubuque, IA: Kendall Hunt.

Bailey, S. (1995, December). *Managing reform efforts—Detecting and gardening multiple change initiatives.* Speech presented at the annual conference of the National Staff Development Council, Chicago.

Ball, D. L. (1996). Teacher learning and the mathematics reforms: What we think we know and what we need to learn. *Phi Delta Kappan, 77*(7), 500-508.

Ball, D. L., & Cohen, D. K. (1995). *Developing practice, developing practitioners: Toward a practice-based theory of professional education.* Paper presented at the National Commission on Teaching and America's Future, New York.

Ball, D. L., & Cohen, D. K. (1999). Developing practice, developing practitioners: Toward a practice-based theory of professional education. In L. Darling-Hammond & G. Sykes (Eds.), *Teaching as the learning profession: Handbook of policy and practice* (pp. 3-32). San Francisco: Jossey-Bass.

Ball, D. L., & Cohen, D. K. (2000). *Challenges of improving instruction: A view from the classroom.* Paper prepared for the Council of Basic Education.

Barnett, C. (1991). Building a case-based curriculum to enhance the pedagogical content knowledge of mathematics teachers. *Journal of Teacher Education, 42*(4), 263-272.

Barnett, C. (1999). Cases. *Journal of Staff Development, 20*(3), 26-27.

Barnett, C., & Friedman, S. (1997). Mathematics case discussions: Nothing is sacred. In E. Fennema & B. Scott-Nelson (Eds.), *Mathematics teachers in transition.* Hillsdale, NJ: Lawrence Erlbaum.

Barnett, C., & Sather, S. (1992). *Using case discussions to promote changes in beliefs among mathematics teachers.* Paper presented at the annual meeting of the American Education Research Association, San Francisco.

Barnett, C., & Tyson, P. (1993). *Mathematics teaching cases as a catalyst for informed strategic inquiry.* Paper presented at the annual meeting of the American Educational Research Association, Atlanta, GA.

Barth, R. (2001). *Learning by heart.* San Francisco: Jossey-Bass.

Beeth, M. E. (1993). *Dynamic aspects of conceptual change instruction.* Unpublished doctoral dissertation, University of Wisconsin–Madison.

Bennett, B., & Green, N. (1995). Effect of the learning consortium: One district's journey. *School Effectiveness and School Improvement, 6*(3), 247-264.

Black, P., & William, D. (1998). Inside the black box: Raising standards through classroom assessment. *Phi Delta Kappan, 80*(2), 139-148.

Boss, S. (2001, Spring). Leading from within. *Northwest Teacher.* Retrieved from www.nwrel.org/msec/nwteacher/spring2001

Bransford, J. D., Brown, A. L., & Cocking, R. R. (1999). *How people learn.* Washington, DC: National Academy Press.

Briars, D. J., & Resnick, L. B. (2001, January). *Standards, assessments—And what else? The essential elements of standards-based school improvement.* Unpublished paper presented at the Horizon Research, Inc. Local Systemic Change meeting, Studying the Effects of the LSC on Students, Research Triangle Park, NC.

Britton, E., Raizen, S., Kaser, J., & Porter, A. (2000). *Beyond description of the problems.* Madison, WI: National Institute for Science Education.

Brown, C. A., & Smith, M. S. (1997). Supporting the development of mathematical pedagogy. *Mathematics Teacher, 90*(2), 138-143.

Bruner, J. (1966). *Toward a theory of instruction.* Cambridge, MA: Harvard University Press.

Burns, M. (1994). *Replacement units: A direction for changing math instruction.* Sausalito, CA: Math Solutions Publications, Marilyn Burns Education Associates.

Bybee, R. (1993). *Reforming science education: Social perspectives and personal reflections.* New York: Teachers College Press.

Bybee, R. W. (1997). *Achieving scientific literacy: From purposes to practices.* Portsmouth, NH: Heinemann.

Campbell, P. (1995). Project IMPACT: Increasing Mathematics Power for All Children and Teachers, final report. College Park, MD: Center for Mathematics Education, University of Maryland.

Carlson, M. O., Humphrey, G., & Reinhardt, K. (in press). Weaving science inquiry & continuous assessment. Thousand Oaks, CA: Corwin.

Castle, S., & Watts, G. D. (1992). The tyranny of time. *A Forum on School Transformation From the NEA National Center for Innovation, 8*(2), 1-4.

Cobb, P. (1994). Where is the mind? Constructivist and sociocultural perspectives on mathematical development. *Educational Researcher, 23*(7), 13-20.

Coble, C. R., & Koballa, T. R., Jr. (1996). Science education. In J. Sikula, T. J. Buttery, & E. Guyton (Eds.), *Handbook of research in teacher education* (pp. 459-484). New York: Simon & Schuster/Macmillan.

Cochran, K. F., De Ruiter, J. A., & King, R. A. (1993). Pedagogical content knowing: An integrative model for teacher preparation. *Journal of Teacher Education, 44,* 263-272.

Cohen, D., & Hill, H. C. (2001). *Learning policy: When state education reform works.* New Haven, CT: Yale University Press.

Cohen, D. K., & Ball, D. L. (1999, June). *Instruction, capacity, and improvement.* CPRE Research Report Series, RR-43. Philadelphia: University of Pennsylvania, Consortium for Policy Research in Education.

Cohen, D. K., & Hill, H. C. (1998). State policy and classroom performance: Mathematics reform in California. *CPRE Policy Briefs* (RB-23-January, 1-14). Philadelphia: Consortium for Policy Research in Education, Graduate School of Education, University of Pennsylvania.

Corwin, R. B. (1997). Talking mathematics: Supporting discourse in elementary school classrooms. In S. N. Friel & G. W. Bright (Eds.), *Reflecting on our work: NSF teacher enhancement in K-6 mathematics* (pp. 187-192). Lanham, MD: University Press of America.

Costa, A., & Kallick, B. (1993). Through the lens of a critical friend. *Educational Leadership,*
51(3), 49-51.

Council of Chief State School Officers. (2000). *Using data on the enacted curriculum in mathe-*
matics and science: Sample results from a study of classroom practices and subject content.
Washington, DC: Author.

Covey, S. R. (1989). *The seven habits of highly effective people: Restoring the character ethic.* New
York: Simon & Schuster.

Cross, C., & Rice, R. (2000). The role of the principal as instructional leader in a standards-
driven system. *NASSP Bulletin, 84*(620), 61-65.

Crowther, F., Kaagan, S. S., Ferguson, M., & Hann, L. (2002). *Developing teacher leaders.* Thousand Oaks, CA: Corwin.

Darling-Hammond, L. (1997). *Doing what matters most: Investing in quality teaching.* New
York: National Commission on Teaching and America's Future.

Darling-Hammond, L. (1999). Target time toward teachers. *Journal of Staff Development,*
20(2), 31-36.

Darling-Hammond, L. (2000). Teacher quality and student achievement: A review of state
policy and evidence. *Education Policy Archives, 8.* Retrieved from Web site: http://
epaa.asu.edu

Darling-Hammond, L., & McLaughlin, M. W. (1999). Investing in teaching as a learning profession: Policy, problems and prospects. In L. Darling-Hammond & G. Sykes (Eds.),
Teaching as the learning profession: Handbook of policy and practice (pp. 376-412). San Francisco: Jossey-Bass.

Davenport, L. R., & Sassi, A. (1995). Transforming mathematics teaching in Grades K-8:
How narrative structures in resource materials help support teacher change. In B. S.
Nelson (Ed.), *Inquiry and the development of teaching: Issues in the transformation of mathe-*
matics teaching (pp. 37-46). Newton, MA: Center for the Development of Teaching, Education Development Center.

Deal, T. A., & Kennedy, A. A. (1982). *Corporate cultures: The rites and rituals of corporate life.*
Reading, MA: Addison-Wesley.

Denmark, V. M., & Podsen, I. J. (2000). The mettle of a mentor. *Journal of Staff Development,*
21(4), 18-22.

DePree, M. (1989). *Leadership is an art.* New York: Dell.

DiRanna, K., Osterfeld, M., Cerwin, K., Topps, J., & Tucker, D. (1995, Spring). *Facilitator's*
guide to science assessment. California Department of Education, California Science Implementation Network, California Science Project, Scope, Sequence, & Coordination
Project, & Santa Barbara County Office of Education Region 8.

Driscoll, M. (2001). *Fostering algebraic thinking toolkit.* Westport, CT: Heinemann.

Driscoll, M. (2002). *Inviting professional growth: The case of the Algebraic Thinking Toolkit.* Retrieved from www.TE-MAT.org/driscoll.shtml

Driscoll, M., & Bryant, D. (1998). *Learning about assessment, learning through assessment.*
Washington, DC: National Research Council, Mathematical Sciences Education Board.

Driver, R., Asoko, H., Leach, J., Mortimer, E., & Scott, P. (1994). Constructing scientific
knowledge in the classroom. *Educational Researcher, 23*(7), 5-12.

Duckworth, E. (1986). Teaching as research. *Harvard Educational Review, 56*(4), 481-495.

DuFour, R. (2000, Winter). Community: Data put a face on shared vision. *Journal of Staff De-*
velopment, 21(1), 71-72.

DuFour, R. (2001). In the right context. *Journal of Staff Development, 22*(1), 14-17.

DuFour, R., & Eaker, R. (1998). *Professional learning communities at work.* Bloomington, IN:
National Educational Service.

Dunne, F., Nave, B., & Lewis, A. (2000, December). Critical friends groups: Teachers helping
teachers to improve student learning. *Phi Delta Kappa International, Research Bulletin,*
No. 28. Retrieved from http:www.pdkintl.org/edres/resbul28.htm

Duschl, R. A. (1990). *Restructuring science education: The importance of theories and their devel-*
opment. New York: Teachers College Press.

Dyasi, H. (1990). Assessing imperfect conceptions. In K. Jervis & C. Montag, *Progressive education for the 21st century*. New York: Teachers College Press.

Dyasi, H. M. (1995). *The City College Workshop Center program for reculturing teachers to teach inquiry-based science in the elementary school*. Unpublished manuscript.

Education Commission of the States. (1995). *Scaling-up math, science and technology education reform: Strategies from the National Science Foundation's statewide systemic initiatives*. Denver, CO: Author.

Educational Research Service. (1999). Professional development for school principals. *The Informed Educator Series* (WS-0350). Arlington, VA: Author.

Eisenhower National Clearinghouse. (1998). *Ideas that work: Mathematics professional development*. Columbus, OH: Author.

Eisenhower National Clearinghouse. (1999). *Ideas that work: Science professional development*. Columbus, OH: Author.

Eisenhower National Clearinghouse and National Staff Development Council. (2002). *By your own design: A teacher's professional learning guide* [CD]. Oxford, OH: National Staff Development Council.

Elmore, R. F. (1996). Getting to scale with good educational practice. *Harvard Educational Review, 66*(1), 1-26.

Elmore, R. F., & Burney, D. (1999). Investing in teacher learning: Staff development and instructional improvement. In L. Darling-Hammond & G. Sykes (Eds.), *Teaching as the learning profession: Handbook of policy and practice*. San Francisco: Jossey-Bass.

Evans, C. S. (1993). When teachers look at student work. *Educational Leadership, 50*(5), 71-72.

Evans, R. (1996). *The human side of school change: Reform, resistance, and the real-life problems of innovation*. San Francisco: Jossey-Bass.

Far West Laboratory. (1990, Summer). *Case methods: A knowledge brief on effective teaching*. San Francisco: Author.

Fazio, R. P., Levine, C., & Merry, D. (2000). Cultivating a garden of educators. *Journal of Staff Development, 21*(2), 16-19.

Fernández-Balboa, J. M., & Stiehl, J. (1995). The generic nature of pedagogical content knowledge among college professors. *Teaching & Teacher Education, 11*, 293-306.

Ferrini-Mundy, J. (1997). Reform efforts in mathematics education: Reckoning with the realities. In S. N. Friel & G. W. Bright (Eds.), *Reflecting on our work: NSF teacher enhancement in K-6 mathematics* (pp. 113-132). Lanham, MD: University Press of America.

Filby, N. N. (1995, November 30). *Analysis of reflective professional development models*. San Francisco: WestEd.

Friel, S. N. (1996). *Teach-Stat: A model for professional development in data analysis and statistics for teachers K-6*. Paper presented at the Professional Development Project of the National Institute for Science Education, Madison, WI.

Friel, S. N., & Bright, G. W. (Eds.). (1997). *Reflecting on our work: NSF teacher enhancement in K-6 mathematics*. Lanham, MD: University Press of America.

Friel, S. N., & Danielson, M. L. (1997). Teach-Stat: A key to better mathematics. In S. N. Friel & G. W. Bright (Eds.), *Reflecting on our work: NSF teacher enhancement in K-6 mathematics* (pp. 197-206). Lanham, MD: University Press of America.

Friel, S. N., & Joyner, J. (1991). *Teach-Stat: A key to better mathematics*. Arlington, VA: National Science Foundation.

Friel, S. N., & Joyner, J. (Eds.). (1997). *Teach-Stat for teachers: Professional development manual*. Palo Alto, CA: Seymour.

Fritz, R. (1996). *Corporate tides: The inescapable laws of organizational structure*. San Francisco: Berrett-Koehler.

Frost, D. L. (1995). *Elementary teachers' conceptions of mathematics staff development and their roles as workshop leaders*. Unpublished doctoral dissertation, University of North Carolina at Greensboro.

Fullan, M. (2000). The three stories of education reform. *Phi Delta Kappan, 81*(8), 581-584.

Fullan, M. (2001). *Leading in a culture of change*. San Francisco: Jossey-Bass.

Fullan, M. (2002). The change leader. *Educational Leadership, 59*(8), 16-20.

Fullan, M. G. (1991). *The new meaning of educational change.* New York: Teachers College Press.

Fullan, M. G. (1993). *Change forces: Probing the depths of educational reform.* Bristol, PA: Falmer.

Fullan, M. G., & Hargreaves, A. (1991). *What's worth fighting for? Working together for your school.* Andover, MA: Regional Laboratory for Educational Improvement of the Northeast and Islands.

Fullan, M. G., & Miles, M. (1992). Getting reform right: What works and what doesn't. *Phi Delta Kappan, 73*(10), 745-752.

Garet, M. S., Birman, B. F., Porter, A. C., Desimone, L., Herman, R., & Yoon, K. S. (1999). *Designing effective professional development: Lessons from the Eisenhower program.* Washington, DC: U.S. Department of Education.

Garmston, R. (1987). How administrators support peer coaching. *Educational Leadership, 44*(5), 18-28.

Gleason, J., Vesilind, E., Friel, S. N., & Joyner, J. (Eds.). (1996). *Teach-Stat for statistics educators: Staff developers manual.* Palo Alto, CA: Seymour.

Goldenberg, L. B., & Outsen, N. (2002). Missed connections can be instructive: Project to link teachers turns setbacks into information. *Journal of Staff Development 1*(23), 28-31.

Goldhaber, D. D., & Brewer, D. J. (2000, Summer). Does teacher certification matter? High school teacher certification status and student achievement. *Education Evaluation and Policy Journal, 22*(22).

Grady, A. (1997). Elementary and middle school math and technology project. In S. N. Friel & G. W. Bright (Eds.), *Reflecting on our work: NSF teacher enhancement in K-6 mathematics* (pp. 207-214). Lanham, MD: University Press of America.

Graham, B. I., & Fahey, K. (1999). School leaders look at student work. *Educational Leadership, 56*(6).

Guiney, E. (2001). Coaching isn't just for athletes: The role of teacher leaders. *Phi Delta Kappan, 82*(10), 740-743.

Guskey, T. R. (1999). Apply time with wisdom. *Journal of Staff Development, 20*(2), 10-15.

Guskey, T. R. (2000). *Evaluating professional development.* Thousand Oaks, CA: Corwin.

Hall, G. E., & Hord, S. M. (1987). *Change in schools: Facilitating the process.* Albany: State University of New York Press.

Hall, G. E., & Hord, S. M. (2001). *Implementing change: Patterns, principles, and potholes.* Boston: Allyn & Bacon.

Hawley, W. D., & Valli, L. (1999). The essentials of effective professional development. In L. Darling-Hammond & G. Sykes (Eds.), *Teaching as the learning profession: Handbook of policy and practice* (pp. 127-150). San Francisco: Jossey-Bass.

Hawley, W. D., & Valli, L. (2000, August). Learner-centered professional development. *Research Bulletin, Phi Delta Kappa Center for Evaluation, Development, and Research, No. 27,* 1-7.

Haycock, K., & Robinson, S. (2001). Time-wasting workshops? *Journal of Staff Development, 22*(2), 16-18.

Heck, D. J., Weiss, I. R., Boyd, S., & Howard, M. (2002, April 2). *Lessons learned about planning and implementing statewide systemic initiatives in mathematics and science education.* Presented at the annual meeting of the American Educational Research Association, New Orleans, LA. Retrieved from Web site: www.horizon-research.com

Heller, J. I., Kaskowitz, D., Daehler, K. R., & Shinohara, M. (2001). *Annual technical report to the Stuart Foundation.* San Francisco: WestEd.

Hewson, P. W., & Thorley, N. R. (1989). The conditions of conceptual change in the classroom. *International Journal of Science Education, 11*(5), 541-553.

Hoff, D. J. (2000, February 23). A teaching style that adds up. *Ed Week, 19*(24), 32-37.

Holly, P. (1991). Action research: The missing link in the creation of schools as centers of inquiry. In A. Lieberman & L. Miller (Eds.), *Staff development for education in the 90's: New demands, new realities, new perspectives* (pp. 133-157). New York: Teachers College Press.

Hord, S. (1998). *Creating a professional learning community: Cottonwood Creek School.* Washington, DC: Office of Educational Research and Improvement (ERIC Document Reproduction No. ED424685).

Hord, S. M., & Boyd, V. (1995). Professional development fuels a culture of continuous improvement. *Journal of Staff Development, 16*(1), 10-15.

Hord, S. M., Rutherford, W. L., Huling-Austin, L., & Hall, G. E. (1987). *Taking charge of change.* Alexandria, VA: Association for Supervision and Curriculum Development.

Horizon Research. (2000). *2000-2001 local systemic change classroom observation protocol.* Chapel Hill, NC: Author.

Horizon Research. (2001). *Local systemic change through teacher enhancement: 2001 teacher questionnaire: Mathematics (6-12).* Chapel Hill, NC: Author.

Huberman, A. M. (1995). Networks that alter teaching: Conceptualizations, exchanges and experiments. In J. Little & M. McLaughlin (Eds.), *Teachers work.* New York: Teachers College Press.

Institute for Educational Leadership. (2000). *Leadership for student learning: Reinventing the principalship—A report of the task force on the principalship.* Washington, DC: Author.

International Society for Technology in Education. (2000). *National Educational Technology Standards.* Retrieved from Web site: www.iste.org

Jonassen, D. H. (1994). Thinking technology: Toward a constructivist design model. *Educational Technology, 34*(4), 34-37.

Joyce, B., & Showers, B. (1988). *Student achievement through staff development.* New York: Longman.

Joyner, J. (1997). TEAM: Teaching excellence in mathematics. In S. N. Friel & G. W. Bright (Eds.), *Reflecting on our work: NSF teacher enhancement in K-6 mathematics* (pp. 223-228). Lanham, MD: University Press of America.

Joyner, J., Pfieffer, S., Friel, S. N., & Vesilind, E. (Eds.). (1997a). *Teach-Stat activities: Statistics investigations for Grades 1-3.* Palo Alto, CA: Seymour.

Joyner, J., Pfieffer, S., Friel, S. N., & Vesilind, E. (Eds.). (1997b). *Teach-Stat activities: Statistics investigations for Grades 3-6.* Palo Alto, CA: Seymour.

Kaser, J., Mundry, S., Stiles, K. E., & Loucks-Horsley, S. (2002). *Leading every day: 124 actions for effective leadership.* Thousand Oaks, CA: Corwin.

Kaser, J. S., & Bourexis, P. S., with Loucks-Horsley, S., & Raizen, S. A. (1999). *Enhancing program quality in science and mathematics.* Thousand Oaks, CA: Corwin.

Katzenmeyer, M., & Moller, G. (1996). *Awakening the sleeping giant: Leadership development for teachers.* Thousand Oaks, CA: Corwin.

Kelemanik, G., Janssen, S., Miller, B., & Resnick, K. (1997). *Structured exploration: New perspectives on mathematics professional development.* Newton, MA: Education Development Center.

Killion, J. (1998, December). Learning depends on teacher knowledge. *Results.* (Oxford, OH: National Staff Development Council)

Killion, J. (2002). Loading the e-learning shopping cart: First examine the product and serve for student results. *Journal of Staff Development, 23*(1), 12-16.

King, B., & Newmann, F. (2000, April). Will teacher learning advance school goals? *Phi Delta Kappan,* pp. 576-580.

Klein, S. P., McArthur, D. J., & Stecher, B. M. (1995, February). *What are the challenges to "scaling up" reform?* Briefing paper for National Science Foundation Conference, Washington, DC.

Kleinfeld, J. (n.d.). *Ethical issues and legal liability in writing cases about teaching.* Unpublished manuscript.

Klentschy, M., Garrison, L., & Amaral, O. (n.d.). *Valle Imperial project in science (VIPS) four-year comparison of student achievement data, 1995-1999* (Research Series No. 1). San Diego: Educational Research Institute, San Diego State University, Imperial Valley Campus, Calexico, CA.

Koba, S. B., Clarke, W. M., & Mitchell, C. T. (2000). Action research: Collaborative efforts in teacher change. In D. L. Jordan, M. A. Henry, & J. T. Sutton (Eds.), *Changing Omaha class-*

rooms: Collaborative action research efforts (pp. 90-102). Aurora, CO: McREL Eisenhower High Plains Consortium for Mathematics and Science.

Kotter, J. (1996). *Leading change.* Boston: Harvard Business School Press.

Kouzes, J. M., & Posner, B. Z. (2001). *Leadership practices inventory, individual contributor, participant's workbook* (2nd ed.). San Francisco: Jossey-Bass/Pfeiffer.

Kovacik, B. (2000). *Transforming learning for science and mathematics teachers by design.* Unpublished paper presented to the NISE Professional Development working group, Andover, MA.

LaBonte, K., Leighty, C., Mills, S. J., & True, M. L. (1995). Whole-faculty study groups: Building the capacity for change through interagency collaboration. *Journal of Staff Development, 16*(3), 45-47.

Lambert, L. (1998). *Building leadership capacity in schools.* Alexandria, VA: Association for Supervision and Curriculum Development.

Lave, J., & Wenger, E. (1991). *Situated learning: Legitimate peripheral participation.* Cambridge, UK: Cambridge University Press.

Leonhardt, N., & Fraser-Abder. P. (1996). Research experiences for teachers. *Science Teacher, 63*(1), 30-33.

Lewis, A. C. (1998). Student work. *Journal of Staff Development, 19*(4), 24-27.

Lewis, C. (2002a, January). Does lesson study have a future in the United States? *Nagoya Journal of Education and Human Development, 1,* 1-23.

Lewis, C. (2002b). Everywhere I looked—Levers and pendulums: Research lessons bring studies to life and energize teaching. *Journal of Staff Development, 23*(3), 59-65.

Lieberman, A. (1986). Collaborative research: Working with, not working on. . . . *Educational Leadership, 43*(5), 28-32.

Lieberman, A., & McLaughlin, M. W. (1992). Networks for educational change: Powerful and problematic. *Phi Delta Kappan, 73*(9), 673-677.

Liptak, L. (2002). It's a matter of time: Scheduling lesson study at Paterson, NJ School 2. *RBS Currents, 5*(2), 1-3. Retrieved from Web site: www.rbs.org/currents

Little, J. W. (1982). Norms of collegiality and experimentation: Workplace conditions of school success. *American Educational Research Journal, 19*(3), 325-340.

Little, J. W. (1993). Teachers' professional development in a climate of educational reform. *Educational Evaluation and Policy Analysis, 15*(2), 129-151.

Loucks-Horsley, S. (1995). Professional development and the learner-centered school. *Theory Into Practice, 34*(4), 265-271.

Loucks-Horsley, S. (1996). Professional development for science education: A critical and immediate challenge. In R. W. Bybee (Ed.), *National standards and the science curriculum: Challenges, opportunities, and recommendations.* Dubuque, IA: Kendall/Hunt.

Loucks-Horsley, S. (1999). Effective professional development for teachers of mathematics. In Eisenhower National Clearinghouse, *Ideas that work: Mathematics professional development.* Columbus, OH: Eisenhower National Clearinghouse.

Loucks-Horsley, S., Harding, C. K., Arbuckle, M. A., Murray, L. B., Dubea, C., & Williams, M. K. (1987). *Continuing to learn: A guidebook for teacher development.* Andover, MA/Oxford, OH: Regional Laboratory for Educational Improvement of the Northeast and Islands/National Staff Development Council.

Loucks-Horsley, S., Hewson, P. W., Love, N., & Stiles, K. E. (1998). *Designing professional development for teachers of science and mathematics.* Thousand Oaks, CA: Corwin.

Loucks-Horsley, S., Kapitan, R., Carlson, M. O., Kuerbis, P. J., Clark, R. C., Melle, G. M., Sachse, T. P., & Walton, E. (1990). *Elementary school science for the 90's.* Alexandria, VA/Andover, MA: Association for Supervision and Curriculum Development/The NETWORK.

Loucks-Horsley, S., & Stiegelbauer, S. (1991). Using knowledge of change to guide staff development. In A. Lieberman & L. Miller (Eds.), *Staff development for education in the 90's: New demands, new realities, new perspectives.* New York: Teachers College Press.

Loucks-Horsley, S., Stiles, K. E., & Hewson, P. (1996). *Principles of effective professional development for mathematics and science education: A synthesis of standards: NISE Brief.* Madison: University of Wisconsin at Madison, National Institute for Science Education.

Louis, K. S., Kruse, S., & Marks, H. (1996). Schoolwide professional community. In F. Newmann and Associates (Eds.), *Authentic achievement: Restructuring schools for intellectual quality* (pp. 179-203). San Francisco: Jossey-Bass.

Love, N. (2002). *Using data/getting results: A practical guide for school improvement in mathematics and science.* Norwood, MA: Christopher Gordon.

Ma, L. (1999). *Knowing and teaching elementary mathematics.* Mahwah, NJ: Lawrence Erlbaum.

Makibbin, S., & Sprague, M. (1991). *Study groups: Conduit for reform.* Paper presented at the annual meeting of the National Staff Development Council, St. Louis, MO.

Massell, D. (2000, September). The district role in building capacity: Four strategies. *CPRE Policy Brief* (RB-32). Philadelphia: University of Pennsylvania.

McCullum, P. C. (2000). 6 points of a partnership. *Journal of Staff Development, 21*(2), 39.

McDiarmid, G. W. (1995). *Realizing new learning for all students: A framework for the professional development of Kentucky teachers* (Special Report, pp. 1-33). East Lansing, MI: National Center for Research on Teacher Learning.

McLaughlin, M. W. (1993). What matters most in teachers' workplace context? In J. W. Little & M. W. McLaughlin (Eds.), *Teachers' work: Individuals, colleagues, and contexts* (pp. 79-103). New York: Teachers College Press.

McLaughlin, M. W., & Talbert, J. (2001). *Professional communities and the work of high school teaching.* Chicago: University of Chicago Press.

Mechling, K. R., & Oliver, D. L. (1983). *Promoting science among elementary school principals.* Washington, DC: National Science Teachers Association.

Merseth, K. (1991). *The case for cases in teacher education.* Washington, DC: American Association of Higher Education/American Association of Colleges for Teacher Education.

Mezirow, J. (1991). *Transformative dimensions of adult learning.* San Francisco: Jossey-Bass.

Mezirow, J. (1997). Transformative learning: Theory to practice. In P. Cranton (Ed.), *Transformative learning in action: Insights from practice* (pp. 5-12). New Directions for Adult and Continuing Education No. 74. San Francisco: Jossey-Bass.

Miles, M. B. (1983). Unravelling the mysteries of institutionalization. *Educational Leadership, 41*(3), 14-20.

Miller, D. M., & Pine, G. J. (1990). Advancing professional inquiry for educational improvement through action research. *Journal of Staff Development, 11*(3), 56-61.

Mumme, J., & Seago, N. (2002, April). *Issues and challenges in facilitating videocases for mathematics professional development.* Paper presented at the annual meeting of the American Education Research Association.

Mundry, S. (2003). Honoring adult learners: Adult learning theories and implications for professional development. In J. Rhoten & P. Bowers (Eds.), *Science teacher retention: Mentoring and renewal.* Arlington, VA: National Science Education Leadership Association/National Science Teachers Association.

Mundry, S., Britton, E., Raizen, S., & Loucks-Horsley, S. (2000). *Designing successful professional meetings and conferences in education: Planning, implementation, and evaluation.* Thousand Oaks, CA: Corwin.

Mundry, S., & Loucks-Horsley, S. (1999). Designing effective professional development: Decision points and dilemmas. *NISE brief.* Madison: University of Wisconsin–Madison.

Murphy, C. (1995). Whole-faculty study groups: Doing the seemingly undoable. *Journal of Staff Development, 16*(3), 37-44.

Murphy, C. U., & Lick, D. W. (2001). *Whole-faculty study groups: Creating student-based professional development.* Thousand Oaks, CA: Corwin.

Murphy, M. (2001, May). Developing skills to embrace parent involvement. *Results.* (Oxford, OH: National Staff Development Council)

National Center for Education Statistics. (2001). *Teacher preparation and professional development: 2000* (NCES Publication No. 2001-008). Washington, DC: U.S. Department of Education.

National Commission on Mathematics and Science Teaching for the 21st Century. (2000). *Before it's too late: A report to the nation from the National Commission on Mathematics and Science Teaching for the 21st Century.* Washington, DC: U.S. Department of Education.

National Commission on Teaching and America's Future. (1996). *What matters most: Teaching for America's future.* New York: Author.

National Council of Teachers of Mathematics. (1989). *Curriculum and evaluation standards for school mathematics.* Reston, VA: Author.

National Council of Teachers of Mathematics. (1991). *Professional standards for teaching mathematics.* Reston, VA: Author.

National Council of Teachers of Mathematics. (1995). *Assessment standards for school mathematics.* Reston, VA: Author.

National Council of Teachers of Mathematics. (2000). *Principles and standards for school mathematics.* Reston, VA: Author.

National Education Commission on Time and Learning. (1994). *Prisoners of time.* Washington, DC: Author.

National Education Goals Panel. (2000, December). Bringing all students to high standards. *NEGP Monthly.*

National Partnership for Excellence and Accountability in Teaching. (2000). *Revisioning professional development: What learner-centered professional development looks like.* Oxford, OH: National Staff Development Council.

National Research Council. (1996a). *National science education standards.* Washington, DC: National Academy Press.

National Research Council. (1996b). *The role of scientists in the professional development of science teachers.* Washington, DC: National Academy Press.

National Research Council. (1999a). *Designing mathematics or science curriculum programs: A guide for using mathematics and science education standards.* Washington, DC: National Academy Press.

National Research Council. (1999b). *Selecting instructional materials: A guide for K-12 science.* Washington, DC: National Academy Press.

National Research Council. (2000). *Inquiry and the National Science Education Standards: A guide for teaching and learning.* Washington, DC: National Academy Press.

National Research Council. (2001). *Classroom assessment and the National Science Education Standards.* Washington, DC: National Academy Press.

National Science Resources Center. (1997). *Science for all children: A guide to improving elementary science education in your school district.* Washington, DC: National Academy Press.

National Science Teachers Association. (1993). Scope, sequence, and coordination of secondary school science. In *The content core: A guide for curriculum designers.* Arlington, VA: Author.

National Science Teachers Association. (2001). [Online survey of NSTA members]. Arlington, VA: Author.

National Staff Development Council. (2001a). *E-learning for educators: Implementing the standards for staff development.* Oxford, OH: Author. Retrieved from www. nsdc.org/standards_tech.html

National Staff Development Council. (2001b). *Standards for staff development.* Oxford, OH: Author.

Nelson, B. S. (1995). Introduction. In B. S. Nelson (Ed.), *Inquiry and the development of teaching: Issues in the transformation of mathematics teaching* (pp. 1-7). Newton, MA: Center for Development of Teaching, Education Development Center.

Newton, A., Bergstrom, K., Brennan, N., Dunne, K., Gilbert, C., Ibarguen, N., Perez-Selles, M., & Thomas, E. (1994). *Mentoring: A resource and training guide for educators.* Andover, MA: Regional Laboratory for Educational Improvement of the Northeast and Islands.

NISE Professional Development Strategies Working Group. (1999). Unpublished report.

No Child Left Behind Act of 2001. Public Law 108-110, amending Title I of the Elementary and Secondary Education Act of 1965 (20 V.S.C. 6301 et seq.).

Norris, J. H. (1994). What leaders need to know about school culture. *Journal of Staff Development, 15*(2), 2-5.

North Central Regional Educational Laboratory. (2000). *Blueprints: A practical toolkit for designing and facilitating professional development.* [CD]. Oak Brook, IL: Author.

Oja, S. N., & Smulyan, L. (1989). Collaborative action research. In *Collaborative action research: A developmental approach* (pp. 1-25). Philadelphia: Falmer.

Olson, L. (1994, November 2). Learning their lessons. *Education Week*, pp. 43-46.

Parke, C. S., & Lane, S. (1996/1997, December/January). Learning from performance assessments in math. *Educational Leadership, 54*(4), 26-29.

Parker, R. E. (1997). Comprehensive school and district restructuring of mathematics: Principles and caveats. In S. N. Friel & G. W. Bright (Eds.), *Reflecting on our work: NSF teacher enhancement in K-6 mathematics* (pp. 237-246). Lanham, MD: University Press of America.

Patterson, J. L. (1993). *Leadership for tomorrow's schools.* Alexandria, VA: Association for Supervision and Curriculum Development.

Peters, T., & Waterman, R. (1982). *In search of excellence.* New York: Harper & Row.

Peterson, K. D. (2002). Positive or negative. *Journal of Staff Development, 23*(3), 10-15.

Pfeiffer, L. (1998). *Becoming a reform oriented teacher.* Unpublished doctoral dissertation, Michigan State University.

Pfundt, H., & Duit, R. (Eds.). (1994). *Bibliography: Students' alternative frameworks and science education* (4th ed.). Kiel, Germany: Institut fur die Padagogik der naturwissenschaften.

Phillips, G. (1993). *The school-classroom culture audit.* Vancouver, BC: Eduserve, British Columbia School Trustees.

Posner, G. J., Strike, K. A., Hewson, P. W., & Gertzog, W. A. (1982). Accommodation of a scientific conception: Toward a theory of conceptual change. *Science Education, 66*(2), 211-227.

Pratt, H., & Loucks-Horsley, S. (1993). Implementing a science curriculum for the middle grades: Progress, problems, and prospects. In G. M. Madrazo & L. L. Motz (Eds.), *Sourcebook for science supervisors* (pp. 61-72). Washington, DC: National Science Teachers Association.

Raizen, S. A., & Michelsohn, A. M. (1994). *The future of science in elementary schools: Educating prospective teachers.* San Francisco: Jossey-Bass.

Ramirez, A., & Barnett Clarke, C. (2000). *Inviting broader participation in the leadership of the mathematics case methods project.* Unpublished manuscript.

Regional Educational Laboratories. (1995). *Facilitating systemic change in science and mathematics education: A toolkit for professional developers.* Andover, MA: Regional Laboratory for Educational Improvement of the Northeast and Islands.

Richardson, J. (September, 2001). E-learning potential: Online staff development has great possibilities—And pitfalls. *NSDC Results*, pp. 1, 6.

Ridgway, C., & Bowyer, J. (2000). Science centers: Give teachers the stars. *Journal of Staff Development, 21*(2), 11-15.

Robbins, P. (1999). Mentoring. *Journal of Staff Development, 20*(3), 40-42.

Roseman, J. E., Kesidou, S., & Stern, L. (1996, November). *Identifying curriculum materials for science literacy: A Project 2061 evaluation tool.* Paper presented at the colloquium of the National Research Council, Washington, DC.

Rosenholtz, S. J. (1991). *Teachers' workplace: The social organization of schools.* New York: Teachers College Press.

Russell, S. J., Schifter, D., Bastable, V., Yaffee, L., Lester, J. B., & Cohen, S. (1995). Learning mathematics while teaching. In B. S. Nelson (Ed.), *Inquiry and the development of teaching: Issues in the transformation of mathematics teaching* (pp. 9-16). Newton, MA: Center for the Development of Teaching, Education Development Center.

Schifter, D. (1994). *Voicing the new pedagogy: Teachers write about learning and teaching mathematics.* Newton, MA: Center for the Development of Teaching, Education Development Center.

Schifter, D. (1996a). A constructivist perspective on teaching and learning mathematics. *Phi Delta Kappan, 77*(7), 492-499.

Schifter, D. (Ed.). (1996b). *What's happening in math class?* (Vols. 1 and 2). New York: Teachers College Press.

Schifter, D. (1999). Reasoning about operations: Early algebraic thinking in Grades K-6. In L. V. Still (Ed.), *Developing mathematical reasoning in Grades K-12.* Reston, VA: National Council of Teachers of Mathematics.

Schifter, D., & Bastable, V. (1995, April). *From the teachers' seminar to the classroom: The relationship between doing and teaching mathematics, an example from fractions.* Paper presented at the annual meeting of the American Education Research Association, San Francisco.

Schifter, D., & Fosnot, C. T. (1993). *Reconstructing mathematics education: Stories of teachers meeting the challenge of reform.* New York: Teachers College Press.

Schifter, D., Russell, S. J., & Bastable, V. (1999). Teaching to the big ideas. In M. Solomon (Ed.), *The diagnostic teacher: Constructing new approaches to professional development.* New York: Teachers College Press.

Schmidt, B. J., & Faulkner, S. L. (1989). Staff development through distance education. *Journal of Staff Development, 10*(4), 2-7.

Schmidt, W. H. (2001). Defining teacher quality through content: Professional development implications from TIMSS. In J. Rhoton & P. Bowers (Eds.), *Professional development planning and design* (pp. 141-164). Arlington, VA: National Science Teachers Association.

Schmidt, W. H., McKnight, C. C., Houang, R. T., Wang, H., Wiley, D. E., Cogan, L. S., & Wolfe, R. G. (2001). *Why schools matter: A cross-national comparison of curriculum and learning.* San Francisco: Jossey-Bass.

Schmoker, M. (1999). *Results: The key to continuous improvement.* Alexandria, VA: Association of Supervision and Curriculum Development.

Schmoker, M. (2002, Spring). Up and away. The formula is well known, now we need to follow it. *Journal of Staff Development, 23*(2), 10-13.

Schön, D. A. (1983). *The reflective practitioner: How professionals think in action.* New York: Basic Books.

Schön, D. A. (1988). Educating teachers as reflective practitioners. In P. Grimmett & G. Erickson (Eds.), *Reflection in teacher education.* New York: Teachers College Press.

Schwahn, C., & Spady, W. (1998, April). Why change doesn't happen and how to make sure it does. *Educational Leadership, 55*(7), 45-47.

Schweitzer, C. (2000, December). Creating a dot-com compatible culture. *Association Management, 52*(13), 28-35.

Sebring, P. B., & Bryk, A. S. (2000, February). School leadership and the bottom line in Chicago. *Phi Delta Kappan, 81*(6), 440-443.

Senge, P. M. (1990). The leader's new work: Building learning organizations. *Sloan Management Review Report Series, 32*(11), 1-5.

Showers, B., & Joyce, B. (1996). The evolution of peer coaching. *Educational Leadership, 53*(6), 12-16.

Shulman, L. S. (1986). Those who understand: Knowledge growth in teaching. *Educational Researcher, 15*(2), 4-14.

Shulman, L. S. (1992). Toward a pedagogy of cases. In J. H. Shulman (Ed.), *Case methods in teacher education* (pp. 1-30). New York: Teachers College Press.

Shulman, J., & Kepner, D. (1994, October). *The editorial imperative: Responding to productive tensions between case writing and individual development.* Unpublished manuscript, Far West Laboratory, San Francisco.

Silver, E. A., Kilpatrick, J., & Schlesinger, B. (1990). *Thinking through mathematics: Fostering inquiry and communication in mathematics classrooms.* New York: College Entrance Examination Board.

Smith, D. C., & Neale, D. C. (1989). The construction of subject matter knowledge in primary science teaching. *Teaching & Teacher Education, 5,* 1-20.

Smith, M. S. (2001). *Practice-based professional development for teachers of mathematics.* Reston, VA: National Council of Teachers of Mathematics.

Smith, M. S., & O'Day, J. (1991). *Putting the pieces together: Systemic school reform* [Policy briefs]. New Brunswick, NJ: Consortium for Policy Research in Education.

Smith, P. S. (1996). *Report of NTEN evaluation activities and findings: January 1995-January 1996.* Durham, NC: Horizon Research.

Sneider, C. (1995). *Global Systems Science: A professional development program for high school science teachers.* Paper presented at the Professional Development Project of the National Institute for Science Education, Madison, WI.

Sneider, C. (1996, June 17). *Summative evaluation report: Astronomy and space science summer institutes for elementary and middle school teachers* (Award No. ESI-9153783). Arlington, VA: National Science Foundation.

Sparks, D. (1994, March 16). A paradigm shift in staff development. *Education Week,* 42.

Sparks, D. (1997, Spring). Maintaining the faith in teachers' ability to grow: An interview with Asa Hilliard. *Journal of Staff Development, 18*(2), 24-25.

Sparks, D. (2001, October). Time for professional learning serves student learning. *Results.* (Oxford, OH: National Staff Development Council)

Sparks, D. (2002a). *Designing powerful professional development for teachers and principals.* Oxford, OH: National Staff Development Council.

Sparks, D. (2002b). Dreaming all that we might realize. *ENC Focus, 9*(1), 18 23.

Sparks, D., & Hirsh, S. (2000). *Learning to lead, leading to learn.* Oxford, OH: NSDC. Retrieved from www.nsdc.org/leader_report.html

Sparks, G. M., & Simmons, J. M. (1989). Inquiry-oriented staff development: Using research as a source of tools, not rules. In S. D. Caldwell (Ed.), *Staff development: A handbook of effective practices* (pp. 126-139). Oxford, OH: National Staff Development Council.

St. John, M. (2002, May). *The improvement infrastructure: The missing link or why we are always worried about "sustainability."* LSCNet Virtual Conference on Sustainability. Retrieved from http://sustainability2002.terc.edu

St. John, M., & Pratt, H. (1997). Factors that contribute to the "best cases" of standards-based reform. *School Science and Mathematics, 97*(6), 316-324.

Stein, M. (1998). *High performance learning communities District 2: Report on year one implementation of school learning communities.* High Performance Training, Communities Project. Washington, DC: Office of Educational Research and Improvement (ERIC Document Reproduction No. ED429263).

Stein, M. K., Silver, E., & Smith, M. S. (1994). *Mathematics reform and teacher development: A community of practice.* Pittsburgh, PA: Learning Research and Development Center.

Stein, M. K., Smith, M. S., Henningsen, M. A., & Silver, E. A. (2000). *Implementing standards-based mathematical instruction: A casebook for professional development.* New York: Teachers College Press.

Stigler, J. W., & Hiebert, J. (1999). *The teaching gap: Best ideas from the world's teachers for improving education in the classroom.* New York: Simon & Schuster.

Strycker, J. (1995). Science first. *Science and Children, 32*(7), 26-29.

A superintendent's view. (2001, Spring). *Northwest Teacher.* Retrieved from www.nwrel.org/msec/nwteacher/spring2001

Taylor, E. F., & Smith, R. C. (1995). Teaching physics on line. *American Journal of Physics, 63,* 1090-1096.

Thompson, C. L., & Zeuli, J. S. (1999). The frame and the tapestry: Standards-based reform and professional development. In L. Darling-Hammond & G. Sykes (Eds.), *Teaching as the learning profession: Handbook of policy and practice* (pp. 341-375). San Francisco: Jossey Bass.

U.S. Department of Education. (1996). *Pursuing excellence: A study of U.S. eighth-grade mathematics and science teaching, learning, curriculum, and achievement in international context.*

(National Center for Education Statistics [NCES] Publication No. 97-198). Washington, DC: Government Printing Office.

U.S. Department of Education. (2000). *Does professional development change teaching practice? Results from a three-year study.* Washington, DC: Author.

U.S. Department of Education. (2002). *Does professional development change teaching practice? Results from a three-year study.* Washington, DC: Author.

Van Driel, J. H., Verloop, N., & De Vos, W. (1998). Developing science teachers' pedagogical knowledge. *Journal of Teacher Education, 41,* 3-11.

Villani, S. (2002). *Mentoring programs for new teachers: Models of induction and support.* Thousand Oaks, CA: Corwin.

Wandersee, J. H., Mintzes, J. J., & Novak, J. D. (1994). Research on alternative conceptions in science. In D. L. Gabel (Ed.), *Handbook of research on science teaching and learning* (pp. 177-210). New York: Macmillan.

Watkins, J. (1992). *Speaking of action research.* Paper adapted from a presentation to the Board of Overseers of the Regional Laboratory for Educational Improvement of the Northeast and Islands, Andover, MA.

Weiss, I. R. (1997). The status of science and mathematics teaching in the United States: Comparing teacher views and classroom practice to national standards. *NISE Brief* (University of Wisconsin–Madison) *1*(3), 1-7.

Weiss, I. R., Banilower, E. R., McMahon, K. C., & Smith, P. S. (2001). *Report of the 2000 National Survey of Science and Mathematics (status report).* Chapel Hill, NC: Horizon Research.

Weiss, I. R., Banilower, E. R., Overstreet, C. M., & Soar, E. H. (2002, March). *Local systemic change through teacher enhancement: Year seven cross-site report.* Chapel Hill, NC: Horizon Research.

Weiss, I. R., Matti, M. C., & Smith, P. S. (1994). *Report of the 1993 survey of science and mathematics education.* Chapel Hill, NC: Horizon Research.

Weissglass, J. (1996). *No compromises on equity in mathematics education: Developing an infrastructure.* Santa Barbara: University of California, Santa Barbara, Center for Educational Change in Mathematics and Science.

Wenglinsky, H. (2000). *How teaching matters: Bringing the classroom back into discussions of teacher quality.* Princeton, NJ: Educational Testing Service.

WestEd. (1996, Fall). Scientists and teachers working together. *SEABA Journal,* p. 9.

WestEd. (2000). *Teachers who learn, kids who achieve: A look at schools with model professional development.* San Francisco: Author.

WestEd and the WGBH Educational Foundation. (2003). *Teachers as learners: Professional development in science and mathematics, a video library.* Thousand Oaks, CA: Corwin.

Wheatley, M. (2002). *Turning to one another: Simple conversations to restore hope in the future.* San Francisco: Berrett-Koehler.

Wilson, K. G., & Davis, B. (1994). *Redesigning education.* New York: Henry Holt.

Wood, P. (1988). Action research: A field perspective. *Journal of Education for Teaching, 14*(2), 135-150.

Index